MICHAEL FREEMAN ON...

COLOR&TONE

The Ultimate Photography Masterclass

An Hachette UK Company
www.hachette.co.uk

First published in the United Kingdom in 2023 by
Ilex, a division of Octopus Publishing Group Ltd
Carmelite House
50 Victoria Embankment
London, EC4Y 0DZ
www.octopusbooks.co.uk
www.octopusbooksusa.com

Design and layout copyright
© Octopus Publishing Group Ltd 2023
Text, photographs and illustrations copyright
© Michael Freeman 2023

Publisher: Alison Starling
Commissioning Editor: Richard Collins
Managing Editor: Rachel Silverlight
Assistant Editor: Jeannie Stanley
Art Director: Ben Gardiner
Designer: Eoghan O'Brien
Picture Research Manager: Giulia Hetherington
Senior Production Manager: Katherine Hockley

ISBN 978-1-78157-871-1

A CIP catalogue record for this book is available
from the British Library

Printed and bound in China

10 9 8 7 6 5 4 3 2 1

MIX
Paper | Supporting
responsible forestry
FSC® C008047

MICHAEL FREEMAN

ON...

COLOR&TONE

The Ultimate Photography Masterclass

ilex

CONTENTS

INTRODUCTION

Color in photography inspires more opinion and argument than does any other image quality, for two reasons. One is that, as I'll show throughout this book, color is in the mind, not in the world in front of our eyes, which just has measurable wavelengths. We judge color only once those wavelengths have been processed at the back of our brains, and we very much do judge. Color triggers likes and dislikes just by itself, and as with all matters of taste it's personal, so there are plenty of differences. The second reason is that most people don't have the faintest idea of what color is about or how it works, and that kind of ignorance is a perfect breeding ground for opinionating.

Given that color happens in the mind, you might think that this relieves any need for hard science, and we can have a comfortable, if slightly vague, time just talking about the aesthetics of color. Far from it, I'm afraid. It's the science that's responsible for getting colors in the world to look the way we think they should, into our cameras and onto our screens and prints. It's also the science that inspires the ways in which we can think and talk about color. Unfortunately, the science is still not fully resolved, and there are different opinions and approaches even among those studying it. I'll try to make this as simple and as practical as possible, staying focused on what our needs are as photographers (rather than color scientists).

As for aesthetics, that's too often used as an excuse for not thinking clearly about what is going on in a picture and the effect it has on us, the audience. In fact, aesthetics can be, and to my mind should be, analytical. Here in the world of color in photography, it's simply not enough to say 'that's nice' or 'this doesn't work', however tempting that may be. We need reasons, not lazy opinion, and reasons do certainly exist, as we'll see.

Color in photography is now so utterly normal and commonplace that for most people taking pictures (that inevitably means on phone cameras), it doesn't even merit the name. It's just a part of what a photograph is. This hasn't always been so. I'm not talking about the historical challenge of getting it to work in the first place, because that has no effect on how we shoot now. Rather, the way in which color overtook black and white, and the timing, created some prejudices and disputes that haven't yet played out. The mass production of color film coincided with the means to use it in mass media – print, that is – and that meant it was first heavily used in advertising and editorial magazine features. It was popular, in other words, and for the photography art establishment of those times, it was therefore tainted. The polarisation of how color photography 'ought' to look began in the 1970s, which is a long time ago for such a fast-moving creative medium – half a century, for heaven's sake – but it has persisted until now. In photography, the art world and the popular world continue to differ on color more than on probably any other aspect. Color in photography is very much an active topic – and disputatious.

COLOR FORWARD

1

Maximizing the color means inevitably taking down some of the other ingredients of a picture, and the most likely candidates are subject matter and moment. Putting this another way, and a little simplistically, the normal concerns of photography are interesting things happening, or simply being, in front of the camera, and these are what normally attract attention. This is called salience, which I introduced back in the first book, *Michael Freeman on... Composition*, and as eye-tracking tests show time and again, people, faces and other clearly defined things take centre stage in photographs, particularly if they're in action and interaction.

Now, color can contribute to this, or it can replace it, and while I'll be dealing with both directions in this book, the second is arguably more interesting – and elusive. I can do worse here than invoke the work of the Austrian-American Ernst Haas, member of Magnum, and in the 1960s and 1970s the most famous color photographer of his time. He did both. His preferred medium was Kodachrome, and he was especially skilful at coaxing the richness out of it, especially the reds and yellows that it was known for. As a commercial and advertising photographer he brought strength of color to such campaigns as *Marlboro Man* (he was the first photographer), composing rich hues to direct attention. At the same time, however, he built up a personal collection of color photography that variously used abstraction, creative framing, selective focus and slow motion to make imagery that was, in his words, 'less descriptive, more creative; less informative, more suggestive – less prose, more poetry'. All by observation, 'without touching my subject'.[†]

That will do pretty well as a manifesto for anyone drawn to color-forward shooting. This is generally about being a colorist photographer, which is a description I'm fairly sure will infuriate some photographers, even those who are called that. The argument is that judging color, working with it, making pictures that are more about it than anything else, demands a skill that not everyone has. Not everyone even wants it. Henri Cartier-Bresson, whose opinions were always worth listening to, thought it a 'complex new element' that could 'prejudice the achievement of the life and movement which is often caught by black and white'. Ian Berry, another Magnum photographer and one-time president of the agency, had no interest in it, and once told me that even though the demands of magazines meant that he had often to shoot color film, he still treated it like black and white. Colorist photographers have often not been particularly articulate about their approach, and it is indeed hard to pin down the methods and styles that will elevate pure color to being the most important ingredient. Hard but not impossible, as I intend to show.

[†] Ernst Haas, 'About Color Photography', *Du* magazine, 1961

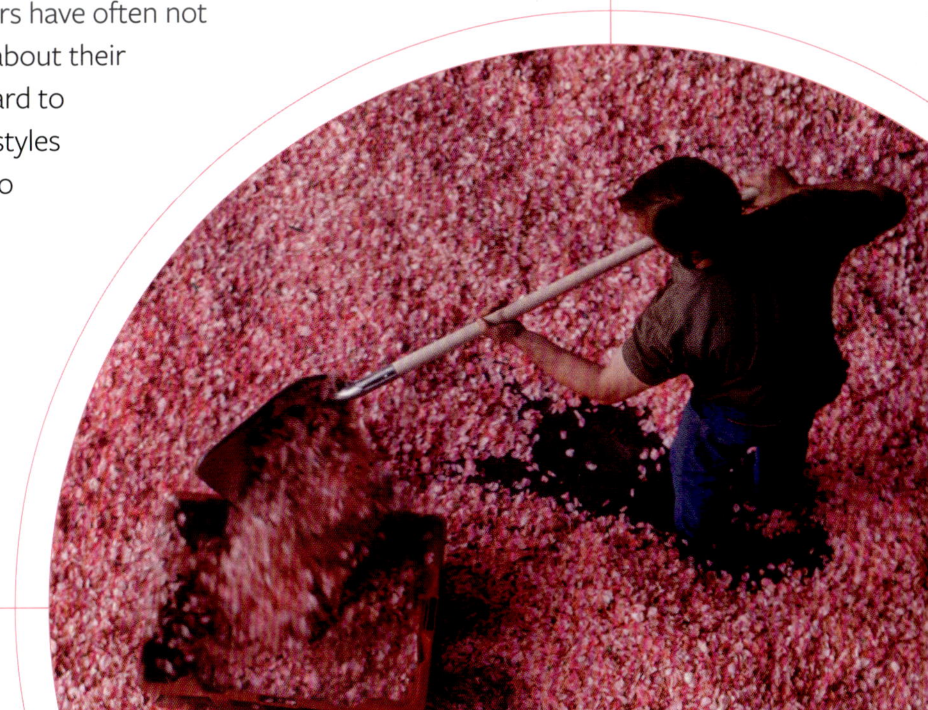

JUST THE COLOR

As I mentioned in my other books, there are about a dozen ingredients that go into the making of a photograph, and they vary wildly from shot to shot.

The pie chart (right, above) shows them evenly divided, but in this book we're interested in when the color ingredient dominates. This is always a mixture of opportunity (interesting color in front of the camera) and personal taste. Not everyone finds color fascinating. There are also photographers who enjoy color in some contexts but commit to black and white in other work. But then, there are photographers who find certain color effects, palettes and combinations their own justification for shooting.

There are also scenes and situations that could play either way, and the main example here is one of these. You too might be in more or less of a mood to explore color for color's sake, depending on the day and the time. In this case, I had been invited to a funeral in a Yi ethnic minority village in the mountains above Lijiang, southwest China. As a photojournalist, my main interest was in how the proceedings played out, with emotions on display and all the delicacies involved in being a stranger present at an intimate rite of passage. Most of the shooting followed this narrative, observing moments and details, such as an aside in which a grandmother adjusts the dress of one of the younger women, who hardly wear traditional attire anymore.

Viewed as a purely color interaction, it becomes an abstract of geometric color fragments popping out of black.

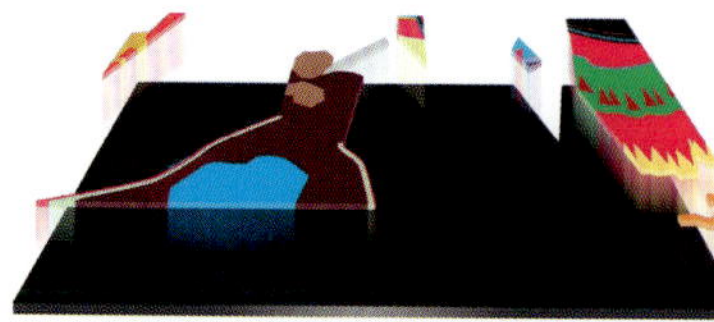

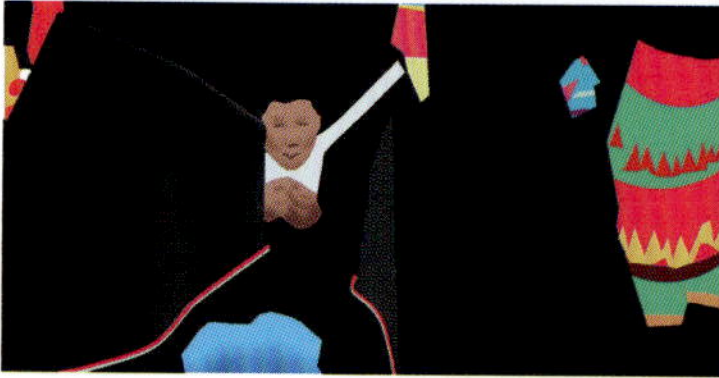

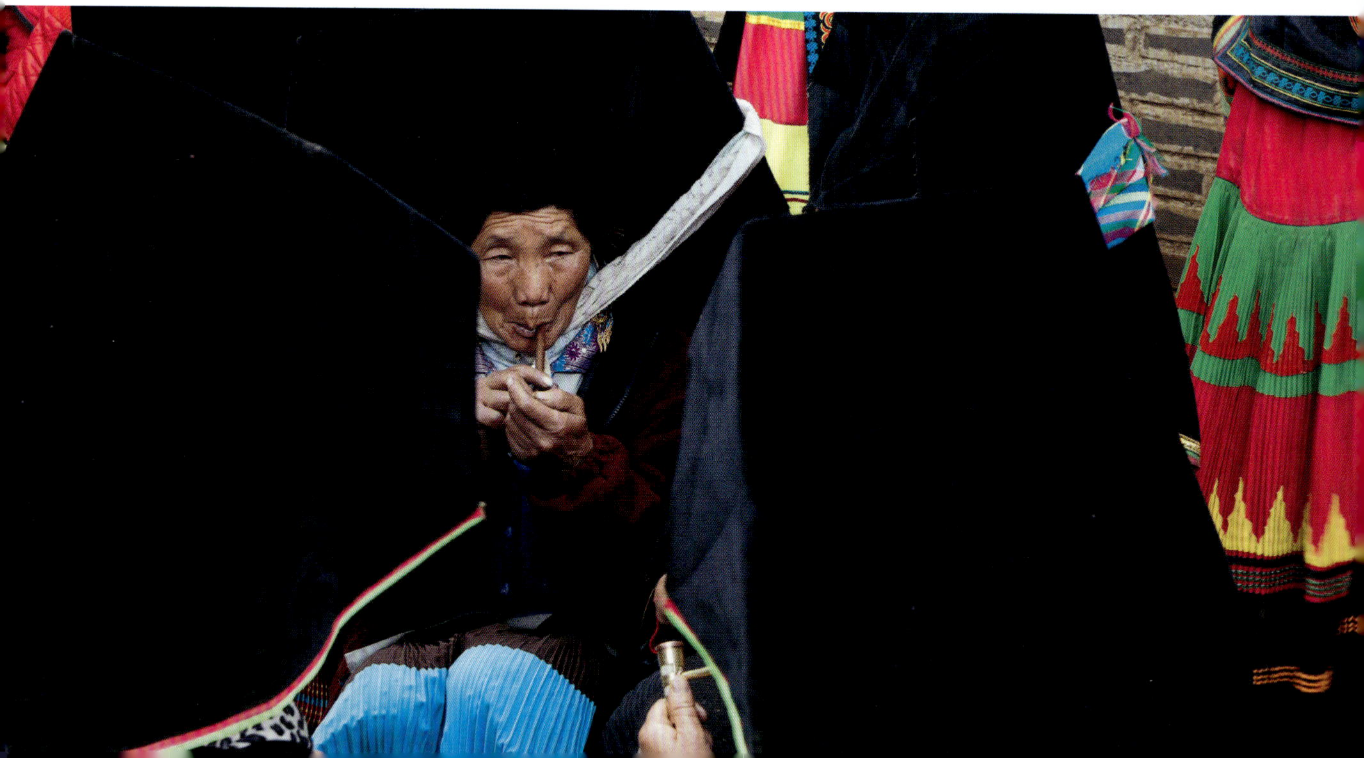

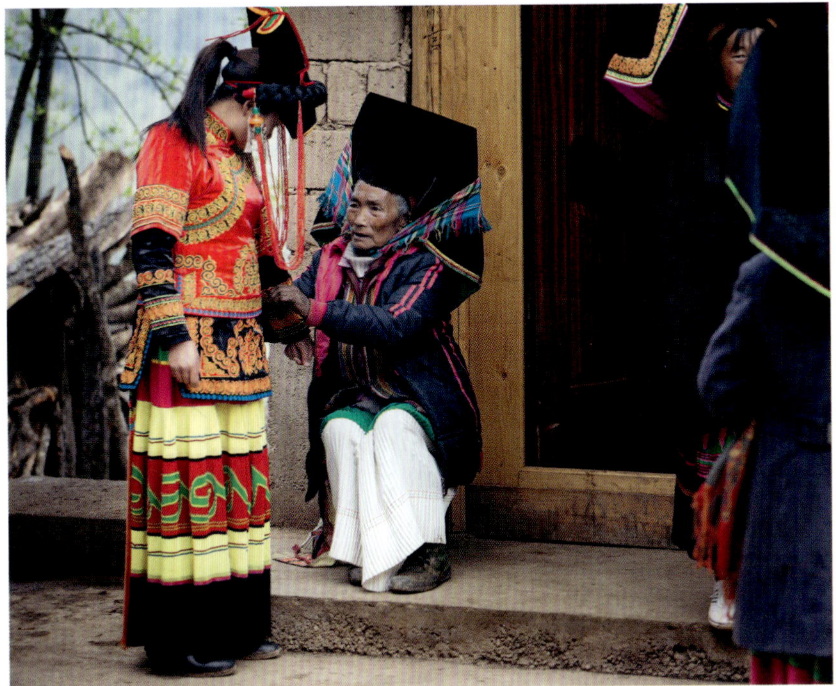

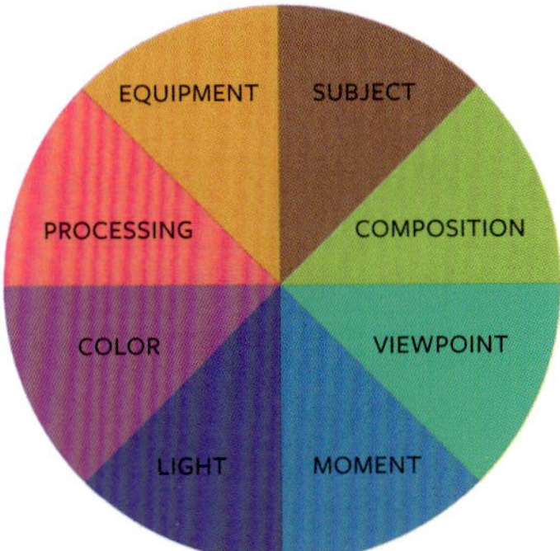

An older Yi woman adjusts the dress of a young woman at the funeral of an elder in southwest China.

The 12 ingredients that go into making a photograph. In any one image they are almost always in varied proportions.

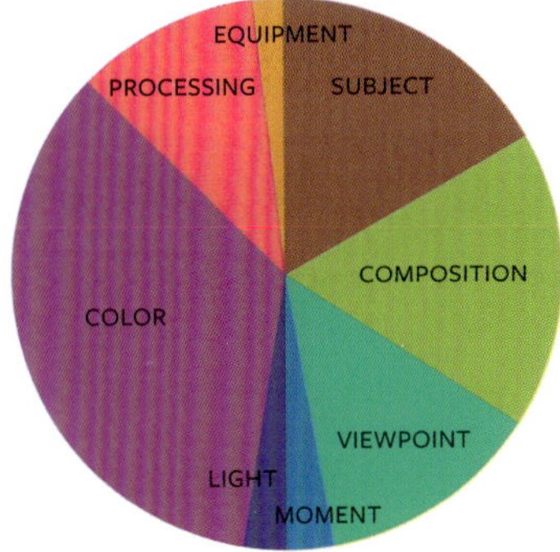

The same 12 ingredients apportioned for the main picture here, with color dominating. Composition and viewpoint were also important, but the equipment, light and moment mattered very little.

- Subject
- Composition
- Viewpoint
- Moment
- Light
- Color
- Processing
- Equipment

Yet at the same time, the traditional dress of the Yi women was graphically striking: large headdresses covered in black velvet and vivid patches of geometric patterns in the skirts and hems. I could see the possibilities of a graphic shot in which fragments of color popped out from a rich black background, and for the picture (left) I stepped aside from the reportage to work on a single shot which would be simply about color.

There are practical differences between shooting normally and shooting for just the color. Normal is a broad term, but is typically driven by clear subjects, scenes and events. Making color the subject takes away the usual undercurrent of documenting what's in front of the camera, which in a sense frees up the photographer to go exploring and experimenting. It also increases the risk of ending up with a meaningless image, because if the color composition doesn't work, there's nothing tangible to fall back on. Most viewers expect a strong image to be 'about' something, so it definitely helps if there remains some inherent subject interest as well. In the case of this shot, the fact that this is a traditional minority dress, rarely seen these days, keeps it grounded.

A major shooting difference here was that there was less urgency, because I temporarily stopped looking for expressions, actions and other things critical to the idea of moment. Most of the day was spent staying alert to just such moments, and this picture was a distinct break from that.

PLEASURE FROM COLOR

T he ultimate driving force behind colorist photography is the simple fact that many people enjoy the sensation of color. That's not quite so obvious as it may sound.

The same strength and variety of likes and dislikes don't apply to image qualities such as light and composition. You might have to coax a reaction out of someone to either of those, but just about everyone seems to have an instant and easy opinion on a color scheme or combination. Entire consumer industries (house paint, lipstick, nail varnish) depend on it. In a sense, this makes color a little like music. They both have a direct sensory appeal that bypasses thinking. Of course, if you want to make music, or color, you have to know a lot more.

Whatever the reasons for this, under-researched and beyond the scope of this book, it provides justification for shooting color for its own sake, irrespective of the subject and action unfolding in front of the camera. This is not a universally held view – it gets short shrift on a news desk – but ever since the photographers of the 1950s and 1960s such as Ernst Haas, Saul Leiter and Helen Levitt (notably all in New York) began experimenting with color palettes and color washes, it became

Color is so subjective that it's virtually impossible to show examples that everyone will like, but this highly colorful, clean shot of a Maldivian woman cycling past a brightly painted wall has broad appeal, pairing saturated hues around her black abaya, which functions as a key or anchor.

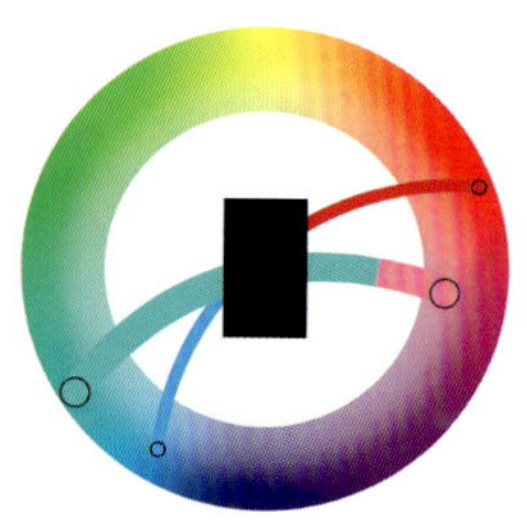

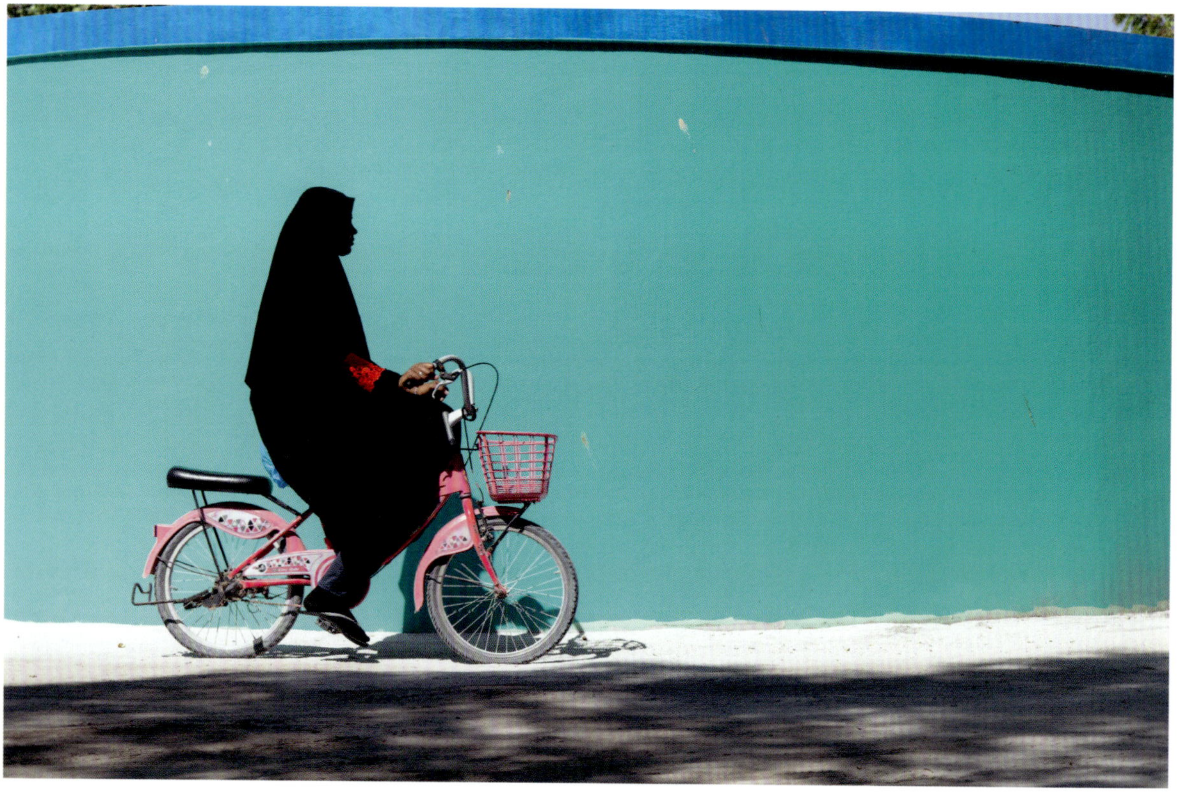

While this shot of workers sorting a tera harvest in Guangdong, China, was taken on reportage assignment for its content, the unexpected and slightly garish counterpoint of pink against green makes it as much about color as about what's happening.

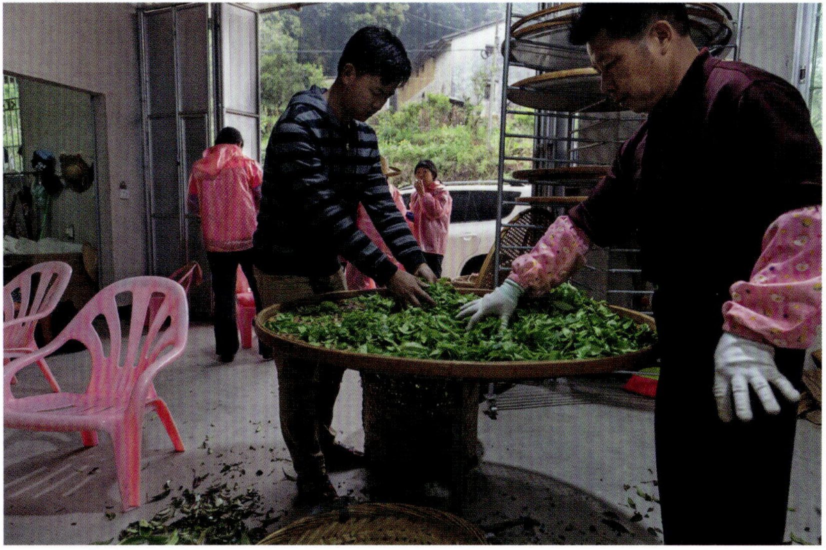

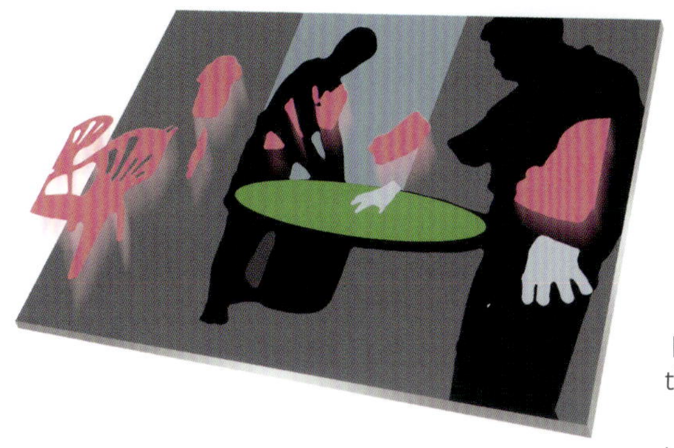

more generally accepted. Other photographers picked up the theme, such as William Eggleston, Harry Gruyaert and Gueorgui Pinkhassov, and what they were all doing was disregarding the accepted subjects worthy of the camera's attention, and looking instead for interesting ways in which colors could fall into the frame. Colors became 'objects' in their own right, and if that doesn't seem so remarkable these days, it was quite radical then. Pinkhassov wrote, 'At some point I became more fascinated by the magic of photography than by its content. Or rather, the magic itself became the content. The metaphysics of pattern replaced the physics of content.'

Of course, not everyone gets the same pleasure from color, or pleasure from the same color. It's slippery. The very uncertainty of color's appeal leads to polar differences in opinion. The so-called New Color movement in America in the 1970s rejected the easy commercial appeal of color up to that point and sought to replace it with a more sophisticated aesthetic. In reality, much of what William Eggleston, the new champion, did had already been done by Ernst Haas, including celebrating intensity of color and printing with the dye-transfer process. Pinkhassov again about a particularly colorful picture that he recently posted: 'I know my group of connoisseurs and what they require of me. I cannot exclude the possibility that the most demanding of them will turn away: they'd say it's kitsch, too beautiful. Is it kitsch? – you may ask. Is it kitsch? – I ask myself. Where is the borderline and what is it? Triviality, sweetness, glamour, an easy route, the desire to please?'

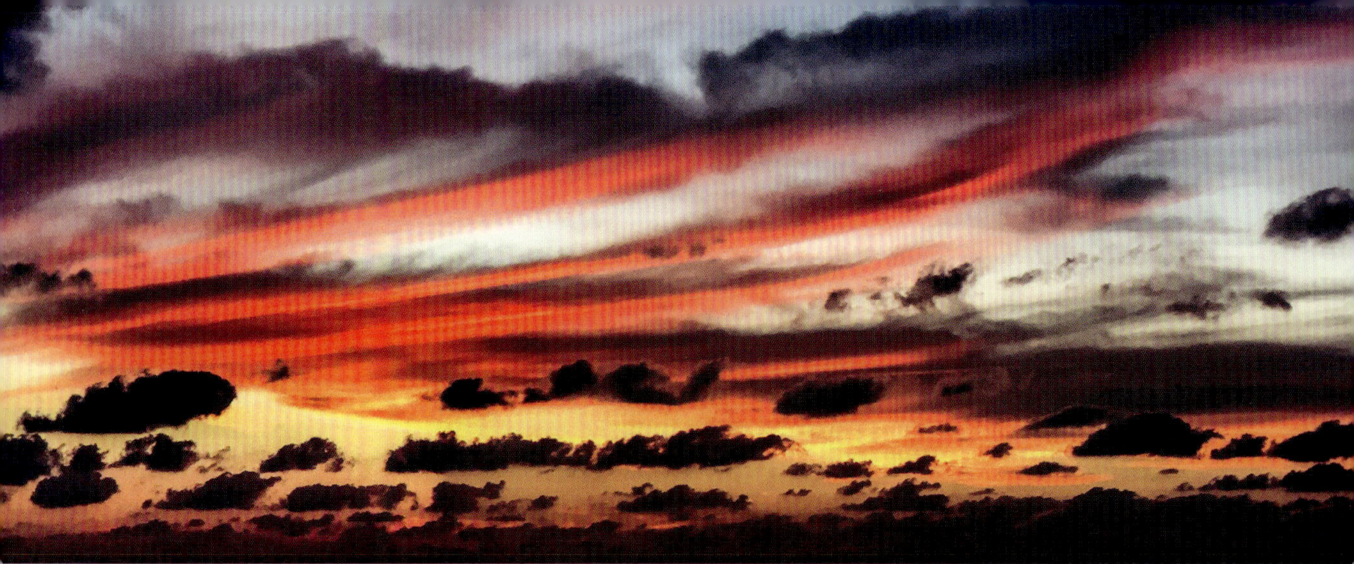

THE SUNSET SYNDROME

Given a clear view and at least a few minutes of free time to watch it, a 'good' sunset or sunrise reliably attracts people. This despite the fact that it happens every day of our lives, and needs only clear weather to see it.

Yes, it's associated with holidays when we're not busy with anything, and beaches because there's a clear view of the horizon, but even so, sunsets give pleasure, which is why it belongs here, directly after the preceding pages. It's the exemplar of pleasure from color. If we ignore the copycat effect in which one person on the beach shooting the sunset (with or without heart-shaped hands framing it) triggers others to do the same, it still catches attention.

At the same time, it attracts scorn in critical and curatorial circles for being populist and shallow, but you might be surprised how many painters and photographers of note have made sunset images. Among photographers, Ernst Haas and Steve McCurry naturally, but also, perhaps less expectedly, William Eggleston (you thought he was above that?), Nadav Kander, Mario Testino and David Alan Harvey. More or less everyone, in fact. Before them, in painting, there was J.M.W. Turner, Claude Monet, Edgar Degas, Henri Matisse and Rembrandt (yes, really). That list goes on, too. If that doesn't reassure you for sometimes having lapsed into a sunset moment, here's Mahatma Gandhi, no less: 'When I admire the wonders of a sunset or the beauty of the moon, my soul expands in the worship of the creator.'

Photography is strongly intertwined with sunsets and sunrises because, apart from the color, there's the attraction of the moment. It's a fleeting moment. Visually, sunsets move quickly, and that triggers one of the essential appeals of photography – capturing that moment in an attempt to preserve it and not let it slip away. The challenge for photography (and that short list above of otherwise serious photographers indulging in it surely convinces that there is a challenge)

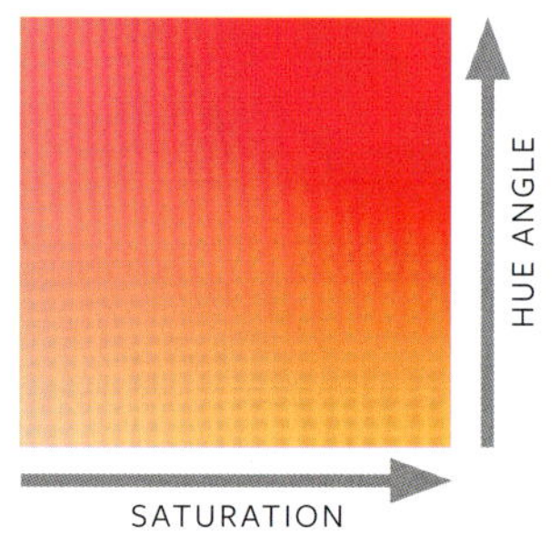

Assembled from a databank of over a hundred sunset and sunrise shots, this square shows the range possible, plotting saturation against hue.

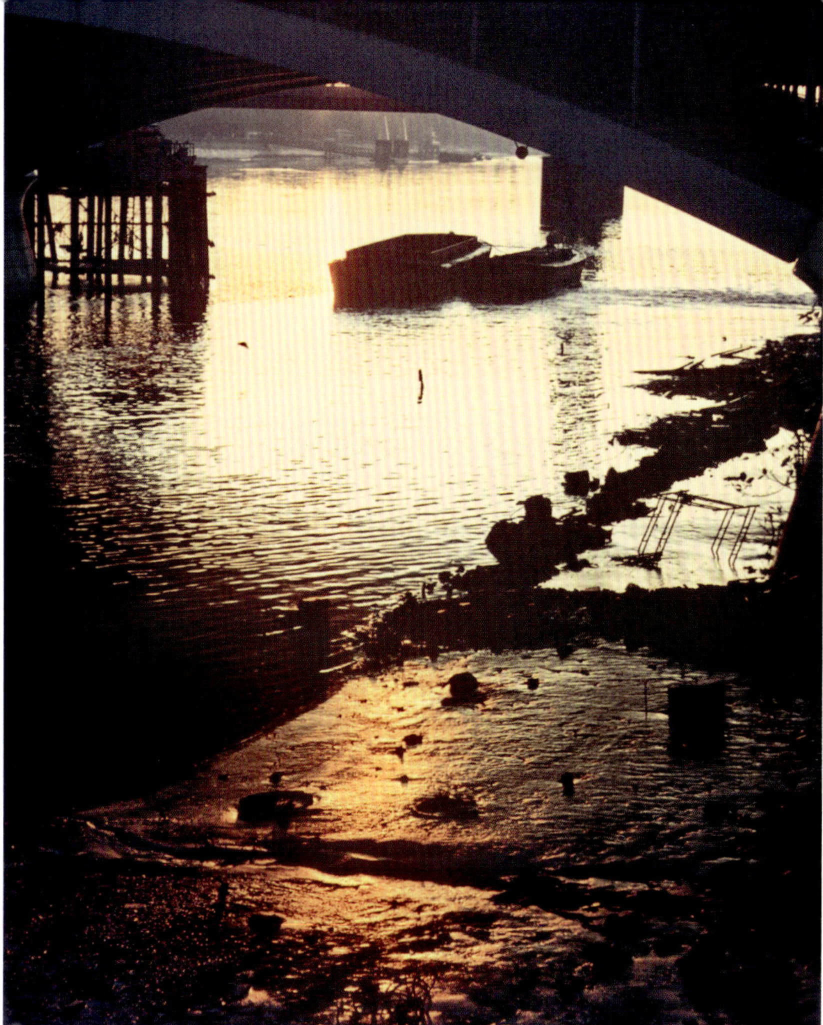

is to be surprising. The typical color range, shown in the hue bar (left), doesn't really cut it if you want to be taken seriously. Finding ways around cliché calls for more effort than usual in viewpoint, anticipation, framing and composition, but ultimately a 'good' sunset shot depends on what's being offered. That's simply not predictable, which makes the situation a perfect challenge for photography – a high failure rate and the need to work very quickly and accurately.

At the heart lies the color palette. I've plotted the range from which it can be drawn (see left), and these are just the sky colors. Other surfaces that reflect, from glass to rock to water, add even more possibilities. Air quality, particles and clouds all play their part, and with the typical limited range to improve on aesthetically, the challenge is worthwhile. There are six sunsets/sunrise images in this book: here and on pages 54 and 56.

HARMONY OR NOT

The idea of color harmony is a hare that has been chased by artists and theorists for centuries. In other words, that certain colors go 'well' together in an image.

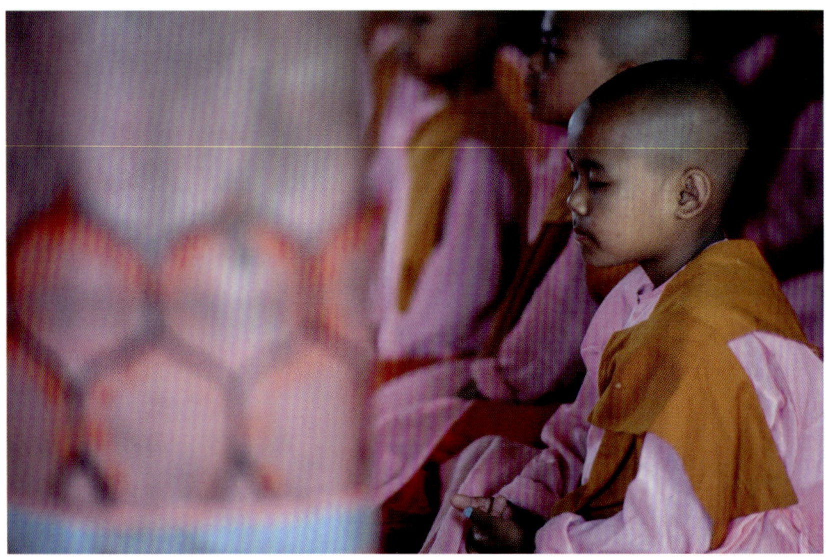

There may be some scientific basis for this, though not a lot, and as an idea it has had cycles of popularity through the ages. Photography may actually have put a bigger dent in it than did any other practice, because it records everything and because our diet of photographic imagery is now so huge that we may simply be getting used to more and more varied color combinations. What has made the idea tempting is the color circle, which we'll come to shortly, and the way different hues are arranged around it. Those next to each other are naturally similar, which is possibly one kind of harmony. Those directly opposite are often called complementary, and are generated by what's known as successive contrast (see page 45), and that traditionally has been seen as harmonious by many. But does it actually work like that?

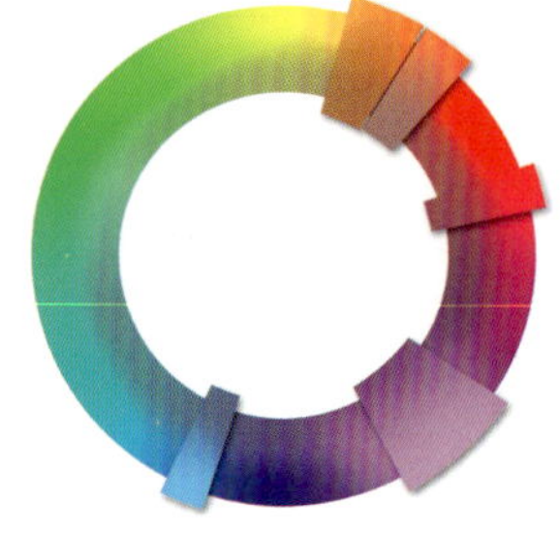

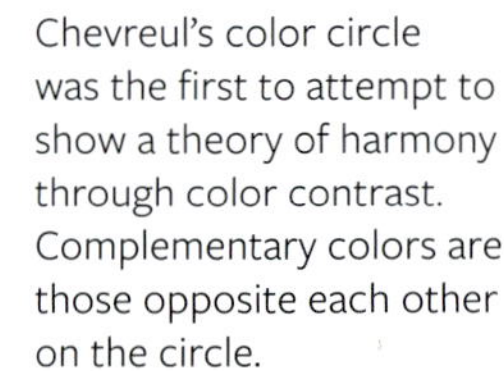

Chevreul's color circle was the first to attempt to show a theory of harmony through color contrast. Complementary colors are those opposite each other on the circle.

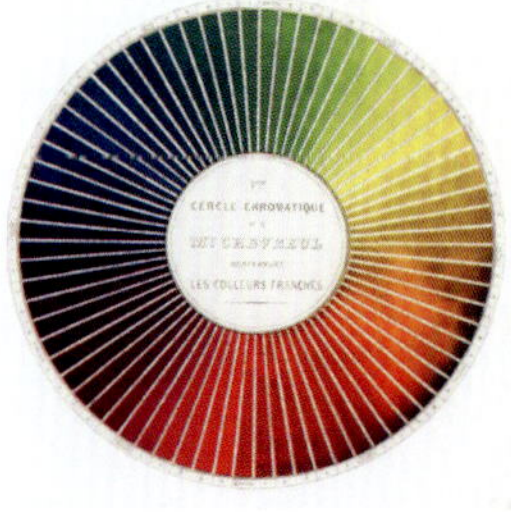

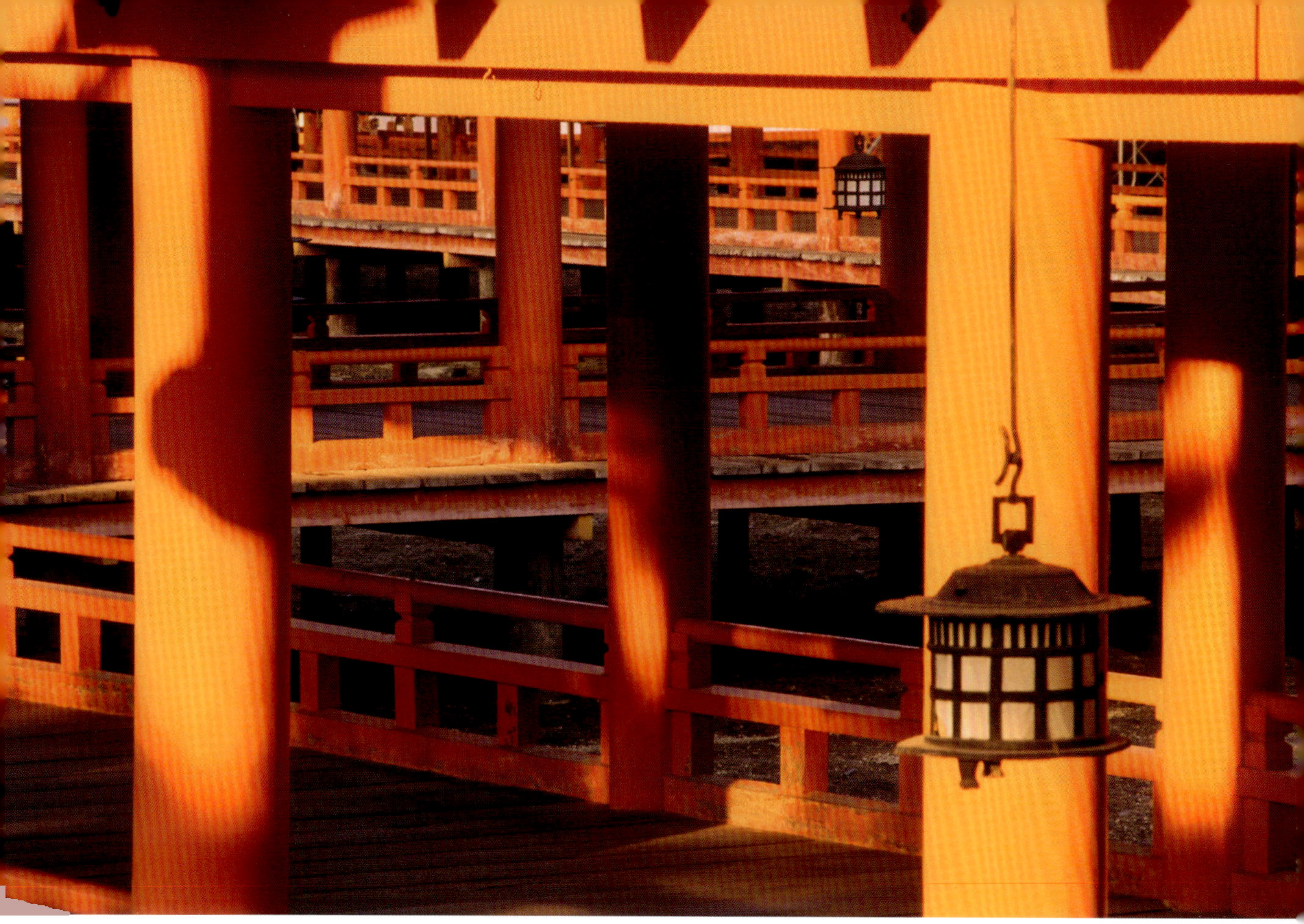

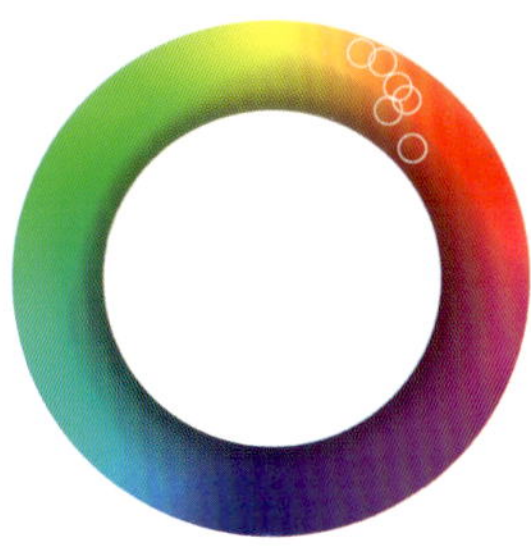

Built on stilts in the shallow waters off Myajima, the Itsukushima shrine is painted the traditional red-orange of Japanese Shinto. Shadows cast by the setting sun expand the range of hues towards deep red. The range seems harmonious for being made up of adjacent colors (see page 116).

Harmony means being pleasing, and it's also about how two or more colors relate to each other – or affect each other – so one of the first basics is to be clear about what we mean by 'a color'. Mainly, and for most people, color means hue, so that ever since the hues of the spectrum were arranged in a circle, by Newton, that simple arrangement became the obvious place to work out harmony. However, Newton turned the linear spectrum into a circle because he was already looking for a kind of harmony. He decided there ought to be seven colors to match the seven notes of the musical scale (although he needed the help of a friend to distinguish them), and because the two ends looked fairly similar to each other and looked fine when joined.

On the circle, colors next to each other have similarity and 'go well' together, but more interesting is that colors directly opposite one another also have some sort of aesthetic connection – the attraction of opposites, if you like. The first to make a theory out of this was the French chemist Michel Eugène Chevreul in 1839, who claimed six color harmonies, of which complementary colors contrast, across the circle were 'superior to every other'. That basic idea, minus the circle, had been around for a long time. Leonardo da Vinci had already written that 'the most fierce' contrast was between 'colors surrounded by their directly contrary color'. In any case, Chevreul influenced the Impressionists, Vincent van Gogh and most colorists since.

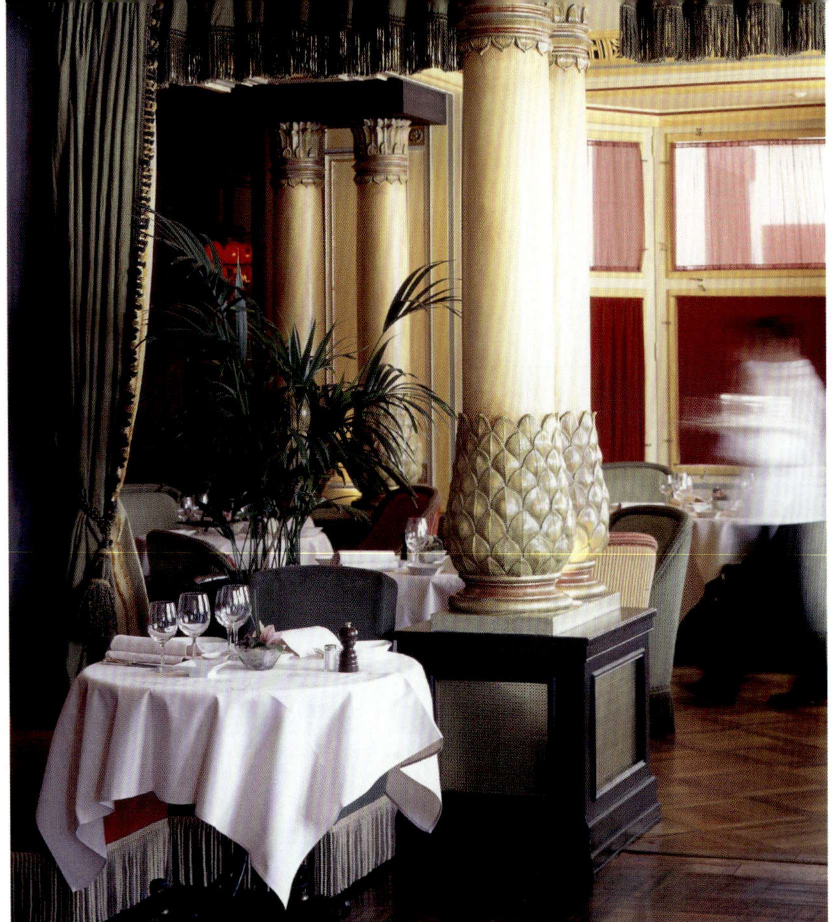

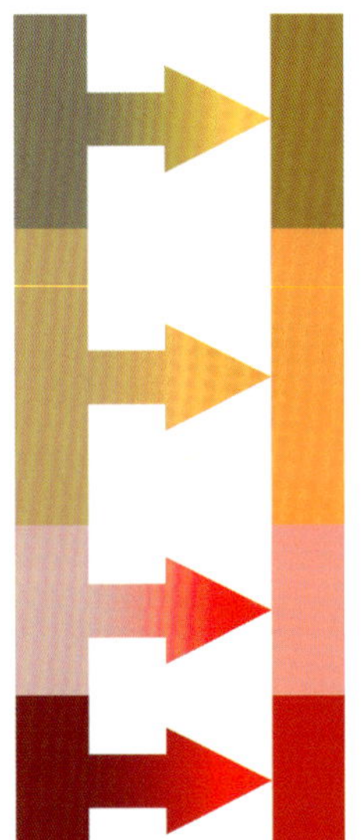

There are two scientific 'proofs' of this special relationship. One is that mixing them together produces a neutral white or grey (according to whether you're using light or pigments). Another is color after-image, also known as color contrast. If you stare at length at a pure solid color and then shift your gaze to a white space, you'll see an after-image of the opposite (complementary) color, and there's an example of this on page 44. So far so good, but how exactly you arrange the colors around the circle makes a big difference. I'm jumping the gun because we'll look at color circles in the next chapter, but Chevreul's circle (see page 16) is not at all the same as the one based on actual perception. For Chevreul and for many painters up to now, the opposite of violet is yellow, so they 'go well' together. The actual after-image of violet, however, is a green – easy enough to see for yourself. But does it matter? Maybe not if we're talking about what's pleasing, as there are so many other things in play.

Ultimately, color harmony matters simply because so many people look for it, but whether it actually exists or not is another matter. There are two problems, both probably insurmountable. The first is the sheer number of variables among viewers, which include age, gender, personality, state of mind, culture, context and trends. Colors that might appeal to a group of Thai school friends shopping for party clothes are hardly likely to be similar to the color scheme for redecorating a living room for an elderly English couple living in the countryside. Yes, that's an extreme comparison, which is what happens when you try to find simple combinations that will attract everyone. Of course, this doesn't stop people in the color business from trying,

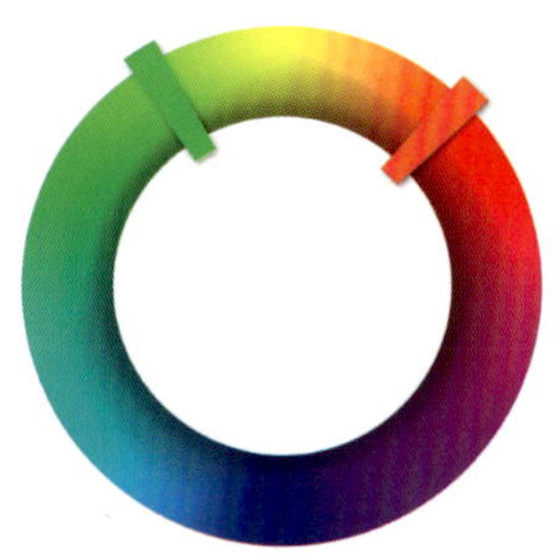

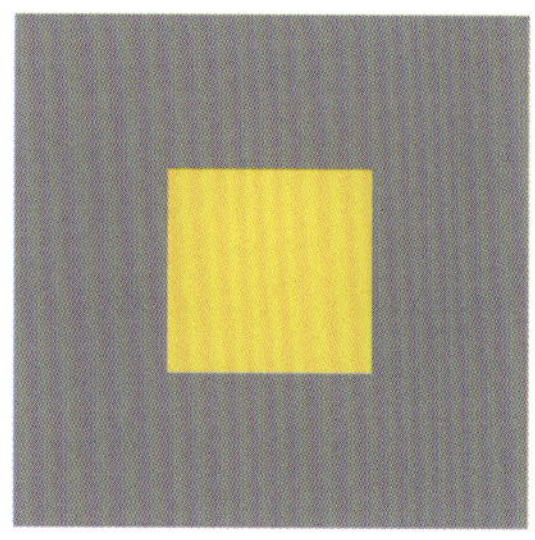

A single color on a neutral ground gains a certain amount of strength from being framed and isolated. Grey is particularly effective because it avoids the high contrast that black or white would give, keeping attention on the hue.

The attractiveness of pairs of colors is subjective, but the saturated green and orange here seem garish to many, probably related to their positions on the color circle – neither complementary opposites nor close enough to be similar.

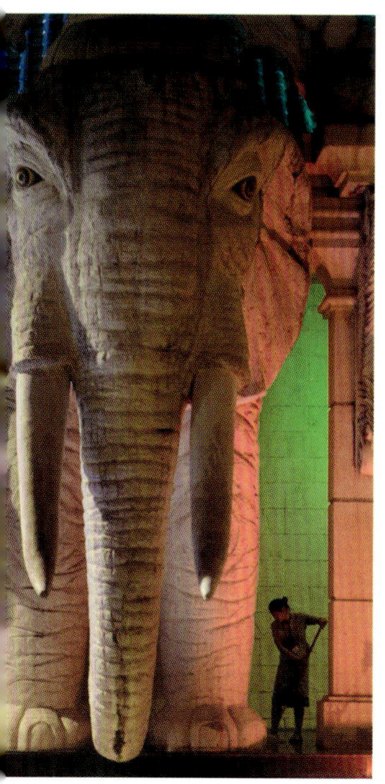

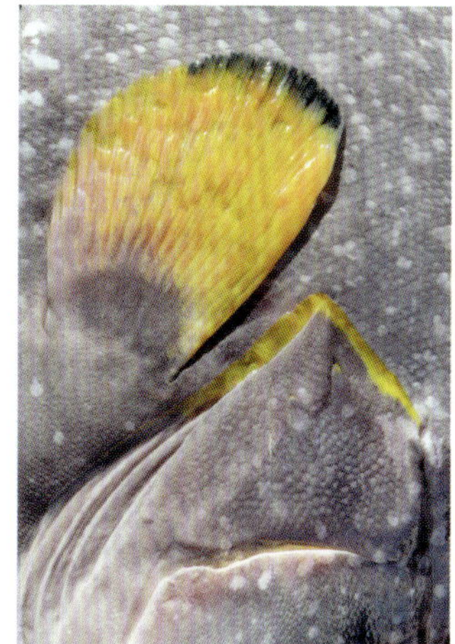

but they tend to stick to well-defined markets. You need only look at fashion and decorating in any one country to see that a yearly or even seasonal change in trending colors is a retail necessity. Pantone has for many years promoted a Color of the Year, just to keep business moving. In the year I'm writing this, it's yellow and grey, or in their terms 'a bright and cheerful yellow sparkling with vivacity, a warming yellow shade imbued with solar power' together with 'Ultimate Gray . . . emblematic of solid and dependable elements which are everlasting and provide a firm foundation'.[†] Actually, you can see just this here (left). The fish beat Pantone to it by a comfortable margin of time.

The second problem is that the 'being pleasing' aspect of harmony means expected, comfortable and essentially conservative. In other words not challenging, instead following what the audience already likes. Now, that's a formula for advertising and marketing, but it's questionable for art and creativity. Naturally, we all want to satisfy some audience, but which one? There's usually a gulf between popular taste and expert taste. The first will get you more numbers, but the second is more likely to get you status and even awards. Challenging popular taste, a.k.a. accepted harmony, runs risks of falling flat, but there's also the opportunity to move ahead of the game.

The history of art and other creative media is filled with upheavals as newcomers deliberately shake up what they see as the boring status quo. I just mentioned violet, which happens to be one of the more uncommon colors. In fact, violet burst into the art world in 1874, when the French Impressionists began their exhibitions. Édouard Manet soon predicted that 'within three years everyone will be painting violet'.[‡] Many critics were outraged at the 'unrealistic' color, but it became fashionable, particularly when paired with yellow, as it often was, to contrast sunlight and shadow (as in *The Four Trees*, 1891 by Monet).

Perhaps it's more realistic to think about different harmonies, and about harmonies that change over time. The violets paired with yellows that seemed discordant to gallery-goers in Paris in the 1870s are now perfectly acceptable. What is certainly true is that people have stronger opinions about stronger colors, so one easy option for harmony is to use less saturated colors, perhaps also varying the brightness to be less strident. The picture on the opposite page illustrates this simple fact of color life. Otherwise, rather than fret over harmony, it might be better simply to explore and see how you feel about the result, which we'll be doing in Chapter 4. If you like the result, maybe it doesn't matter if some others don't.

[†] Pantone Color of the Year, www.pantone.com/uk/en/color-of-the-year-2021

[‡] David Scott Kastan, *On Color* (Yale University Press, New Haven and London, 2018)

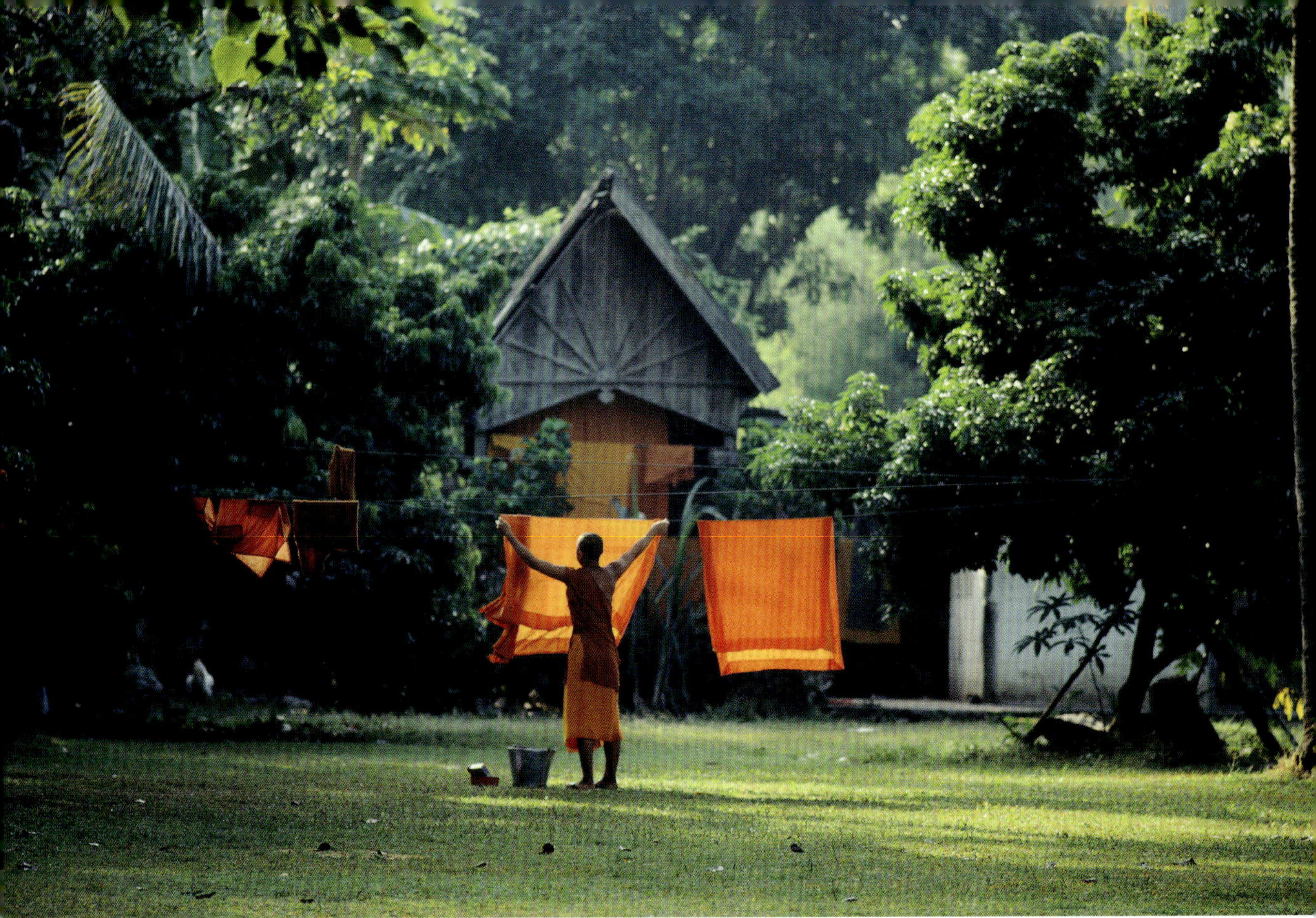

DELIVERED OR DISCOVERED

This is about authorship, and it's a special concern for color in photography. If a picture is more about color than anything else, how much does it matter where that color came from or more specifically, who created the color, you or someone else?

If you copy a painting (which is a branch of photography, after all), then it's clearly a record of the artist's work, not your creativity. It would be almost the same with street art, though that depends on the context. If it's a wall painting and nothing else – let's say a Banksy creation – it's still a record of Banksy's work. But if you include the surroundings, or wait for a passerby, then what? I'm not talking about copyright, which is another issue that you would face if you decided to sell the photograph, but about where it puts you as the creative author of the picture.

Backlighting from an early morning sun helps to make the shot, as does capturing the short moment of this monk in northern Thailand hanging his saffron robes out to dry, and the small patches of orange standing out against the many greens. Briefly glimpsed color combinations like this have the pleasure of unpredictable found pictures.

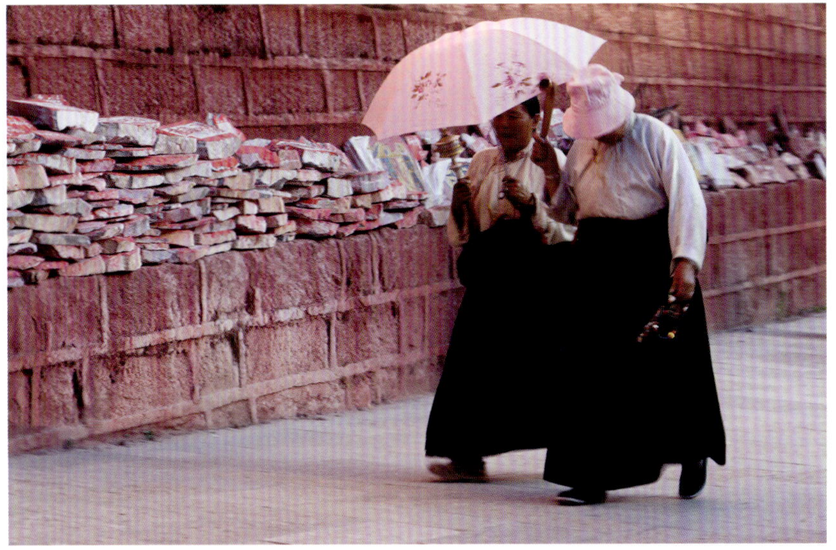

More unexpected is color coincidence, which is similar to the sort of coincidences of unexpected things coming together in street photography. Walking around the sacred Scripture House in Dege, western Sichuan, two Tibetan women add the pink of a parasol and hat to the color of the stone walls and broken prayer stones.

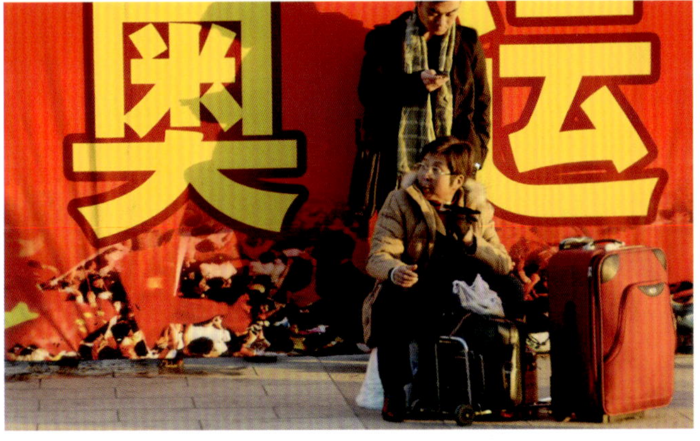

The colors of signage outside one of Beijing's rail stations are striking and rich, but perhaps a little less satisfying for being already provided. Fortunately, the matching red suitcase was a little more of a discovery.

Not everyone bothers about this, though I do. In the same way that I don't have all that much time for pictures about words (where what you can read in the picture is largely its point), I can't get as excited about a scene where someone else has been responsible for the coloring than when I've made the discovery. In signage, or even in colorful house façades, I've had a key part of the picture delivered to me on a plate. That doesn't stop me shooting, I'll admit, but I'm not quite so proud of the finished image.

You may see where this is going. Discovering color in situations where it might not be so obvious or predictable feeds into the larger issue of skill in shooting. As in the other titles in this series, I'm writing not so much about the aims and purposes of photography, but about its practice, and that is heavily skill-based. The first skill called upon in taking a photograph is observing at a heightened level of awareness and alertness. If you admit the competitive nature of creative photography, that means staying alert to the possibility of a unique image – unique because only you saw it or thought of it – and a situation that isn't likely to be repeated. Skill in color very much starts with finding a combination and recognizing it, quickly followed by capture. All color-forward photography is about some sort of combination.

DOMINANT COLOR

The simplest color statement you can make in photography is one strong hue covering most or all of the frame. Nearly all notable colorist photographers, like Pete Turner, Harry Gruyaert and Ernst Haas, have done this more than once, and the appeal of staying within one hue goes back to color field painting of the 1950s and 1960s.

This grew out of Abstract Expressionism, and while most color field painting involved relationships between blocks of color, Mark Rothko and Barnett Newman in particular experimented with modulations on a single color. The aim, in any case, was that 'color is freed from objective context and becomes the subject in itself'.[†]

Unlike abstract painting, however, the question of where the single, strong hue actually comes from affects the success of the photograph. The easy way would be to use a colored filter over the lens or simply use extreme controls during processing or post-production, but anything like this is so instant and lacking in skill that it's hardly worth a second glance. Already-painted surfaces are an obviously important source, but as we saw on the previous pages, if there's nothing else going on photographically – such as viewpoint, framing, composition – there's not much point to the picture. However abstract a photograph becomes, there is nearly always the sense that there is some reality being captured. There's a strong argument for making sure that there is some interest or intrigue in where and how the suffusing color comes from. It adds to the story a little, as in the examples here.

Daylight filters through blocks of ice at the Ice Hotel in northern Sweden, a seasonally constructed resort built entirely of ice each winter. The interior is at a constant -5 degrees to -7 degrees and all the furniture and beds are of ice. The blue color that permeates throughout is because ice absorbs the red wavelengths of light.

LED lamps being stress-tested in an industrial oven. The atmosphere inside not only diffuses the light but spreads the narrow range of color, from yellow to orange, across the whole picture frame, which was cropped to maintain the sense of a single color.

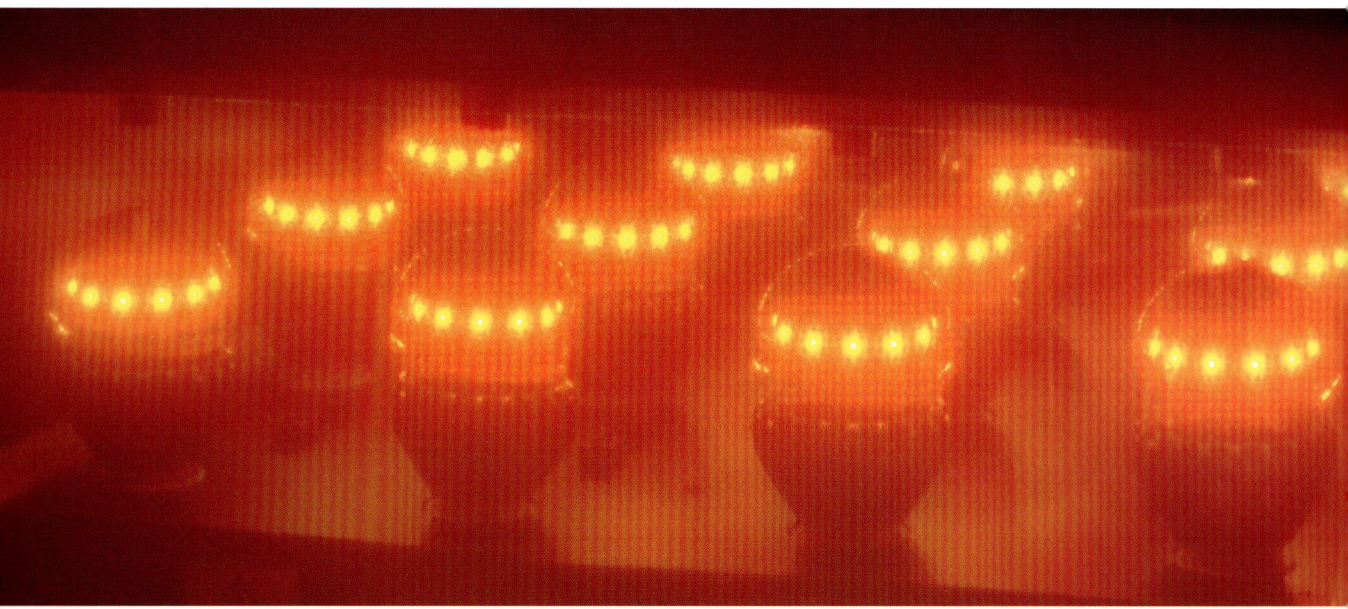

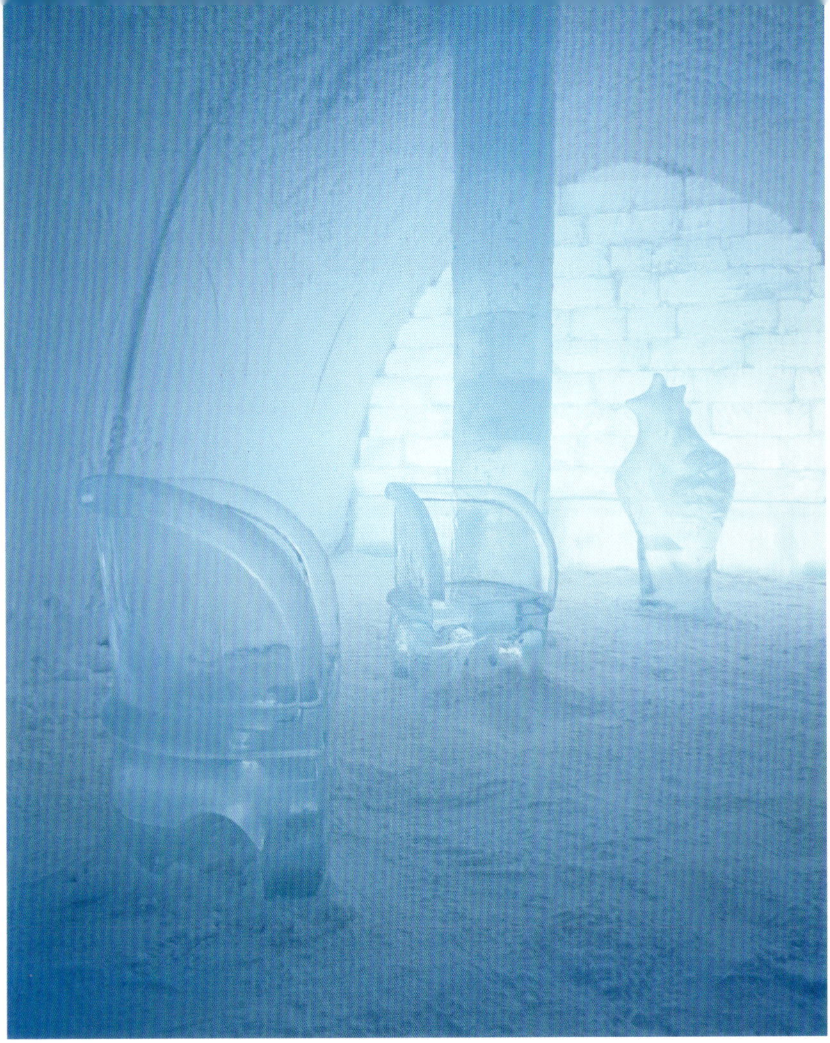

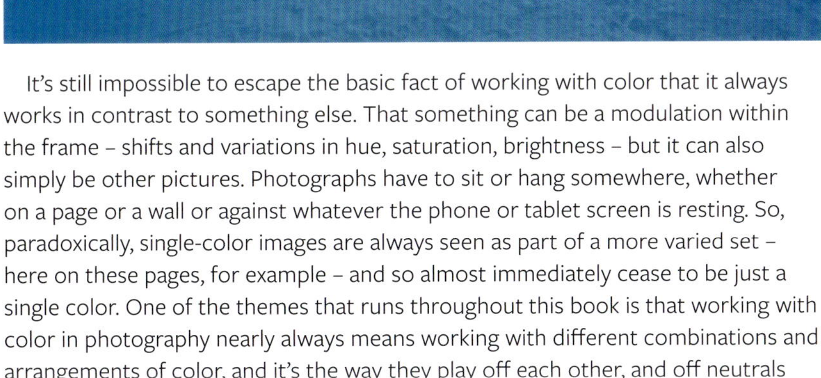

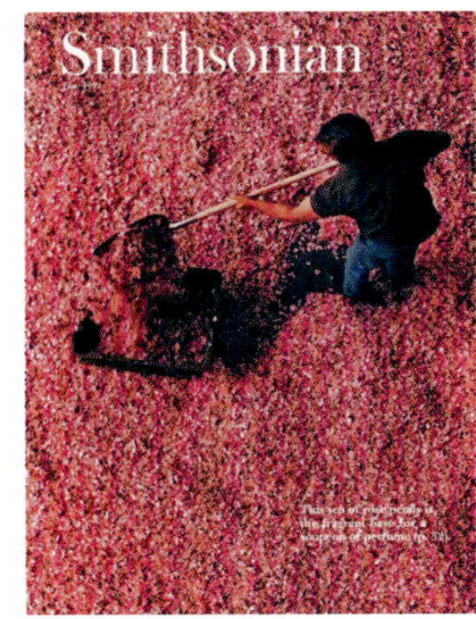

For a story on perfume, the cover was planned to be a striking single color, rose pink, achieved by shooting down onto a mass of harvested roses spread out on a factory floor to dry.

It's still impossible to escape the basic fact of working with color that it always works in contrast to something else. That something can be a modulation within the frame – shifts and variations in hue, saturation, brightness – but it can also simply be other pictures. Photographs have to sit or hang somewhere, whether on a page or a wall or against whatever the phone or tablet screen is resting. So, paradoxically, single-color images are always seen as part of a more varied set – here on these pages, for example – and so almost immediately cease to be just a single color. One of the themes that runs throughout this book is that working with color in photography nearly always means working with different combinations and arrangements of color, and it's the way they play off each other, and off neutrals and backgrounds, that ultimately satisfies.

[†] *Themes in American Art: Abstraction* (National Gallery of Art, June 2011)

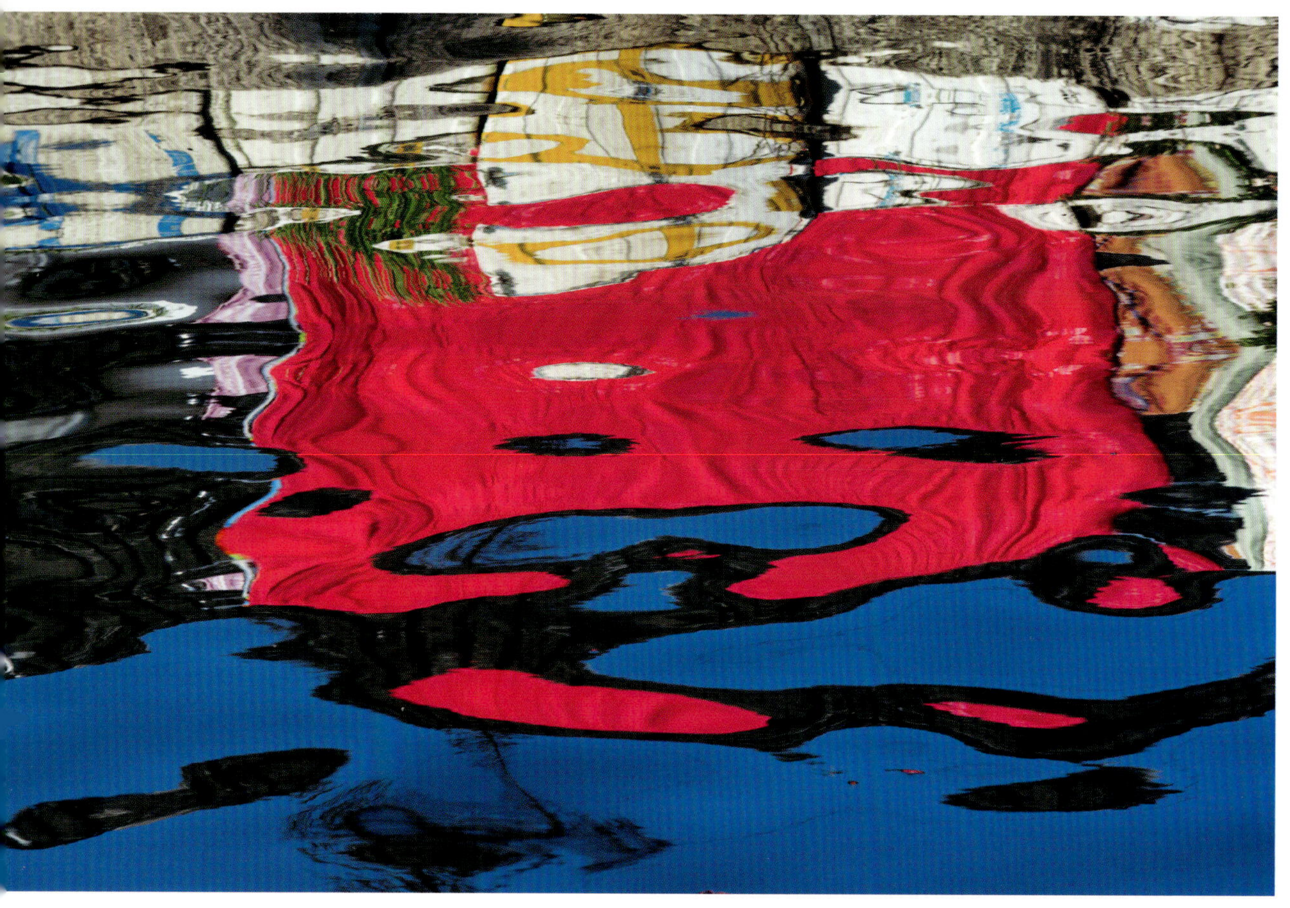

REFLECTED COLORS

Reflections play a special role in the photography of colors. They do in all photography, because they have the capacity to bring a second layer into an image, but with color they help to abstract.

In other words, as long as the reflective surface isn't perfect and they are not exact, adding colors to an image in this way helps to make their origin less obvious. As I mentioned at the beginning, pushing color forward inevitably means pulling other image qualities back – and recognizable content is a prime candidate. Nevertheless, there's a practical limit to this in photography, as we saw on the previous pages. Reducing the importance of content isn't the same as eliminating it entirely.

A brightly colored blanket hanging out to dry on the banks of a canal in a water town in the Yangtze delta, China, becomes a pure abstract reflected in the water, against a blue sky.

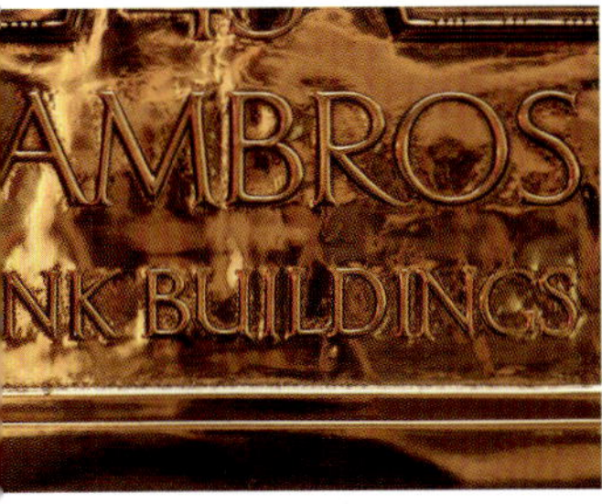

The polished brass plaque of a bank in the City of London acquires a new and ambiguous color interest as it catches the reflection of a passing double-decker red bus, itself in sunlight.

The slightly metallic glaze on Middle Eastern decorative tiles adds its own sheen to the colors of a sunlit garden that they reflect.

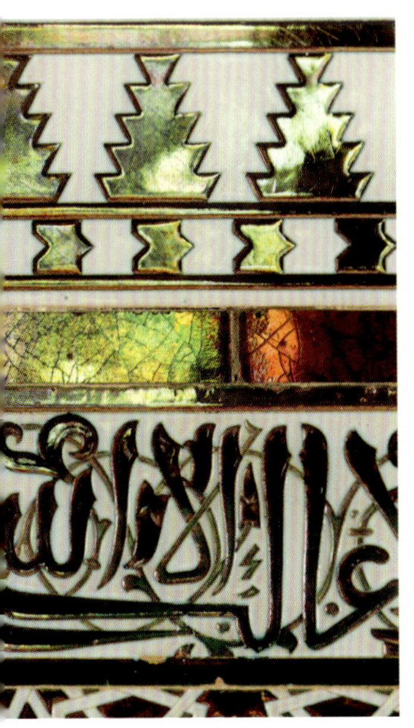

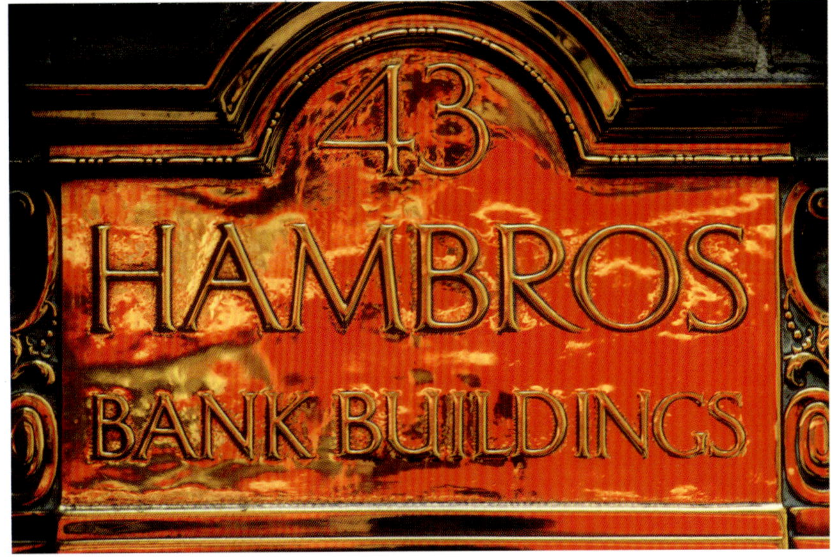

This falls into the same category as the slow reveal in composition and deliberately obscuring parts of the image, both of which are in *Michael Freeman on... Composition*. It uses ambiguity to try and be more intriguing. There's the usual risk of confusing or irritating the viewer, but it's arguably less in this case because color patterns and arrangements have long been accepted as images worth looking at in their own right. For this we have decades of abstract painting to thank. Even if the unexplained color addition is simply an invitation to guess where it might be coming from, as in the old bank plaque above, most viewers are prepared to play along. It's a kind of game in which the photographer looks for the unexpected that other people might not notice. Distortion often plays a part in this, by bending the original shapes and forms and making them harder to interpret. In fact. there's nothing new in this kind of showing off. Many classical painters excelled at playing with reflections to bring other layers into the picture. As Eugène Delacroix wrote, 'The more an object is polished or brilliant, the less you see its own color and the more it becomes a mirror reflecting the color of its surroundings'.

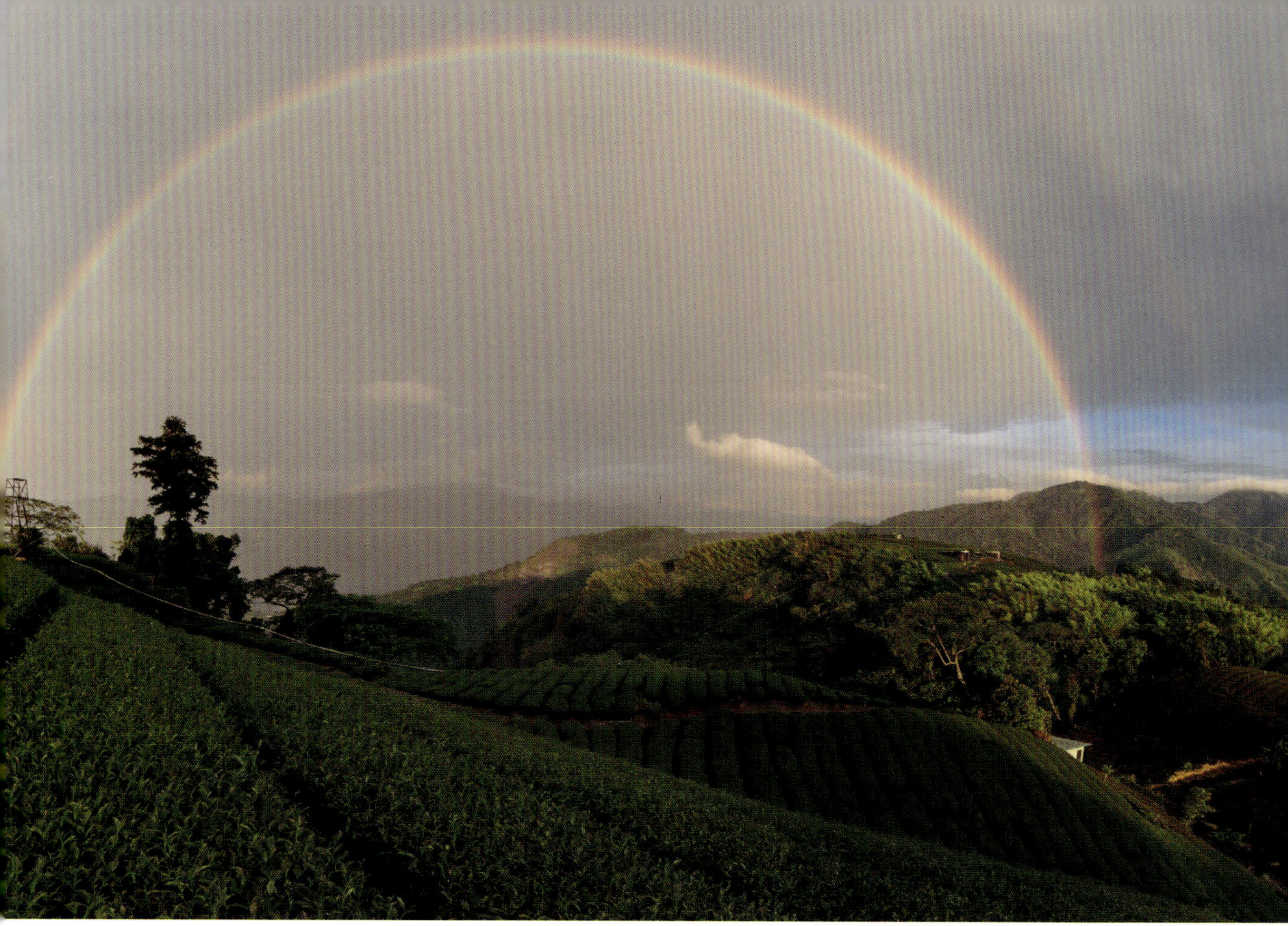

SPECTRAL COLORS

F ew colors in the natural world are pure, in the sense of fully saturated and optimally bright, but there's one exception that continues to fascinate photographers, and that's the set of spectral colors that Newton first discovered.

The spectrum, or at least a good part of it, doesn't occur often, and probably most people's experience is in the form of a rainbow. That's not frequent either, and short-lived, so the relative scarcity of these multicolor and pure color displays is a large part of their appeal. There are a few related causes, though I'll skim over them because they don't affect the photography, which is pretty straightforward once you've found the subject. Rainbows happen by refraction, like a prism but in large numbers of small droplets, and the different wavelengths that make up 'white' light bend at different angles, so get separated. Oil film and soap bubbles get their color effect by thin-film

A particularly full rainbow, with a faint double, because the sun behind the camera is lower than usual (this is a mountain top in Taiwan). The way the spectral colors merge into each other leaves room to dispute how many there are: seven or less?

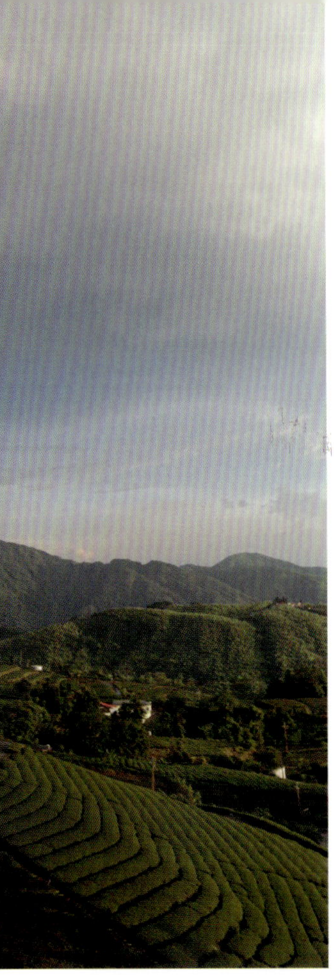

interference, with slight differences in the thickness of the 'skin' affecting some wavelengths more than others. The polished shell of an abalone, shown on page 172, displays its iridescence mainly because of diffraction through the thin layers of nacre.

This raises a perfectly valid and practical question: how many colors are there in the spectrum? I'm getting ahead of myself here, as we'll be dealing with the spectrum in the next chapter, but the naming of colors is an important part of how we perceive them. It's complicated, not least because meanings and definitions change between languages, but crudely put, we give names to those colors that we see as being distinct. If it's a color that we see as clearly different from others, it has a name. Anyway, even on the clearest of days and in the best conditions, I wonder how many people could see all seven 'traditional' colors in a rainbow. Try it yourself the next time you see one. Even Newton wasn't certain.

Apart from the natural fascination in coming across spectral colors in a group, being both colorful and uncommon, there's also a photographic history of shooting them, from Ernst Haas' oil slicks on New York streets to Galen Rowell's rainbow over the Potala in Lhasa, Tibet. For purity, it's the ultimate photographic excursion into color, which is why I'm showing it here. It's probably a good job that these happen rarely, as a regular diet of intense color would be too much for most of us. They set a kind of aesthetic limit to color in photography, and for me at least are a convincing argument for spending more time with the opposite – more delicate and less insistent colors.

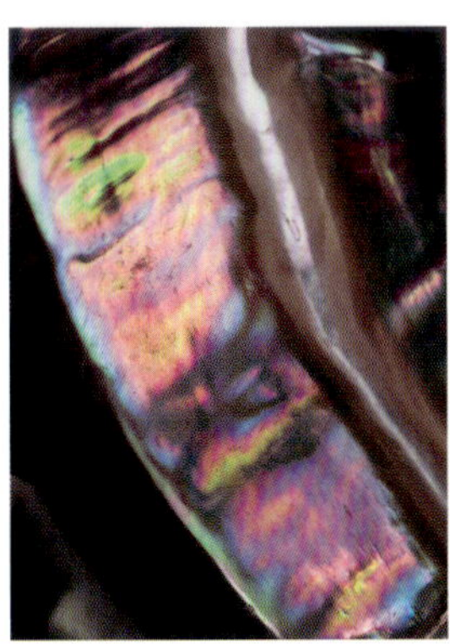

Two other surfaces which divide the light spectrally: a polished turban shell above (diffraction) and soap bubbles right (thin-film interference).

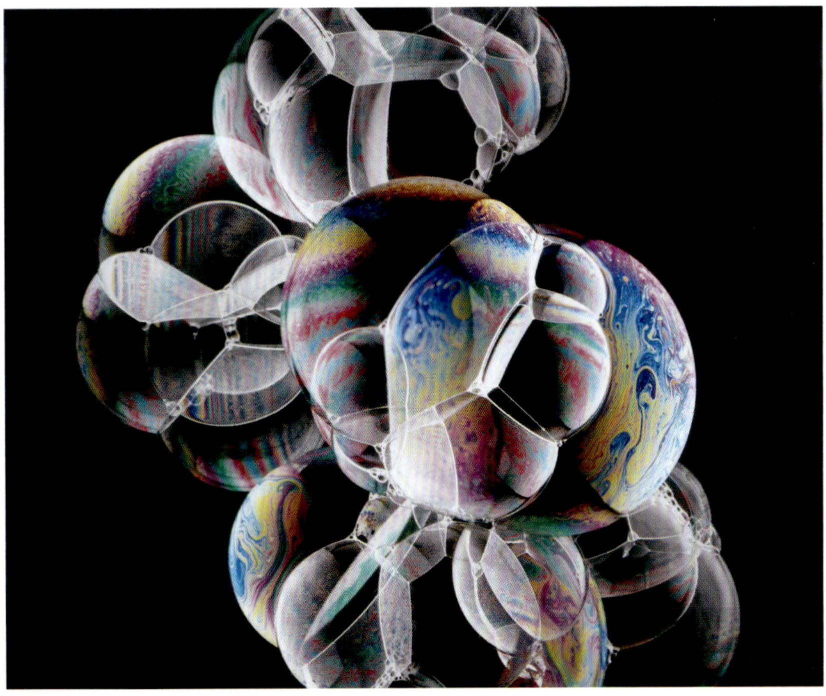

COLOR PERSUASION

As we'll see in the next chapter, color is in the mind. That's where it's processed and recognized, so it shouldn't come as any surprise that we can be influenced in how we react to colors – basically to like or dislike, and to have feelings that might persuade us to, well, buy a product. Advertising uses positive or associative words to promote everything from home decorating paints ('fresh clean minty blue') to lipsticks ('light peach shimmer') to holiday resorts ('candy-hued' evenings).

This is the world of color semantics, where words influence perception, and in photography it applies to color more than to any other image quality I can think of. You can prime the audience's response, because color pulls on emotions. I did an analysis of more than 30 books and catalogues with critical writings on photography (basically everything relevant in my library), pulling out the adjectives used to describe color, and the results intrigued me.

On a scale from vivid to muted (these are neutral terms), approval and disapproval were concentrated at the far ends, meaning that critics and commentators had extreme opinions of extremes of color, as you might expect. The vocabulary is extensive, and you can see some of it on either side of the two images here, and what's most telling is that these words are used to justify personal taste rather than to be descriptive. Neutral terms are quite rare; instead, adjectives are almost always used to try and persuade the reader that the writer's judgement is correct. This has an inevitable result: the most extreme approval and disapproval words can be used for the same color images. In today's universe of color in photography, this is the biggest divide.

More than that, there's a clear division between what's popular and what the refined art photography world likes. Popular taste tends towards stronger, definite colors, art-critical taste towards muted, and each side complains about the other. This rift in color photography began in the 1970s, first in America with New York's Museum of Modern Art at its centre, before spreading to Europe. It acquired a name – New Color – with a manifesto that rejected colorfulness as being crass and the proper preserve only of advertising and low culture. Refinement meant austerity in color. The underlying idea is that if most people like it, it stops being art, which is an argument that doesn't bear much looking into, yet still persists. With this in mind, you'll hopefully see that I'm trying to stay neutral in my descriptions. In fact, parts of me like both extremes, but in small doses, not as a constant diet.

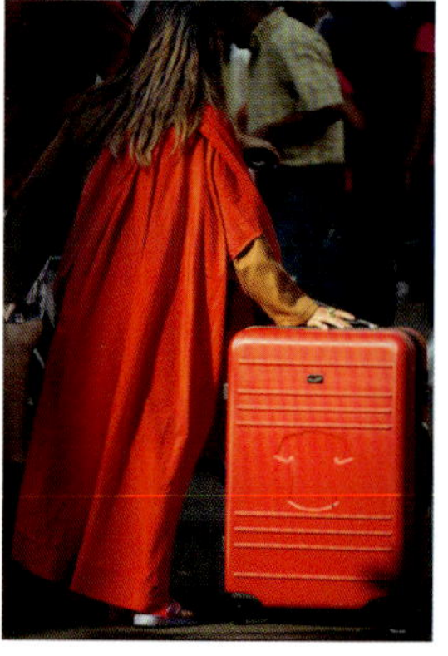

Objectively, the marked differences between the two pictures at right can be expressed simply in terms of hue relationships, saturation and brightness, but in terms of taste, each can be described in polar opposite terms.

A generalized view of the contrary color opinions between popular and the established art world, as applied to color photographs. The scale from approval (green) to disapproval (red) is reversed.

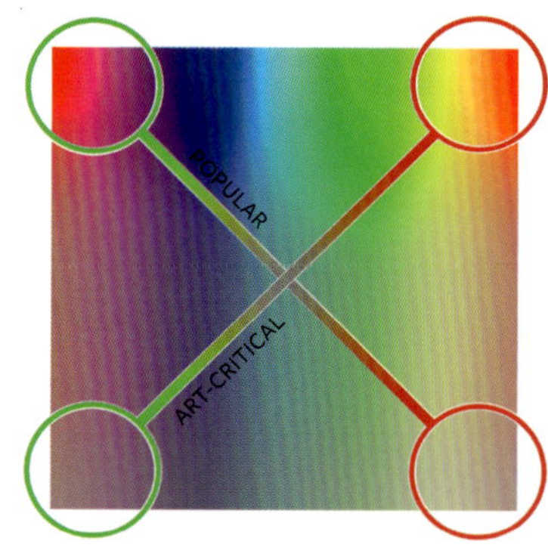

<table>
<tr><td>

Exuberant
Rich
Intense
Expressive
Vibrant
Spectacular
Bold
Dramatic
Funky
Popping

</td><td>

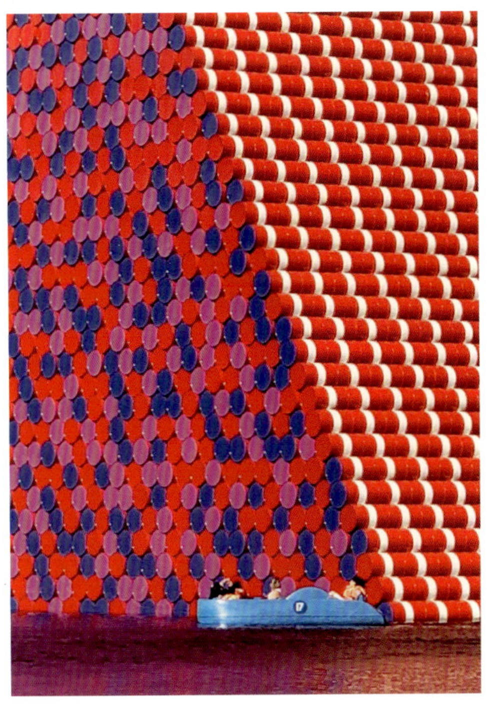

</td><td>

Lurid
Jolting
Vulgar
Sensational
Kitsch
Garish
Brash
Raucous
Exaggerated
Slick
Clashing
Theatrical

</td></tr>
<tr><td>

Subtle
Understated
Nuanced
Restrained
Delicate

</td><td>

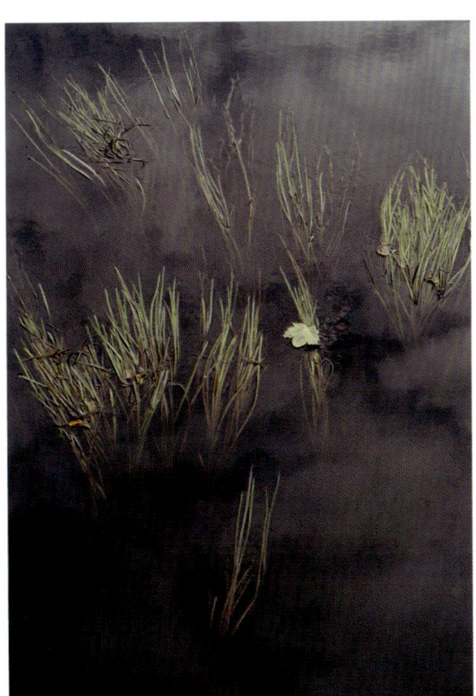

</td><td>

Dull
Muddy
Insipid
Flat
Bland

</td></tr>
</table>

2

COLOR SCIENCE

You'll see that there are lots of threes in this chapter. There are three kinds of color receptor in our eyes, three colors in the filter in front of our cameras' sensors, three colors in the screens we look at, and indeed we need three numbers (axes if you like) to define any color. You'll also see three color models, three color spaces and three color profiles, though this last one is because I've selected the only three of each that are standard, basic and useful for photographers.

For anyone interested in using color in photography (or anywhere else for that matter, but photography's what I'm focused on), many of the most fascinating questions are best answered by the science. Why are purples and violets tricky to capture? Why are they relatively rare? Why is yellow brighter than any other color? Why is red so strong and why is it often exaggerated in digital capture? And why, despite the many claims to the contrary on the web, are we more tolerant of differences between greens than any other color? It's all in the science; it isn't painful and doesn't involve equations, and ignoring it results in such wrong assumptions as that last one about green.

That probably came about because we are more sensitive
to green than any other wavelength, but that's not the same
 as being able to discriminate fine differences, and once a
myth takes hold, it gets repeated by everyone who prefers
not to think.

Treat this as the reference chapter of the book. It may seem far
from the creativity and pleasure of color, but it deals with the
underpinning. And it really does help explain why we react to
certain colors and color combinations in the way we do.

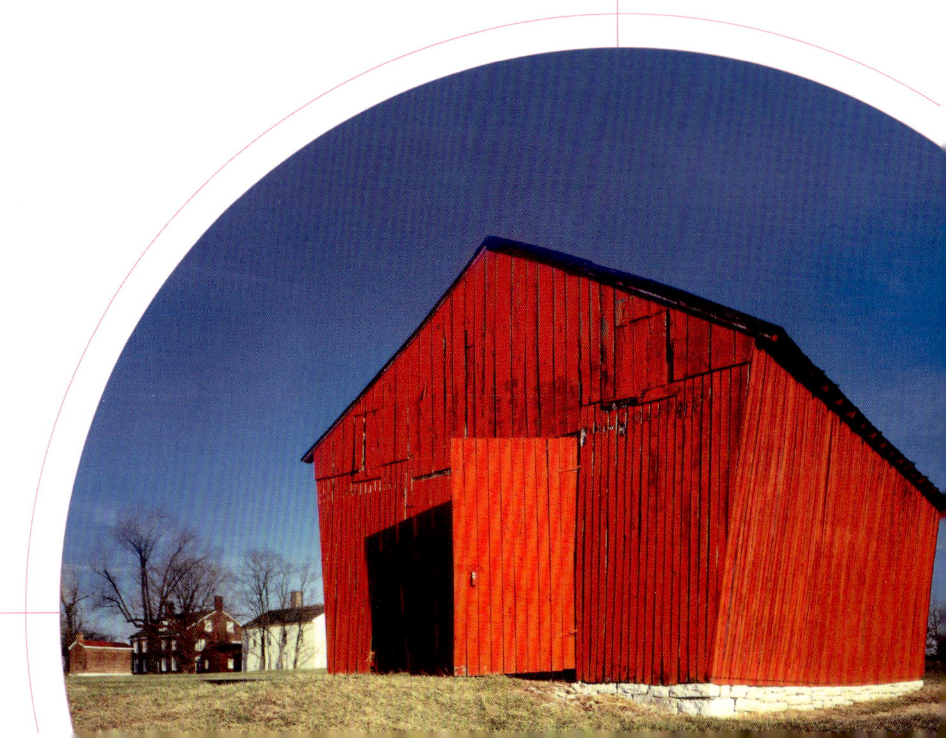

WAVELENGTH IN THE EYE...

olor science essentially began with Newton, who found not only that visible light can be divided into wavelengths of different colors, but that once separated, these colors could not be changed.

As shown in the band illustrated opposite, what we can see goes from just above ultraviolet to just below infrared. These are the spectral colors, and it's worth bearing in mind that most of the colors we see day to day are not these, but rather reflected light that's a mixture of wavelengths. We normally don't look at light sources because they can be uncomfortable (and seriously damaging in the case of the sun).

The photoreceptors in our retinas that react to these wavelengths are the cones, and there are three types, each sensitive to a different spread of wavelengths across this spectrum. Named after the wavelengths they are most sensitive to, they are short (S), middle (M) and long (L), and, as you see opposite, they overlap considerably. The L cones are very close in sensitivity to the M, and it actually peaks (i.e., is at its most sensitive) in yellowish green. Notice also the small bump at the far left in both the M and L which, added to the peak in the S, accounts for the reddish component of violet. For more on the 'difficult' range between violet and purple, see page 37.

The essential takeaway is that our eyes have evolved a tristimulus method of recording color, meaning we can distinguish millions of colors from just three signals. How many millions is open to discussion, but probably between about eight and ten million.

Sunlight refracted through a glass roof projects a spectrum onto a wall: a clear spread of the visible wavelengths similar to those on pages 26–7. The brightest colors are in the centre, as expected from the illustration below right.

Saturation, or rather lack of it, can confuse our sense of hue. Very rarely is it pure (as in the picture opposite). More usually it's intermediate, as in the picture of Burmese women carrying rice baskets below. The sequence of three goes from desaturated to fully saturated, with the accurate capture in the middle.

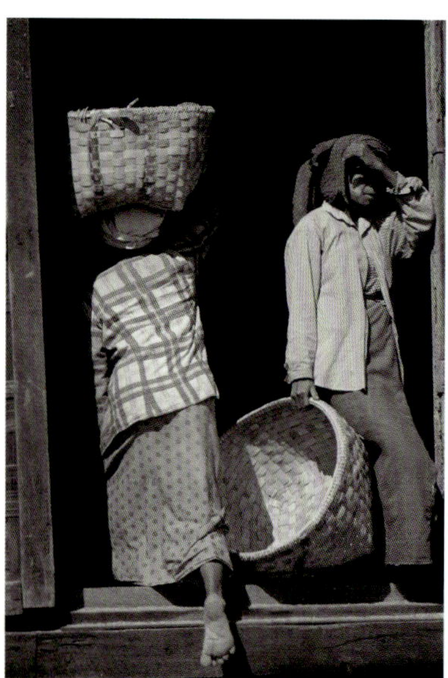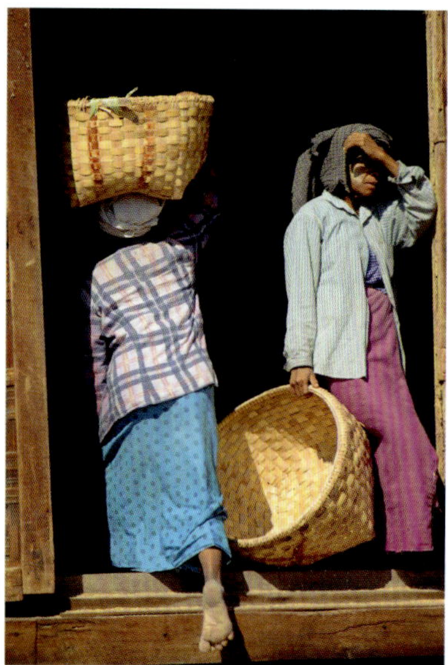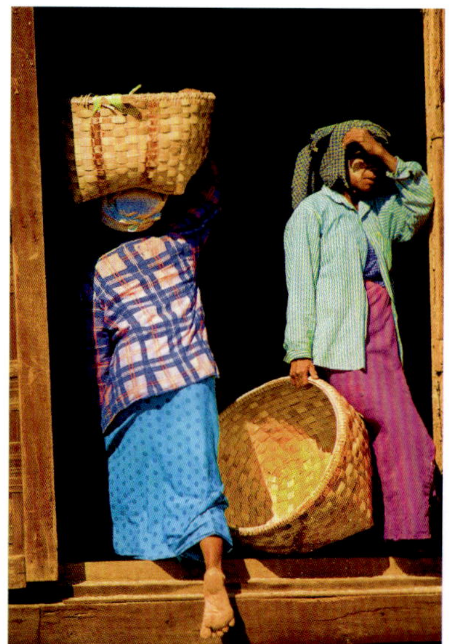

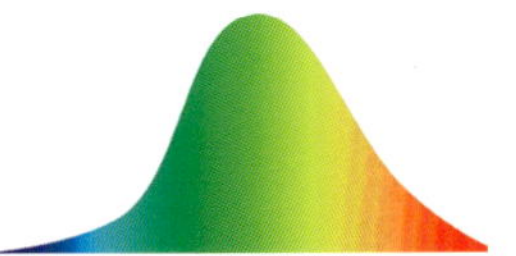

The illustration below shows how the retina responds to different wavelengths of light along the visible spectrum (shortest left to longest right). The three types of cones sensitive to wavelength are called short, medium and long, but they don't divide the spectrum equally, and both the medium and long peak close to each other in the green-yellow area. As a result, the Luminosity Curve above peaks strongly in green and yellow.

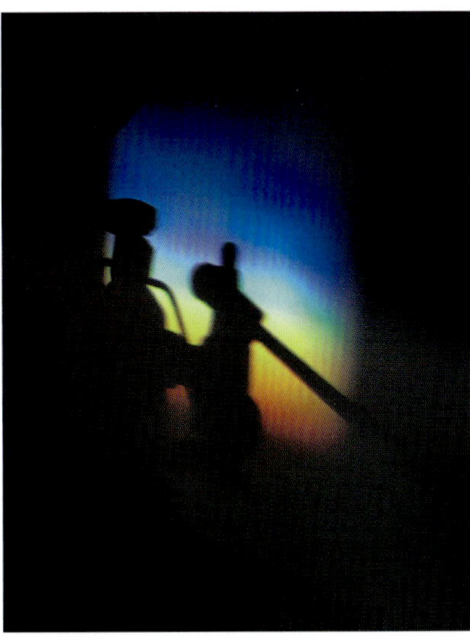

Combined, these three types of cones give a response curve (shown left). This is the luminosity curve and it peaks quite strongly in yellowish green. If you look at the difference in sensitivity between blue and green – about 20x for the wavelengths marked – it's clear that for our eyes, spectral blue is dark and spectral greens and yellows are bright. Fast forward to camera sensors (see page 50), and that explains why the green filters in a Bayer array are used to measure brightness as well as color (and why some manufacturers have used yellow instead of green in the array to gather almost half as much extra brightness information).

Also obvious from just looking at the spectrum is that the colored wavelengths merge smoothly into each other, so that raises a simple question: how many colors are there? It's considered normal to 'see' seven. From long to short they are red, orange, yellow, green, blue, indigo violet (one mnemonic is Richard Of York Gave Battle In Vain, another is ROY G BIV), but you could have as many – or as few – as you like. We'll look more at this later (page 36), but Newton started with five, and later added indigo and violet. Orange, in fact, didn't enter European languages as a color until the late 16th century, when the fruit that gives it its name also started to arrive. And what about cyan? That lies between blue and green, so you could label that if you wanted. We use color words for convenience, but they are just descriptions.

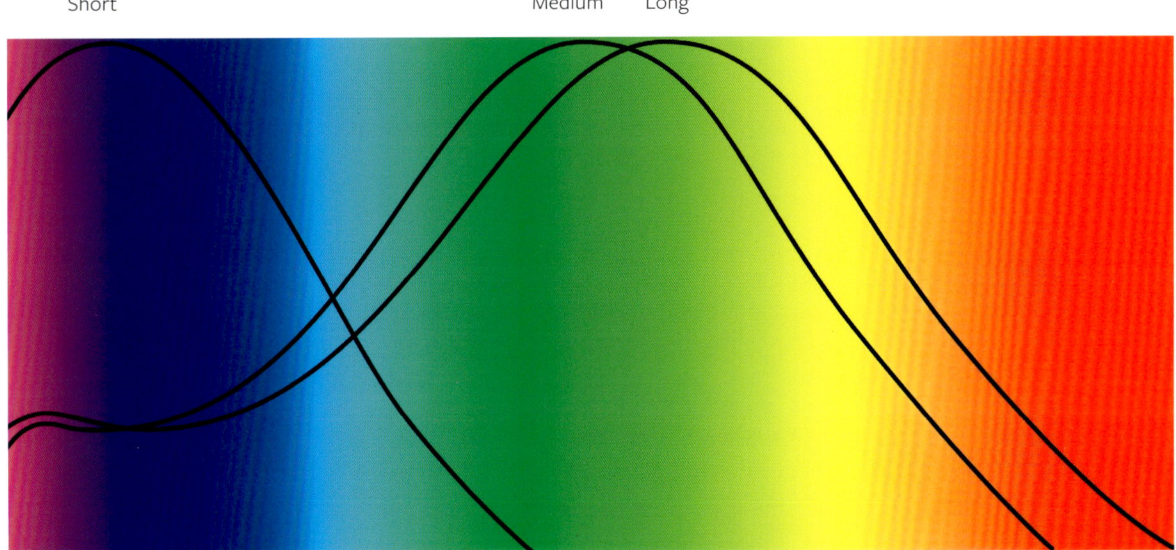

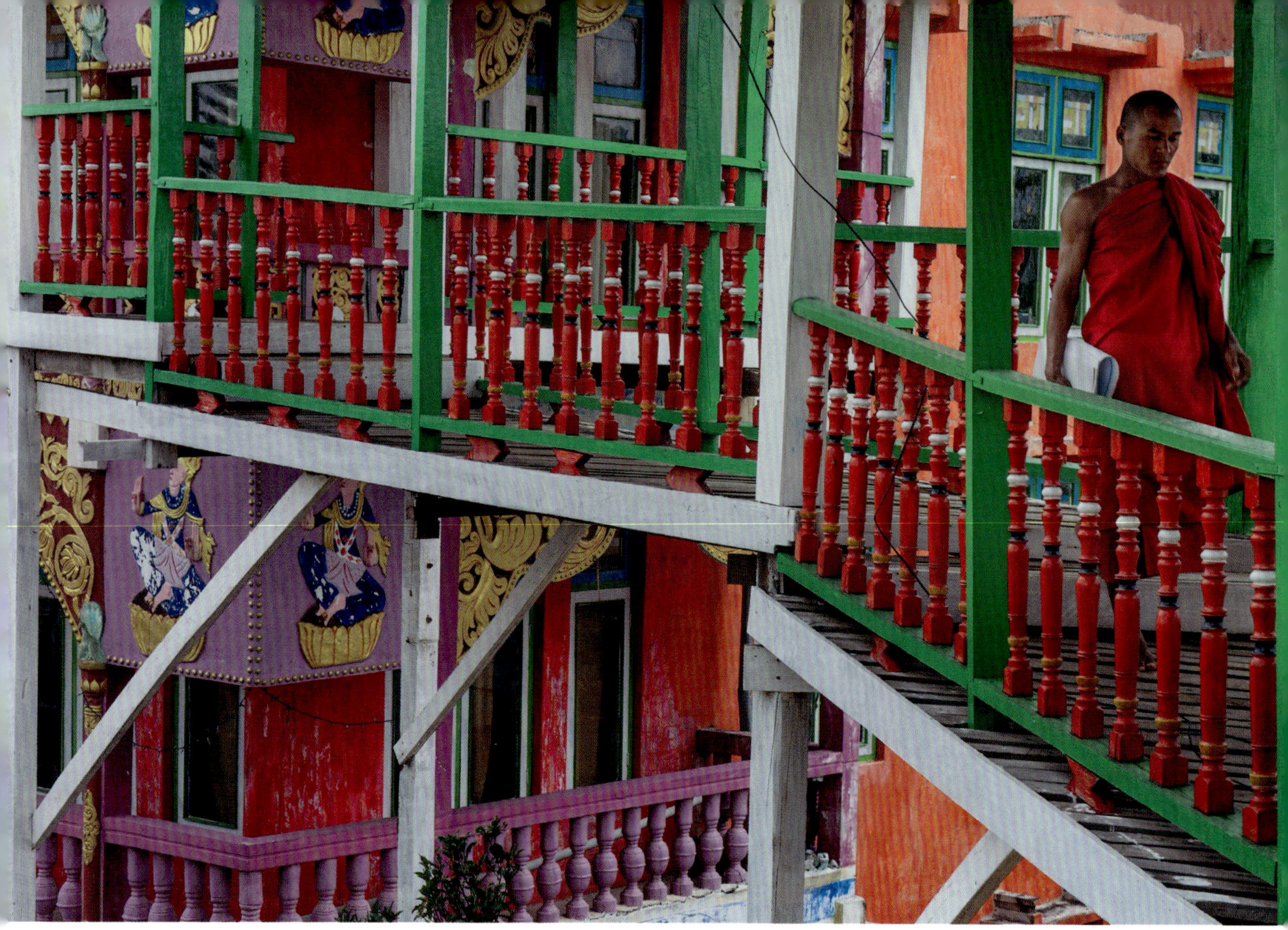

...COLOR IN THE MIND

The cones in the retina are just the start of the color vision pipeline, which physically goes straight to the back of the brain in the occipital lobe and then on for higher processing to the temporal and parietal lobes in the middle.

It's this processing that lets us recognize color and do things with it like consider relationships and make judgements. Color in the ways we'll look at in this book is very much in the mind. Also, colors and tones are always relative, and this is at the heart of everything to do with using color creatively in photography. They mean something only when we compare them with other colors or tones. One color next to or on top of a different color changes the way we look at it.

So, while the eye's color system is trichromatic – RGB (red, green, blue) basically – the mind's color system is different, and works on opposites. It's still a system based on three measurements (as I said earlier, there are lots of threes in color), but these

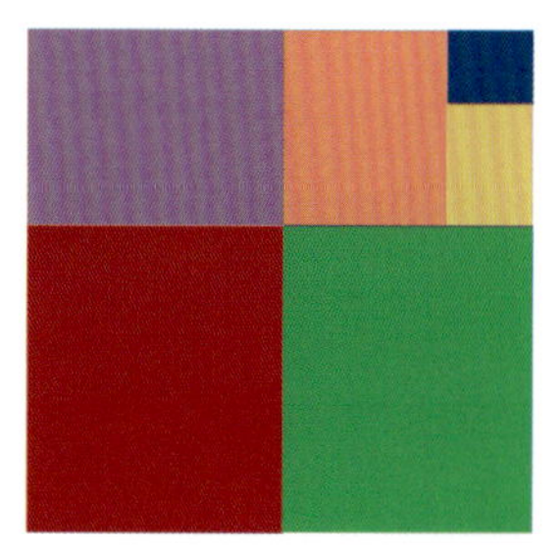

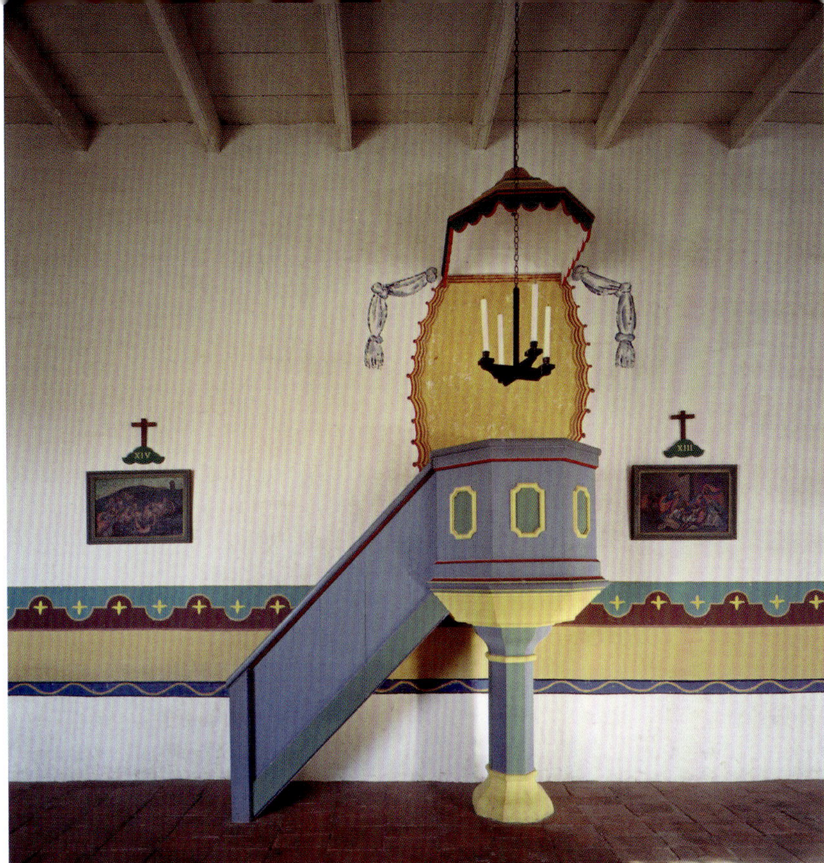

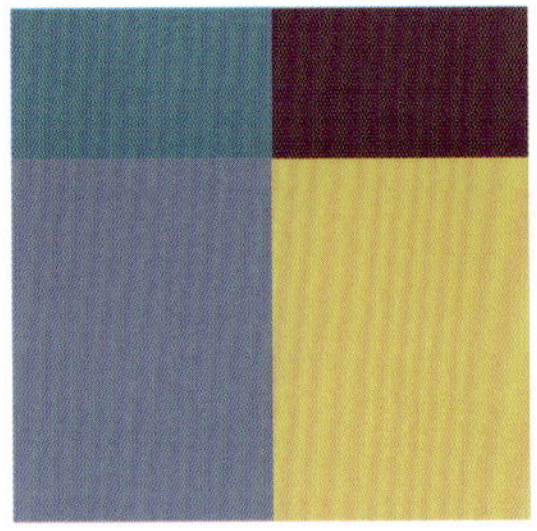

As in the picture opposite, the color scheme of this pulpit in the Mission San Francisco Solano, California, has been painted to satisfy the community's visual tastes. The hues are less saturated but still varied, and chosen because they intuitively 'go well together'.

The idea of being colorful, as this picture in a Burmese Buddhist monastery is, is entirely a mental construct, and revolves around good saturation and a number of very different hues.

are scales that go from one extreme to the other. One is luminosity, from black to white, and the other two are color opposites, red to green and blue to yellow. This is called the color opponent system, and it's important to grasp this very basic human way of perceiving – it goes further than color. It's basically a one-thing-or-another approach.

The color opposites are more complex than, for instance, the opposites of bright and dark. In the way we understand color, red and green are opposites – there's no such thing as a reddish-green – as are blue and yellow. It's not the way we describe color to each other or think about it consciously (we'll get to that later, see page 120), but it is the way our minds recognize it. As we'll see on the following pages, an important color model and color space (available for us to use in Photoshop *et al*) was created entirely around this: L*a*b*.

The important thing is that the wavelengths along the spectrum that we can measure, along with whatever happens to them as the light bounces around (muddying them, brightening them, darkening them), get translated by the eye and the mind into what we call color, and that is an experience, not reality. It seems like reality to each of us, but that's just because we believe our mind – and that's something skilled photography can play with.

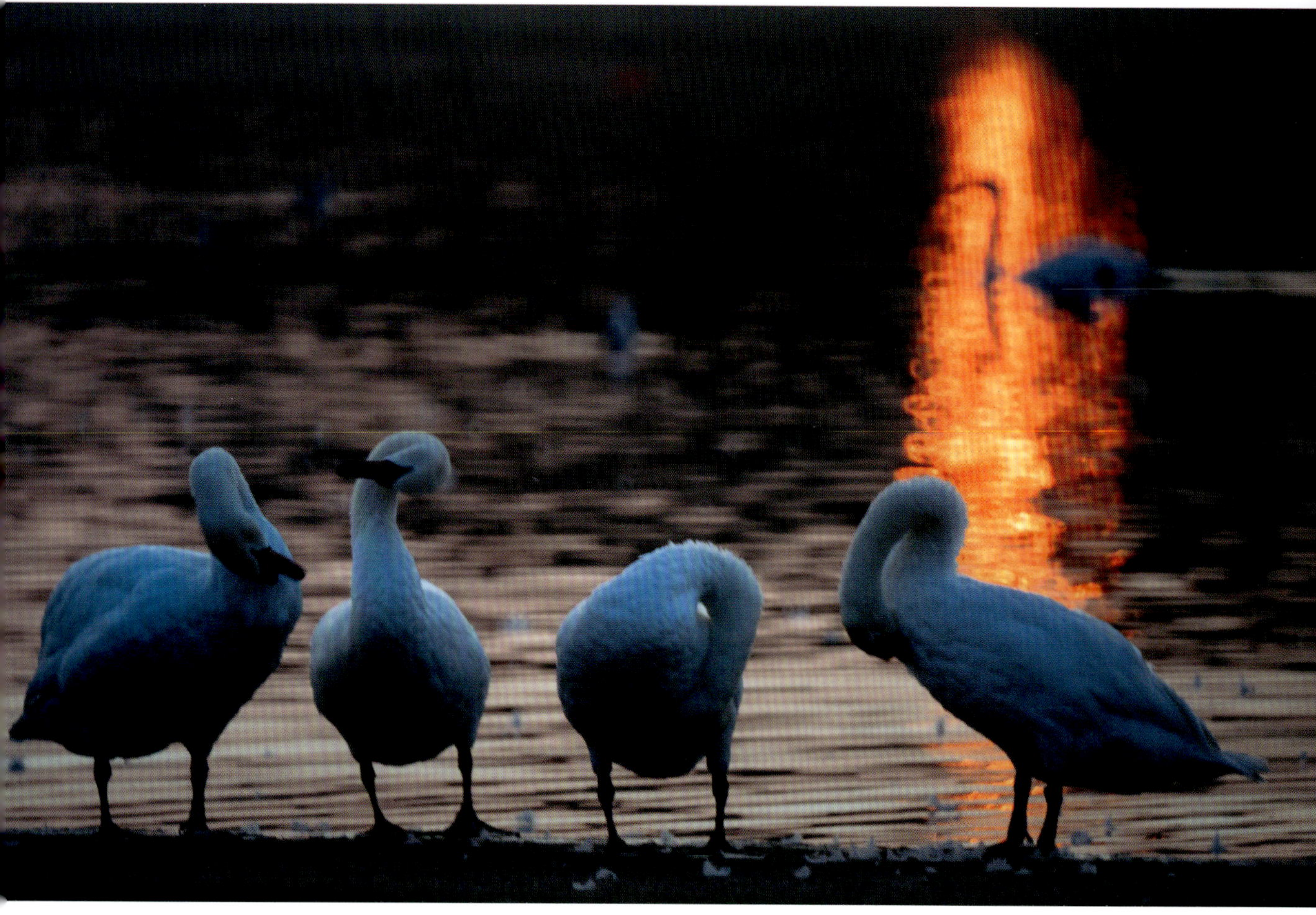

COLOR MODELS & SPACES

Simply to be able to start talking about colors, we need a way of arranging all of them into a space that we can visualize. If this sounds like it shouldn't be necessary if all we're doing is taking photographs, please bear with me, because it's fundamental to capturing images, processing them and evaluating them.

Most people are used to seeing colors arranged into a circle, and I'll be using this a lot in this book, but even so, this circle needs to come from somewhere. The way the colors progress is standard and comes from the spectrum – shading from blue

Swans at sunrise show the color temperature range that we can see, from the deep orange reflections of the low sun to the white feathers reflecting the blue sky behind the camera – the central curve in the color space opposite.

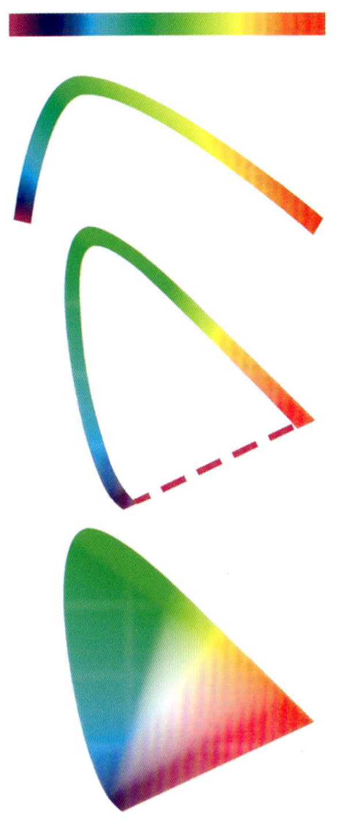

In effect, the linear color spectrum bends to became a horseshoe-shaped color space, fully saturated at the edges but neutral in the centre. The straight line that bridges the gap is the 'line of purples' that we can see but isn't spectral.

This is the standard CIE 1931 color space, a slice out of a 3D model, and contains (as well as can be shown on a printed page) the colors we can see. Wavelengths (black) and hue angles (red) are around the curve, while the black curved line in the centre (the Planckian locus) shows color temperature. In the middle is neutral, the color of the sun at midday.

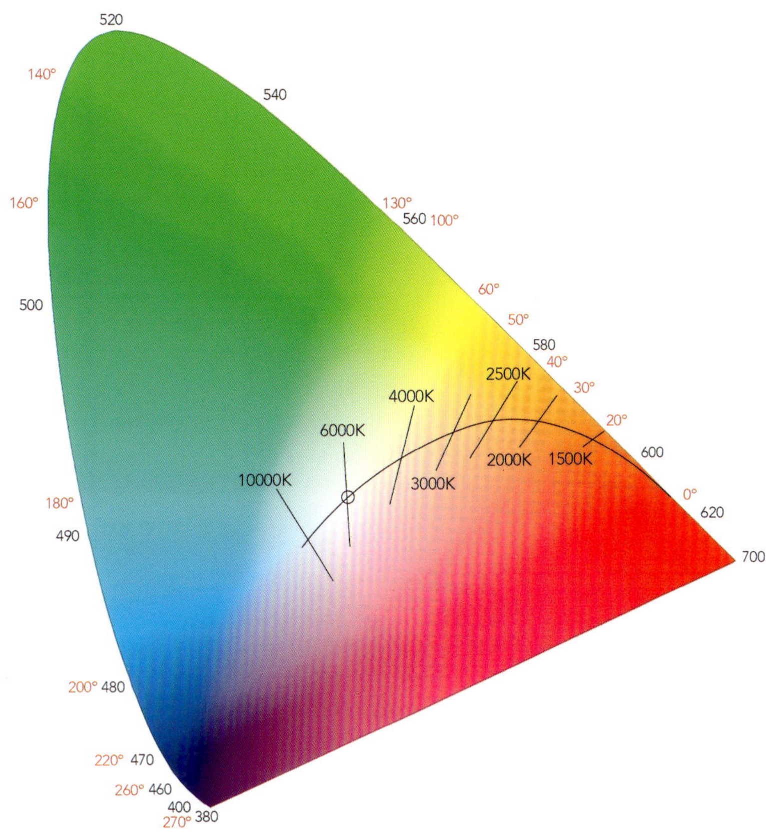

to green to yellow to red – but how much of the circle should each color take up? And what goes opposite what? Search on the web and you'll see many variations.

There is, in fact, a universally recognized standard. It comes from the CIE, short for Commission international de l'éclairage (International Commission on Illumination), the authority set up at the beginning of the 20th century. The horseshoe-shaped or tongue-shaped diagram familiar to anyone working in color is the CIE 1931 color space, which shows all the colors visible to someone with average eyesight. For convenience, this is a flat slice out of a more irregular solid model, and to be accurate it's called a chromaticity diagram.

The shape becomes less strange when we look at how it's constructed. The scale of visible wavelengths runs around the curve, and the elongation towards greens is because our eyes are especially sensitive to them. The straight edge at lower right is not on any wavelength, and is called the 'line of purples', made up of varying mixtures of violet and red (which are on the spectrum at either end). There is no purple light, just purple reflections, even though some mixtures of red and blue can be identical in color to violet. Because our sensitivity to violet and to far red is relatively weak, all of these purples are quite dark. Finally, the black line, known as the Planckian locus, is the range of color temperature that most photographers are familiar with as the difference between blue skies, midday sunlight, sunset and tungsten lamps. For more on this, see page 65.

This is the standard flat color model, and also color space (see Color Models vs Color Spaces below), and among other things we can lift a circle straight out of it. Now, while this is the color space for what we can see, in photography we have more limited color spaces for the colors we can record, process and view. Neither camera nor screens can show all of what the eye is capable of.

There are three basic kinds of color space useful for photography, each taking a different approach to color. One is based on how colors are created by mixing the three basic ones: red, green and blue – from now on I'll just say RGB. As we saw on page 32, our eyes record light using three kinds of cones, each sensitive to a different wavelength, and pass on the three signals down the pipeline to the brain. By definition (because color is what we can see), any color can be made by these three, and also that's how a camera sensor records color and how a screen displays it.

There's a second based on how we normally think about and describe colors by their hue, saturation and brightness: HSB. And there's a third based on how our brains handle color, which is in terms of opposites: L*a*b*. Each of these models and spaces is useful for some part of the business of dealing with color in photography. So we need all three; that's a model each for making, describing and perceiving. As I mentioned in the introduction, three different measurements are needed to pinpoint any color, and obviously they differ between the three color models, but what they have in common is that they are all in three dimensions. Because this is not very convenient to visualize as a still image, typically the color spaces you'll see are actually slices from a 3D shape. And one place you can see them all together is in Lightroom, Adobe Camera Raw and other processing software.

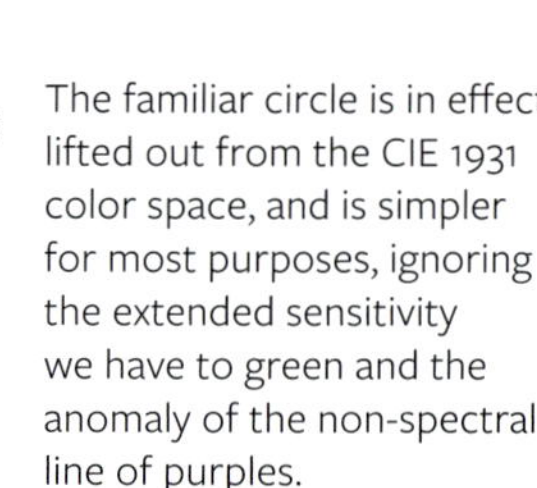

The familiar circle is in effect lifted out from the CIE 1931 color space, and is simpler for most purposes, ignoring the extended sensitivity we have to green and the anomaly of the non-spectral line of purples.

Maple leaves on a forest floor in New Brunswick, Canada. The saturated colors occupy the right half of the color spectrum, from green in the middle through yellow and orange to red.

COLOR MODELS VS COLOR SPACES

The difference between a color model and a color space is that the model is a mathematical system, while the space is a specific version of it with absolute values. The distinction is important for a color scientist, but not practically for photographers.

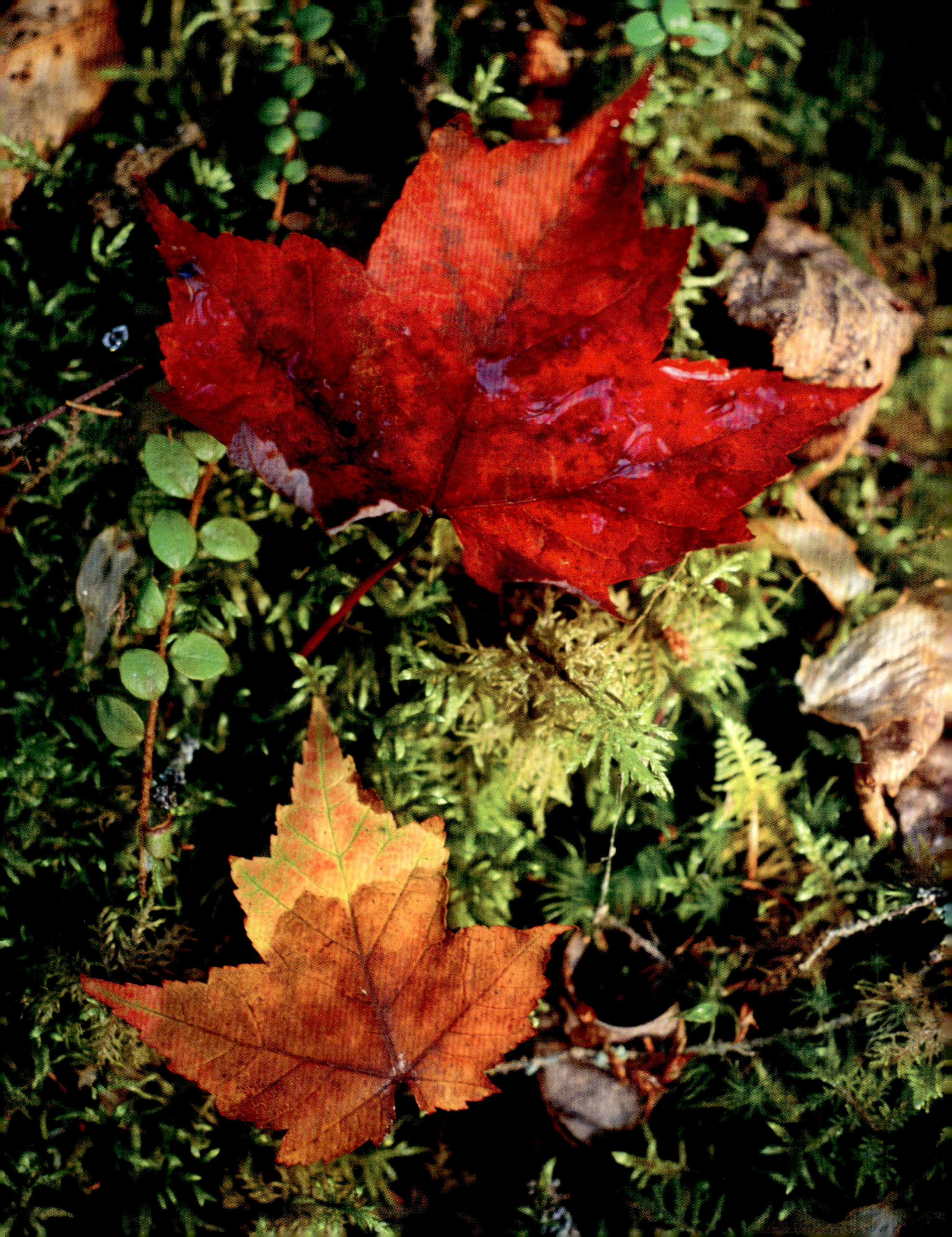

RGB FOR MAKING

The idea of the RGB color space is to stick to the principle of how our eyes work, with three primary colors, and it's also the way our equipment works, from camera sensor to screen or print.

The color space for a finished photograph depends on where it will be viewed, and there's a basic choice of two. sRGB (Standard RGB) was created for viewing on screens, and is relatively small because most screens don't handle a large color space well. Adobe RGB (1998) was created as a larger color space for printing, because it converts well to the CMYK inks used by printers. In other words, the reason for having different sizes of color space for photography is because of the different capabilities of the devices we use: the cameras and the ways of displaying, from phone screens to monitors to print. The better cameras capture many more colors and finer nuances than the poorest displays, so on the one hand you don't want to throw away color information unnecessarily when you process, but on the other hand you want to make sure that the image you're going to post on Instagram, for example, is optimized for viewing on the least sophisticated phone.

Most cameras offer this choice between sRGB and Adobe RGB (1998), but it applies only to TIFFs and JPEGs that the camera processes itself. Of course, if you shoot on a phone camera and post it directly without doing anything to the

Working in a higher color space for viewing in a lower one calls for the profile to be converted once finished. Otherwise, there's a noticeable color loss, as in the three versions below: properly converted (left), unconverted from Adobe RGB (1998) to sRGB (centre), and the more severe loss from ProPhoto RGB to sRGB (right).

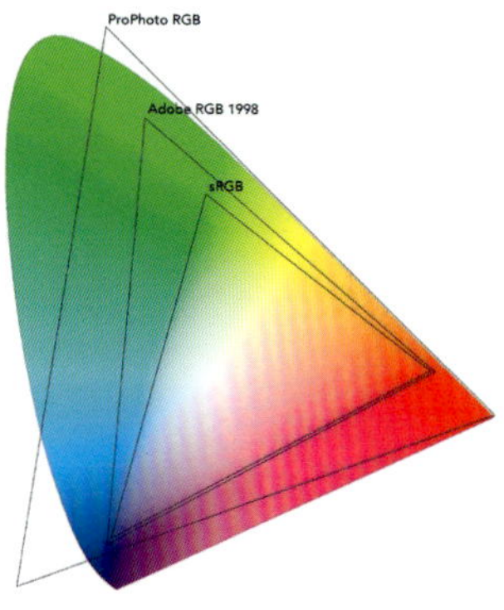

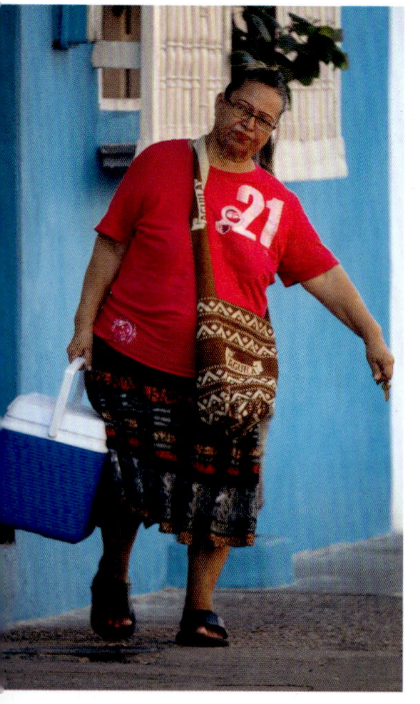

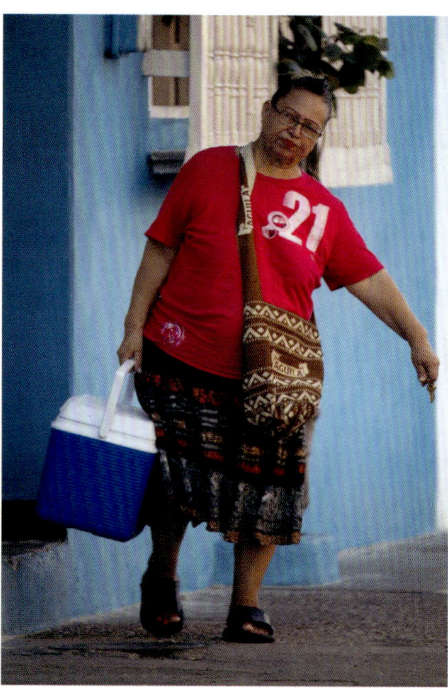

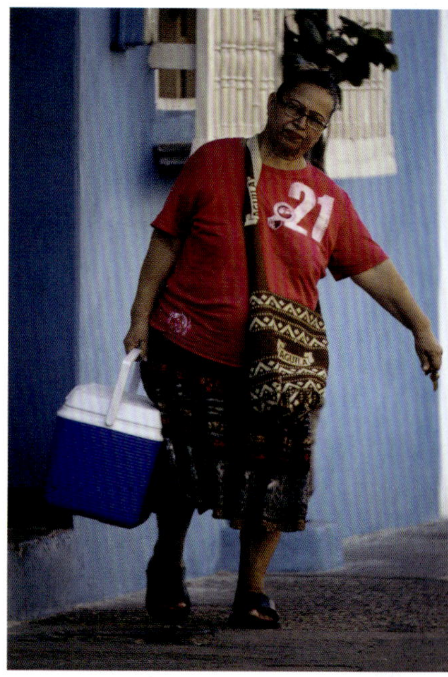

The three main color spaces for photography are triangles, shown here overlaid on the full color space that we can see. None of them can encompass the range of green that our eyes are capable of.

The three triangles below show the colors lost to the three important color spaces in photography, from ProPhoto RGB (top) to Adobe RGB (1998) (centre) and sRGB (bottom). ProPhoto RGB is a working space, while Adobe RGB (1998) was designed to encompass most of the colors used in CMYK printing. sRGB is the standard for displays such as monitors, tablets and phones.

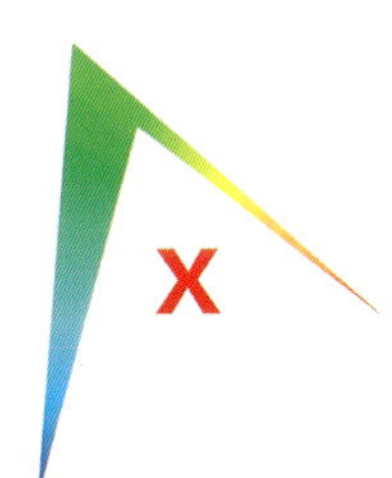

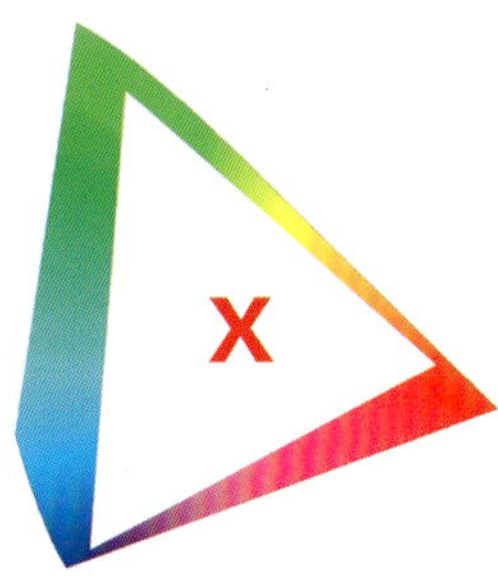

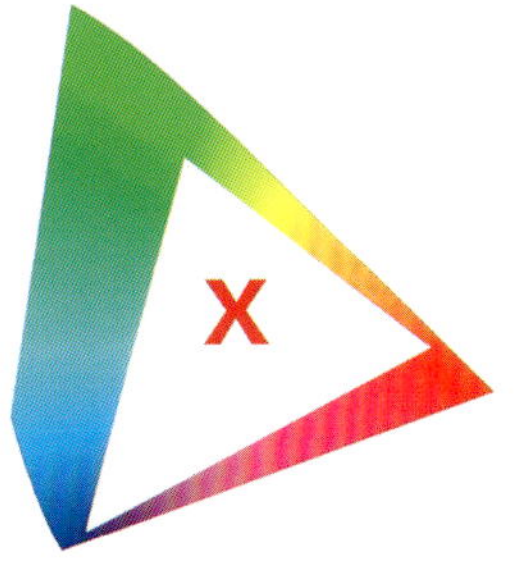

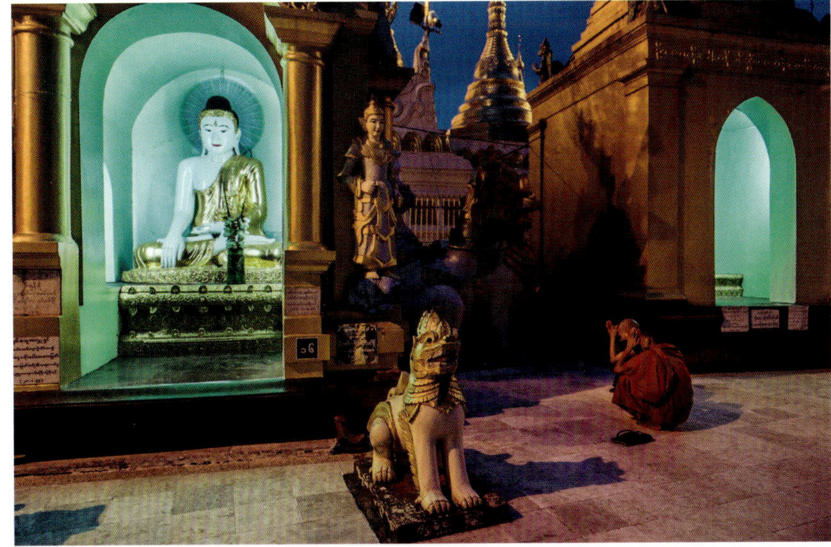

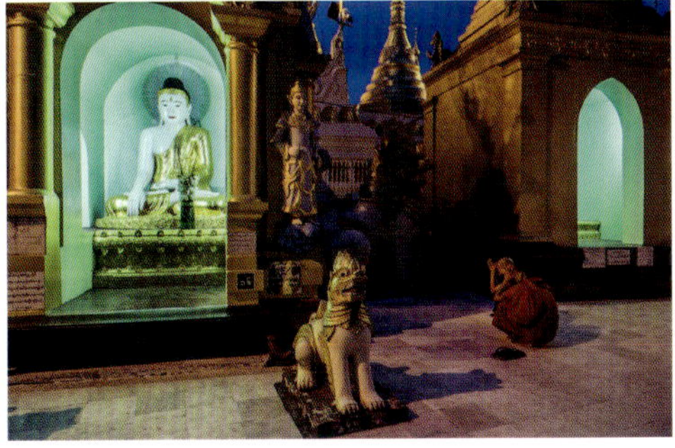

image, it will stay in the same color space (which is sRGB for the web) and there's nothing to think about. Well, not much at the moment, but phones themselves differ in their screen displays, and not only are they improving, but manufacturers produce a range of models, so that if you take a shot with, say, the latest top-of-the-range Huawei, it isn't going to look the same on a five-year-old iPhone. If you shoot Raw, as most serious photographers do, there is no color space until you start to process, and whenever you process, edit, save and export an image, you'll have to decide which of three color spaces (not two) to work in. The third space, and the largest of all, is ProPhoto RGB, and it's useful at the processing stage for being able to handle extremes of color, but no use for viewing, so the image will always need to be finally converted to a smaller space. That means we use color spaces in photography in two ways: for processing and for viewing. It often means using two color spaces, one for the working space and the other for the device on which the picture will be displayed. This can cause confusion, not helped by the many opinions (sometimes wrong) shared on the internet. I'll deal with this specifically in Chapter 6: Process & Grading.

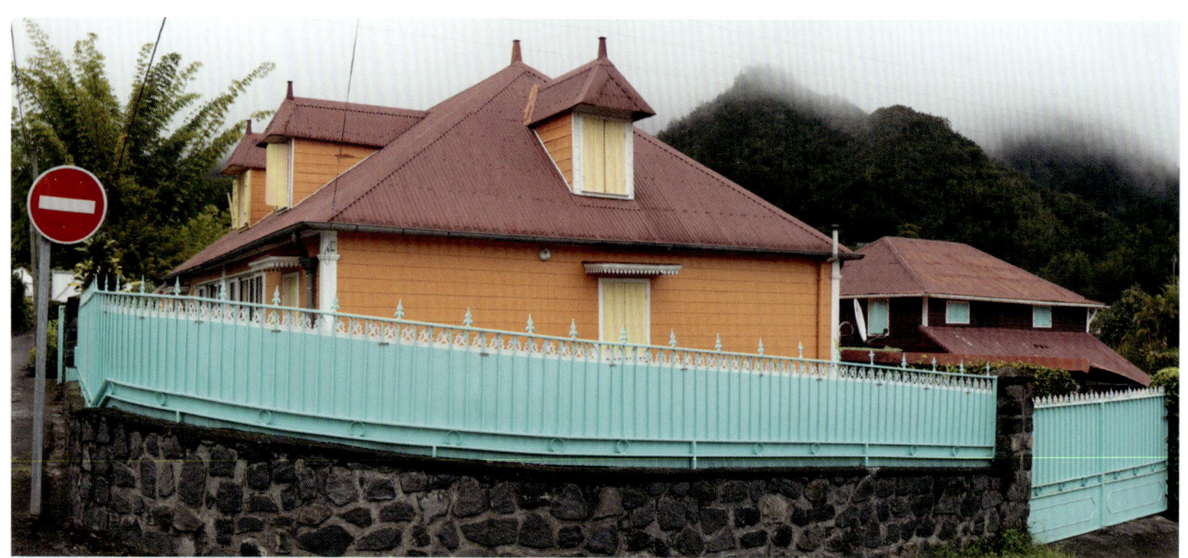

HSB FOR DESCRIBING

Most of us who do even the least amount of image processing in Lightroom or similar know about RGB, but it's practically impossible to judge colors on their RGB values. Look at any color near you.

Can you imagine how much of red, green and blue it contains? The way most people think about colors (when they think at all, which may not be all that often) is first by hue. If I asked what the dominant color is in the upper-right picture, the answer is going to be 'green'. Generally, before we get to other qualities of color, we talk about its hue.

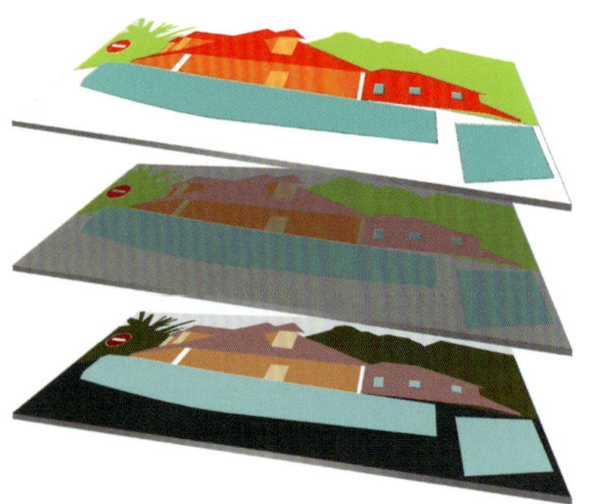

But then there's how strong, rich or vibrant that hue is, and the quality here is saturation. A fully saturated hue is pure, but we can lower the saturation all the way to grey, which is what most people would call colorless (again, that shows how much we're in thrall to the hue of a color).

The third quality to complete this natural way of talking about color is brightness. You'll also see the word lightness used, and value, and while there are technical

Brightly painted houses are typical of this area of the island of La Réunion, Cirque de la Salazie, so they make a good example. In the diagram, from top to bottom are the pure hues at 100-percent brightness, then desaturated to an equal 50-percent brightness, and finally modified by the actual brightness.

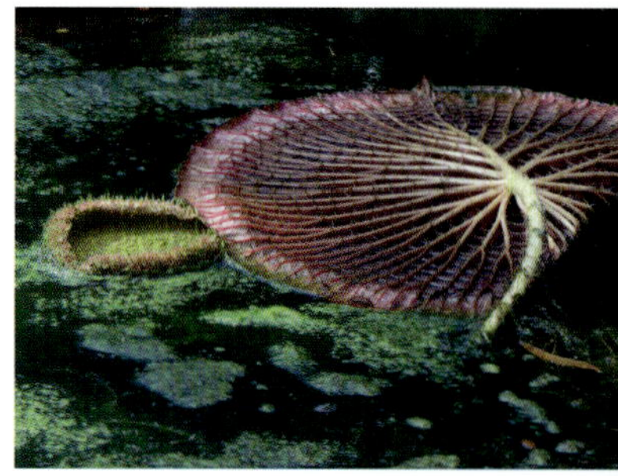

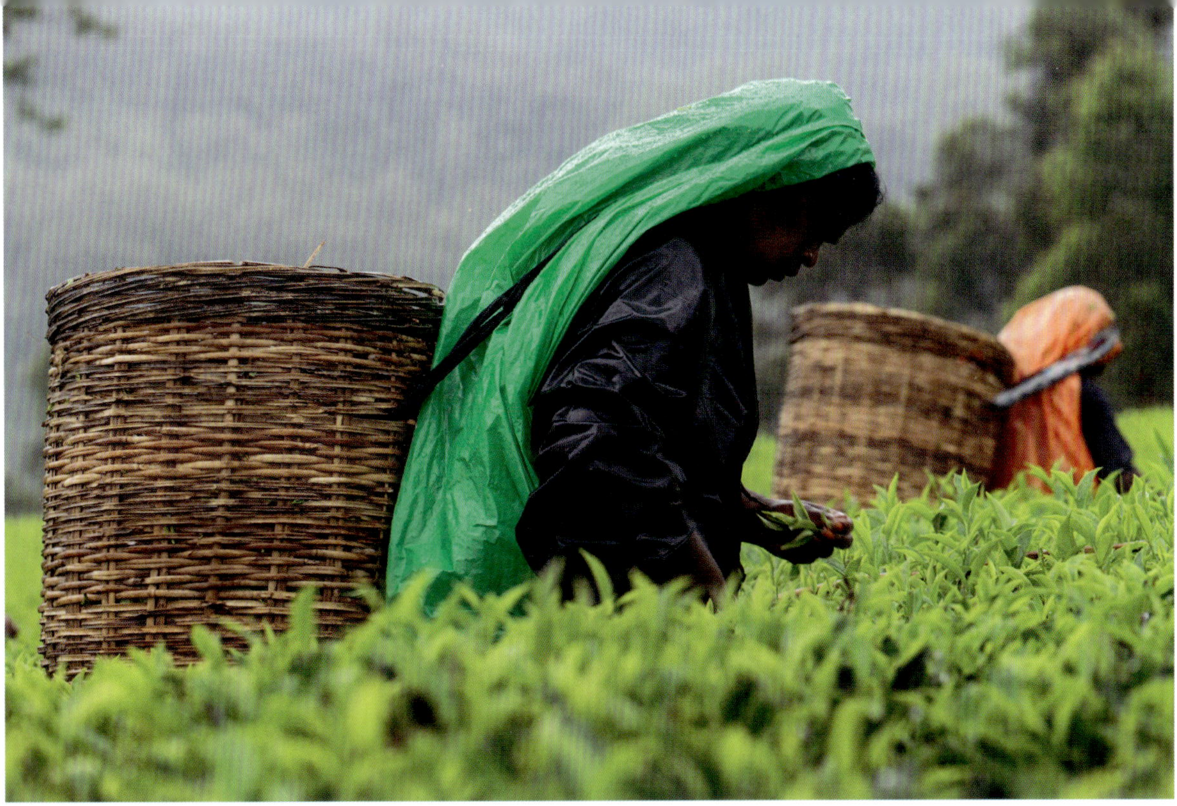

In the picture of a Sri Lankan tea-picker in the rain, there are four colors that we would lump together as green, perhaps calling them emerald, yellow-green, leaf green and grey-green. What unites them in our minds is the greenish hue range, even though they are strongly divided by saturation.

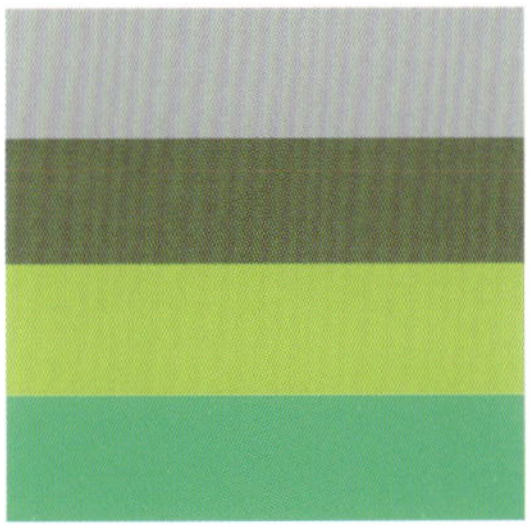

The pleasure we get from contrasting colors in a picture, as in the upturned Victoria Regia lily (left), depends very much on our ability to describe them as (in this case) pinks and greens.

differences important in color science, I'll stick with the most common term, brightness, and the three together – hue, saturation and brightness – are known as HSB.

Actually, this gets complicated and uncertain when you start to dive deeply into describing colors, because it involves language and culture, and these are minefields. One of the most influential studies, but also quite hotly disputed in some areas (Berlin & Kay 1969), ranked societies by how many different basic colors they have words for. Now, when pressed to pay attention, we can normally discriminate between millions of colors, yet the most 'advanced' color-language societies have around only a dozen basic words. Without getting into the many arguments surrounding this, they typically include black (or dark), white (or light), red, green, yellow, blue, brown, purple, pink, orange and grey. Naturally, with more attention there are others, especially if you're choosing house paint or lipstick, but these are the basics.

L*a*b* FOR PERCEIVING

However, while RGB and HSB are fit for different ways of dealing with color, and you can see and use them side by side in Lightroom and Adobe Camera Raw, neither correspond with the way we actually perceive color.

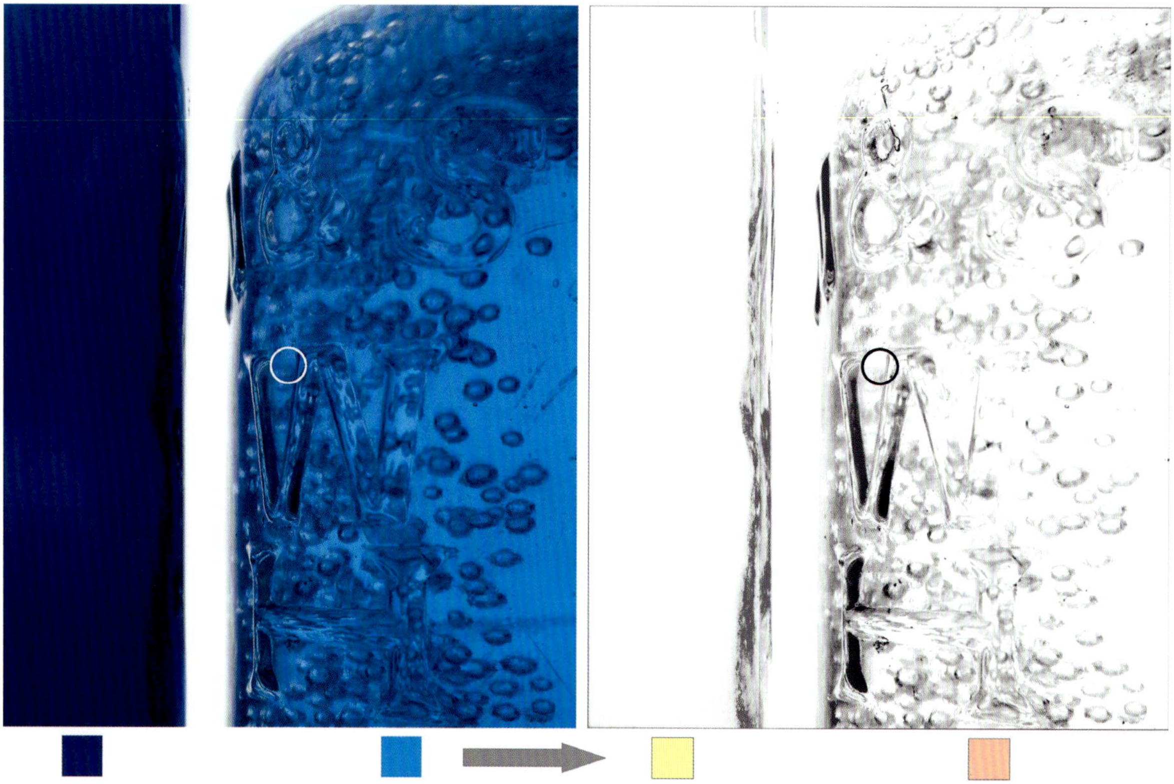

That's based on what's called color opponent theory. As before, we need three qualities – left's say three intersecting axes – that go from one extreme to the other. One is light-dark, which is easy to understand, as they're the opposite of each other. The other two opposites are maybe a little less intuitive: two color axes crossing each other, one from red to green, the other from yellow to blue. Red and green are opposites in the sense that there's no such possible color as a reddish-green. So too are yellow and blue (there are no yellowish blues or bluish yellows). On the color circle (see page 38), the red-green axis is at right angles to the yellow-blue one, so that without taking into account brightness you can define any color by its red-to-greenness and its yellow-to-blueness.

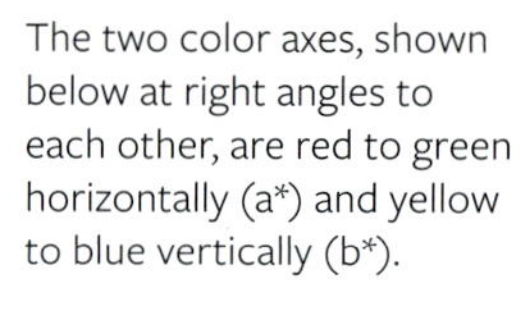

The two color axes, shown below at right angles to each other, are red to green horizontally (a*) and yellow to blue vertically (b*).

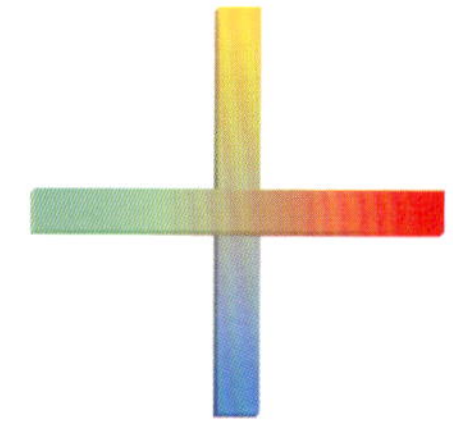

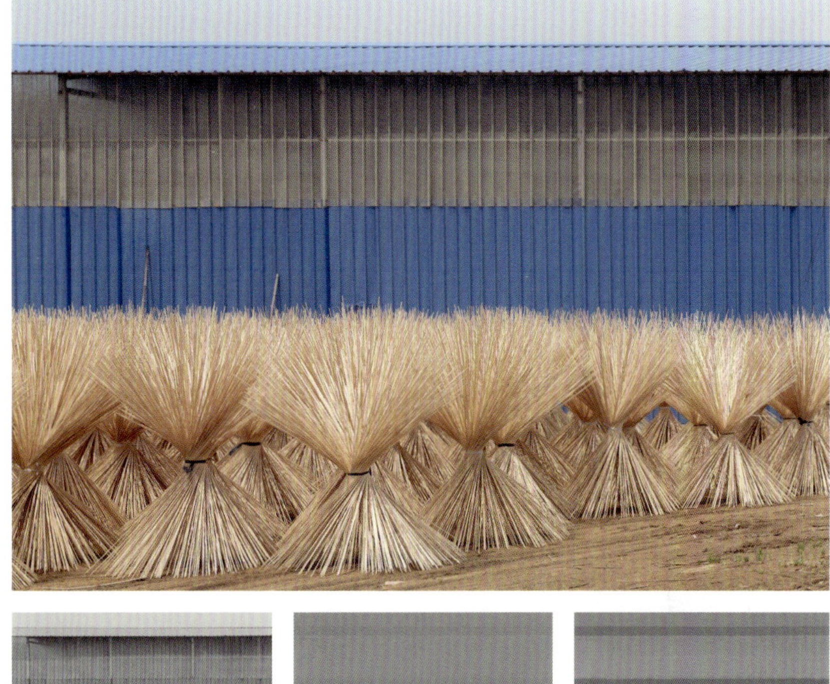

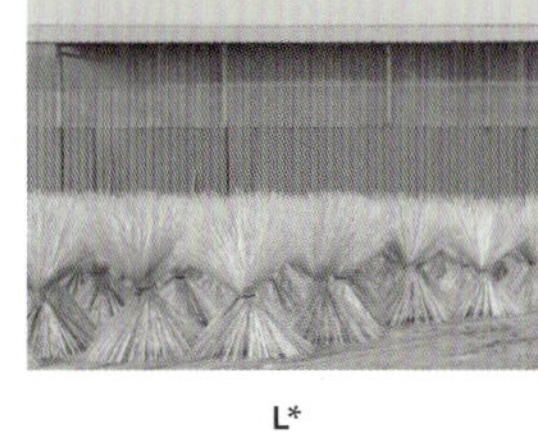

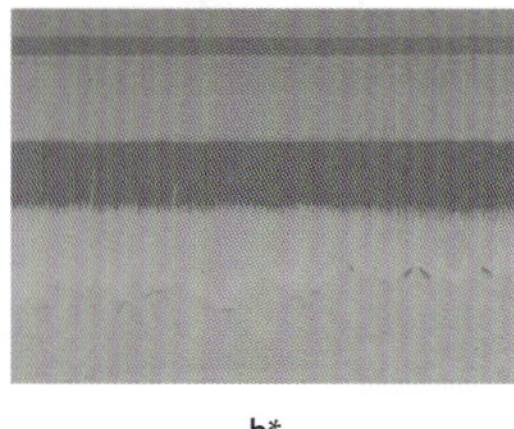

L*   a*   b*

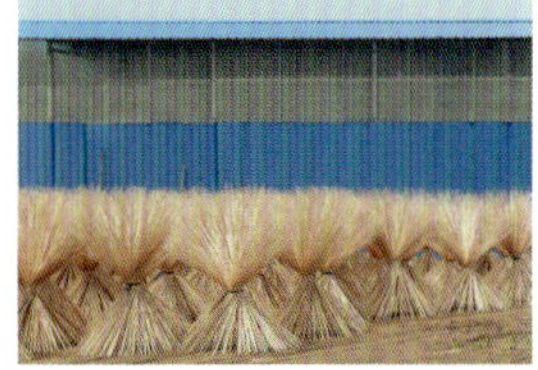

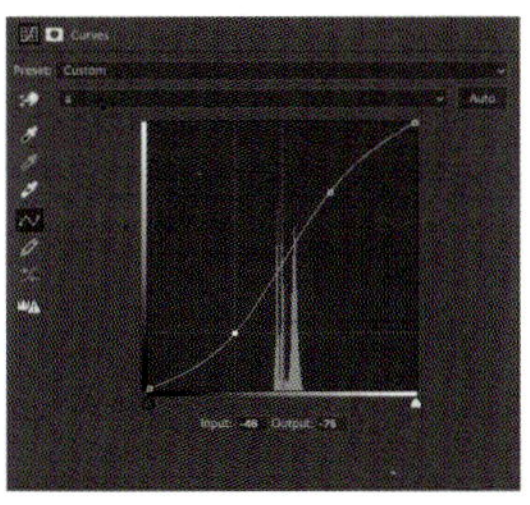

There's practical evidence that we perceive this way, in terms of opposites, and one of the easiest ways to demonstrate it is by what's called successive contrast. If you stare at a single, preferably strong, color long enough for your receptors to get fatigued (about half a minute) and then immediately switch your gaze to a blank white surface, you'll see the opposite hue. In the example opposite left, I've taken a strongly blue image and then placed on its right a completely desaturated version. Stare at the small white circle in the centre for at least half a minute (the circle keeps your gaze fixed), then quickly look at the small circle in the grey image to the right. You'll see weaker opposites of the two blues – a yellow and a kind of pink. This has more than just trick value for color photography, as we'll see in Chapter 4: Composing with Color, because opposites across the color circle 'help' each other in a picture.

This is probably the closest model to how we perceive color (though obviously there's no separate saturation 'slider', so it's not so good for the way we describe), and in the world of color science it was developed in 1976 by the CIE. L* (also called Lstar) is the lightness value from white to black, a* is the axis from red to green, and b* the axis from yellow to blue. It's also referred to as CIELAB, and a good place to become familiar with it is Photoshop's Color Picker, which displays it alongside RGB and HSB.

CAMERA COLOR

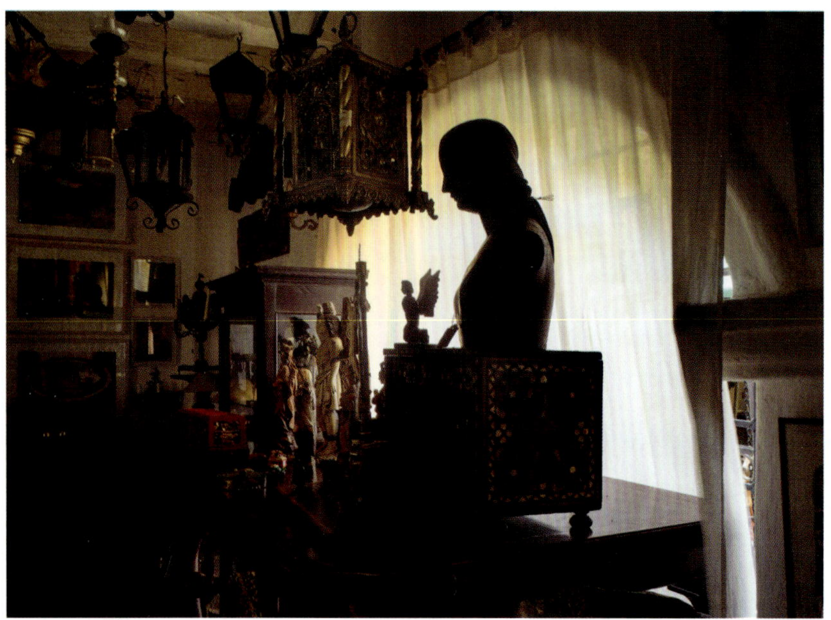

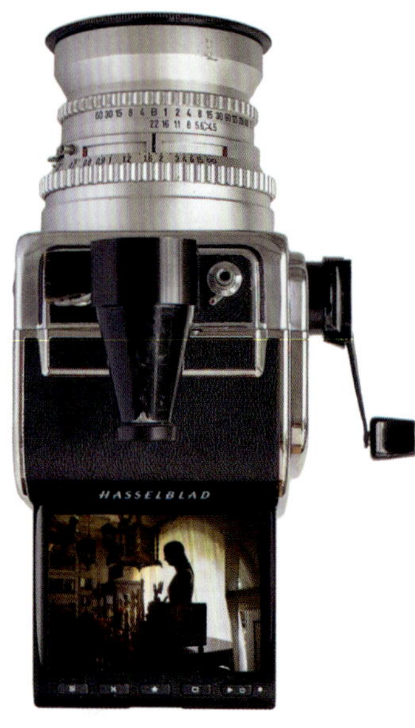

The first step in getting these colors into the final photograph is, of course, capture by the camera. As this involves a lens, a recording medium, then a way of processing the data from it, there's no possibility of a simple, direct translation.

With film, still used by a few of us and in any case still residing in countless archives that can be scanned, the chemistry was created by different manufacturers, each attempting both to reproduce colors as accurately as possible and to make them pleasing to customers (an impossible mix, but they tried nevertheless). Kodachrome was for long a kind of gold standard, famous for rich reds, browns and yellows – and longevity – while Fujichrome's Velvia competed on more saturated blues for the skies and greens for vegetation. There were many others, of course, and Kodak in particular created different films for different kinds of shooting, such as portraits with pleasing skin tones. Transparency film offered little opportunity to influence the color rendering during processing, other than by making mistakes, but color negative film allowed yet another step, in the darkroom when printing.

Camera manufacturer Hasselblad claims that its color management system, which includes a special look-up table (LUT), curve and other processing methods, delivers a color look that is more natural and 'film-like'.

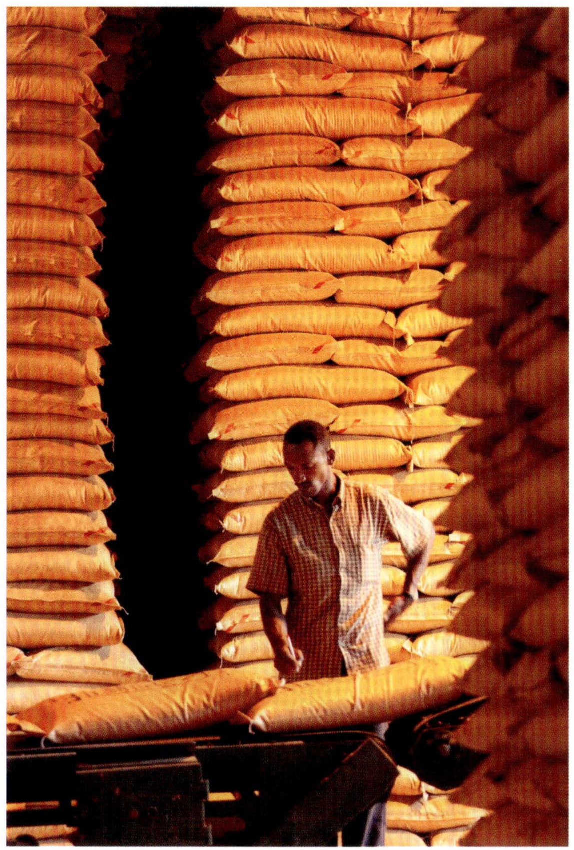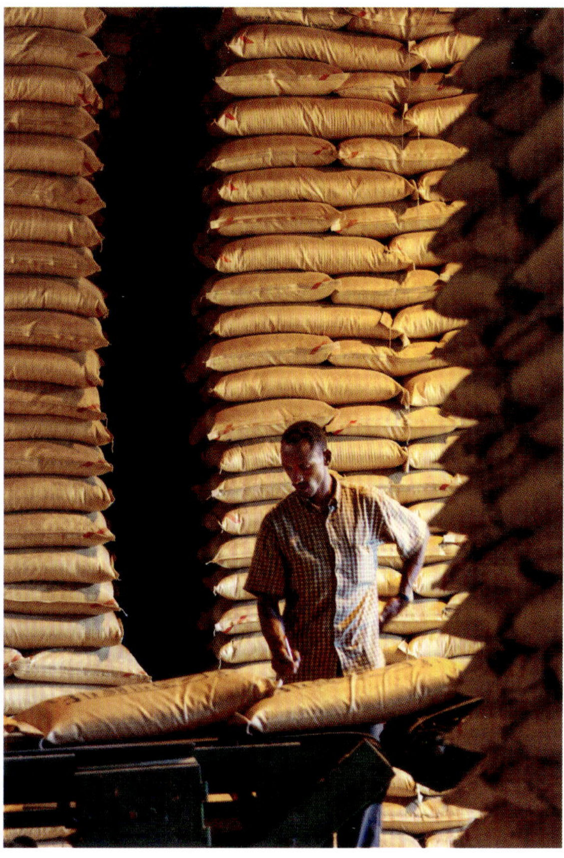

The unprocessed files from an early Nikon digital camera (left) had a tendency to oversaturate oranges, calling for a strong profile correction to bring the scene back to the way it was seen (right).

Digital capture, while completely different from film in the process, has many similarities in principle. Camera and sensor manufacturers (often not the same) now do the work of the film companies, and compete with each other on the same two incompatible goals: accuracy and being pleasing. Crudely put, professionals want accuracy because they know how to manipulate that kind of data to suit their needs, while most users just want the colors to look good straight out of the camera. There are three stages available for this, and together they create many more opportunities, and problems, than with film. They are the color filter in front of the sensor, the size and quality of the sensor itself, and the way of converting the data recorded into digital, including applying deliberate styles.

That's a lot of potential for difference between the color look from one camera to the next, and this is both enhanced and warped by the many opinions posted on the web. The color from certain cameras acquires a reputation among some user groups, and while that might seem to be just a distraction from the actual science of color rendering, color and its judgement is ultimately subjective, so it can't be ignored.

THE FILTER

Sensors work by measuring the quantity of all wavelengths of light striking them, so they record a greyscale.

The solution for color photography is a filter in front that allows only a specific wavelength – one color, in other words – to strike each photodiode. First, though, a clear filter right at the front removes ultraviolet and infrared so that the sensor can record just the *visible* wavelengths.

Each pixel, then, is made sensitive to just one color. For most cameras this is a Bayer filter, named after the Kodak technician who invented it, and the most common pattern of three colors is red, green and blue. This makes sense because it mimics our trichromatic vision (see page 34), and it also corresponds to the way displays work. As the close-up below shows, the usual pattern is RGGB, doubled up on the greens to mimic our eyesight, which is much more sensitive to green wavelengths than to others. So, in a block of four pixels, one will have all wavelengths but red filtered out, one will have all but blue removed, while the other two record only green.

That means the color resolution of the image is much coarser than the tonal resolution, and has to be interpolated as described in The Conversion (page 52). This might sound like a big loss of accuracy but, as we'll see later, it actually sits quite happily with the way the human vision system works, as we detect detail mainly by tonal contrast rather than by color. The green pixels are also used for luminance.

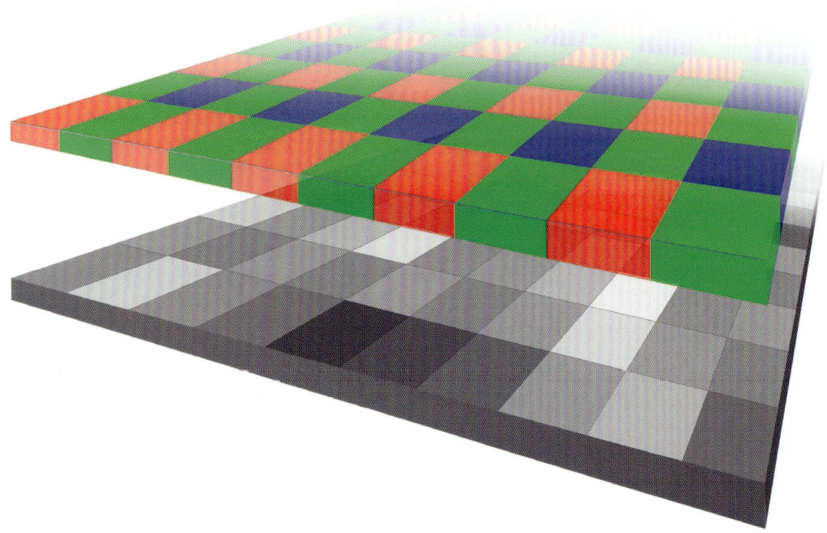

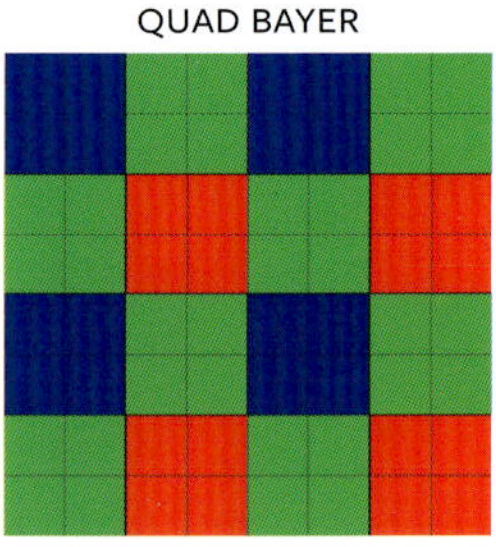

QUAD BAYER

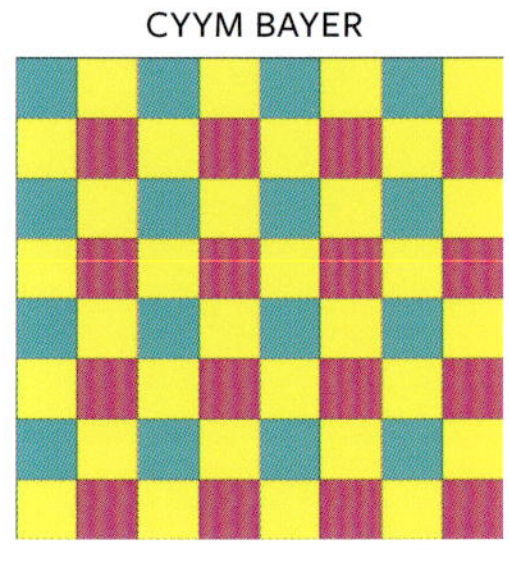

CYYM BAYER

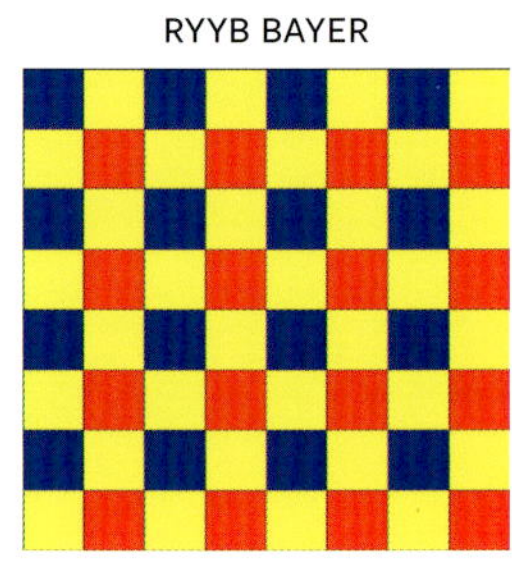

RYYB BAYER

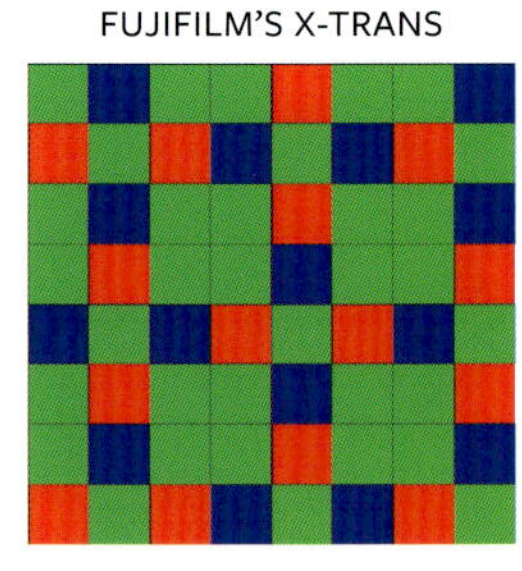

FUJIFILM'S X-TRANS

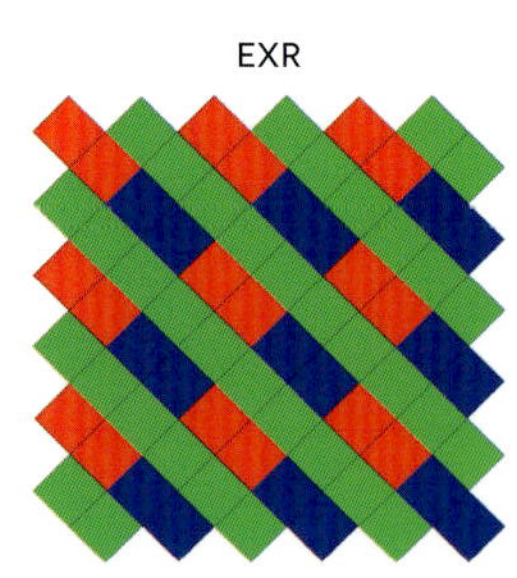

EXR

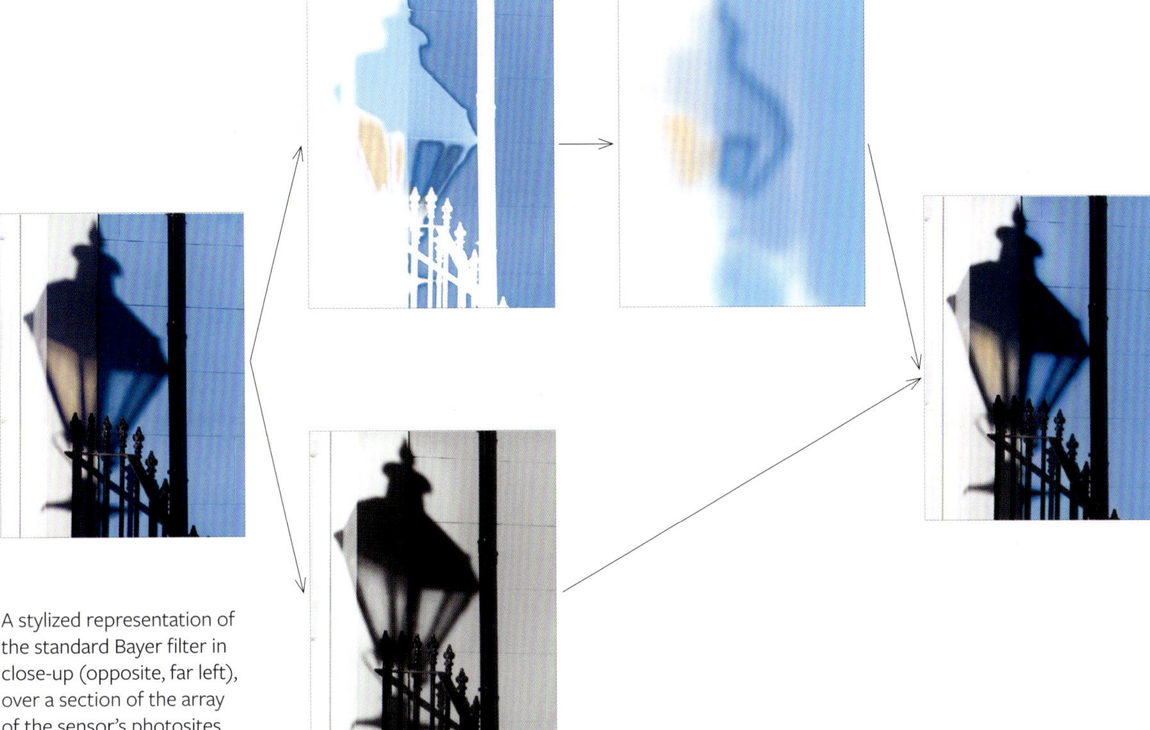

A stylized representation of the standard Bayer filter in close-up (opposite, far left), over a section of the array of the sensor's photosites that record only tones. One color in the filter sits over one photo site and blocks all wavelengths except its color. There have been variants and improvements from this original filter design, including Quad Bayer, CYYM Bayer, RYYB Bayer, Fujifilm's X-Trans and EXR.

On this page is a simple demonstration of how color detail doesn't matter as much as tonal detail. The image at left was split into color (above) and tone (below), then the color was blurred strongly and recombined (at right) with the black and white. There is hardly any visible difference between the original and the new color-blurred version.

However, there are other filter possibilities. One tried earlier was CYYM, using the *complementary* colors to RGB (they happen to be the colors used in printing). This allows more light to reach the sensor and so, in principle, better resolution from the same number of pixels. However, the demosaicing is much more complex, and this pattern never went anywhere. Another is RYYB, effectively replacing the green filters in a standard Bayer with yellow. This increases light transmission by 40 percent, with the yellow being used for luminance as well as color, and green can be reconstructed from the combination, albeit with complex algorithms.

Even with a standard RGB Bayer, camera manufacturers have room to play with color by adjusting the exact wavelength of the filters. The red, for example, can be shifted slightly towards orange, which has some advantages in rendering common light skin tones (see also page 72). The result of all this is that different cameras *do* record slightly different colors.

THE SENSOR

Sensor technology has to balance two conflicting issues: pixel size and pixel density. Larger pixels give better quality, but more pixels closer together give better resolution.

The larger the photosite for each pixel, the higher the saturation capacity, meaning the more photons (which are converted to electrons by the photodiode) it can hold before overflowing. Once it overflows, the pixel delivers a white image – that is, nothing at all. So, large pixels are the basic way to high quality because, with appropriate methods of reducing temporal dark noise, they allow a higher dynamic range. That's to say, they don't overflow so easily. The ideal answer is a large sensor in a large camera, but that's too inconvenient for most people, and too costly. The problem for manufacturers is combining high resolution with pixel size, at its most acute with phone cameras, which simply have very little space to play with. For comparison, looking at 50-megapixel sensors at the time of writing, the size of each photodiode in a Huawei phone camera is 1 micron, in a Canon full-frame camera 4.1 microns, while on a Hasselblad medium-format 5.3 microns.

The second way to high quality is bit depth, also known as color depth. This is how much color information can be stored in each pixel. Most sensors and screens use 8 bits each of R, G and B, making 24 bits; 2^{24} gives almost 17 million distinct colors, comfortably more than the approximately 10 million the human eye can distinguish. Better than this is deep color, 30-bit (10 bits per channel), which gives one billion colors, and beyond this is 36-bit (12 bits per channel), 42-bit (14 bits per channel) and 48-bit (16 bits per channel). To confuse matters, descriptions of bit depths often use the per-channel number. High-end sensors capture 14 bits per channel and then move it into 16-bit color space. If you want the highest-quality color, it comes from a large sensor backed by good processing in a high bit depth.

Let's put to bed one strangely persistent myth – that cameras record in one of the two most common color spaces, sRGB or Adobe RGB (1998). They don't. They gather much more data than either of those, and the best cameras capture most of the colors that we can see. The confusion comes from cameras offering either sRGB or Adobe RGB (1998) as the color space for the JPEGs or TIFFs they produce. And that happens only if you choose to shoot JPEGs or TIFFs. Most casual camera users do, but most serious photographers do not, because all of the actual captured image data can be saved as a Raw file, which is an option that the better cameras offer. As we'll go into in more detail in Chapter 6: Process & Grading, the Raw data has to be processed to make it viewable on a screen or a print, which means throwing away much of what's not viewable. You can let the camera do this on the fly, or you can preserve the full image data and choose for yourself later. Not surprisingly, I go for the latter.

WHAT MATTERS IN SENSOR PERFORMANCE

Quantum efficiency (QE) measures how efficient a pixel is at converting light (photons) into an electrical charge (electrons) at a specific wavelength (nm). The higher the percentage the better, as less light is needed to make an image.

Saturation capacity is how many electrons (that the photodiode has converted from photons) a pixel can store before overflowing (which would give white in an image). The more the better, which gives large pixels an advantage. Also known as full well capacity.

Temporal dark noise is random unwanted noise from surrounding sensor electronics and pixel components when no light is entering the sensor. The lower the better, as it will result in cleaner-looking images, especially in low-light conditions.

Signal-to-noise ratio (SNR) measures useful image data between the signal and noise (that is, the 'noise floor'). The higher the better, giving a clearer image.

Dynamic range is the ratio of the maximum signal (saturation capacity) to the minimum (temporal dark noise). The higher the better in coping with high-contrast scenes.

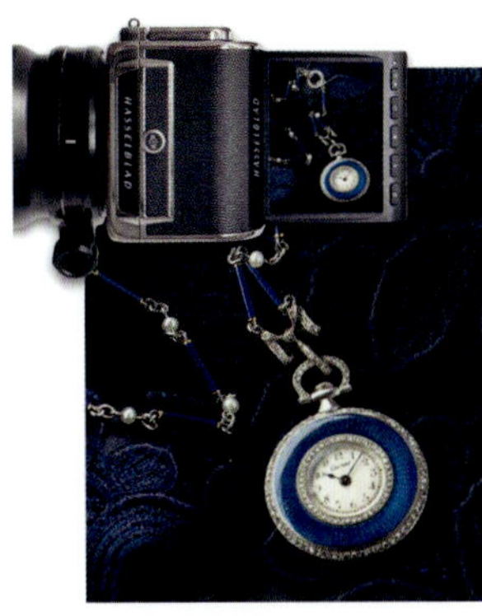

The same shot under controlled studio lighting of a pendant watch taken with a Hasselblad 907X 50C medium-format and a Huawei P40 phone camera. Both use 50MP sensors (a real achievement for the phone camera), but the size difference means that the Hasselblad photosites are five times larger.

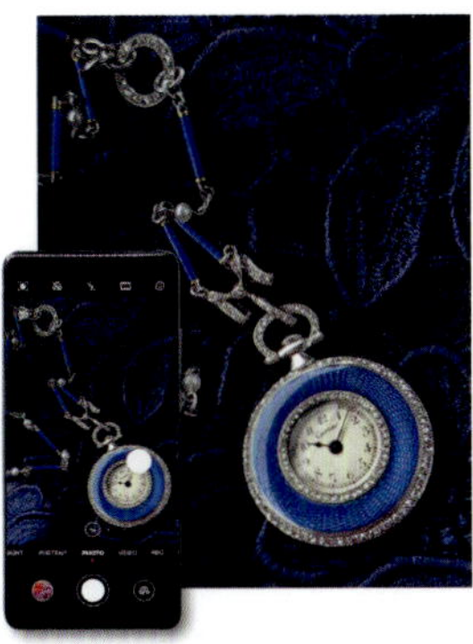

At a modest enlargement there seems little visible difference, although the P40's color conversion is more vivid. The difference is in the detail.

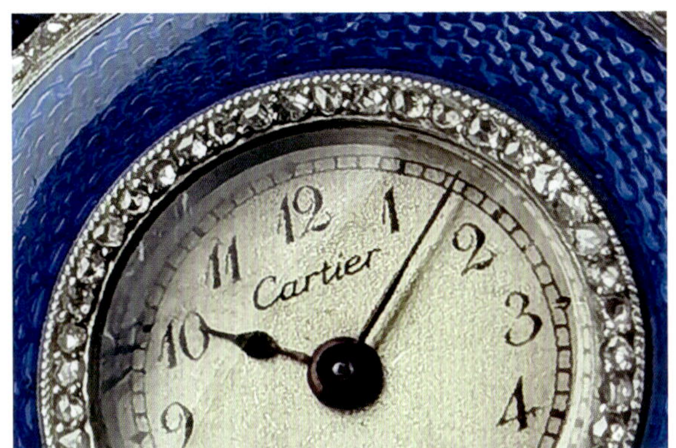

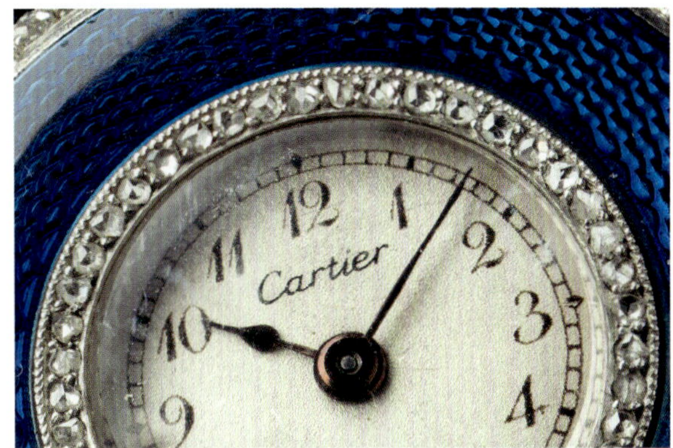

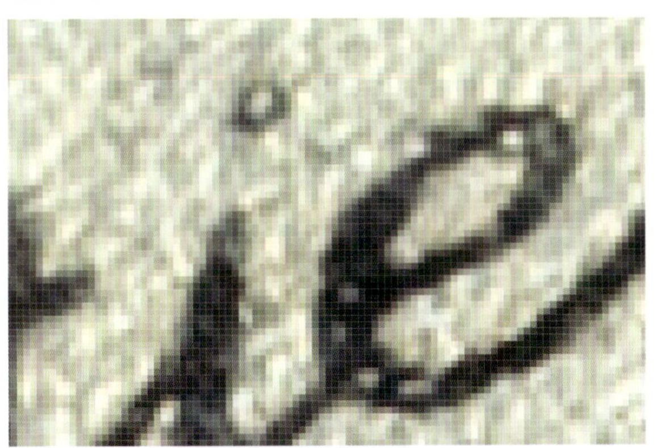

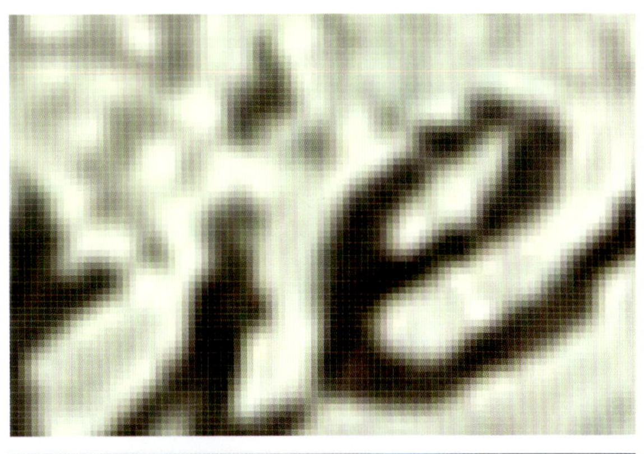

THE CONVERSION

How the data is read out from the sensor is another area for camera manufacturers to distinguish themselves from each other, particularly in interpolating the color – the demosaicing, or debayering – and the algorithms are generally complex.

One obvious goal would be to aim for accuracy in every color across the board, as Hasselblad attempts, for instance. However, many photographers want a color rendering that pleases them straight out of the camera, and so most camera manufacturers offer a choice, which they may call color profiles, picture controls or color styles. In any case, they are different ways of rendering the overall color to suit different photographers' needs, and include such styles as neutral, natural, flat, vivid, portrait and landscape, among others. Color is, as I keep repeating, largely in the mind and so is subject to individual preferences that resist argument. The priorities for many photographers are the kind of subject they prefer shooting, with portraits and landscapes heading the list. The most pleasing skin tones, for example, are not likely to be compatible with the most pleasing greens and blues of sea, sky and trees. These may be small differences, but in the competitive world of camera manufacture (especially in phones, which are by far the largest manufacturers), a great deal of attention is paid to pleasing the user.

A tiny section of a medium-format image file enlarged to the point at which the individual pixels are just visible. In particular, the coarser pattern of the color filter over the sensor needs to be demosaiced so as to reconstruct a smooth color image from the incomplete data.

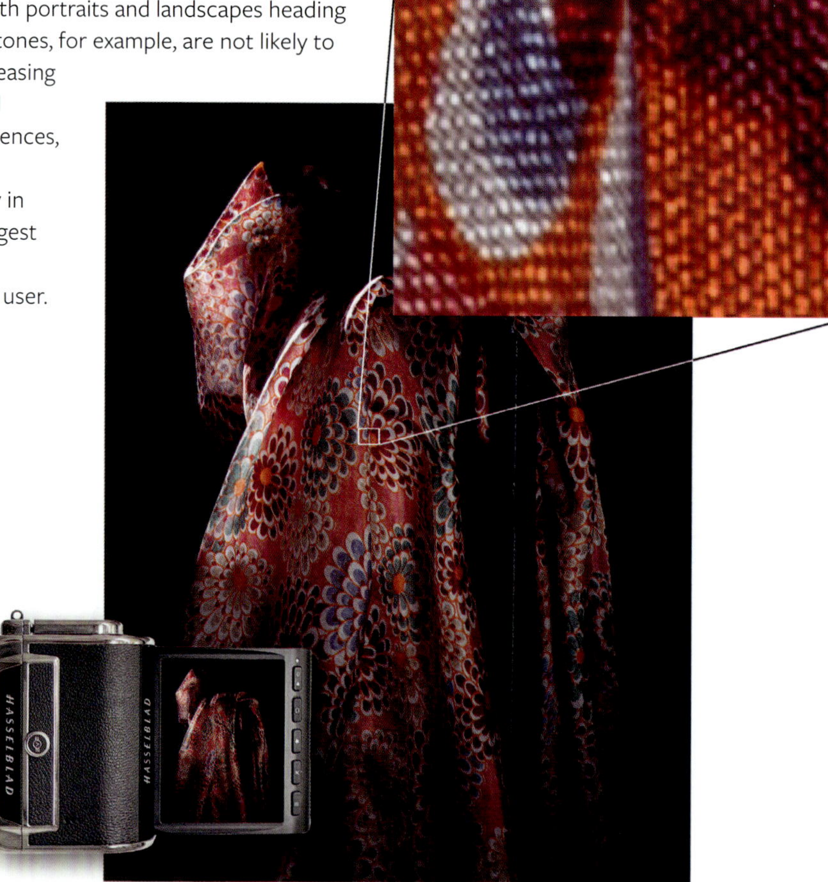

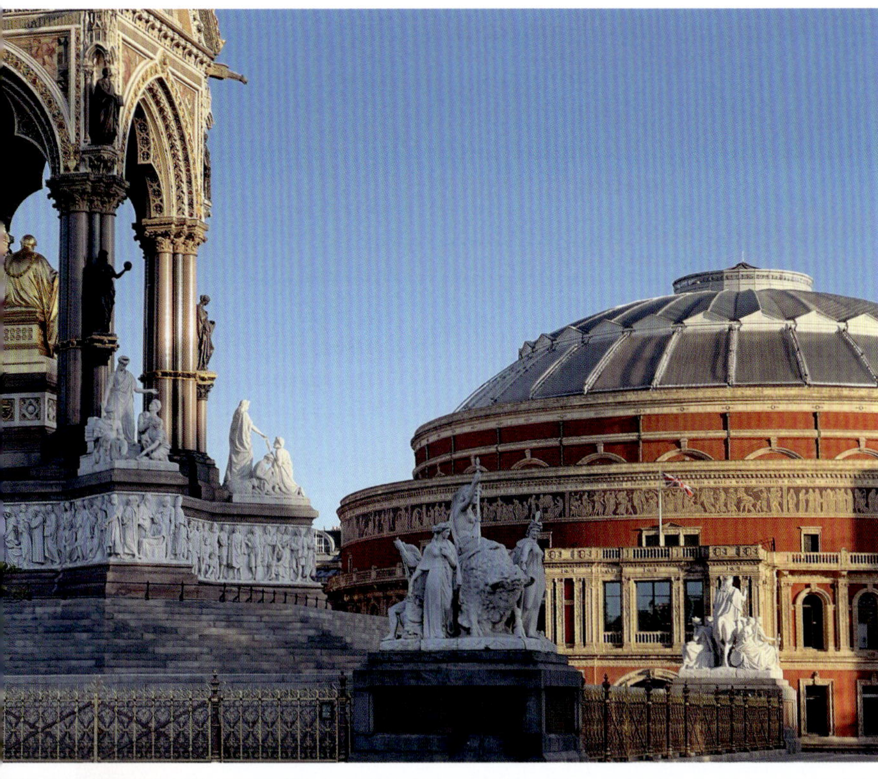

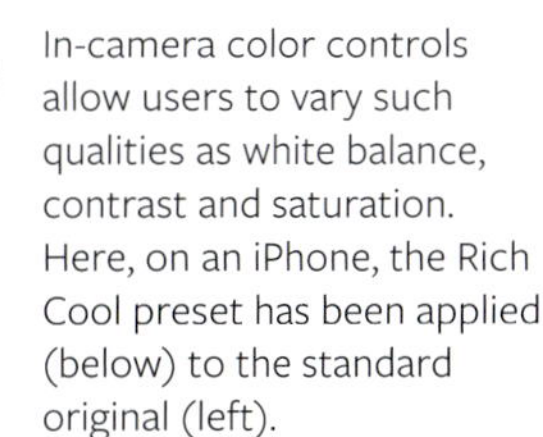

In-camera color controls allow users to vary such qualities as white balance, contrast and saturation. Here, on an iPhone, the Rich Cool preset has been applied (below) to the standard original (left).

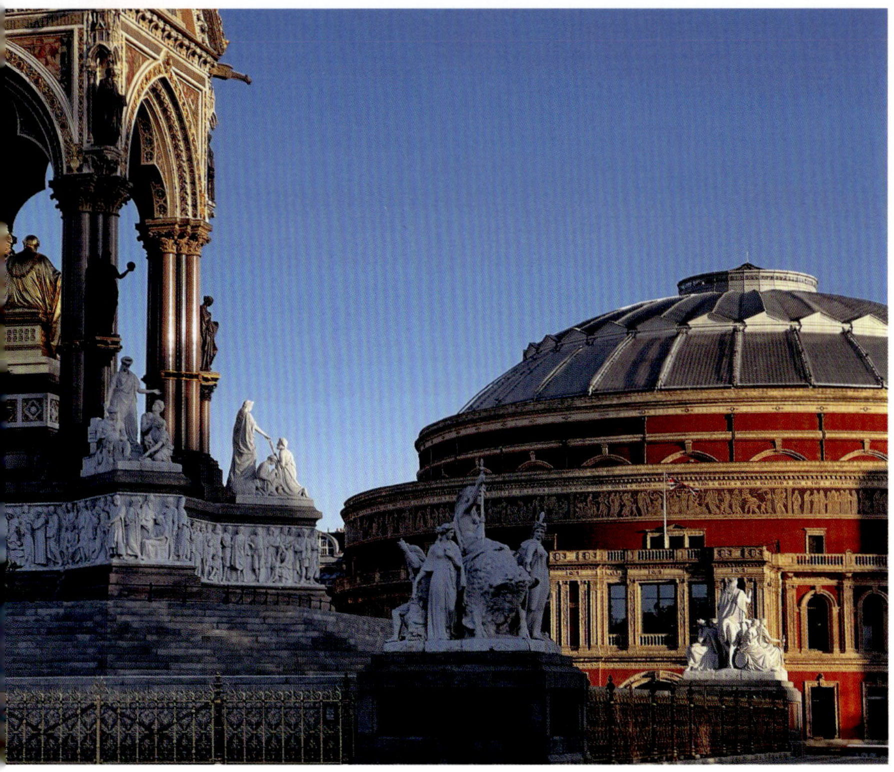

COMPUTATIONAL

I said there were three stages in translating the colors from the lens to the final viewable image, but I fudged this by leaving out computational processing. This was invented for phone cameras, partly because the tiny lenses and sensors need computational help in order to deliver a quality image, and partly because the processing power on a modern phone enables intensive computing.

There are two procedures important for us here. One is multi-frame capture, the other semantic masks (which I introduced in *Michael Freeman on... Light & Shadow*), and they are able to deal with the data from the sensor in ways that are different from the traditional conversion process and color styles.

Multi-frame has more than one use. One of the most practical is to reduce noise for cleaner colors and tones in low light, by combining many short exposures to collect the necessary amount of light that would normally call for a long exposure (the different patterns of noise can be averaged out). Another is to avoid motion blur by computationally aligning displaced elements. Yet another is to computationally increase the dynamic range (useful because this is less in a small sensor than a large one) by combining different exposures. Basically an HDR operation, this really impacts color in very bright highlights, such as in a glowing, high-contrast sunrise or sunset. What typically happens here is a nasty color shift,

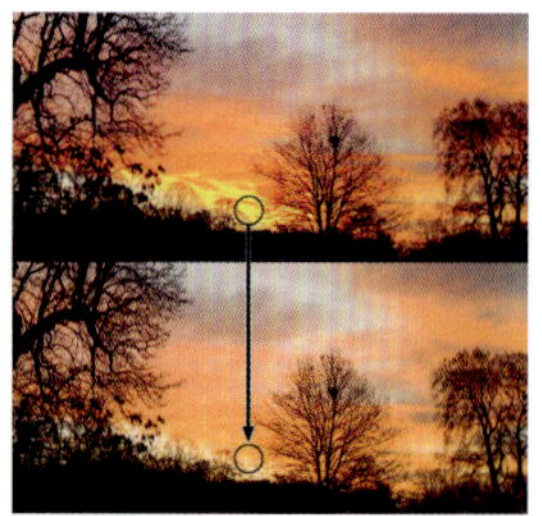

A typical issue with many sensors in sunrise and sunset conditions is a sharp color shift towards yellow in bright areas (top), calling for a selective hue correction (bottom).

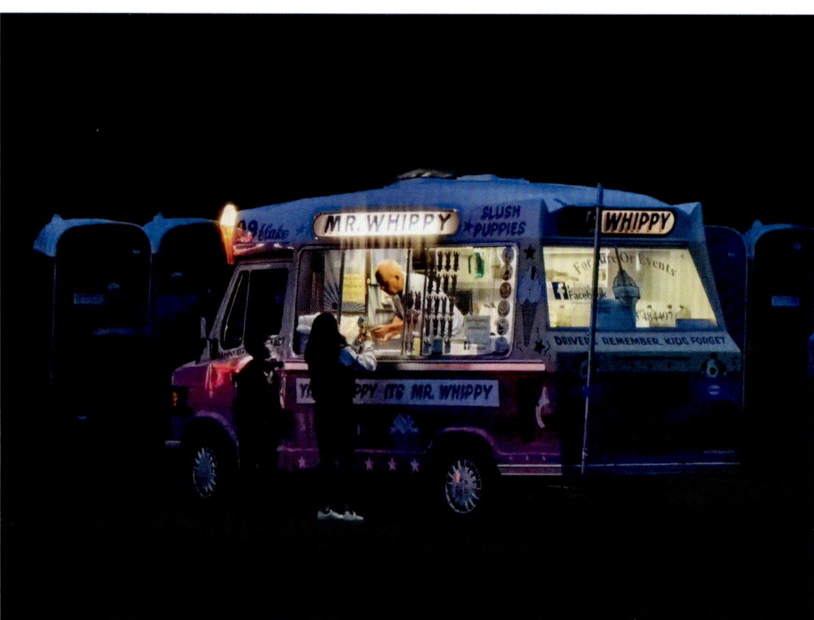

Night mode uses multiple frames captured over a period that can be up to a few seconds to reduce noise and increase the dynamic range, with proprietary algorithms heavily at work. Here, a technically impressive capture at night using a 10x lens on a handheld phone camera.

Another well-developed content recognition is for skies, which allows selective enhancement by first masking (here in green) and then increasing saturation slightly and if necessary tweaking the hue.

Content recognition is now extremely good on faces and human figures, which allows the manufacturers to apply their own algorithms to, for example, boost exposure on the face in backlit situations like this.

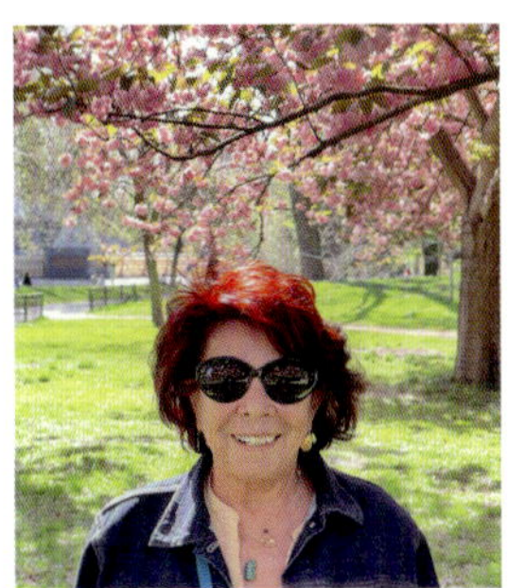

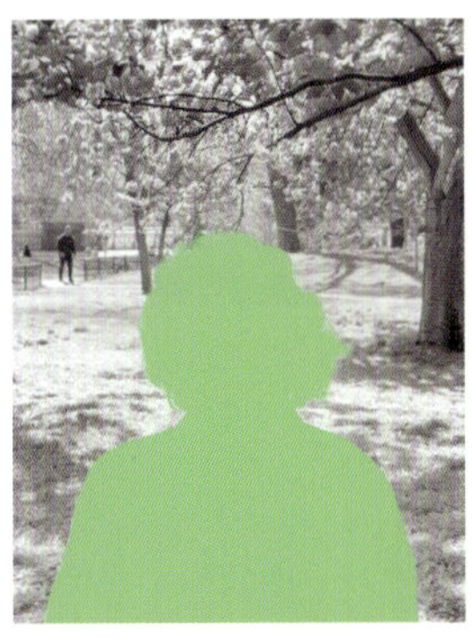

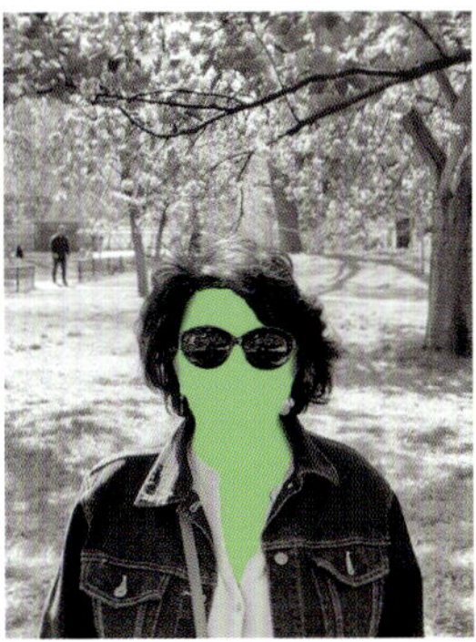

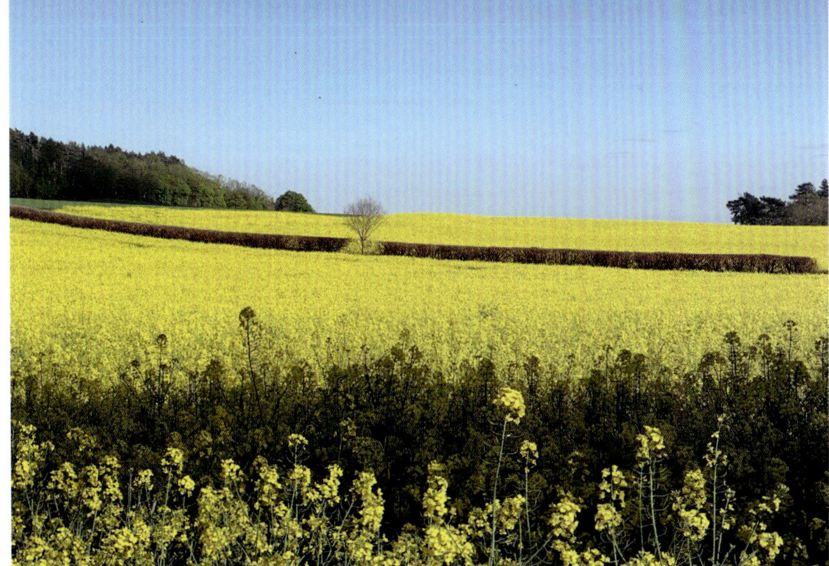

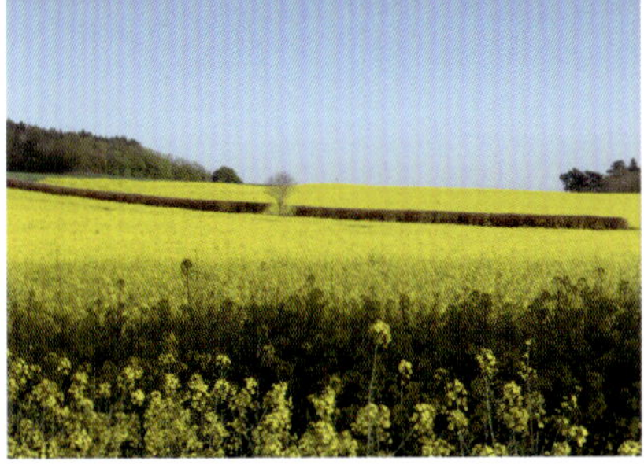

as in the example shown opposite, top. The right algorithm, however, can catch that and correct it. Compare the performance of a modern phone camera with that of an earlier model, and you'll see how useful this is.

Semantic masks allow parts of an image such as faces to be given their own unique tone and color. As you can see in *Michael Freeman on… Light & Shadow*, if the camera can isolate a face in the image at the time of capture, it can make sure that it appears just the right tone and color, regardless of what the light is like in the rest of the picture. People have been doing this in Photoshop for ages (since Photoshop 2, as I remember), but now it can be done within the camera's capture process.

Interestingly, this is changing the game when it comes to Raw processing. The advice for retaining full control over color is still to shoot Raw, and the argument gets stronger as the dynamic range of sensors increases, and as software processing engines such as Adobe Camera Raw and Capture One improve constantly. However, under some circumstances the computationally processed JPEG or HEIC file out of a phone camera may be better than you could achieve with the Raw DNG, because it's handling more data, such as several frames shot microseconds apart. Night mode is a case in point. This is a fluid area, so expect changes to come in what may be possible.

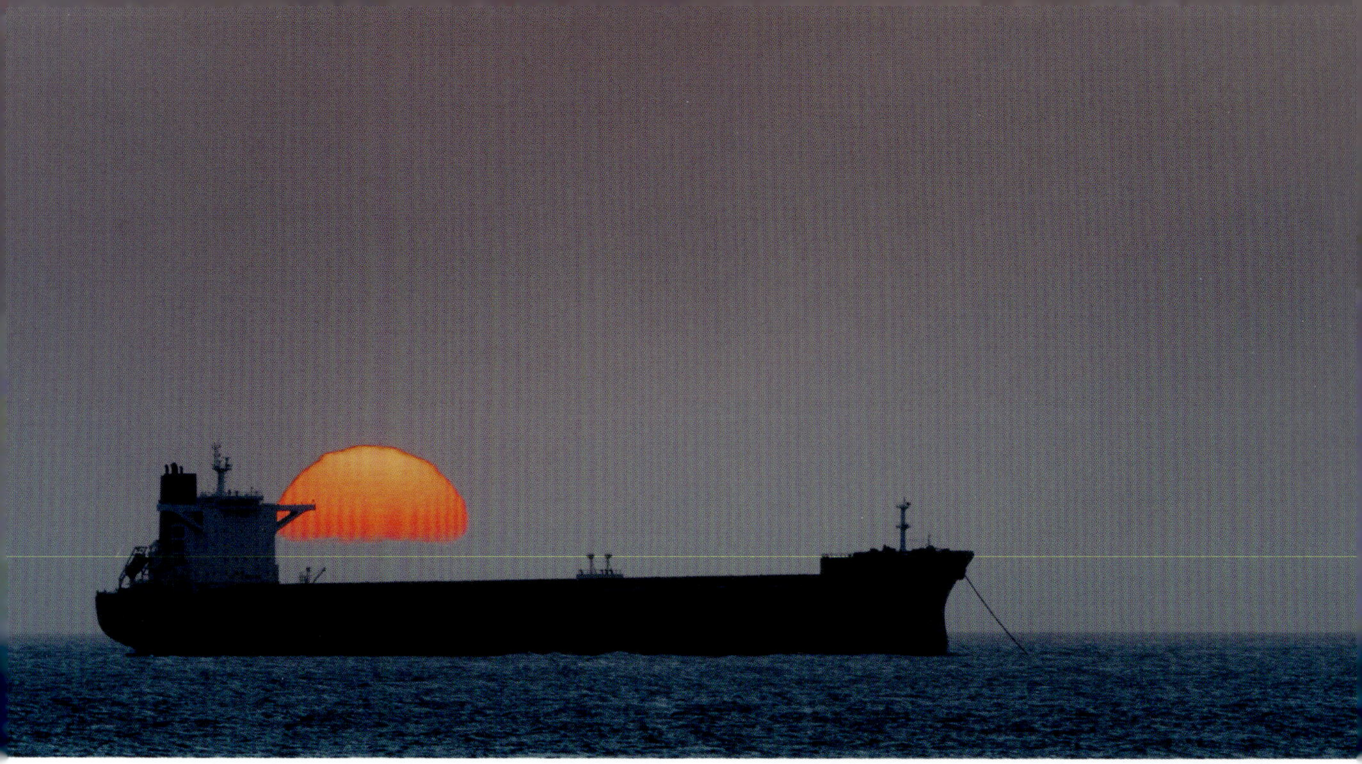

 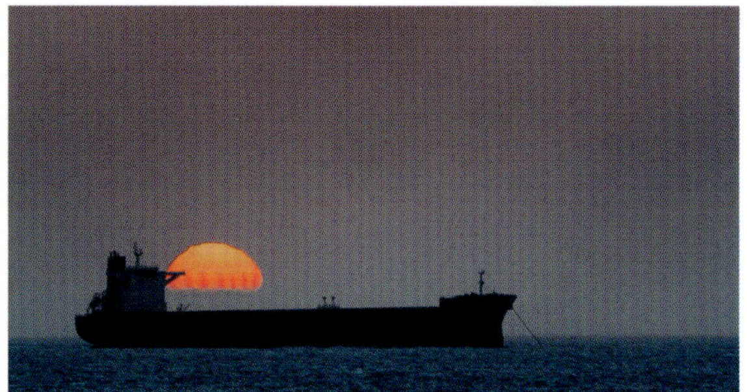

PULSATING COLOR

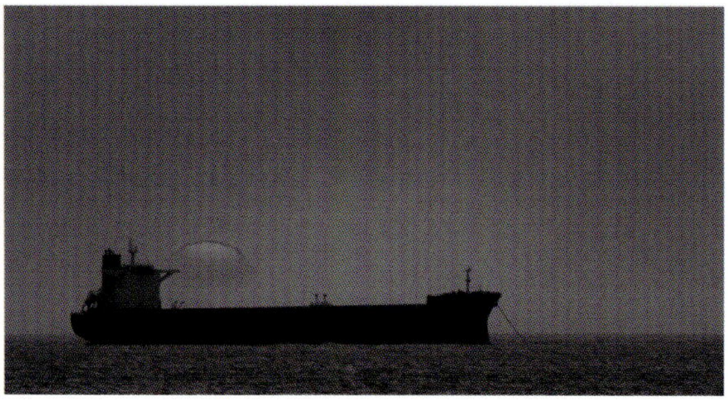

A strange but occasionally useful color effect happens when two colors are the same brightness, and the same applies even if one of them is a colorless grey. At the border between them there's a kind of vibration or switching effect, sometimes described as unstable or jittery.

The cause lies deep in the early stages of the brain's processing system. Luminance and color information take two pathways from the eye, known as the 'Where' and the 'What' systems. The Where system locates things and handles depth,

Tanker off the coast of Santa Marta, Colombia, with the sun the same brightness as the surrounding sky on the horizon. (In black and white, it becomes invisible.) The pulsating effect that this causes brings extra life to the sun, compared with the original version in which it is slightly brighter.

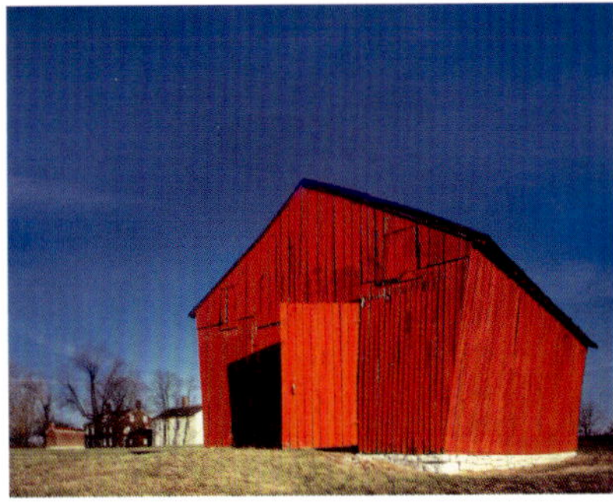
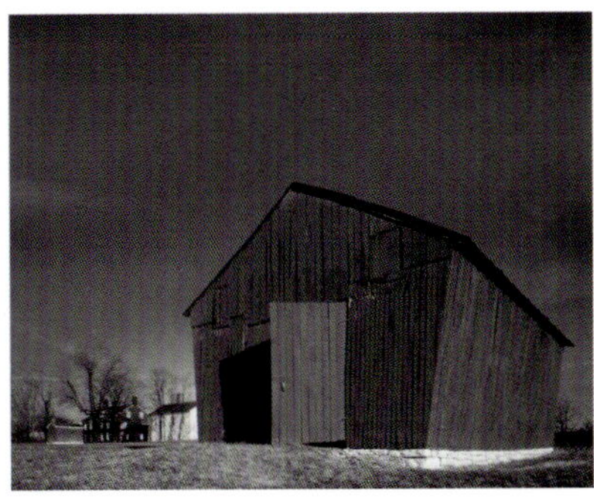

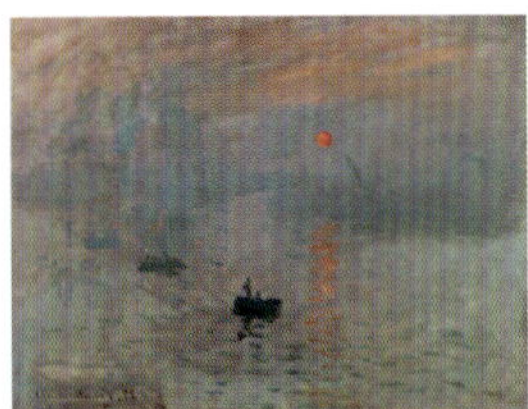
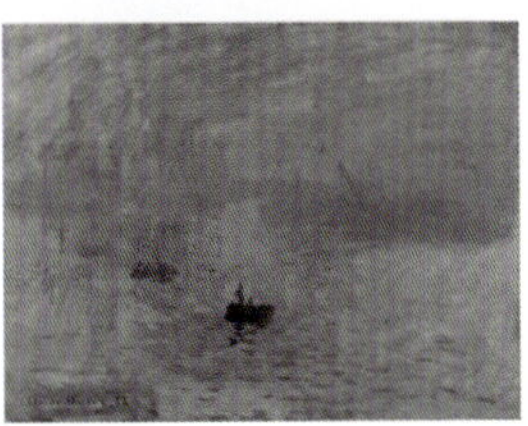

Impression, Sunrise, 1872,
by Claude Monet, who used
the equiluminance effect to
give the sun more energy. In
black and white, it becomes
invisible.

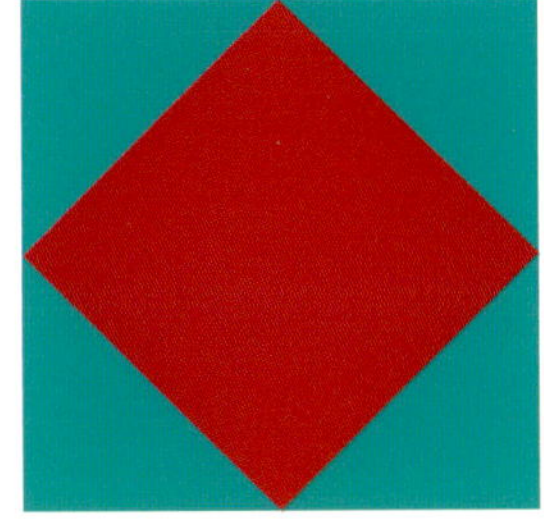

Two complementary
colors at exactly the same
brightness. The edges seem
uncertain to the eye.

motion and general organization of the scene, while the What system allows us to recognize objects, including faces, and colors. The Where system is color-blind, so that when two colors are the same brightness, it cannot distinguish between them, and that puts it at odds with the What system. While the Where system sees the colors, the What system isn't able to position them, hence the floating, unstable, even uncomfortable experience of looking at them.

Can this be useful for photography? Certainly it can, if you want to create a kind of tension, a sense of jittery movement and activity. Some artists already did, notably some of the Op Art painters of the 1960s, but also Monet. In his 1872 painting *Impression, Sunrise*, the red sun seems not only intense, but to pulsate, because it is exactly the same brightness as the bluish clouds around it. The neurobiologist Margaret Livingstone in her book *Vision and Art: The Biology of Seeing* shows a manipulated version with the sun lighter and paler, which as she says, 'has lost its quavering luminosity. It now seems paradoxically less bright.'

This is something to bear in mind when processing and in post-production, where there are a number of tools to make this happen. In the example here, there's a similar situation to Monet's sunrise (actually a sunset in this instance), where haze has darkened the setting sun as it sinks behind a distant bank of clouds. The smaller version is as shot, without any significant processing, and while it works perfectly well, with an attractive color opposition between the sun and the water, I wanted to see what would happen if the sun and the sky were the same brightness. They were already fairly close, at least at the base of the sun, so this took a small adjustment. I'm not sure which is 'better', but there is certainly an instability and a kind of pulsating to the sun in the main photograph. As a way of making the sun powerful, we've substituted this illusion of activity for the original straightforward brightness.

3

THE RIGHT COLOR

To some people 'the right color' might sound like the only goal for color in photography, and one for engineers. There are colors in the scene in front of the colors, and the aim, surely, is to get those exact same colors on the screen or print in front of the viewer.

There's a yes-and-no answer to this. Whether it's film, or sensors and the algorithms applied to them, it's certainly true that you can measure the wavelength, saturation and brightness at the start and at the finish and make a comparison. As I hope the last chapter showed, however, what we see as colors also involves the science of our vision system, made up of both the physiology and the psychology. That complicates matters, but perhaps more easily for most of us, it throws the judgement of what's accurate back on our own judgement.

Even if we're not concentrating on color, just looking at it in photographs we bring quite a lot of undeclared baggage, and most of this is in the form of what we expect from what we know already. Experiences of what the colors of various things look like merges easily into expectations of how they should look in a photograph. Crudely put, we have fairly fixed ideas about what we see a lot of and what we find important. As we'll get onto in several pages, so-called memory colors loom large in any judgement we have about which colors look right. Skin, blue sky, greenery and things we know to be neutral (such as concrete and pavements) lead the way.

Taking some of these further, they invite 'improvement', meaning adjustment, to match the part of our expectations that strays into desirability. Blue skies bluer? Eyes browner? Skin tone deeper? This is surely what the idea of 'right color' is up against. Yes, but it's also in some ways what 'right' means to some people. On the edges, this is not quite such a rigid area.

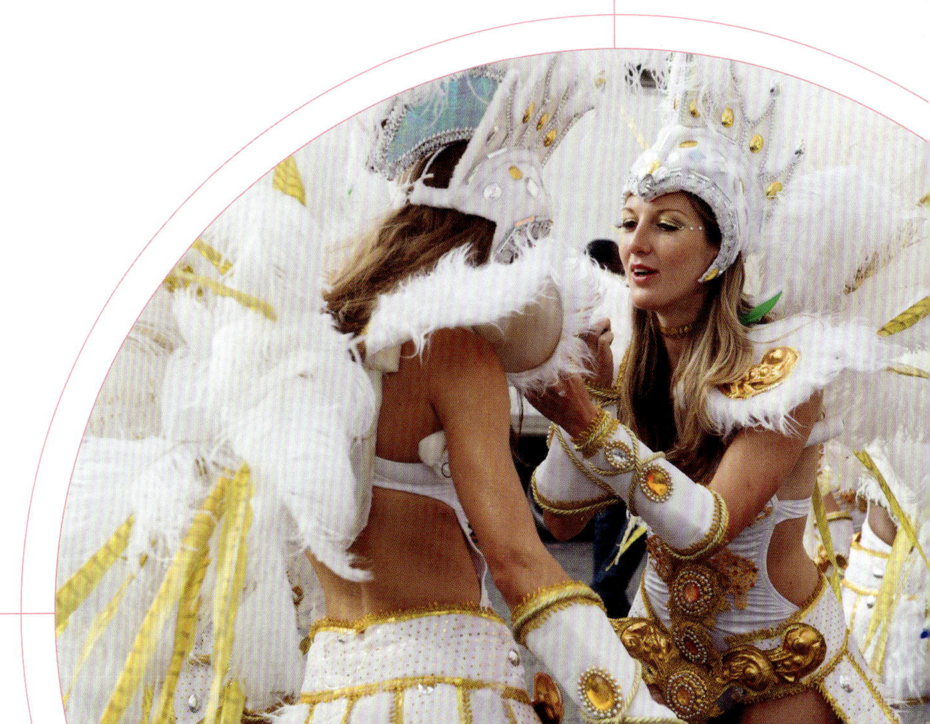

COLOR TRUTH

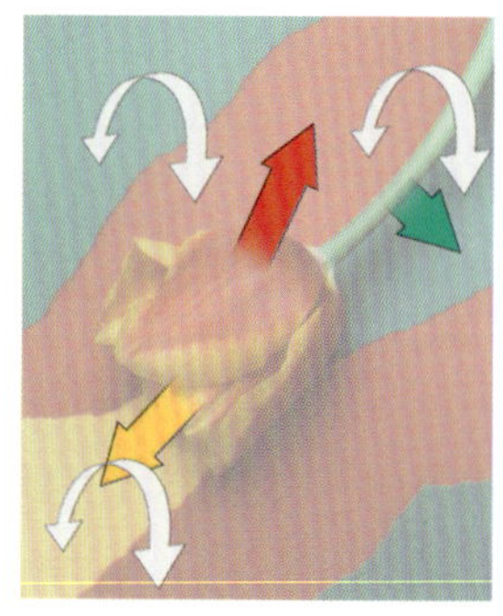

Ground truth is an essential idea in science when the work aims towards an ideal result, meaning something that can be measured as it really is (though reality itself isn't always certain). Machine learning relies on it, and it sounds straightforward, but with color there are complications, because color exists in our minds – along with experience and expectations. This goes back to the color models and spaces on page 36 onward.

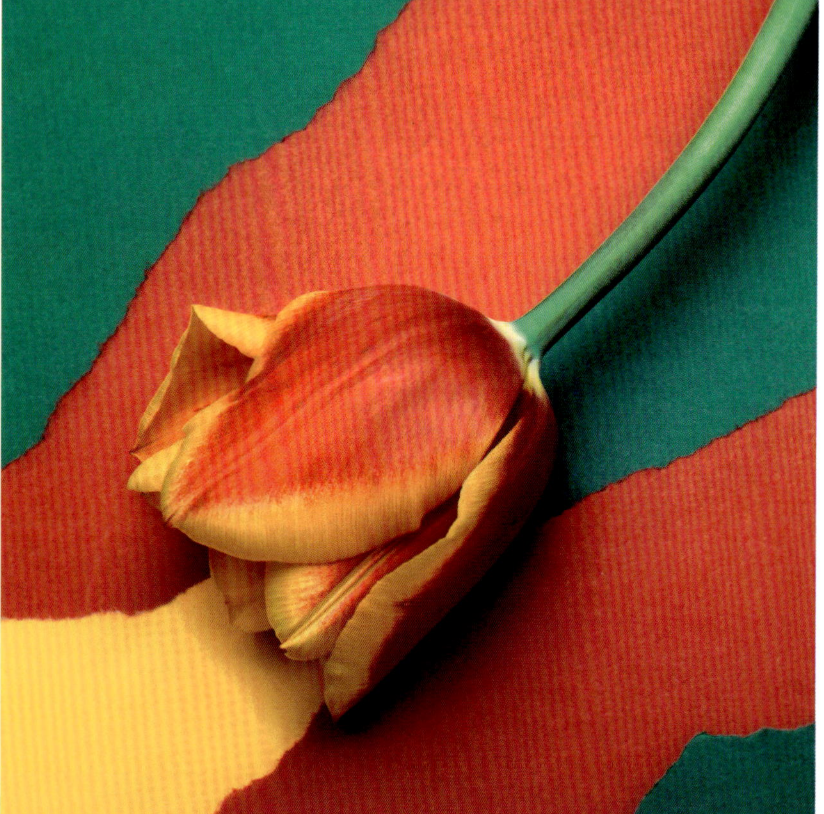

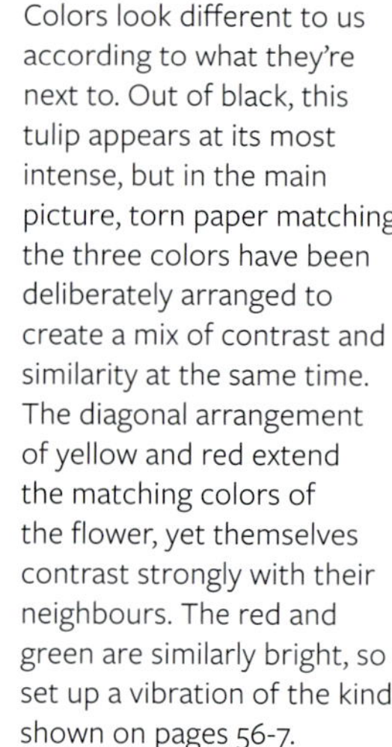

Colors look different to us according to what they're next to. Out of black, this tulip appears at its most intense, but in the main picture, torn paper matching the three colors have been deliberately arranged to create a mix of contrast and similarity at the same time. The diagonal arrangement of yellow and red extend the matching colors of the flower, yet themselves contrast strongly with their neighbours. The red and green are similarly bright, so set up a vibration of the kind shown on pages 56-7.

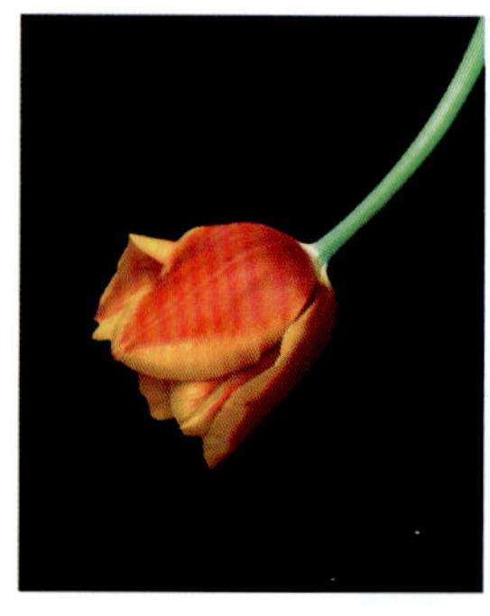

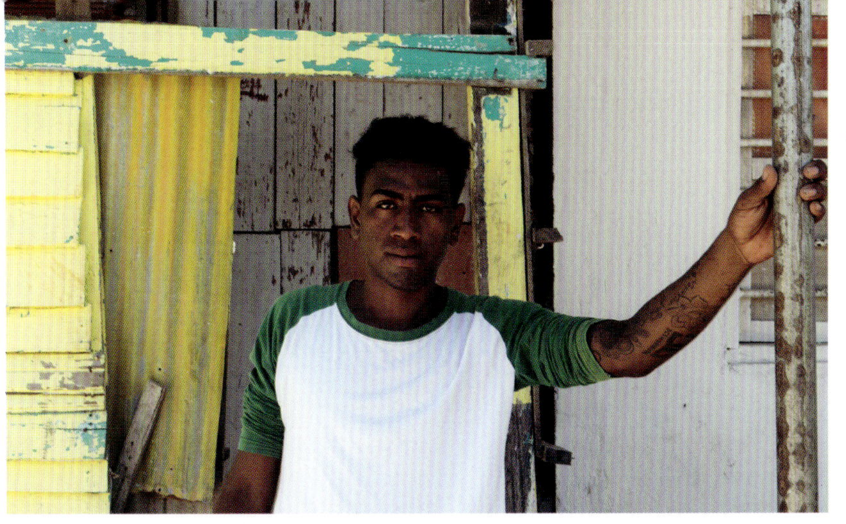

The darker skin is, the more it reflects surrounding colors. In this portrait in Cartagena, Colombia, reflections include a yellow cast from the left and uplighting from the white-fronted T-shirt.

We can measure the wavelength and the brightness and the purity, but that doesn't automatically mean that we know how a surface or lighting appears to a viewer. Our vision system adapts so wonderfully to changing conditions that it easily overrides, so to speak, the reality on the ground. There are many examples of that happening in this book. We're dealing with color in photography here, not color in the abstract, so appearances mean everything.

That's not to say that we need to look for the truth of color only in the mind, but if you want to meet expectations when you photograph color, there has to be a balance between what can be measured and what 'looks' right. And that's a shifting balance, so there's no simple formula. When it comes to measurement, most of the time in photography we're dealing with reflected light, and the colors of things are a mixture of their surface qualities and the light falling on them. A reflectance spectrophotometer or a colorimeter, like the one shown here, is placed on the surface, shines its own light onto the sample and measures the color of the light reflected back. Use it on a branded pack of cereal or soap or whatever, and you'll get the exact values that the manufacturer intended. How it looks, however, is going to be influenced by such things as the setting or background, as the tulip photograph shows.

The more we know what a color should look like (or more accurately, the more we think we know), the more useful a measurement like this is. That gives memory colors (see page 70) more of a ground truth, and the best example is skin, which comes later in this chapter. Not only are we highly sensitive to skin color, and immediately aware of any 'wrong' shifts, there is a massive cosmetics industry built around this. Not surprisingly, skin color and tone have been endlessly measured (yes, with spectrophotometers), and the more obvious color aim in portrait photography is getting it the way it measures. The less obvious goal is getting it to look the way we would like, which is a different matter.

A spectrophotometer of the kind used for measuring such critical surface colors as skin.

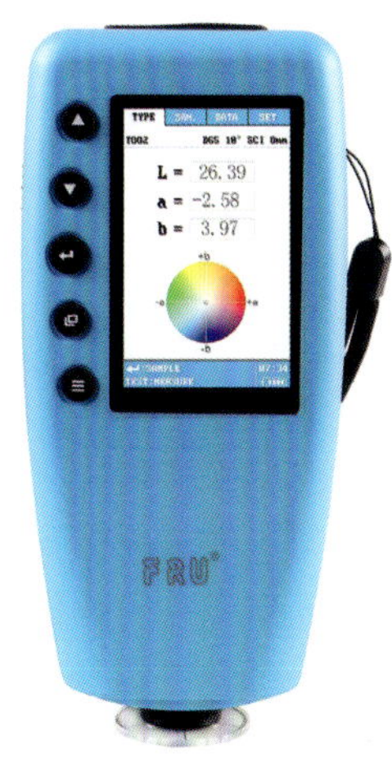

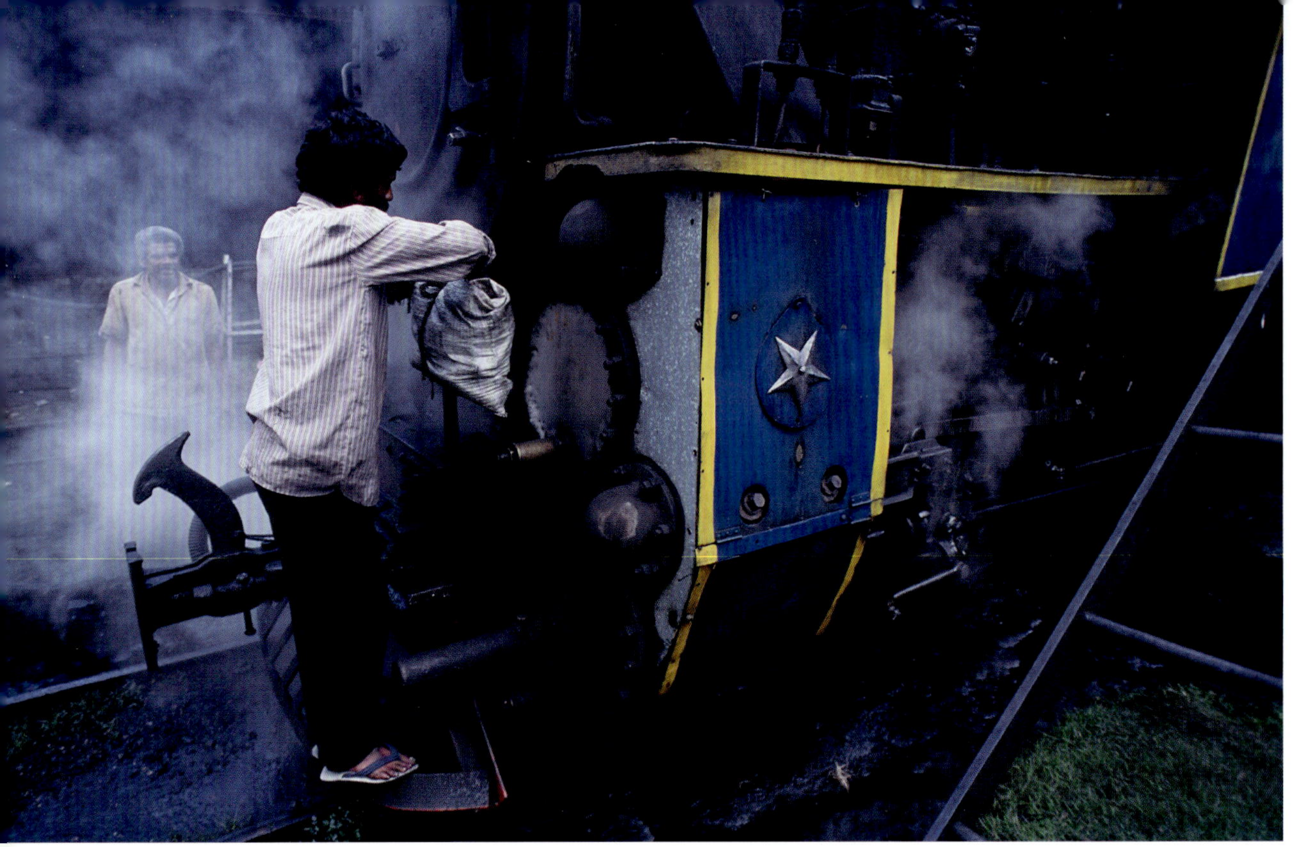

TOLERANCE

An essential step on the way to getting colors right is color tolerance – how accurately we can distinguish between small shifts of color. There are differences between individuals, certainly, but taking average vision we respond consistently to differences between colors.

The measure of tolerance is ΔE, usually called Delta E, and it puts a number on how much of a shift in color it takes before we notice. Below one we can't detect a shift, four and above we definitely can. Also, we're roughly twice as sensitive to shifts in hue as to changes in brightness.

The way of visualizing this is in the standard CIE color space, in the form of ellipses as here. These are sections from a 3D space, and are called MacAdam ellipsoids. As you see, they vary both in size and in narrowness. The smaller and narrower they are, the more sensitive we are to changes. The largest and the fattest are in the greens

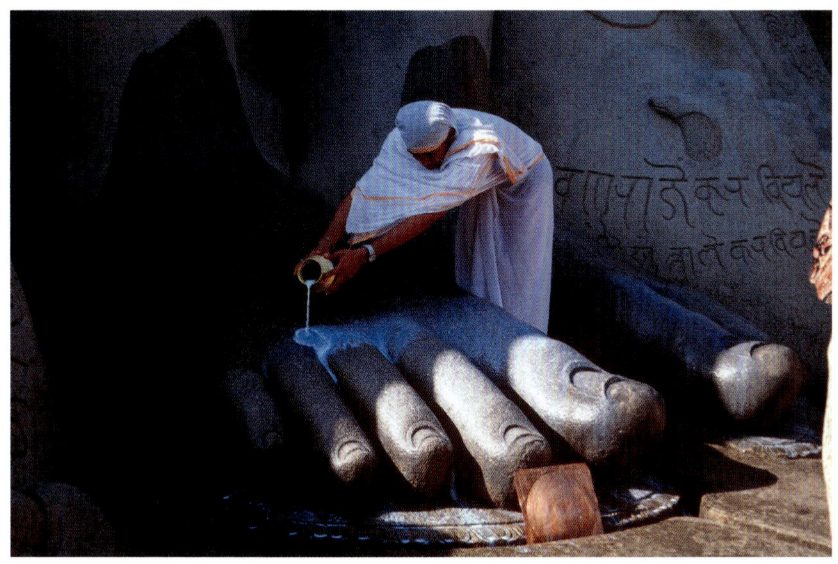

and green-blues, which means that, despite the many wrong opinions passed on the web, we don't discriminate very well among greens. This is even though we have extra sensitivity to green, but it shouldn't be too surprising because what most of us call green stretches from yellowish (lime, for example) to bluish (teal, for example), which is quite a chunk of the circle, almost 100 degrees. Green is especially the color of vegetation, and as we'll see when we come to memory colors (pages 70–1), we're well accustomed to a wide range of green leaves. Basically, we're particularly tolerant of shifts in green.

Yellow is especially narrow, meaning we're very sensitive to shifts from greenish-yellow to orange-yellow, and I'll come back to this later, on page 91. We also have a fairly precise sense of oranges too, and it so happens that human skin color, irrespective of lightness or darkness, is approximately within this range, at quite low saturation. For reasons we'll get to on page 72, we are hypersensitive to skin tones, and it doesn't take much of a color shift when shooting to create a 'wrong' color. The smallest ellipses are in the saturated area of blue to violet, but these also are the colors we come across least in daily life.

Another type of tolerance is color constancy, which factors in experience and expectations. Just as lightness constancy means that if we're familiar with how bright something normally appears, we 'see' it that way even if it's partly in shadow, so the argument goes that if we 'know' we're looking at a particular color, we can override the evidence of our eyes. Or can we? The evidence is that color constancy works some of the time, but not always. Often there's a conflict, because while we may know from common sense that a surface is all the same color in light and shade, the colors do look different. And depending on the camera sensor and conversion, they may even measure differently.

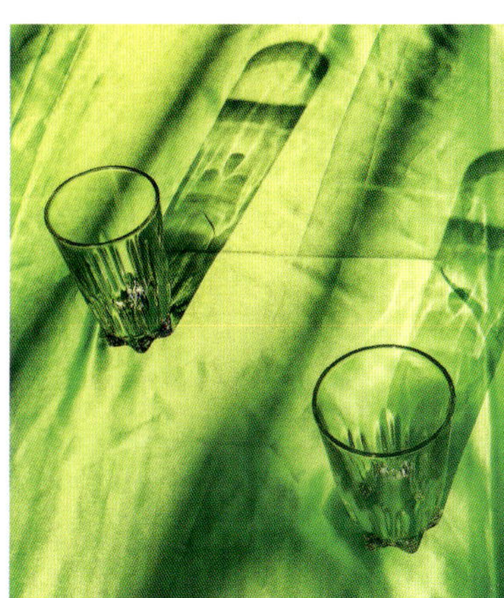

A single-color scene (a green tablecloth lit by a low sun, with neutral glasses and their shadows) offers no clues to accuracy, and is accepted by most viewers as simply colorful.

COLOR TEMPERATURE

Color temperature is a special case, but one that's highly relevant for photography simply because it relates to the changing color of sunlight through the day and to traditional indoor lighting – one of the most obvious constants in color photography.

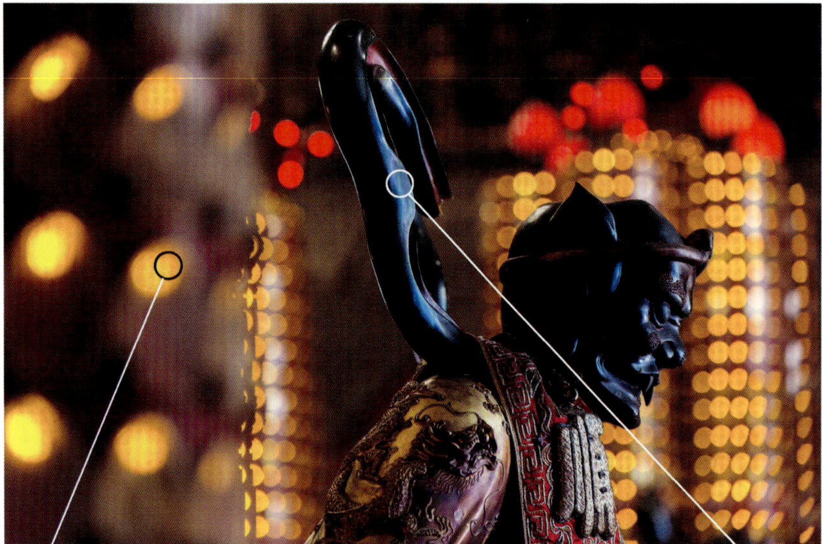

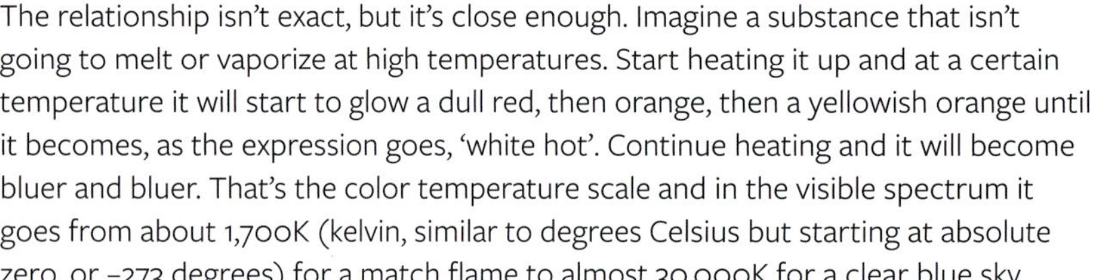

The relationship isn't exact, but it's close enough. Imagine a substance that isn't going to melt or vaporize at high temperatures. Start heating it up and at a certain temperature it will start to glow a dull red, then orange, then a yellowish orange until it becomes, as the expression goes, 'white hot'. Continue heating and it will become bluer and bluer. That's the color temperature scale and in the visible spectrum it goes from about 1,700K (kelvin, similar to degrees Celsius but starting at absolute zero, or –273 degrees) for a match flame to almost 30,000K for a clear blue sky.

It applies to incandescence – burning – and in our experience that includes flames, heated filaments in tungsten lamps, halogen lamps and the sun. Beyond white into blue isn't a part of our experience, although there are some stars like Rigel in Orion that burn so brightly and hotly that they are blue-white. What we do have in daylight that's blue is a clear sky, and while it isn't incandescent and its color comes from the selective scattering of sunlight, the range of blues is a good fit for the high end of the color temperature scale. This is called correlated color temperature, but that's good enough for photography.

STANDARD ILLUMINANTS

White standards for monitors and publishing viewing booths, among other applications, are:

CIE D50	**5,000K**
CIE D55	**5,500K**
CIE D65	**6,500K**
CIE D75	**7,500K**

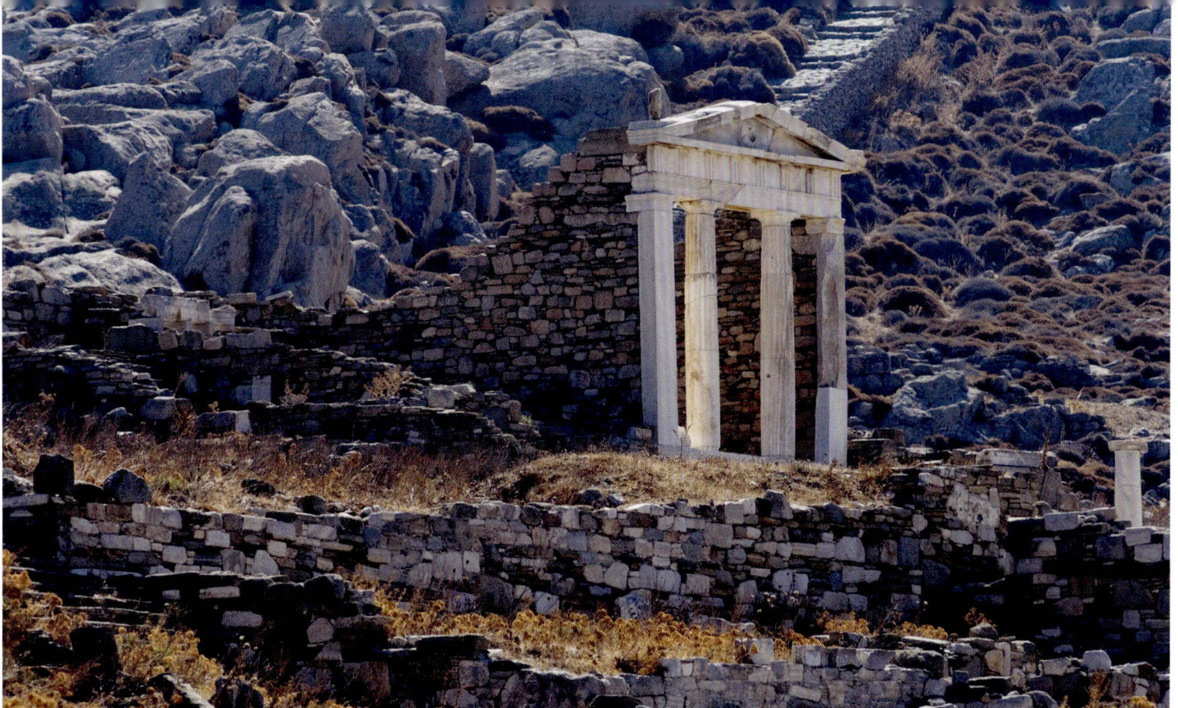

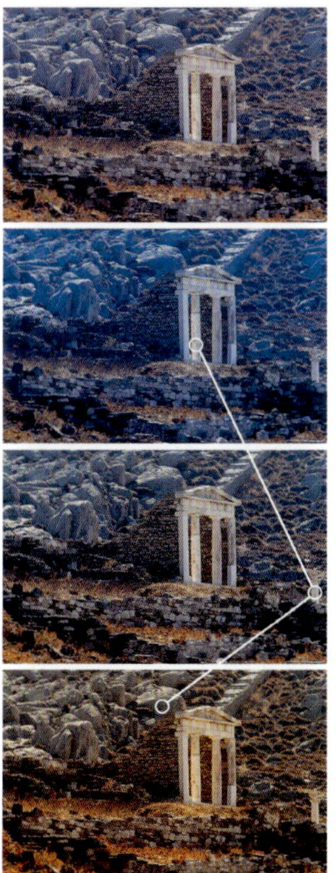

As you can see on page 37, the scale itself fits into the CIE color space, though with a special curve called the Planckian locus (that means path) that goes exactly through the neutral centre. White is essentially unaltered sunlight, and to our eyes is neutral, colorless, because it's the basic illumination under which we evolved. Measured on this scale, though, there are slightly different whites. The sun above the atmosphere is about 5,900K, while the daylight balance long agreed for film is 5,500K. Higher temperatures than this look cooler, which is a possible source of confusion, going way above 15,000K for a blue sky, while lower temperatures, which look warmer, start to kick in when the sun is lower than about 20 degrees above the horizon and can sometimes be a deep red at sunset and sunrise. For more on how and why this happens, see page 14.

Two things come from our familiarity with color temperature (the light at least, if not the numbers). One is that for most scenes we're reasonably tolerant of warmer or cooler color casts along this scale, and in fact expect shots taken close to sunset and sunrise to look warm. The other is that it's a scale used for adjusting white balance by both camera manufacturers and processing software such as Adobe's. A word of caution here. Lightroom and Adobe Camera Raw, among others, offer basic color adjustment with two opposed sliders: 'Temperature' from bluish 50,000K to yellowish 2,000K, and 'Tint' from green to magenta. This is indeed a color opponent system similar to the one described on page 35, but not exactly. The system devised by CIE for L*a*b* (see page 44) uses red-green and yellow-blue. Visually, in the CIE color space, the b* line is straight while the color temperature line is curved.

COLOR TARGETS

The guaranteed way to make sure that the colors captured by the camera stay true in the final photograph is to shoot a test control that has colored patches that can be measured. In practice, this means shooting one frame with a color target, then processing that so that the result matches it on the numbers.

The principle is very simple, but of course it does take some time and effort, so it's best suited to the kind of shooting where you can plan, and for subjects and scenes where absolute color accuracy genuinely matters. As you'd expect, it's standard practice in commercial portraits, fashion shoots with models and clothes, and product photography. It relies on the target having color patches that are both stable and rigorously standardized with known values, so naturally these cost. There are different makes, and the one here is the SpyderCheckr from Datacolor with 48 patches. As the values are known, in L*a*b*, sRGB and Adobe RGB, it's a straightforward matter for the accompanying app, once the photographed target has been loaded and aligned, to calculate the adjustments needed to get all patches to their correct values. This is saved as a calibration preset that you can then use in Lightroom, Adobe Camera Raw, Phocus or whatever.

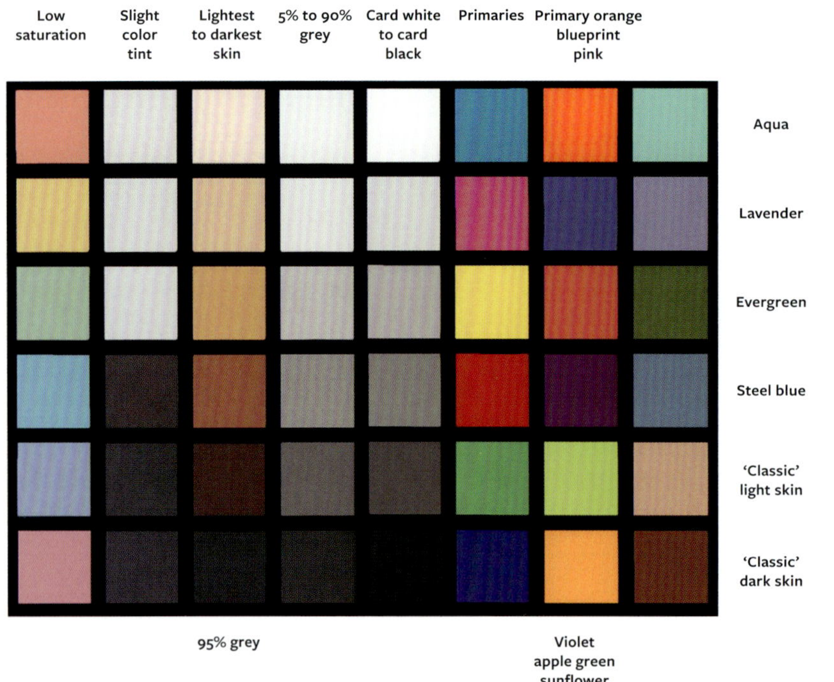

A 48-patch target from Datacolor with the manufacturer's descriptions. On the right are industry-standard patches, on the left additional targets for more precise skin tones, medium-saturation colors and extra near-whites and dark greys.

The same color target in use, opened and mounted on a stand. The small red patch in the lower-left corner warns against fading from prolonged exposure to light by turning yellow-orange.

The target used in an indoor setting. At the same time, the color cards can be flipped over in the holder for a greyscale set to set the camera's white balance.

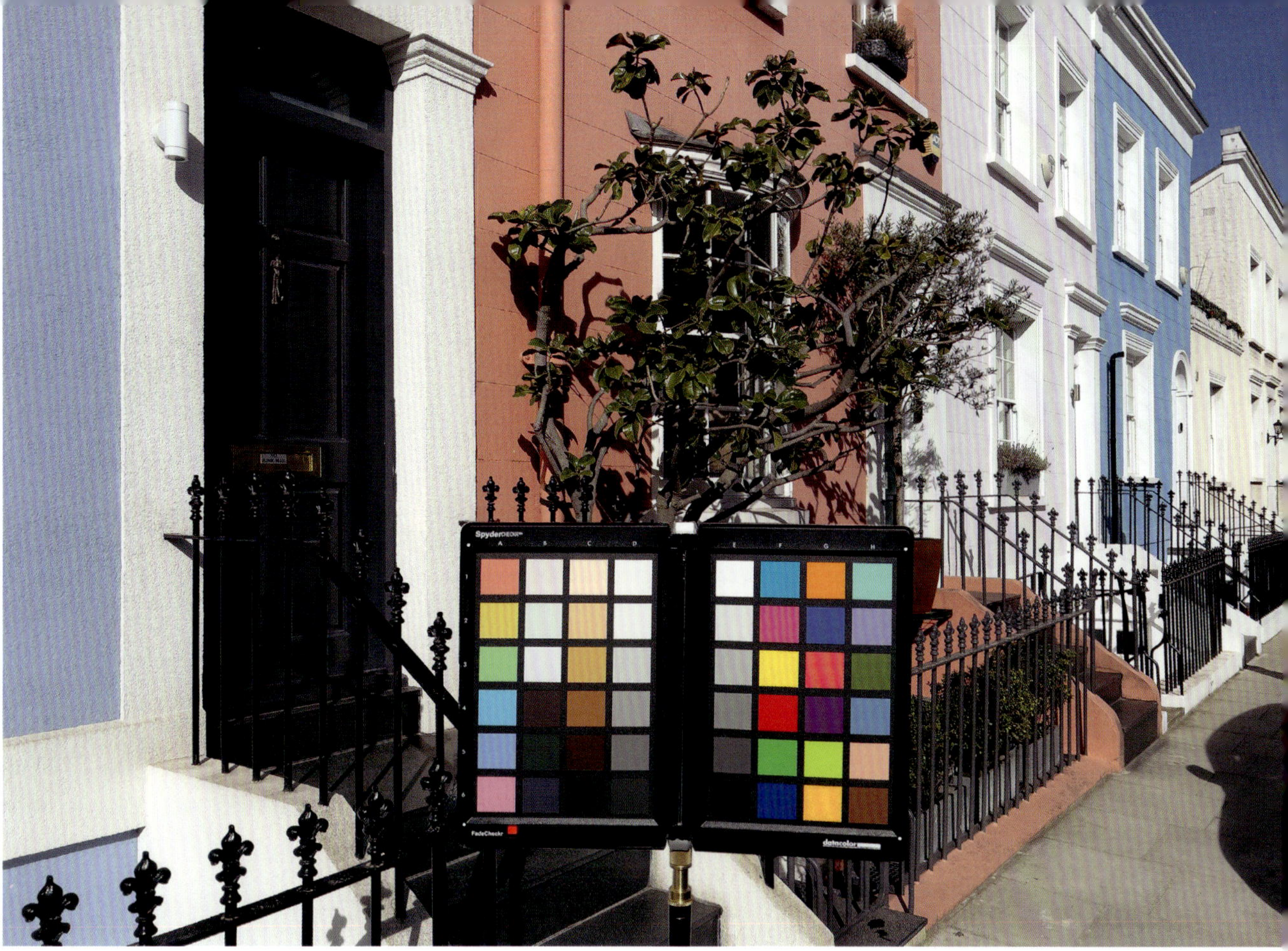

The patches can also be used visually as reliable references for skin, as an example. As we'll come onto later in this chapter, we're extremely sensitive to color accuracy for skin color, and having a number of patches for different tones (there are eight in this target) is useful for a quick reference. Neutral grey is also important, as we'll see on the following pages.

So, when there's time and a need to use a color target, the usual procedure is to set up for the shoot and include the target in the first frame. Once that has been processed and the calibration preset created, the preset will work for all the other shots. Important to remember is that this works only for the same lighting conditions, which includes various reflections from behind or to the side of the camera that you might not be aware of. If you're shooting outdoors, there will be differences in color temperature if there are clouds moving across the sun or a haze building up.

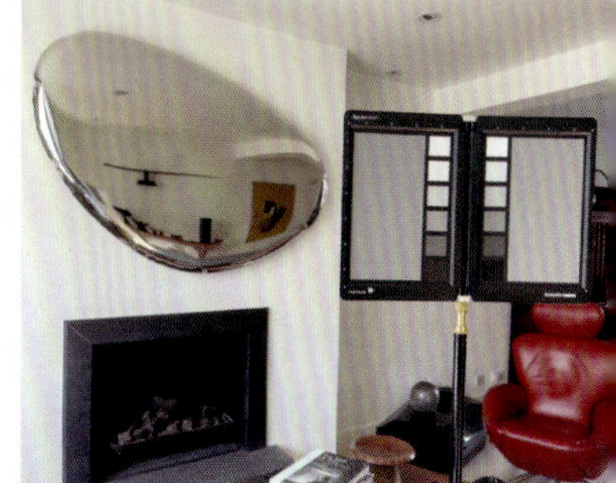

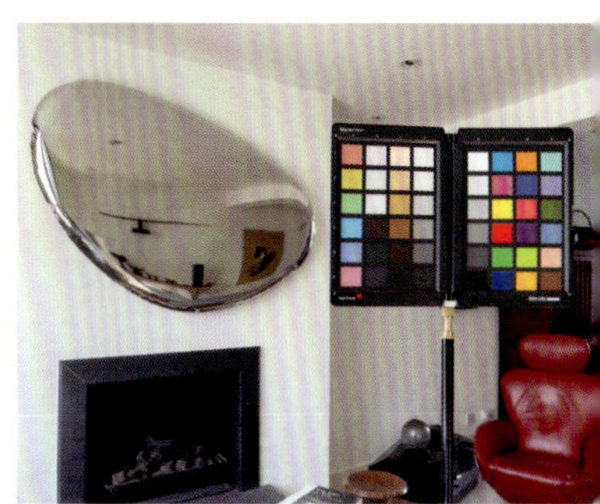

GREY ANCHOR

The simplest means of detecting a color cast is a grey surface. The very word grey means a tone somewhere between black and white, and we are highly sensitive to its neutrality. In most scenes, any drift towards a color in grey is immediately obvious, and you can compensate for it when shooting or correct it later when processing.

When true color accuracy is important and there's enough time, the best practice is to include a grey reference in the frame. The color target shown just now has a bottom row of grey patches, or you could use a mid-tone grey card, or better still a three-dimensional grey object that shows the color from different directions, like the SpyderCUBE shown here. Shoot one frame with one of these in view, then in processing use an eyedropper on the grey, and the color shift from this will work on every other frame you shoot under the same lighting.

These are guaranteed methods, but remembering that most photography deals with appearances rather than measurements, grey targets like these aren't even normally necessary. Our eyes are very well attuned to what ought to be

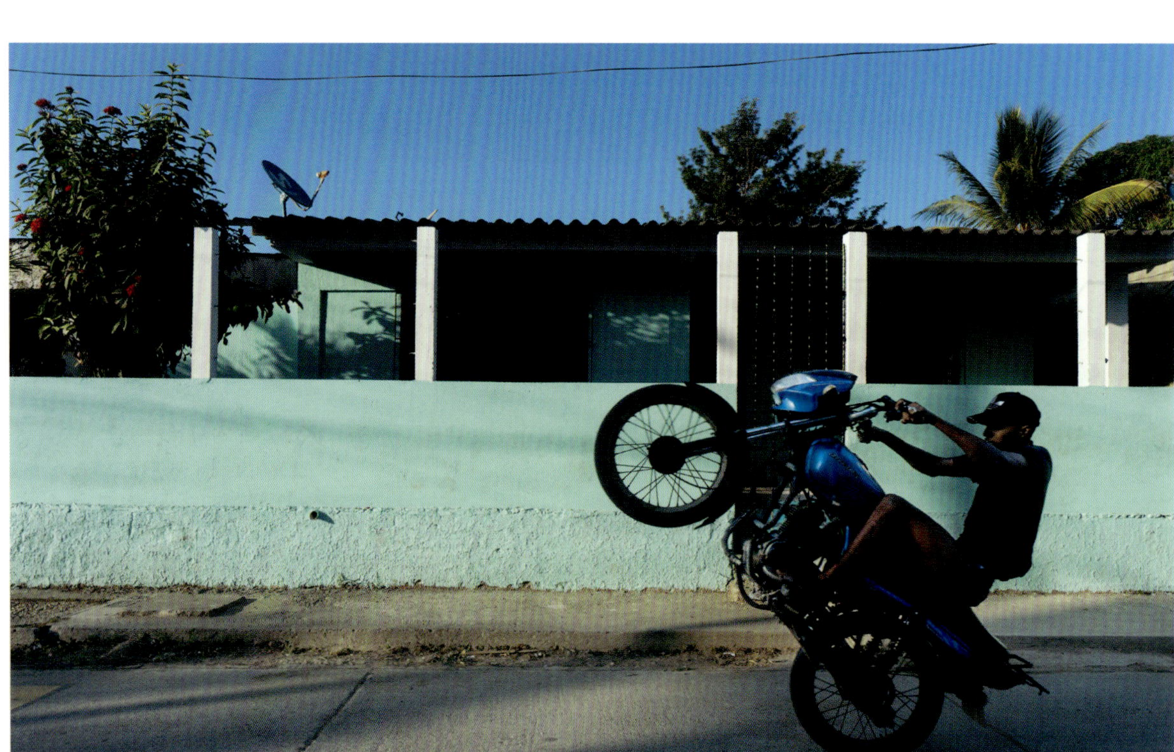

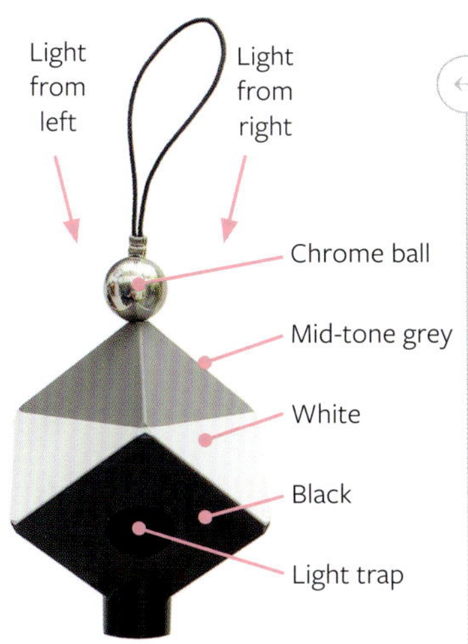

neutral grey, through experience. This includes concrete, most stone, unpolished steel, darker areas of clouds that are not facing blue sky, fog and grey hair. These sound loose and not particularly reliable, but they are good enough for most situations. Interestingly, our vision system is efficient at picking out surfaces that seem like they should be grey, as in the picture here.

If you can find something in the frame that works as grey for you, eyedropping it gives you a working neutral color balance for the entire picture. I also use an on-screen color meter to check without getting into processing – in HSB mode what should be grey should have zero saturation.

In other words, greys anchor the color balance of a scene. When they occupy a large area they are certainly critical, but even when small they are useful for balancing when processing. This doesn't necessarily mean that they have to stay neutral; think of this operation as a starting point. As we just saw, color temperature in low sunlight is expected to look warmer (actually a lower color temperature), and a grey surface is a good place to measure this. The picture of a barrio motorcyclist doing a wheelie is a good example. The shadows show how low the sun is, and the road is in both light and shade. Whoever mixed the concrete, it still works as grey, and the difference between sunlit and shadowed in the main picture is just as you'd expect. Shot with Auto White Balance (my default), it was a little too cool, so the procedure was simply to eyedrop the sunlit concrete and lower the color temperature from 4800K to 4130K. Note that the color of the shadows are exactly the same as the upper part of the sky, as they should be because they reflect it.

Setting white balance by eye when processing the Raw file. As described in the text, the Eyedropper tool is used on sunlit concrete then shifted down 15 percent to look warmer because of the low sun. The hue angle of the blue sky and the shadows on concrete are, as you'd expect, the same.

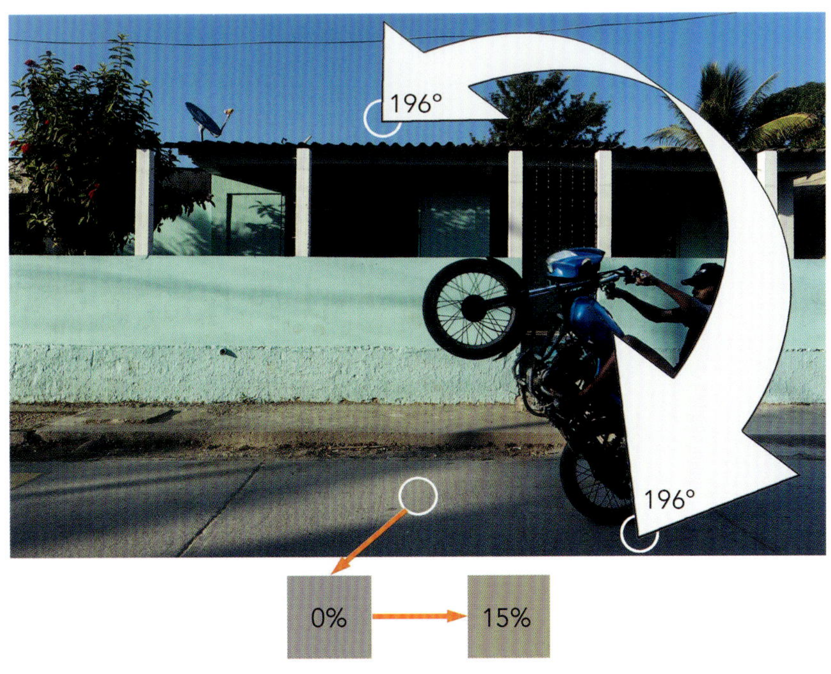

MEMORY COLORS

We read colors through the filter of experience, and I don't mean that as just a cute phrase. It's highly practical. One result is that we're most judgemental about colors that are the most familiar.

These are called memory colors, also canonical colors, and they're in our faces every day. Skin, sky and greenery top the list for everyone, with additional specialities according to what interests you or what you do for a living. Sommeliers and wine enthusiasts discriminate fine shades of red, for example, and if you're into jewellery you'll probably have a good eye for the purity of gold by its color. And so on.

This means that there's more pressure to get memory colors right, all the way from shooting to processing. That includes camera manufacturers, and while dedicated cameras work to improve color globally, across the entire image, phone cameras are more focused on targeting specific areas. Facial recognition and adjustment is at the forefront, as we'll see shortly. Another way of putting it is that we have less tolerance for the colors important to us being different, and so the Delta E on page 62 isn't the last word. As soon as we see a color in context, which is what photography is all about, tolerance changes. Against that, color constancy can, at times, make a photograph with skewed memory colors seem acceptable.

Greenery is also a powerful memory color for evolutionary reasons, and in addition we're more sensitive to its variety than to any other color. There are at least nine distinct greens in this landscape, varying by hue, saturation and brightness.

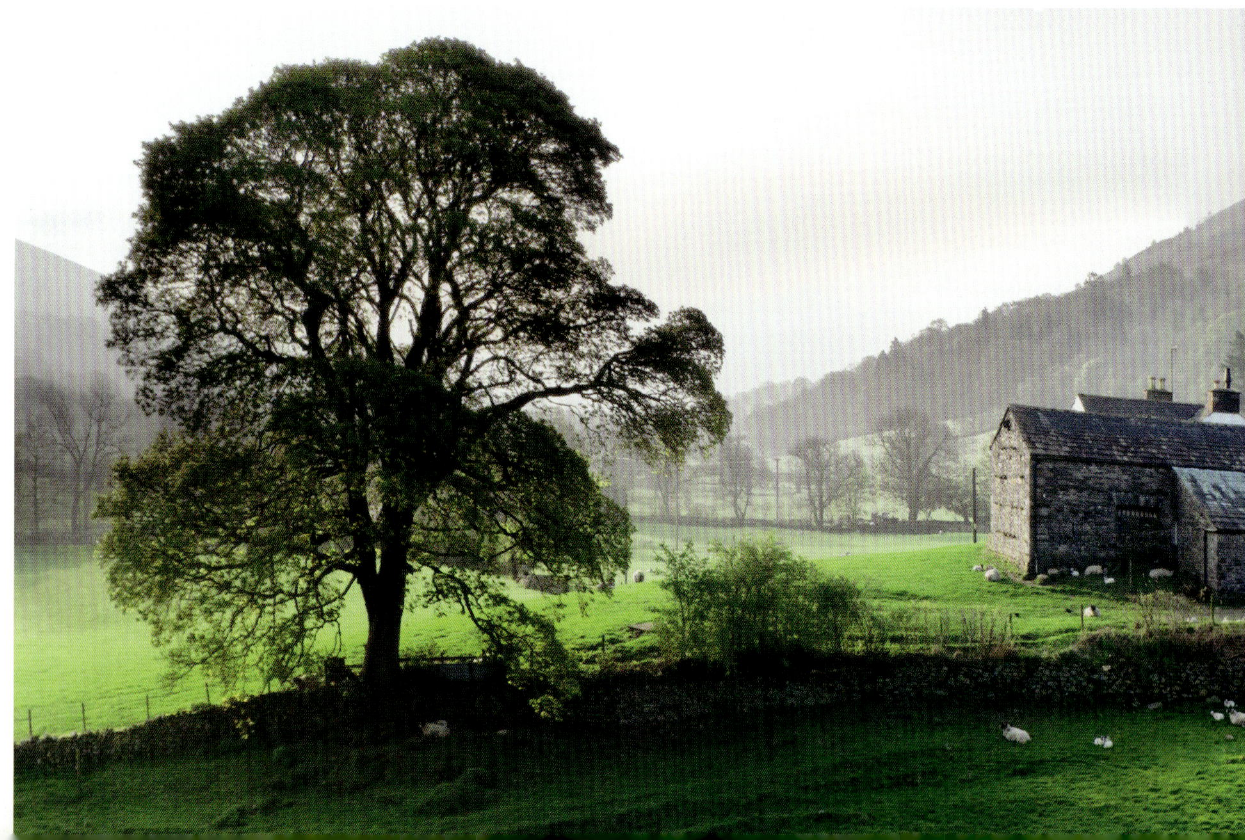

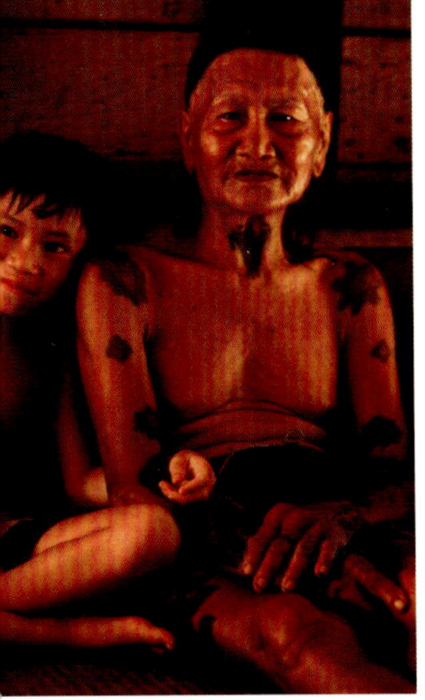

The picture of an Iban man and boy in a longhouse in Sarawak shows skin color that is way too orange and 'hot', but as this applies also to the wooden wall behind them, we simply assume that the entire photograph has a color cast (in fact caused by using daylight film in an interior partly lit by candles). What's not 'right' to our eyes is the overall color cast rather than the skin color.

Memories, however, are often unreliable, and influenced by other things going on in our minds. This calls into question the very idea of 'rightness'. We can measure color, but if the result in a photograph surprises us because we had a different idea about it, what then? Which is more right, the measurement or our judgement? There's no answer to this that would satisfy everyone. You can choose either, or somewhere in between.

Shifts in memory get mixed up with another complication: our preferences and ideals. We'll see a few cases of this over the next few pages, but I'll mention just one now. Blue skies are notorious for this in photography, because they're generally associated with fine weather, good times, even holidays. Popular taste favours saturated blues, professional and art-critical the opposite, and this translates into deeply held views on taste and elitism, as we saw on pages 28–9.

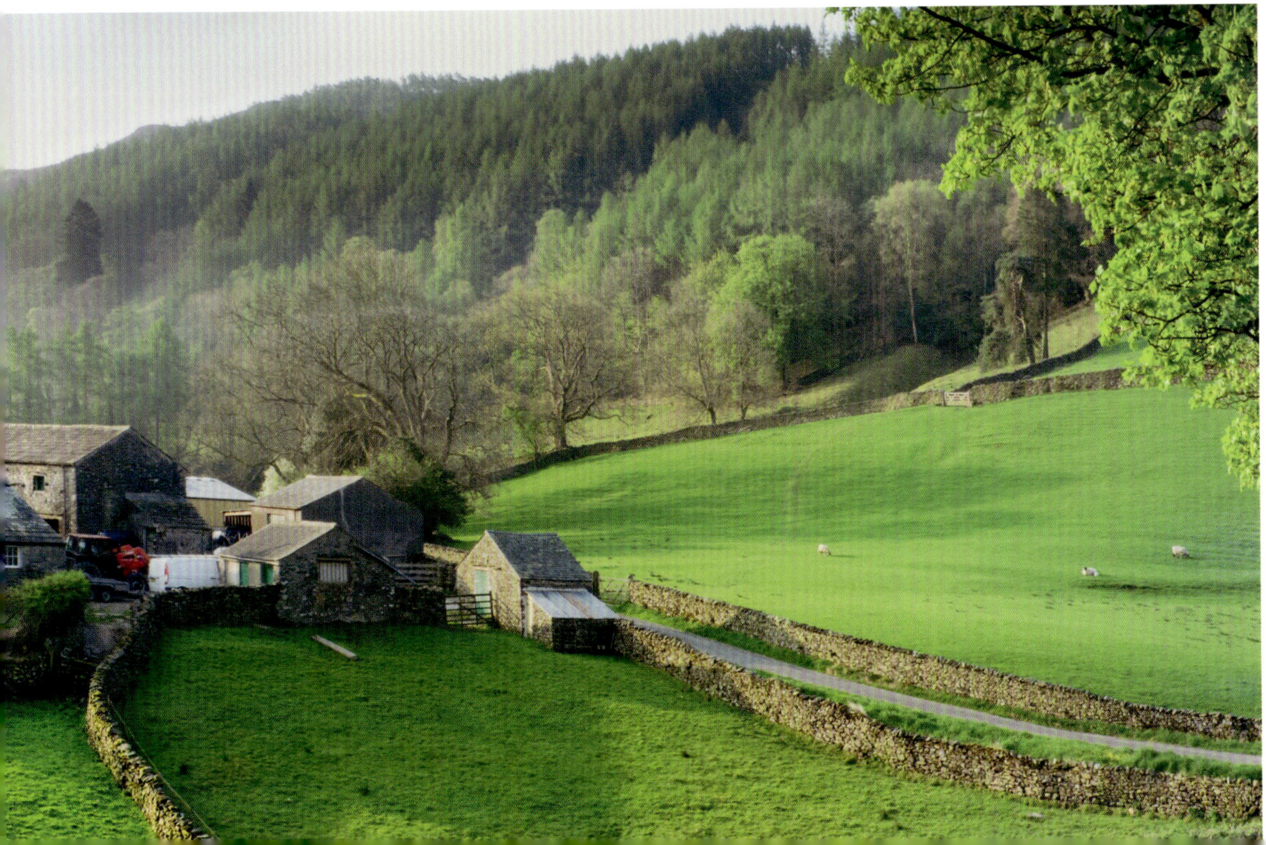

Skin tones are among the most critically judged memory colors, but as described in the text, they are judged against the overall lighting in a scene (here very warm) – in other words, relative to other surfaces in the picture.

UNIVERSAL SKIN

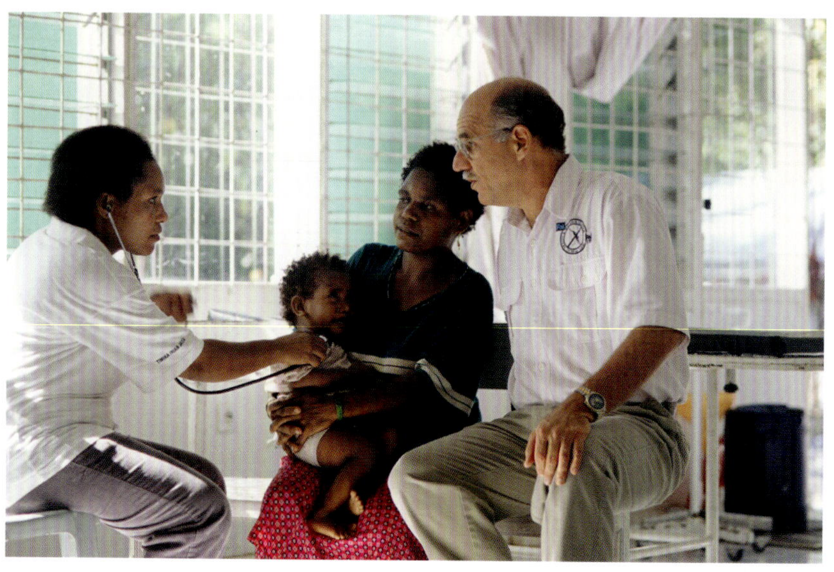

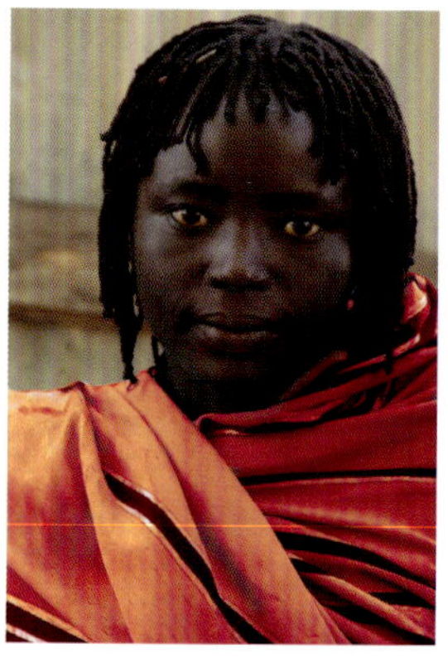

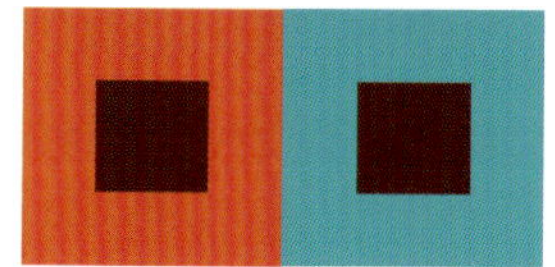

S kin color ought to be a straightforward matter for photography because it's more consistent than many other surfaces in our daily lives, but it's far from that.

We bring a lot of expectations and opinions to it, to do with beauty and differences in society, and we're sensitive to the tiniest differences. As a memory color, it has more layers of complexity and nuance than any other, for a number of reasons. One is that it's tied not just to our general familiarity, but to individual people. We care most about how we ourselves, our loved ones and friends look, naturally. After that, we're more concerned about our own skin type, however that's defined. This is where it gets tricky, because it enters the area of culture and race.

Another complication is that when it comes to judging fine differences in skin color, memory is not such a great tool. Even remembering how the skin color looked minutes after shooting a portrait can be difficult. Vague memory merges with wishes – how we'd prefer to see our skin color. This puts getting skin color right in a photograph at odds with getting it to be pleasing, and most photography for most people is indeed about creating pleasing images.

The range of normal skin tones and colors mapped by brightness against hue (saturation varies little, between about 25 percent and 40 percent). The hue changes are subtle, from yellowish to reddish, across no more than about 5 percent of the color circle.

Because all skin tones are low in saturation compared with other surfaces, their appearance is affected by nearby colors, especially if these are strong, as in the case of a southern Sudanese girl wearing her blue tobe. Shifting it by processing to orange-red alters the apparent color of her face.

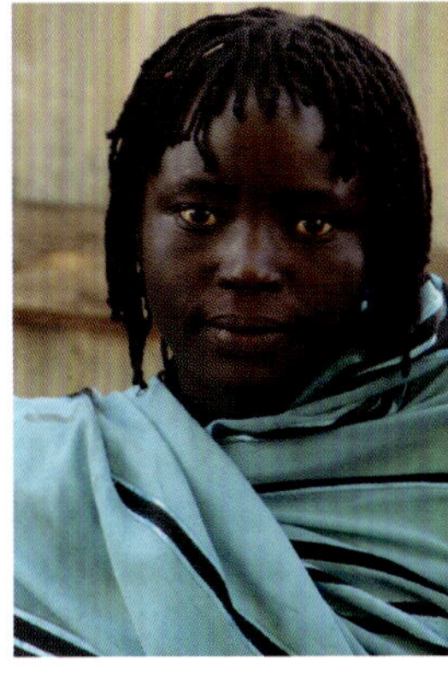
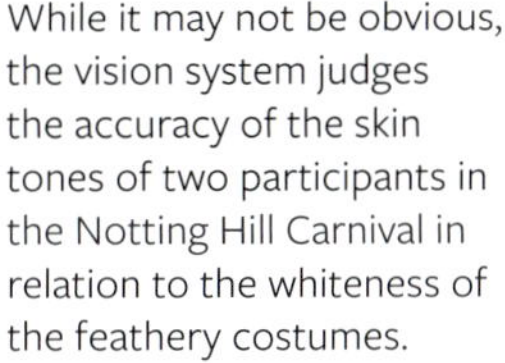

While it may not be obvious, the vision system judges the accuracy of the skin tones of two participants in the Notting Hill Carnival in relation to the whiteness of the feathery costumes.

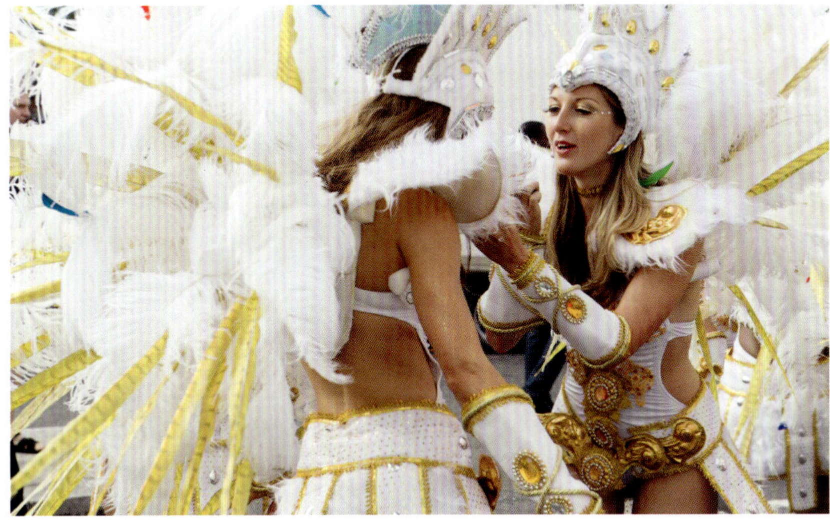

The safest place to start, even if it's not what we're going to end up with, is measurement – the facts of skin color. I'm focusing more on the color of skin here than on the brightness, which I did in *Michael Freeman on... Light & Shadow*, and by color I mean specifically hue, which ranges from yellowish to reddish, though by small amounts. There have been a number of surveys of skin color around the world, but the two best-known are by Pantone and L'Oréal. Pantone's comes from spectrophotometer readings directly on skin, while L'Oréal uses what they call a Chromasphere, which lights the entire face with controlled and very diffuse lighting. The results are not quite the same, but reasonably similar. Both divide the results into single color patches, which works easily for matching colors, but is less realistic than what I'm showing here, a continuous gradient of hue crossed with brightness.

What's immediately obvious is that the saturation is low and doesn't vary much – most skin is between about 20 percent and 50 percent – so for most purposes we can ignore it unless something goes drastically wrong (as it can occasionally do with computational). Also notice that differences in hue are more noticeable in the mid-to-light tones. They don't appear so obviously in very dark and very light skin. Even at their most obvious, the actual difference is at most around 20 degrees of hue angle, which looks not very much in a diagram like this. That we do find the differences marked in real life shows how important skin color is to us, for better or worse.

LIGHT ON SKIN

The facts of skin color are only part of the story. Measurements like those on the previous pages are made in neutral lighting, but that's rarely the case in normal shooting.

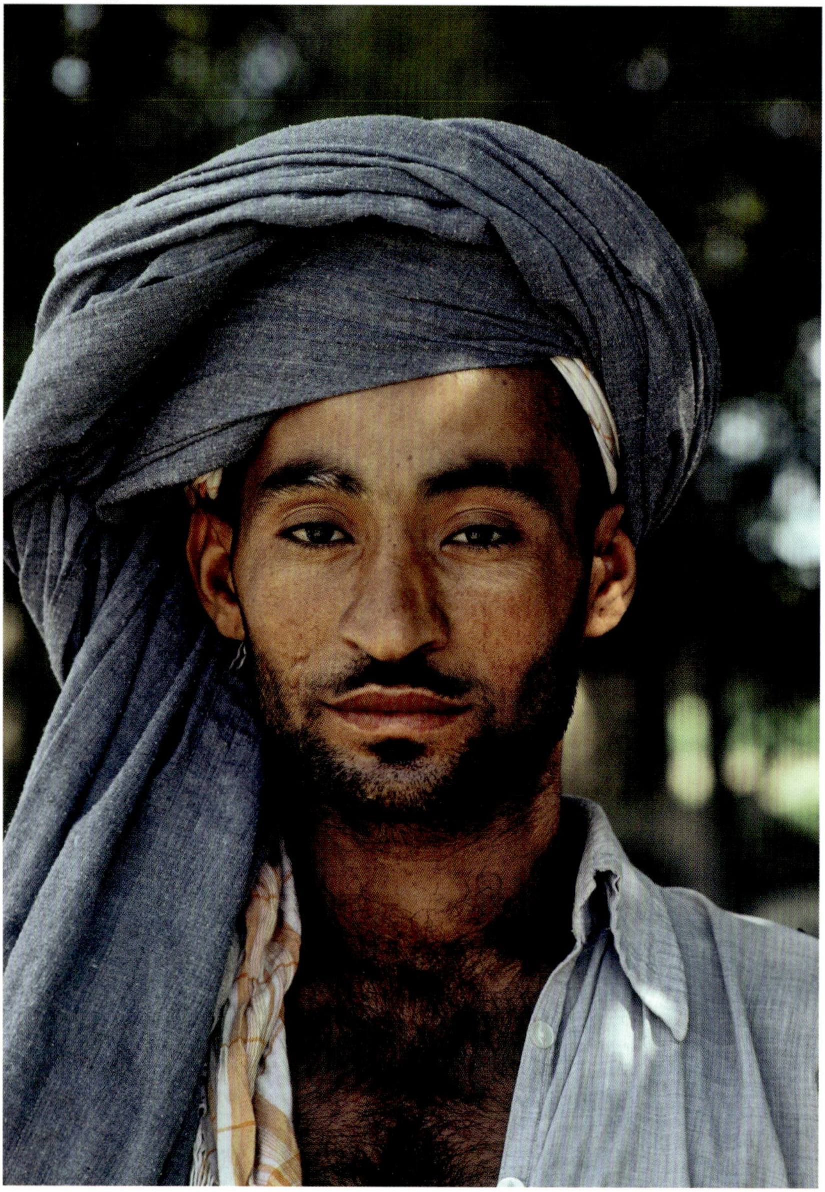

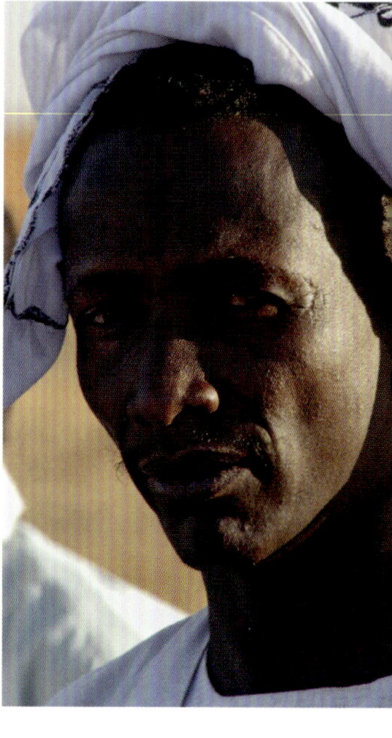

The darker the skin, the more that specular reflections outweigh the diffuse reflections, and the result in sunlight is as here, on a Nubian man photographed in a market near Khartoum, Sudan, in high contrast. The late afternoon sun lights up the side of his face four times brighter than the rest in shade, and at a lower color temperature.

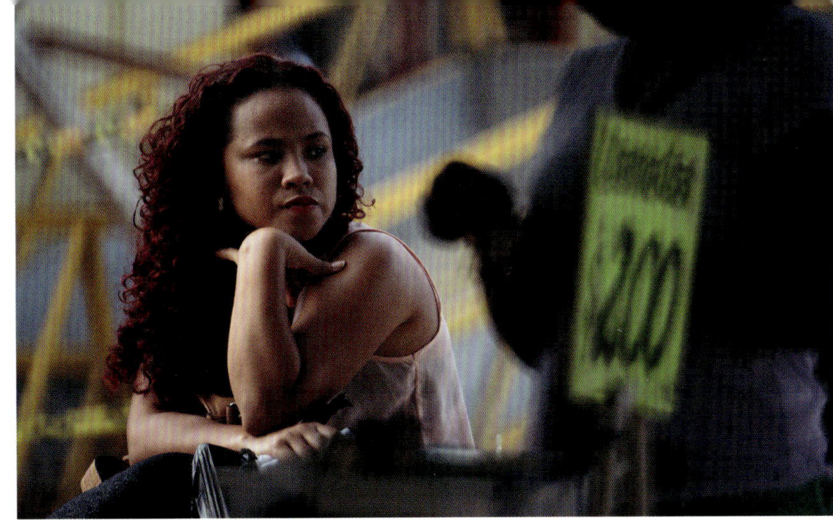

A street shot in which the light sources have to be inferred. Taken in shade in the afternoon, the young woman is lit more or less equally on both sides, from buildings that are sunlit. Like giant reflectors, their own color accounts for the difference between left and right.

A Pathan man in Pakistan's Northwest Frontier Province, photographed in dappled midday shade. Apart from the two sunlit flecks, the main source of light is reflections from sky and surrounding trees, which gives a slightly cool color cast (this was shot on daylight-balanced film).

First, there's color temperature, such as between daylight and the usually warmer interior lighting, and between sunlit and skylight. As we saw on page 64, much depends on what white balance setting you choose, but as long as you're shooting Raw, all those settings are stored separately and you can choose and alter when you process.

Then there are multiple sources of light, more and more of an issue for photography as sensor improvements make night-time and interiors important shooting scenarios. Two or three colors of lighting on one face create havoc with skin color, even allowing for our tolerance. Because of the shape of the face, the most common split from two light sources is between left and right. The simple answer, at least for a starting point, is to make sure that the person you're photographing is more in one light than the other, and then correct for that. When processing, this is a case for targeted color (page 148) or even masking (page 151). Computational photography in phone cameras is moving in this direction with semantic masks that allow color and tonal adjustments. This varies from make to make, and is generally hidden from the user, so if you are shooting computationally it's worth testing to see what the camera is doing to faces. You can be sure that all major phone camera brands are detecting and making some adjustment to faces.

Finally, there are reflections, and while you wouldn't expect any on a well made-up face, skin can be shiny and pick up colors from surroundings. A blue sky is one of the obvious candidates, but so too is sunlit greenery and brightly painted walls in urban scenes. This isn't necessarily unpleasant, but it tends to be less obvious at the time of shooting than later on a screen. Apart from the sheen itself, whether from sweat or oil, darker skin shows reflected colors noticeably more than light skin does. These are specular reflections (see also page 61), different from the other kind of reflection, diffuse, which is scattered. The reason is that on light skin they tend to be overwhelmed by diffuse reflection.

SKIN DESIRES

I t's not surprising that our finely tuned sensitivity to skin color makes many people want it to look better in some way. The entire cosmetics industry feeds this wish, and photography is increasingly the way of displaying the results, on social media.

It's complicated because it's based entirely on opinion, and this varies considerably according to what kind of skin you have and what the lighting is. More than this, there's a cultural element to it which overlays whatever personal wishes people may have for skin appearance. The cultural ideals for skin in China, for example, are very different from those in India, and different again from those of darker-skinned people in the US. Cameras can get the blame for pictures not living up to people's expectations, but at the same time computational cameras are equipped to deal with such issues. Indeed, with its Pixel 6 model, Google was the first manufacturer to lay claim to actively managing and optimizing dark skin in portraits, and other manufacturers have followed. The answer is a combination of improving facial detection and rendering the faces differently according to their color and tone.

East Asian skin ideals, especially among women, are almost universally towards very light with very little color, as in this picture of a Chinese tea master in Zhejiang province. This is remarkably consistent across 20 percent of the world's population.

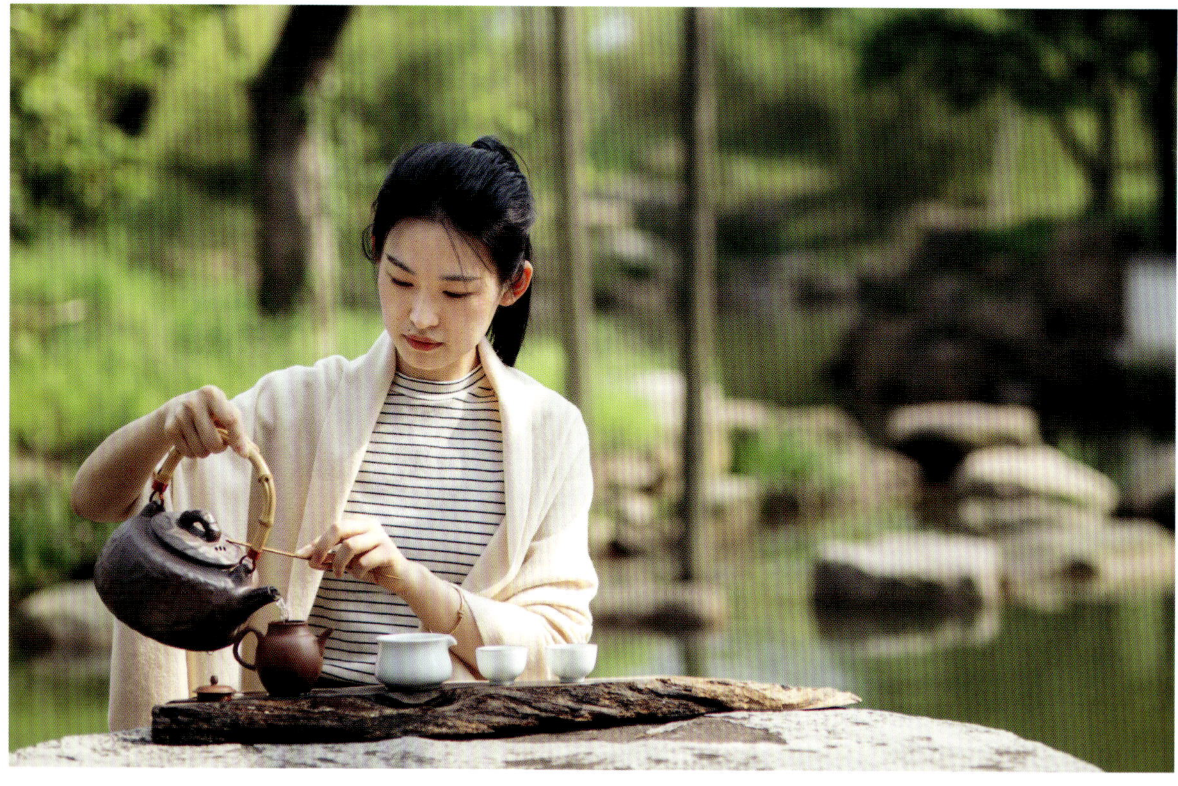

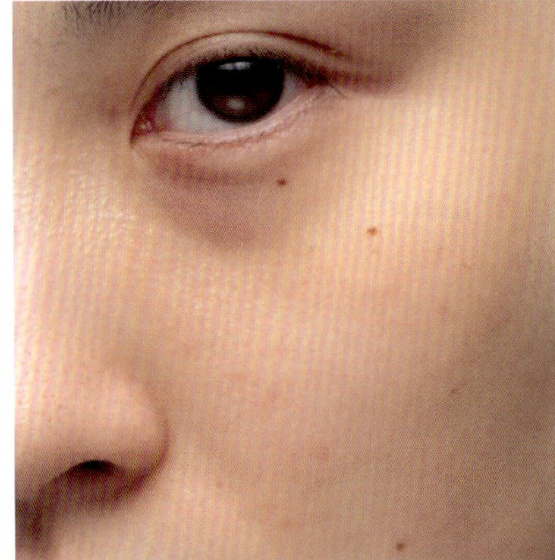
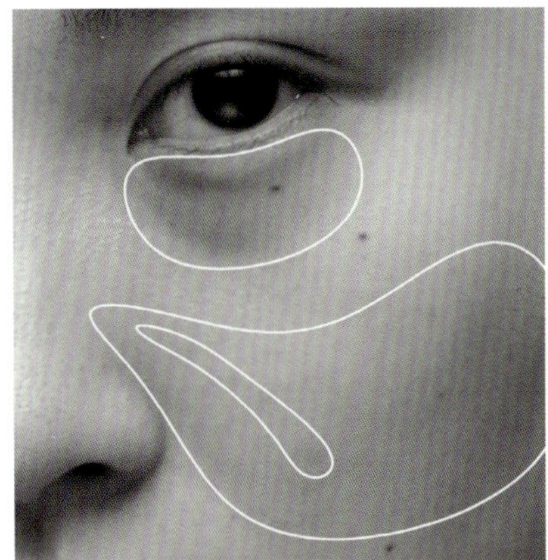
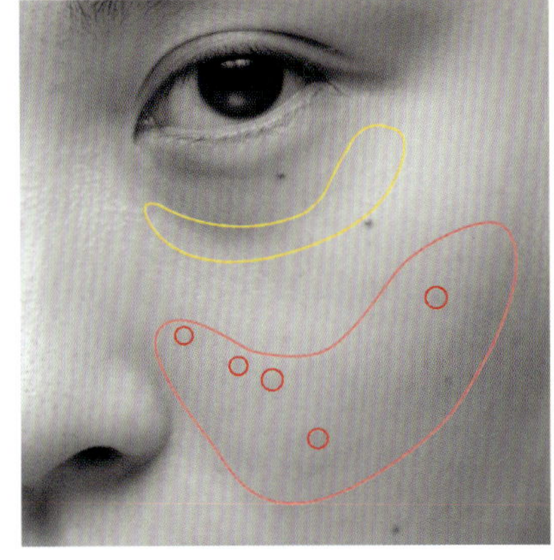
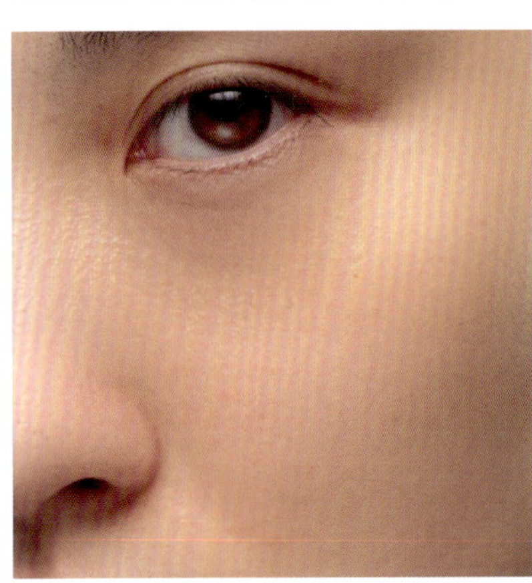

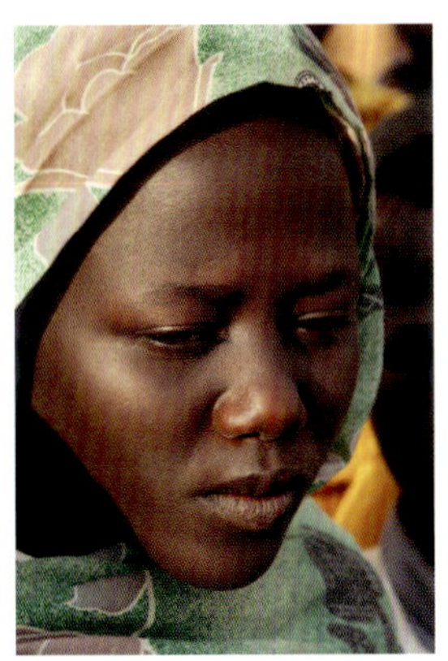
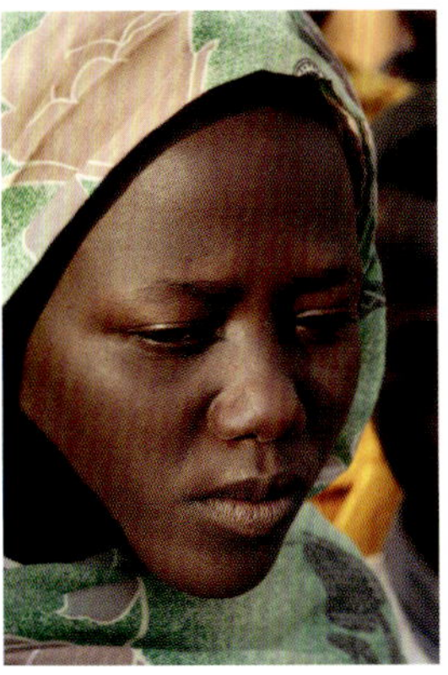

Dark skin issues in photography are in fact similar to the color issues for other kinds of dark tones, including shadows, that we look at in this book – but with the addition that failures naturally upset people. Common issues are: too dark to show facial detail, unnatural over-brightening, too shiny, desaturated. The shiny problem we just covered on the previous pages, and I hope that by the end of this book you'll be able to see all of what causes each of these valid problems.

There are light skin issues also, and they're different. Tints in the form of overall color casts are simply more obvious on lighter surfaces, so that in China, for example, especially in the southeast, there's a strong and consistent demand for makeup that lightens. And while color differences across a face – blotchiness in other words – are universal, they too are more obvious on light skin. There are retouching solutions for this, especially Frequency Separation retouching, which divides the process in large-scale low frequency and small-scale high frequency. Reducing color blotchiness belongs to the former.

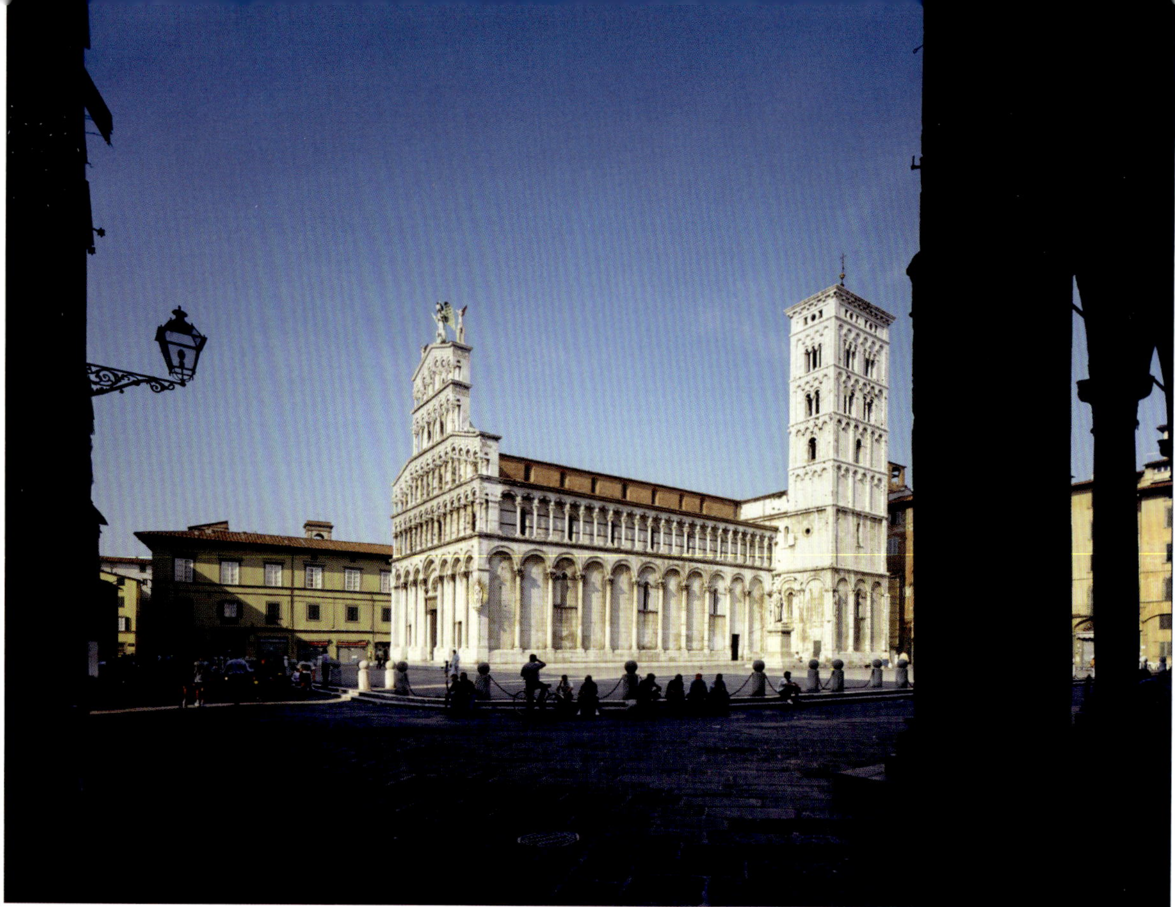

BLUE SKY

Maybe against expectations, the color of the sky varies only a little around the world. Take away clouds, and a blue sky over Europe looks essentially the same as over, say, South America or East Asia.

This shouldn't really be a surprise, because the color comes from a universal phenomenon known as Rayleigh scattering. Air molecules, which are smaller than the wavelength of light, scatter it – and importantly, they scatter the shorter wavelengths much more. These are the blue wavelengths, hence we see the sky as blue (though rarely a true 'Rayleigh blue' because of other stuff in the atmosphere). The X-Rite ColorChecker actually has one patch described as 'blue sky', and the all-important hue angle is 215 degrees. That matches both measurements and expectations for this quite deeply embedded memory color, and if you stray more than about 10 degrees towards cyan or purple (more green or more red), it simply looks wrong. There is, nevertheless, a slight difference depending on how high above the horizon you look or shoot. There's a very slight shift towards cyan closer to the horizon, and a slight shift away (towards purple) the higher you look.

A typical, mid-latitude clear sky with a wide-angle lens, here over the church of San Michele in Lucca, Italy, has a smooth gradient that lightens down towards the horizon and shifts slightly towards cyan.

This means that the wider the angle of lens that you use, the more variation in color, and in tone, there'll be in the sky.

Certainly there are some conditions. One is that we're talking about the main part of the day, when sunlight is mainly white, or else facing away from the sun when it's low. Also, reasonably close to sea level, because at serious altitudes like high mountains and the Tibetan Plateau, there's less atmosphere to scatter. At 3 miles (5km) (that's western Tibet), the atmosphere is about half the density at sea level, and the sky overhead is so dark as to seem almost black. Then there are other particles in the air, like water droplets, dust and pollution. Mainly, because they are much larger than the wavelength of light, they just add white or a pale grey to the sky rather than change the color, but for the most part they make it less saturated.

In fact, saturation is the main issue in photography, from capture through to processing. Simply put, saturated blue skies are popular and, like rich red sunsets, tend to divide people on taste. This is nothing new. When Fujichrome Velvia was launched to compete with Kodachrome slide film, sky blue was intentionally saturated, and it appealed to the mass market. This continues today, notably with some phone cameras, which use content recognition to identify skies. ColorChecker blue sky is 38 percent saturated and 62 percent brightness, and it's a reasonable average to work around if you feel tempted to ratchet up the color when processing.

Looking upwards to Mount Kailash in western Tibet from an altitude of over 5,000 metres, the density of the air is about half that at sea level, and so the sky is an extremely dark blue.

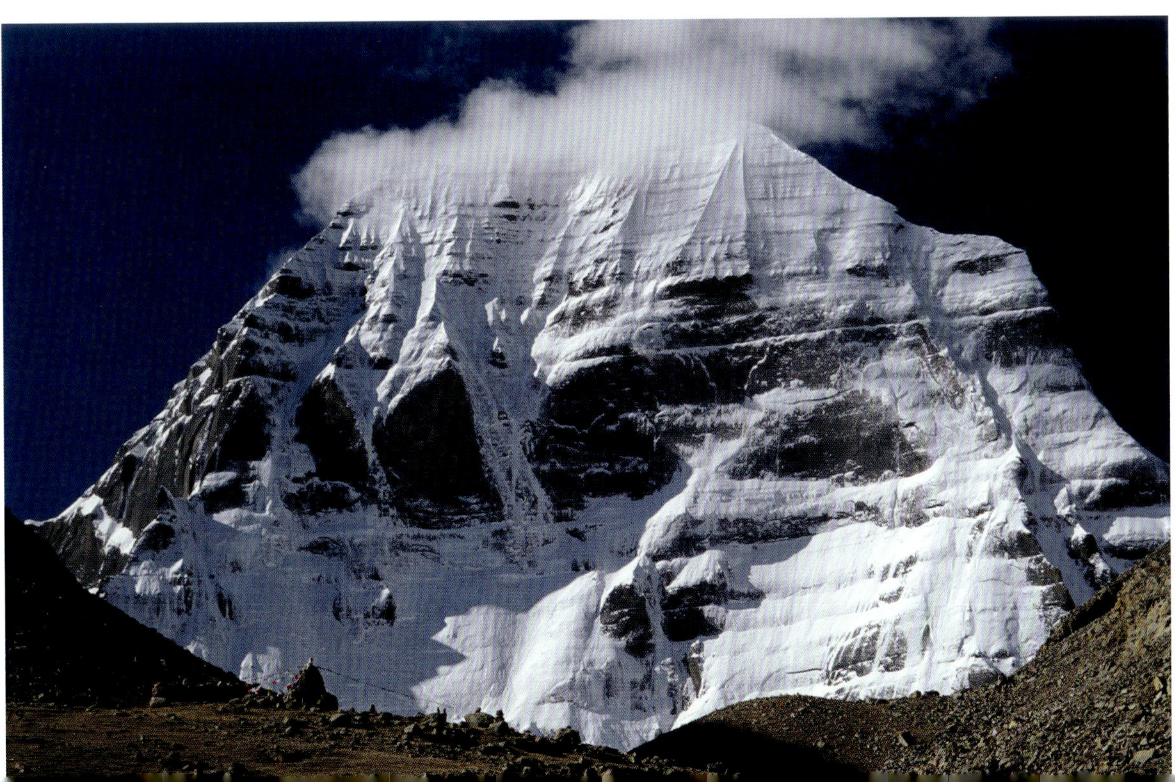

GOLDEN HOUR

In stark contrast to blue skies, color standards start to fall apart when the sun is close to the horizon. The overall color shifts towards yellow and orange, but not only does it vary from day to day and place to place, we don't see this warmth in the same way as a camera.

The reason is that our vision adapts to changes in the color of light – not our eyes, but the way we process them. As we saw on page 62, standard color for us comes from natural light around the middle of the day, and when it changes, we more or less get used to the change so that we either don't notice the color difference, or notice it less. In other words, to some extent we discount the yellowish tint of late afternoon sunlight. It doesn't at the time seem as strongly colored as it would to a camera that's set to daylight balance. That was very much the case with daylight-balanced color slide film. When it came back from being processed (that time lag is completely unfamiliar now, and it had an effect on viewing pictures), the slides often simply looked rich and colorful beyond what was expected. Not that anyone minded. Far from it, rich golden scenes were and remain almost universally attractive.

There's no easy answer to exactly how 'golden' the Golden Hour should look. Despite our color adaptation, we all very much like not just the golden intensity

The sandstone from which Angkor Wat in Cambodia was built is a neutral grey, and so in clear air reflects and takes on the color of a sun almost touching the horizon. This seems all the stronger for contrasting with its complementary opposite: the blue of the sky.

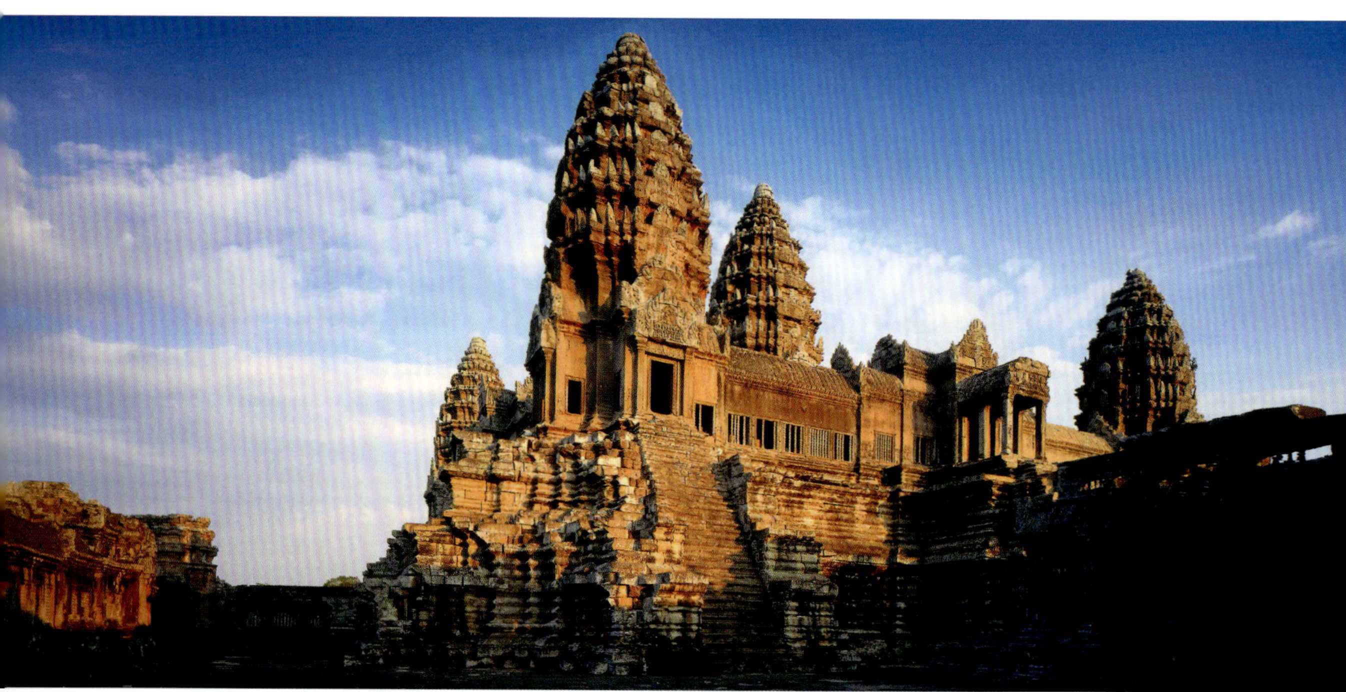

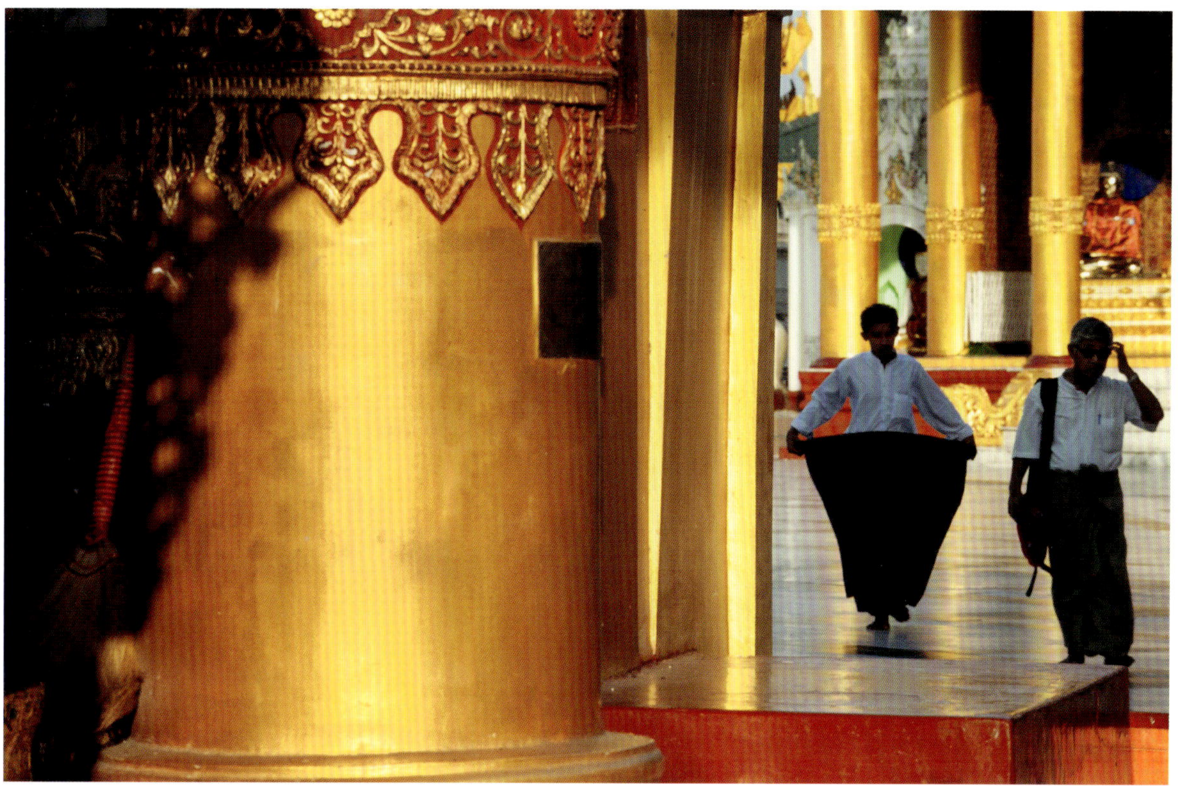

of things lit by a low sun, but also the complementary color cast from the blue shadows reflecting the blue sky opposite the sun. Leonardo da Vinci noted this: '...because the sun is red towards the evening, and the sky is blue, the shadow on the wall not being enlightened by the sun, receives only the reflection of the sky, and therefore will appear blue; and the rest of the wall, receiving light immediately from the sun, will participate of its red colour.'[†]

This becomes a processing issue, and we'll return to it on page 140. The problem is where to set the white point. If on a lit surface, the scene would lose the expected warmth and look wrong. In fact, there are two white points – adopted and adapted – and for a scene to look right they need to be equal. Adopted white point is the one you use in processing, while adapted white point is your vision system's internal assumption at the time of shooting or viewing. They should be similar, but, as Paul Hubel said, 'any deviation of these two white points will cause noticeable and sometimes catastrophic image quality degradation'.[‡]

[†]Leonardo da Vinci, *A Treatise on Painting* (1632)

[‡]Paul M. Hubel, 'The Perception of Color at Dawn and Dusk', *Journal of Imaging Science and Technology* 44: 371–375 (2000)

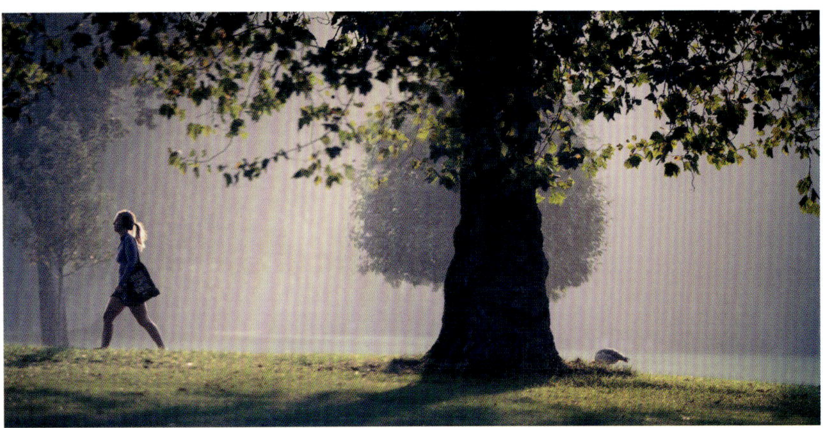

GREENERY

V egetation is all around us, and most of it is green, so it's little surprise that we're familiar with it. It's not as much around us as it used to be in the past, but grass and leaves are still an important part of most people's visual experience.

More than that, as we saw in Chapter 2, our eyes are much more sensitive to green than to any other color. At the same time, however, as we saw in Tolerance on pages 62–3, we don't discriminate as well between greens as we do between other colors. That means that small shifts of hue don't register so well. Add to this many different shades of green in vegetation, from agave and blue fescue at the bluish end to choiysa and gingko at the yellowish end, and it's not surprising that we're relatively tolerant when it comes to green. The hue range goes from an angle of around 50 degrees to 150 degrees (there's a lot of latitude). If you happen to be familiar with a particular plant, then the tolerance is going to be less, and there's one kind of vegetation that most people are familiar with, and that's average grass. That narrows the numbers: typically grass in direct sunlight is around 60 degrees to 75 degrees in hue, with upper-middle saturation and quite high brightness.

Apart from this, there's a general expectation in a photograph that most greenery should be bright and well-saturated. Dull greens, meaning darker and with low saturation, are generally not well regarded in a landscape shot. This sometimes leads to greenery photographs being tweaked to up the saturation, with the usual risks of becoming unrealistic.

The kind of low backlighting from early morning and late afternoon strengthens the impression of greens like the grass here still covered with dew, but the effect comes mainly from brightness and contrast, not usually saturation, which is here around 50 percent.

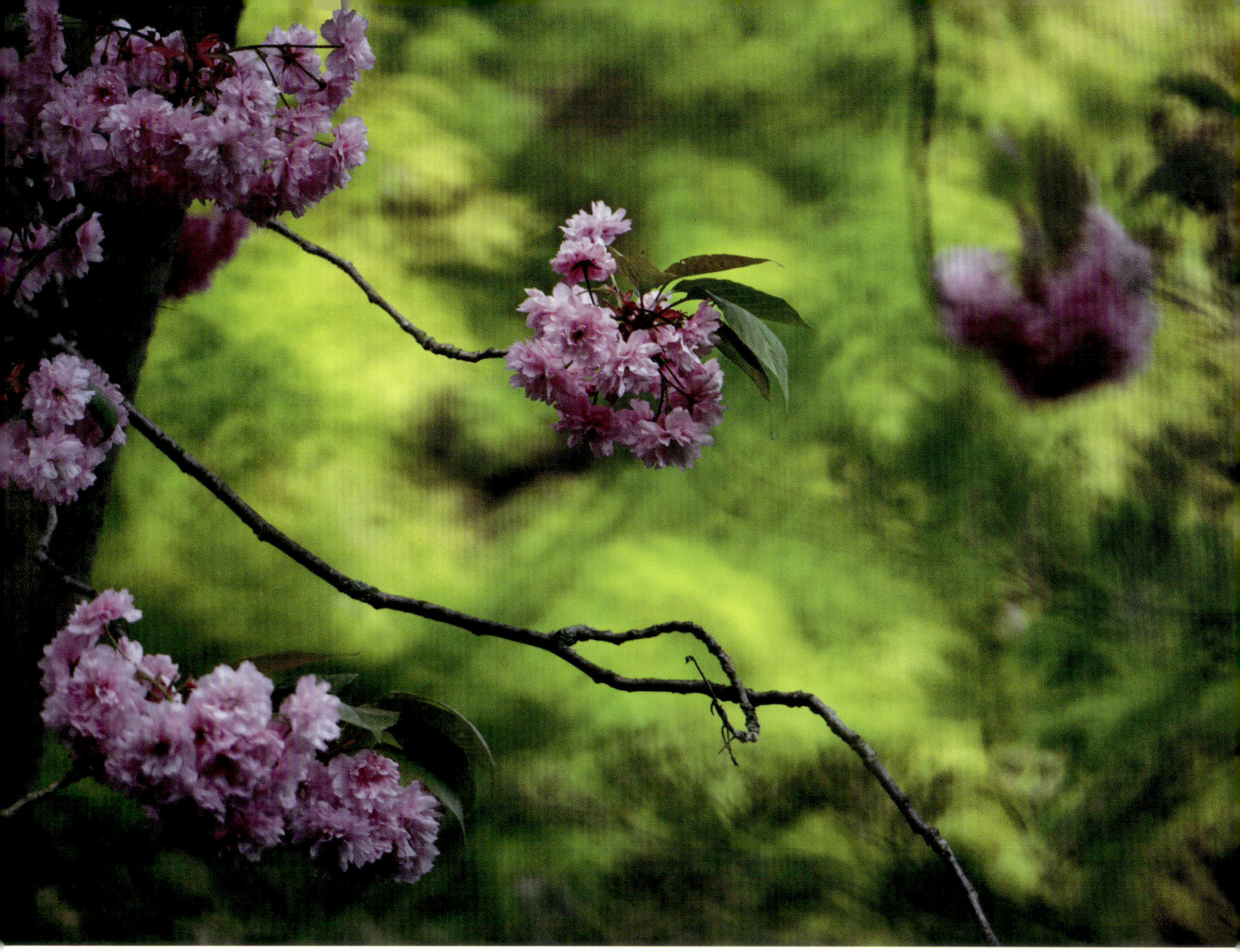

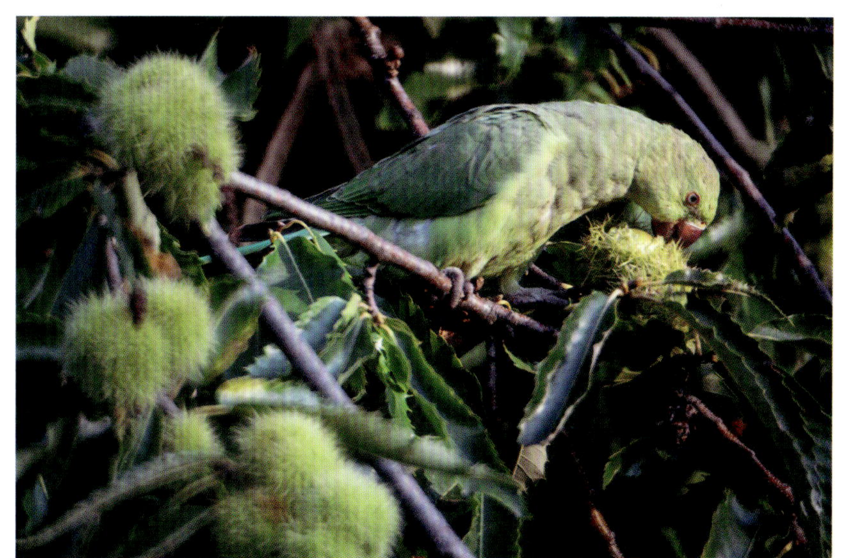

Natural green at its strongest, with no interference during processing. As we'll see in Chapter 5: Composing with Color, a strongly contrasting color, such as these pink blossoms, strengthen the out-of-focus sunlit yellow-green foliage.

A parakeet and chestnut tree share the same range of greens, which is surprisingly long, from the yellow chestnut on which the bird is feeding to blue in the shaded centre of the long leaves. Saturation is not high, which helps tie the colors together.

FOOD COLORS

f any single photography subject went suddenly from being a niche speciality to global phenomenon, it's food. Among the very top Instagram subjects, it now draws huge attention.

Effective food photography leans heavily on good color, for two main reasons. One is that viewers have strong and usually fixed ideas about what is right and wrong about the color of foodstuffs, the other is that in the relatively small images posted on social media, splashes of color are a useful way of getting attention.

The reason why correctness is an issue is that fundamentally people are conservative about what they eat, and color reflects this. However jazzed up food packaging and settings might be, foodstuffs themselves have predictable color coding, and it follows a very specific pattern. Very little of what we eat is colorful. Without getting bogged down in detail, in the United States, for example, half of the daily diet is from cereals, grains and starchy roots, about a quarter each from meat and from dairy and eggs, with just a small fraction from fruit and vegetables. Therefore, warm neutrals dominate, especially browns and creams. Strong, vivid colors are scattered, found mainly in fruit and vegetables (for instance, strawberries, carrots, tomatoes, peppers), with just one or two notable exceptions from the animal world (egg yolk, raw tuna, salmon roe, boiled lobster).

Why does this matter for photography? Because food color has primal associations. Browns and other desaturated reds and yellows look right for meat, bread and breakfast cereals, while whites and creamy tones are good for fish and potatoes, and greens for leaves, but these colors don't cross boundaries. A hint of green in meat means putrid, and brownish for leaves means wilted. And blue,

High-end Chinese dim sum uses strong colors that become more acceptable for small bites than they would be for a main dish.

A Moroccan chicken tagine (lower dish) with rice. A side plate of colorful pickles and a brightly colored bowl offsets the low color values of the main food.

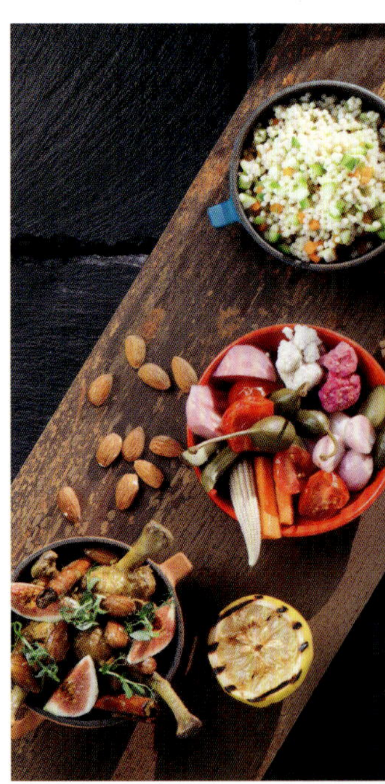

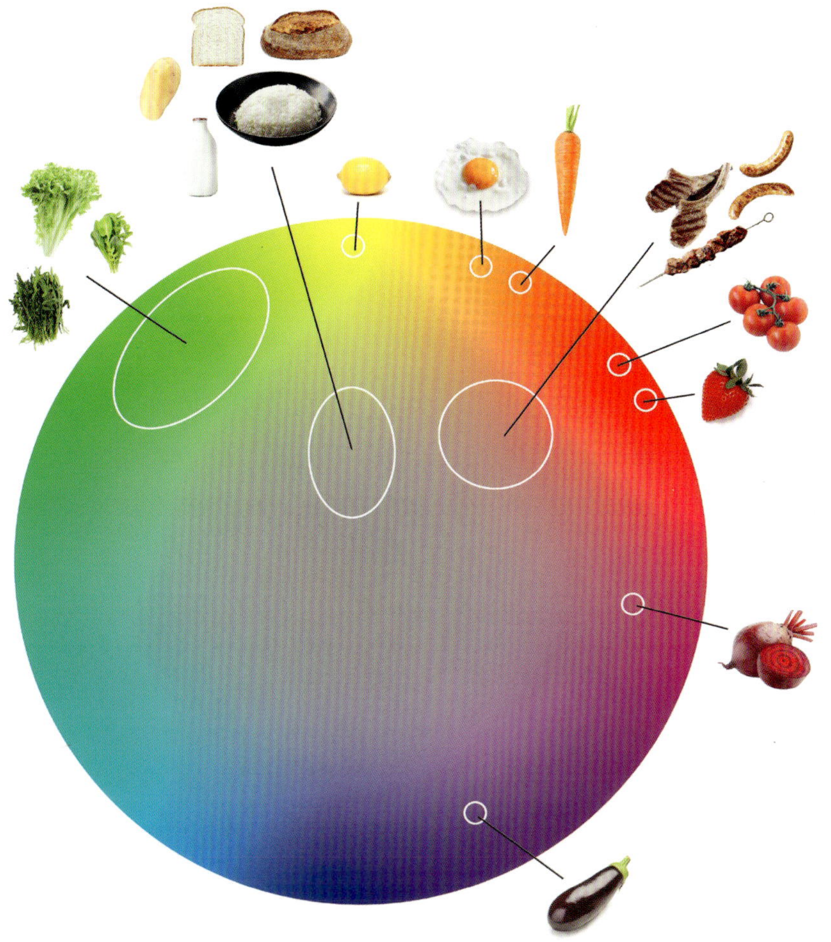

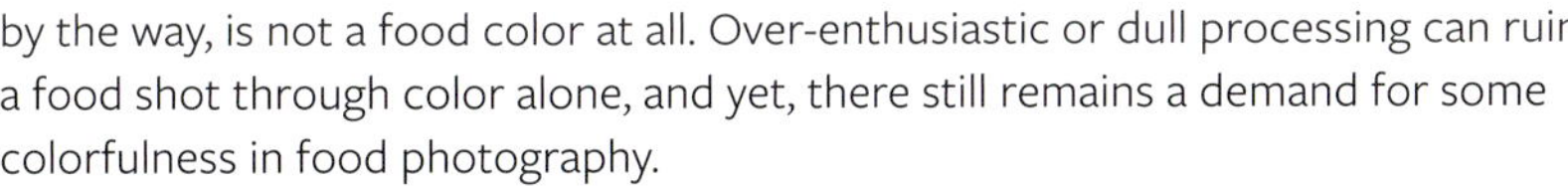

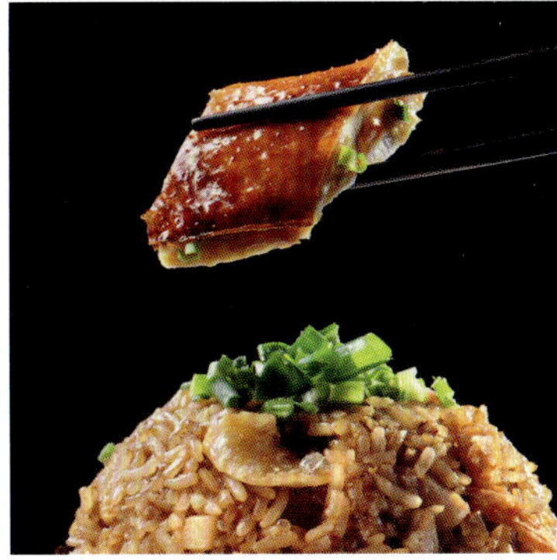

Crispy duck with fried rice. All the colors are in a range of browns, which makes the addition of a colorful garnish – chopped spring onion – all the more important for presentation.

Foodstuffs on the color circle. Leaf vegetables are clearly green, but the majority – cereals, grains, starchy roots, dairy products and meats – are very desaturated with a bias towards warm hues. Brightly colored foods are limited and specific, but mostly between yellow and red. Very few are as far as violet (aubergine), and none are in the area of bright blue to blue-green.

by the way, is not a food color at all. Over-enthusiastic or dull processing can ruin a food shot through color alone, and yet, there still remains a demand for some colorfulness in food photography.

This is a dilemma as important to a chef building a dish as to a photographer shooting it. There are three solutions. One is to prioritize vegetables wherever possible, such as in a side dish, and this also fits the current move towards eating less meat. The second is, broadly speaking, garnish. That means incorporating color accents (see also page 112), from chillies to watercress to edible flowers. It's why garnishes exist, but I argue for color more than for any other reason. The third is realizing that non-staple foods allow more color experimentation, in particular 'entertainment' foods such as desserts and patisseries, and cocktails (stretching the definition to include beverages). Even high-end dim sum, as here.

4

COLOR & TONE

The science of color, as we've seen, revolves very much around the pure, spectral hues. That's fine and necessary, but it's not completely realistic for daily life, which is where most photography happens. If we're talking about managing and manipulating colors from the camera, science and spectral are essential, but when it comes to observing and shooting, no one in my experience thinks like that. Certainly that's not the way most people look at scenes or, more relevantly, look at photographs.

This means thinking about color in more familiar, even ordinary ways, and that includes the names we give to colors. Far from letting go of precision, it's actually necessary, and the clue is in the second chapter – Color in the Mind on page 34. Quite apart from wavelength, lenses and filters, it's how we see color, think about it and talk about it that matters in photography. In case you wondered why this book is titled *Color & Tone* and not just *Color* alone, it's because as viewers (and photographers) we perceive color in quite a mixed way. And people vary individually. It's usual to say that what most people mean by color is actually hue (HSB for Describing, page 42). That's generally true, but not completely, because there are colors that depend on their brightness for being what they are. Yellow is only bright, as is pink. There are no dark versions of them. Brown is a darker and less saturated orange, but we never think of it in those terms; it's simply brown. And, strange though it may sound, most skin of all 'colors' is a version of orange.

More than this, in photography we're always dealing with light and shade, so when a shadow falls across a color, how it looks in a photograph on either side of the shadow edge is going to matter. Darker colors are different from lighter colors, either because we think of them like that or because of the light falling on them, so there's plenty to explore here.

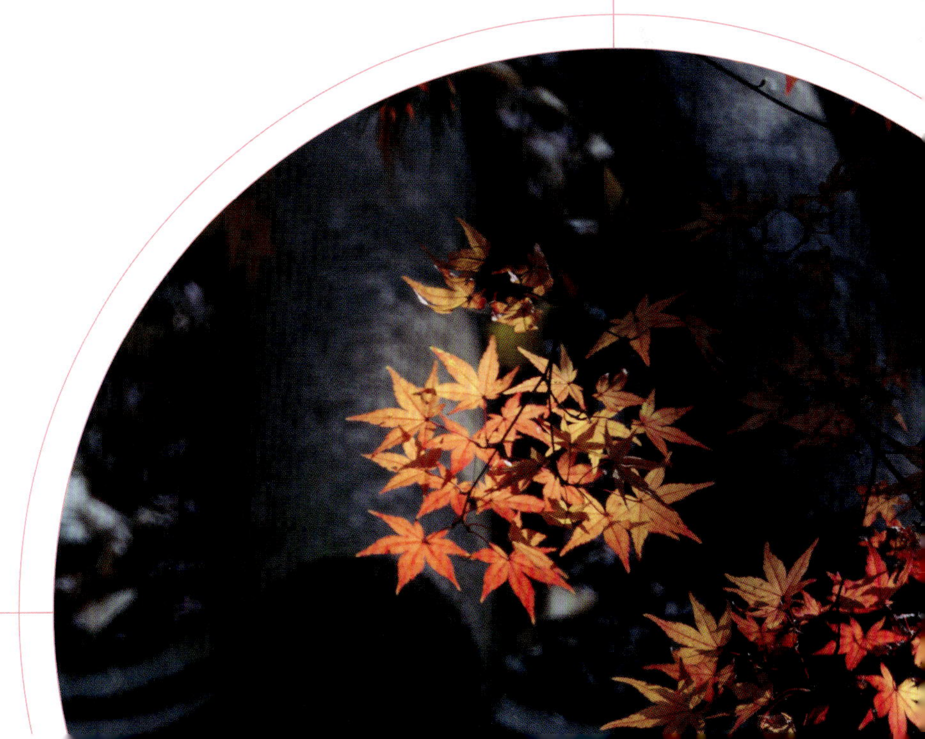

COLORS TO US

W hat makes a color distinct? That is, different enough from others to qualify as a color in its own right, rather than a version of something else. Much more important than where it is on the color circle is how we choose to recognize it, and whether it's visually 'useful'.

One of the most obvious cases is pink. By the numbers, it's simply a very pale red, but to most people's eyes it has its own characteristics and its own associations. In other words, it's a distinct color, and one worth giving a name to. As for red, which you could think of as the familiar baseline for an entire family of colors, it shades in different directions by hue, saturation and brightness, and up to a certain point in any direction we still think of it as red. There are no edges to this, and different people make different judgements, but move far enough away from pure red and we 'see' a different color. Pink is beyond that limit. In the opposite direction, going mainly darker, down through reds with qualifying names like cadmium red, carmine red and madder red (mainly from paints), by the time we reach maroon, which is very dark, we've stepped beyond reds. As for hue, orange is on one side and violet on the other, so that flame red is getting close to being orange while in the opposite direction fuchsia is its own color.

A blue door in raking sunlight. To many people there are two distinct blues here, not counting the deep shadows, but the hue is exactly the same. For more on what we call colors, see pages 94–5.

A simple and definite color, emphasized by being not only alone but offset by grey, is unambiguous because it has a name – pink – that practically everyone understands. Despite being technically a less saturated, paler red, we see it as distinctive enough to be its own color.

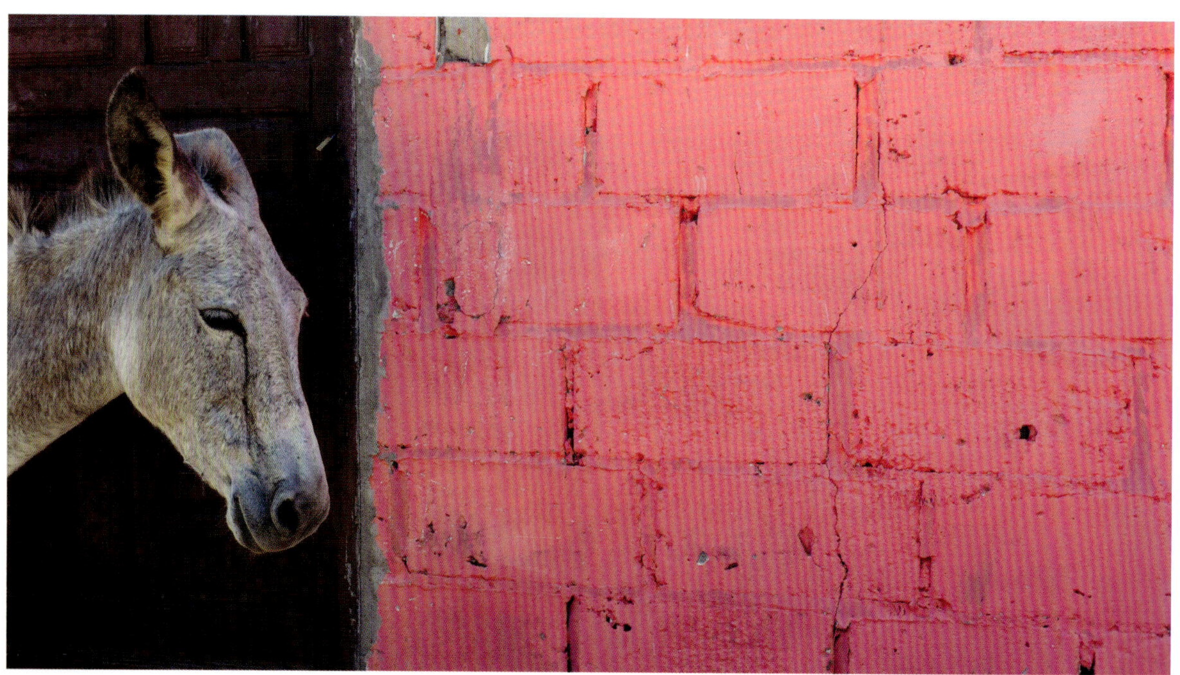

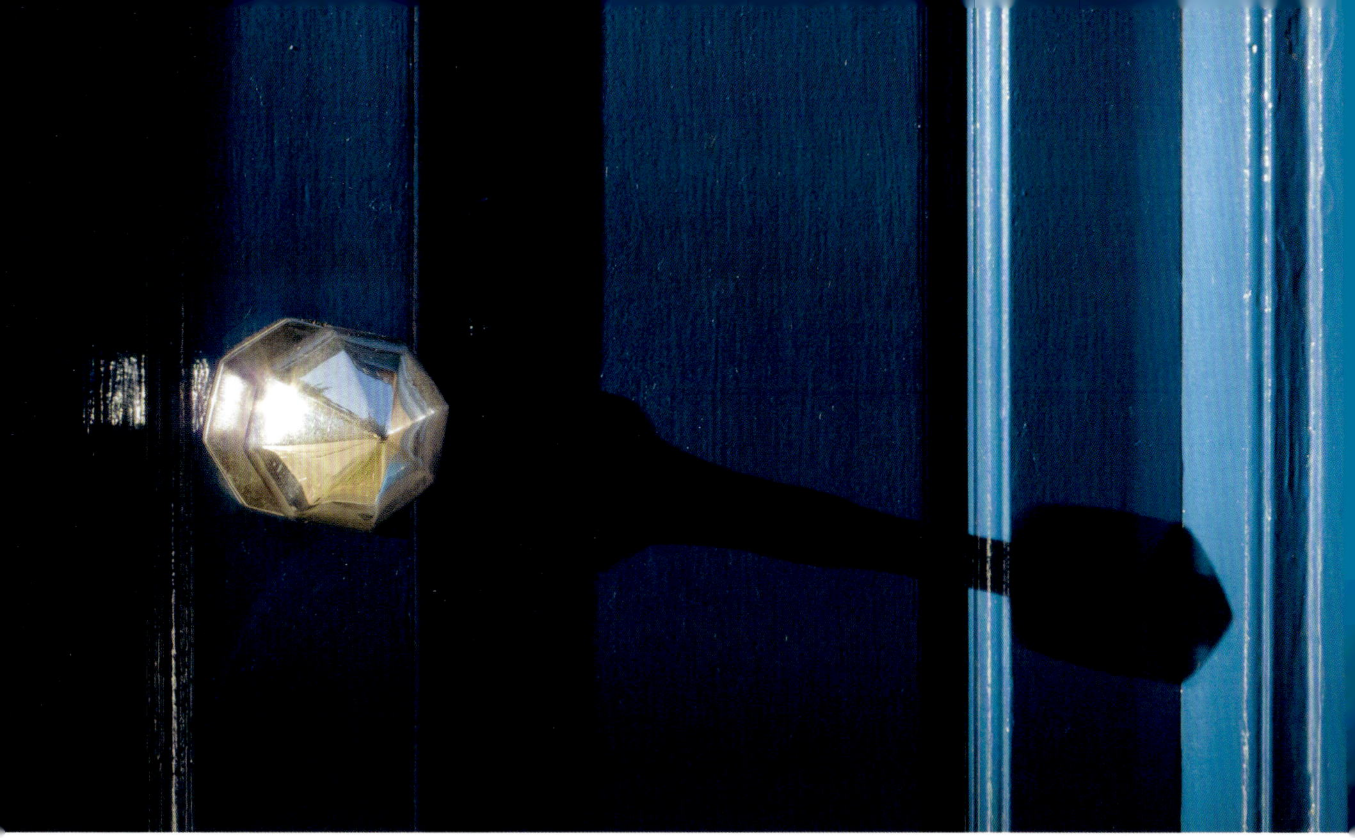

None of this is firm, and indeed none of the actual colors – pink, maroon, fuchsia and so on – are universally agreed. The American painter James Whistler wrote, 'Mauve? Mauve is just pink trying to be purple.' You can find online several 'standard' color charts, including Pantone and HTML, and you can see that they vary. The nearest we have to a universal standard of color description is the ISCC-NBS System, begun in the 1930s, and if you want the color coordinates for any color, that's usually the source. However, there are different interpretations, as we'll see. For each generally recognized color, there is an increasingly fuzzy area around it, and the neat blocks in the chart are there only to simplify. And what I haven't yet mentioned is that color names don't necessarily mean the same thing in different languages. I'm writing this in English, but if you're reading a different language version, we've had to make some adjustments. Celadon is one example. The ISCC-NBS color coordinates are

123 degrees 24 percent 88 percent, but actual celadon glazes cover a range of hues all the way from 50 degrees to 195 degrees. The Chinese name for its color is 青 (*qing* pronounced 'ching'), and famously inexact because it covers all the uncertainty of firing the pottery: 'From light to dark green and light to dark blue, all the colors of celadon can be described as 青.'[†]

If pushed to simplify, most Chinese people would call it a kind of blue.

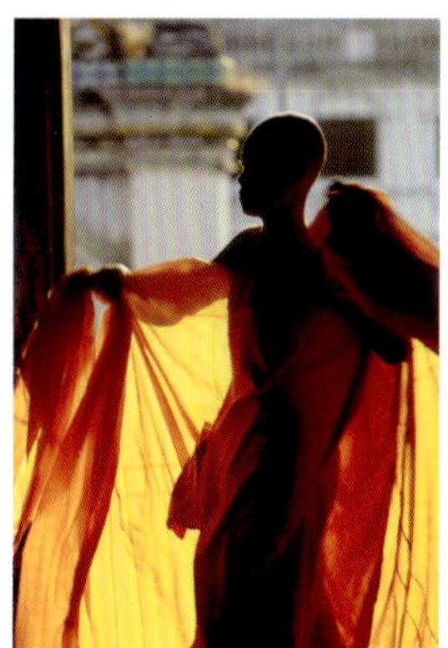

Yellow-orange dominates this shot of a Vietnamese monk, not least because of its intensity (full saturation and brightness in the lit area). We sense this all the more strongly because we know from the context that the saffron robe is backlit by the sun.

† Derek Au, The Color of Celadon, https://derekau.net/2021/07/23/the-color-of-celadon/

NATURALLY LIGHTER

Just a glance at the color circle on page 38 – or at the color space on page 37 – shows that the brightness varies. That's to our eyes, of course. In fact, desaturate it completely and, surprising though it seems to most people, all of these colors have the same luminance.

That doesn't look right at all, but it forcefully underlines how different color perception is from color physics. And for photography, we're dealing with the perception, so the apparent differences in brightness are absolutely real. Appearance is everything, and yellow is the brightest color. The reason is, as we saw in Chapter 2: Color Science, that we are especially sensitive to this wavelength because both the L and M cones peak together close to here (page 33).

In fact, yellow shading into green is on the undisputed bright side of the color circle. Also perceived as bright, though slightly less so, is cyan. Most people see these as naturally bright colors, and this confers some special qualities. For a start, they attract attention strongly, and if you compose with these colors, they will always pop out and tend to dominate the picture.

The lighting design in this contemporary Chinese tea shop features lime green and yellow to create an unarguably light and bright impression. Their bright association comes from their position on the Luminosity Curve (see page 33).

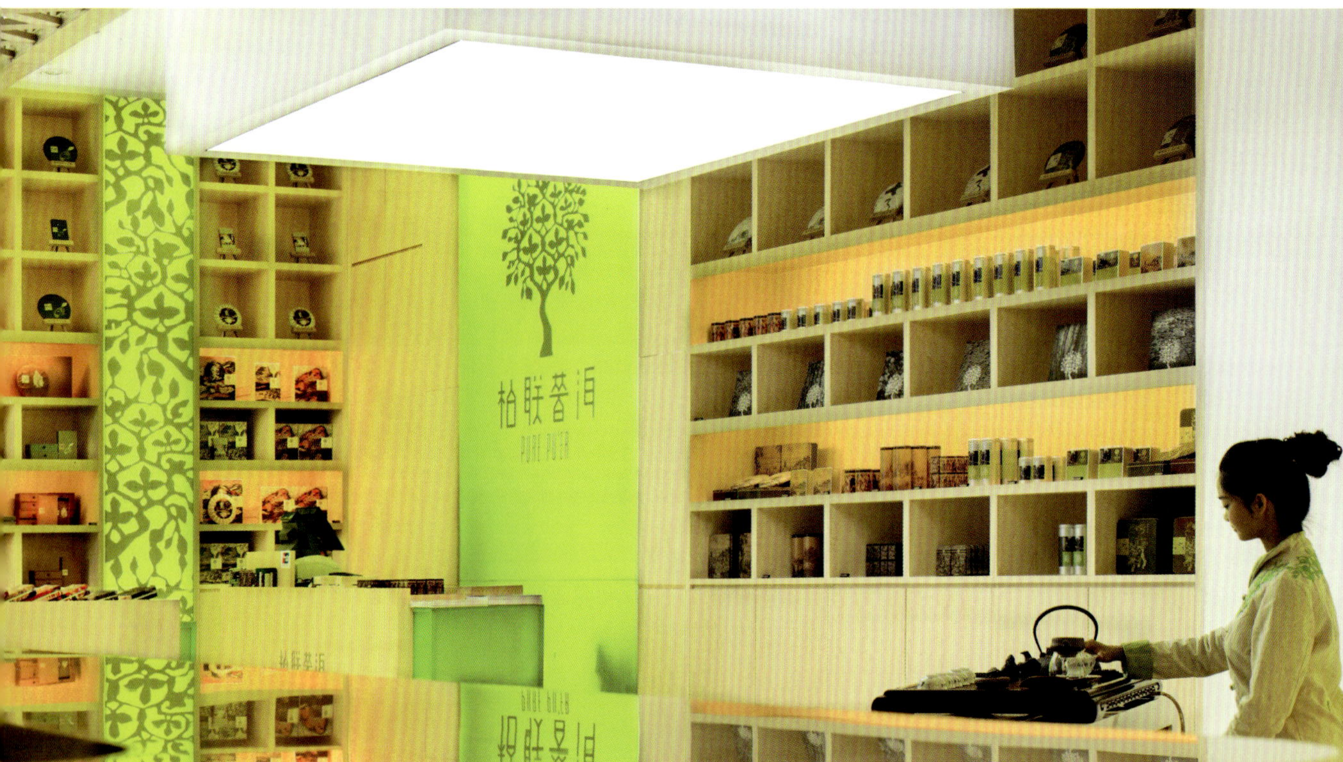

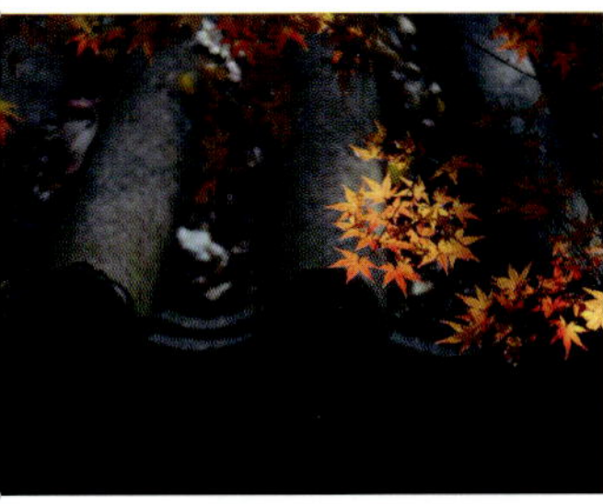

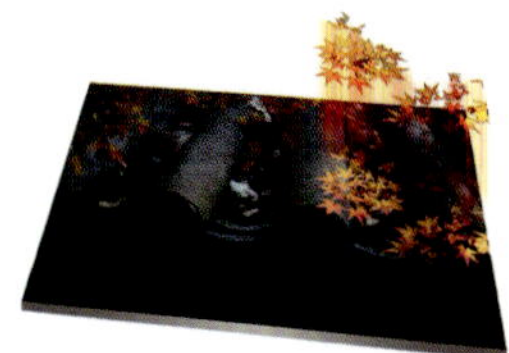

Autumn leaves by the roof of a Chinese temple pop out very strongly by virtue of both their color and the low afternoon sunlight.

Yellow, pink and pale blue are all light colors. In combination here, with yellow dominating, they go well together mainly because they share a higher register. It gives them a kind of similarity. Note, however, that the word 'pale' sets this sky apart from the natural associations of blue, as we'll see next.

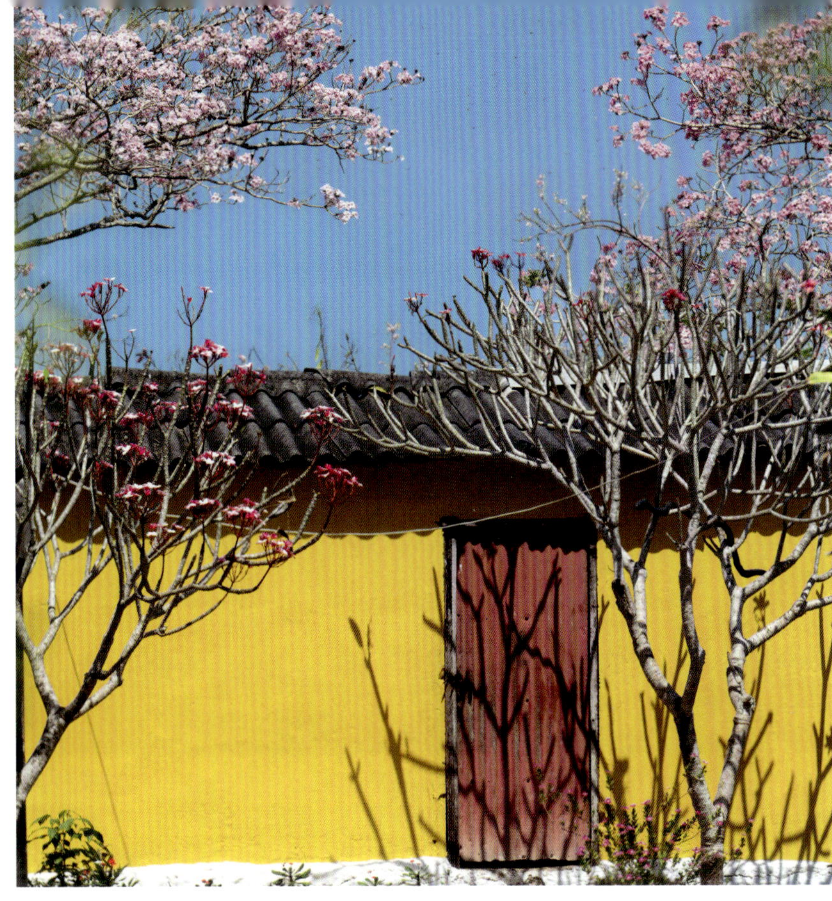

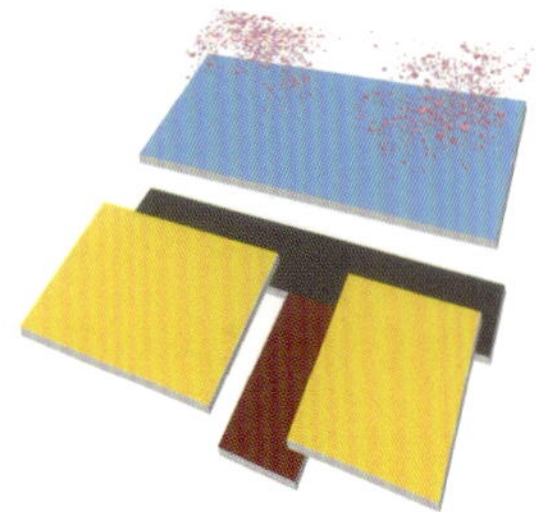

More than that, as the brightest of all colors, yellow is the 'narrowest' in hue, saturation and brightness. We saw on page 33 how sensitive we are to precision in this wavelength, and on top of that it's a named color and there's very little leeway in what we accept as being yellow. For example, a dark yellow is a contradiction. Around 580nm is the wavelength, and that translates to a hue angle of 40 degrees, but reduce the brightness by half, and it simply isn't accepted as yellow. It's now olive, or possibly ochre, depending on how you care to define these two.

Another peculiarity of yellow is that it doesn't make a good base for a range of adjacent colors, as we'll see when we get to Chapter 5: Composing with Colors. Not only is it 'narrow' in the sense that it takes up only about 12 degrees of the circle, the two directions it can go in, towards green and towards orange, appear very different from each other. For instance, if you take a modest range around any other color on the circle, it will look unified and similar. Do this with yellow, however, drifting towards lime green on one side and orange on the other, and the result is not a similar set. The greenish shades and the orangey shades look at odds with each other, so this kind of harmony doesn't work.

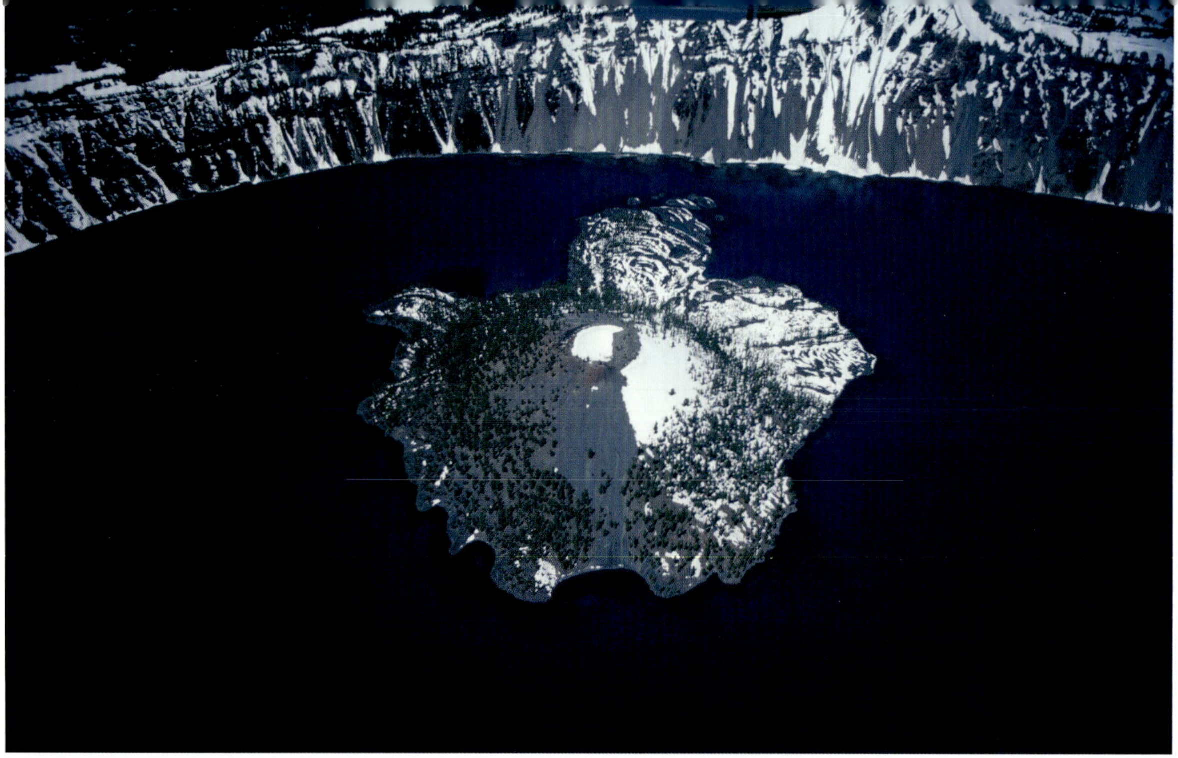

NATURALLY DARKER

Just as yellow is the brightest color, its opposite on the circle is the natural darkest – blue – or to be more accurate, blue drifting towards indigo and violet. And purple, even if it's not on the spectrum.

Again, it's all appearances, because on a desaturated color circle blue and yellow are the same shade of grey, even though they look wildly different. By no means are they simple opposites, however. While you could say that there's only one yellow – with little room to wriggle – we recognize a wide range of blues, in hue and in brightness. The painter Raoul Dufy wrote, 'Blue is the only color which maintains its own character in all its tones... it will always stay blue; whereas yellow is blackened in its shades, and fades away when lightened; red when darkened becomes brown, and diluted with white is no longer red, but another color – pink'. This makes it difficult to pinpoint the actual blue that's darkest to our eyes, as we have only appearances to go on, but generally it's towards the violet side. The explanation is the same as for yellow being bright: this part of the spectrum, at around 470nm, is where the coverage from our L, M and S cones is at its weakest, as the illustration on page 33 shows. This is about 270 degrees, and for reference, spectral blue is 'cooler' at 240 degrees. You can dial this up easily in Photoshop, either with that angle in HSB at full saturation and brightness, or simply 100 percent B in RGB.

Crater Lake, Oregon, is famous for its deep blue water, due to selective absorption that is both very clear and very deep (at its maximum almost 600m/2,000ft).

A market scene from Cuzco, Peru. Most people would distinguish four or five blues, but the major distinction between them is less the hue than the variation in brightness and saturation.

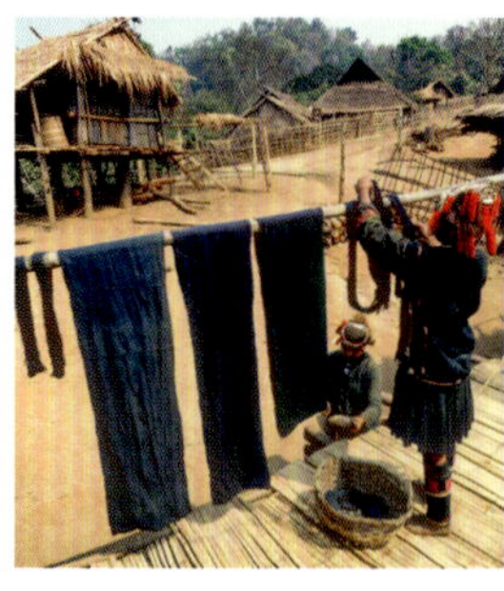

We're quite tolerant of differences in blue, and added to this is how widely we use the word in English, so that it varies by as much as 60 degrees between green and violet, and considerably also in saturation and brightness – on the color chart on page 94 between navy and cornflower. In fact, whenever the color crops up, it's pertinent to ask 'which blue?' For example, the blue in painters' primaries (red, yellow, blue) is not the same as the blue in RGB. Also, languages differ. Russian, for example, has separate words for dark blue and light blue, which sounds practical for what we're talking about here.

It perhaps doesn't help that the most amount of blue that we see day to day is a clear sky, and that's universally accepted as being bright. Blue sky, a typical sunny day in mid-latitudes, averages out at around 62 percent in brightness, definitely not the same as the pure dark blue we're talking about here. Only a few places on the planet are so high and so clear that the sky seems in any way dark, such as western Tibet, and even then, looking upward.

Nor does it help that the darkest 'blue' in the spectrum is actually where the word indigo is used. A major problem with indigo is that few people have any firm idea what color it actually is, apart from being dark and bluish. It isn't a color that has much impact in our daily lives, and that it exists on the spectrum at all is because Newton named it, while also admitting that his eyes were 'not very critical in distinguishing colors'. It's named after a vegetable dye, which confuses matters because the dye, as you can see from the small picture opposite, below, is quite dull (or you could say subtle), and nothing like spectral violet in appearance. There is no general agreement about where spectral indigo lies on the spectrum, and you certainly don't find it in natural textiles. It's yet another instance of blue confusion.

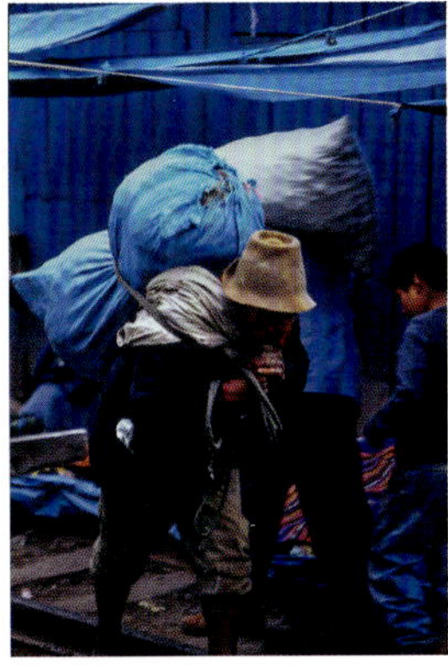

A traditional curtain hanging in front of the entrance to a Kyoto restaurant. Violet and the nearby non-spectral color purple need to be dark (if light they become mauve or lilac), and this is a less saturated version. These are among the most difficult of colors to discriminate.

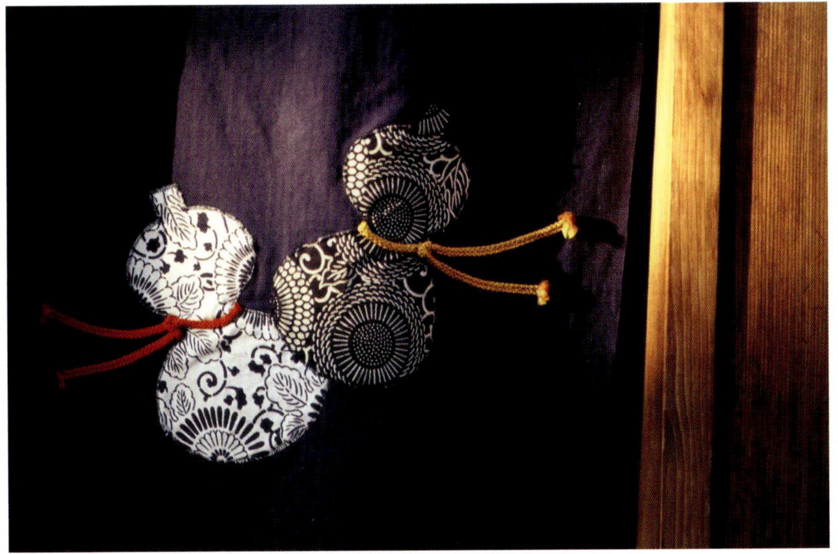

A traditional curtain hanging in front of the entrance to a Kyoto restaurant. Violet and the nearby non-spectral color purple need to be dark (if light they become mauve or lilac), and this is a less-saturated version. These are among the most difficult of colors to discriminate.

BRIGHTER COLORS

Yellow and blue drifting towards indigo and violet are just the two extremes of tonal color. In between there are countless nuances, and I'm going to group them into brighter and darker.

The logic behind this is that as we've seen when it comes to judging colors, we tend to use hue first, followed by brightness. Bright colors – those above the line in the color chart on page 37 – can be bright for two reasons. One is that their surfaces reflect more (a daffodil, for example, or pale skin). The other is lighting, as in the picture on page 87.

What we think of as bright, however, isn't just about luminance. It also involves saturation. The purer, more saturated a color is, the brighter it seems to be. This is measurable, and it's called the Helmholtz-Kohlrausch effect. It's not just academic. It affects color composition, as we'll see in the next chapter. If you look back at the color chart on page 66, turquoise, saffron and fuchsia all look bright, but in fact they're average, and it's their high saturation that convinces us of their brightness.

Practically for us as photographers, there are actually two effects. One is that colored lights look brighter than white, which is counter-intuitive but true. In fact, the sunsets on page 56 show this at work, even apart from the jittery edges

On either side of a narrow band of pure, fully saturated colors are those sufficiently distinctive to have their own names, and are mainly lighter (above) and mainly darker (below). These 28 are the most commonly recognized, although of course it's possible to expand the list and even invent new names.

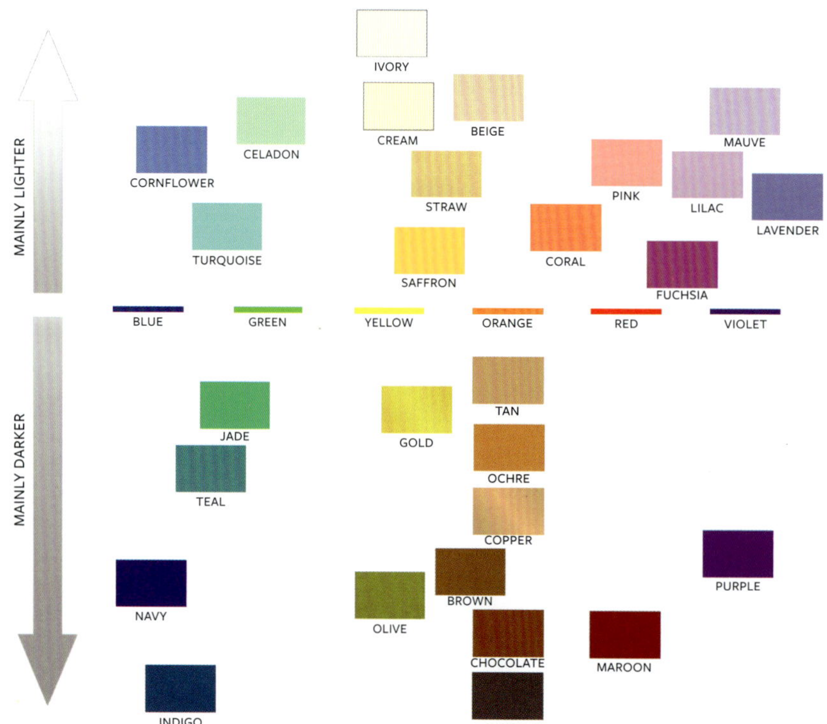

A detail of an old-fashioned Chinese bedroom, with green and gold predominating.

With a typical Japanese sensitivity towards the delicate, a box of higashi – dry confectionery used in the tea ceremony – are unified in their light colors.

that come from equiluminance. The other is that the more saturated a color, the brighter it appears. In fact, for most viewers the two qualities become linked. Bright means intense, and intense means bright. Not only this, but the strength of this effect is quite strongly biased towards magenta and red, to the extent that these hues can easily look excessive as mid-to-light tones.

This matters for photography because the sensor captures colors as they are, not as we see them. There's one situation in particular where you're likely to come across this effect, and it can be both puzzling and bothersome. A saturated magenta or red patch in a scene will appear too bright and too saturated unless the camera's color engine is programmed to take care of this in the onboard processing. You might think that by now this wouldn't be a problem, but even high-end cameras, whether dedicated or in phones, can slip up. That's the manufacturer's choice, of course, and not every person sees this intensifying effect to the same degree, but it's one more reason for shooting Raw and being prepared to process to correct. I'll return to this in Chapter 6: Process & Grading. This is complicated by how the photograph is viewed. In print, as on these pages, the effect isn't quite as strong as on a screen, but screens are where most photographs are displayed these days.

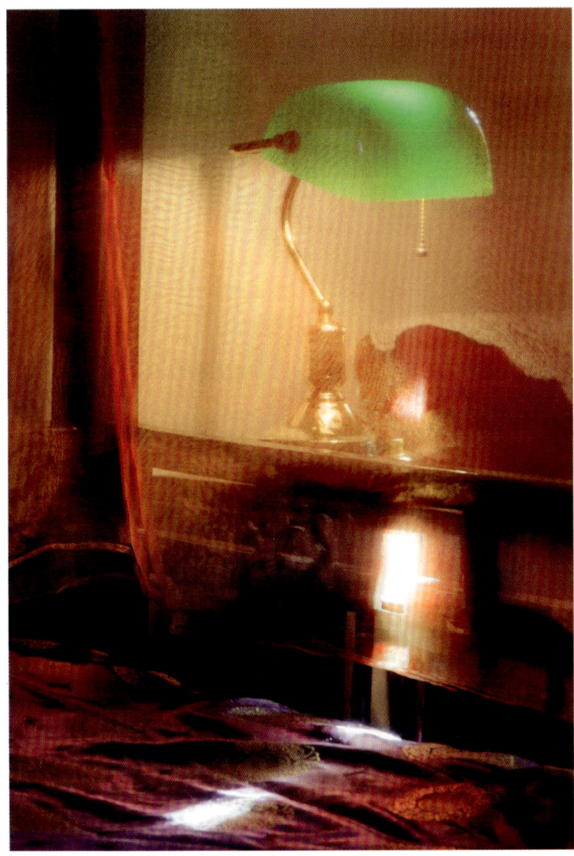

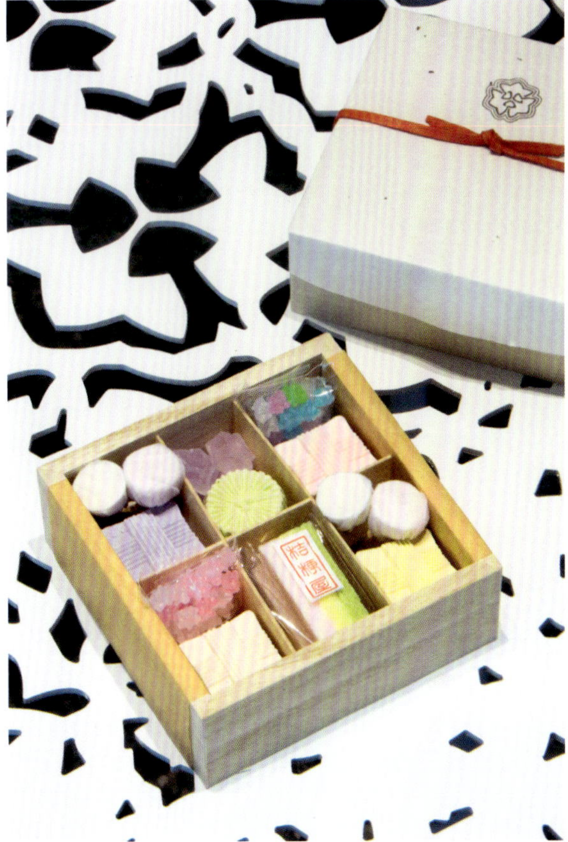

SHADOW COLORS

The contrasting group of colors is on the darker side – below the line on the color chart – and just as bright colors are the way they are because they reflect more or have light shining on them, dark colors too owe their appearance either to being naturally dark, as we just saw, or more usually, to being in shadow.

This complicates matters, because not only are the brightest parts of a photograph the ones that normally catch the attention, but when most colors go darker, they look as if they're less saturated, even when they're not. The exceptions are the 'naturally dark' colors we saw a few pages back: deep blue, purple, violet and indigo, all of which tend to look properly saturated at their typically low brightness level. Others, however, like reds and greens, tend to lose their punch, and the reason is that saturation and brightness get mixed in our perception. When both are high, as we saw on pages 90–91, the color grabs attention, sometimes even more than wanted. Here we run into the opposite situation – there often tends to be less saturation than we want. Going darker tends to reduce the intensity. In the color chart on the previous page, the entire row of dark colors – navy, olive, brown, chocolate, maroon and purple – are fully saturated, and yet most of them, with the possible exception of navy and purple, don't seem to sing out intensity. Here, opposite, woollen cloaks in a Shaker tailoring workshop show the issue perfectly. The picture underneath is as shot, on large-format film, while the one on top has been processed specially by targeting the shadow areas and then increasing the saturation to maximum. They don't seem to be, but the three cloaks

Mist at sunrise turns all the mid- and light tones grey, and this pushes color attention into the shadows.

Brightening (top) and darkening (bottom) has opposing effects on apparent saturation. In fact, the saturation doesn't change at all, yet the lighter version looks purer and the darkened version more muted.

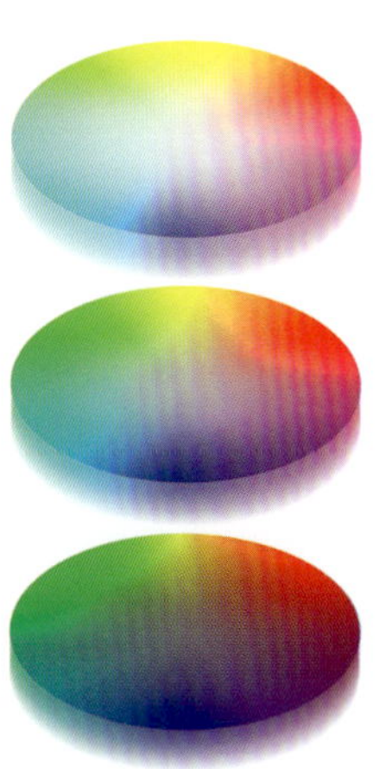

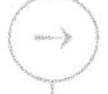

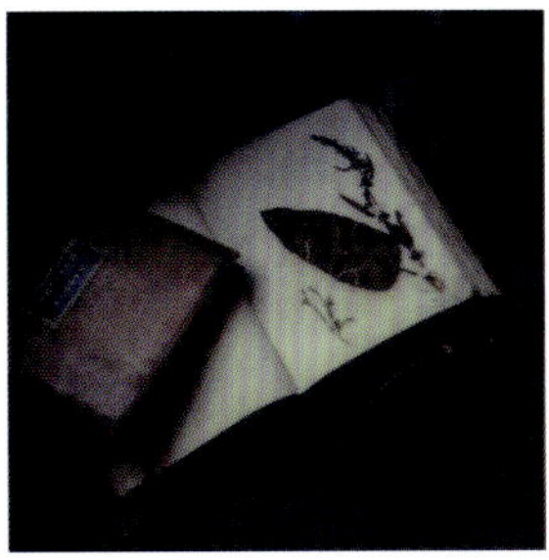

are at 100 percent saturation, and there isn't much difference with the version underneath because that too has almost full saturation in the shadows.

This is an extreme case of shadow colors resisting intensification, and it's quite often a useful processing strategy – to target shadow colors and increase their saturation while leaving mid-to-brights alone. In fact, the idea of 'rich' as a stylistic choice is one to explore in Chapter 7: Styles. All this assumes, of course, that you want richness in shadow colors, and while that's normal, another approach is to let them go subtle so that they can sink back together with the tones, and share in the kind of receding effect that I describe in the Shadowlands chapter of *Michael Freeman on... Light & Shadow*. The picture of the old plant book, above, is one such instance, and the reason for my choosing Polaroid SX-70 as the film was that it was never known for strong saturation.

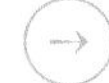

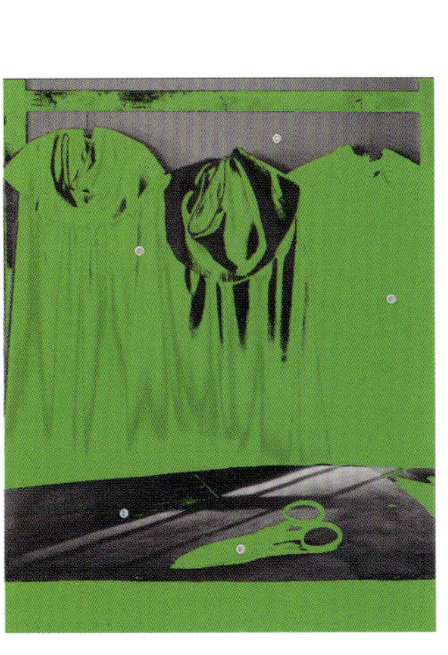

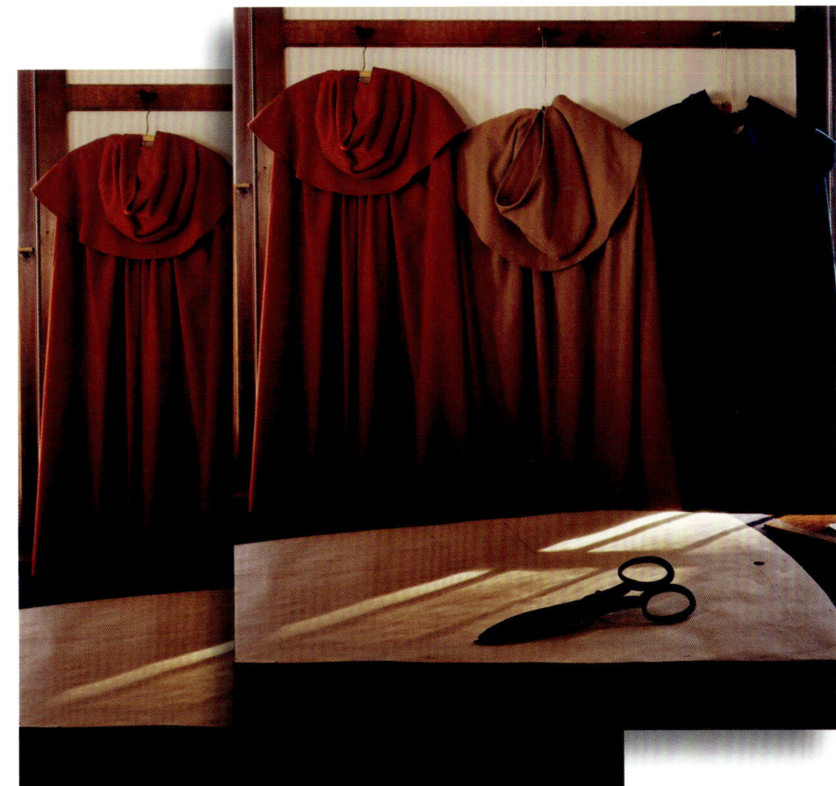

THE COLORS OF NIGHT

N ow that sensors work perfectly acceptably at low light levels with tolerable noise, and high-end phone cameras use multi-frame capture for dedicated low-light shooting, night-time photography has boomed.

The noise floor, explained on page 50, is no longer much of a problem. However, our vision developed under daylight, for which we have an innate sense of correctness for color balance, average brightness and so on. By contrast, we haven't evolved much of an experience as to how night scenes should look, and certainly not how they should look in a photograph. There are simply no generally accepted standards, particularly when it comes to color.

Lit only by moonlight, the color palette of a scene by the Mekong River in northern Thailand is as open to interpretation as it has been for painters throughout history. Here, the color temperature has been chosen for an expected blue cast to the sky and shadows, but the relationship between this, the moon, its halo and reflection has not been altered.

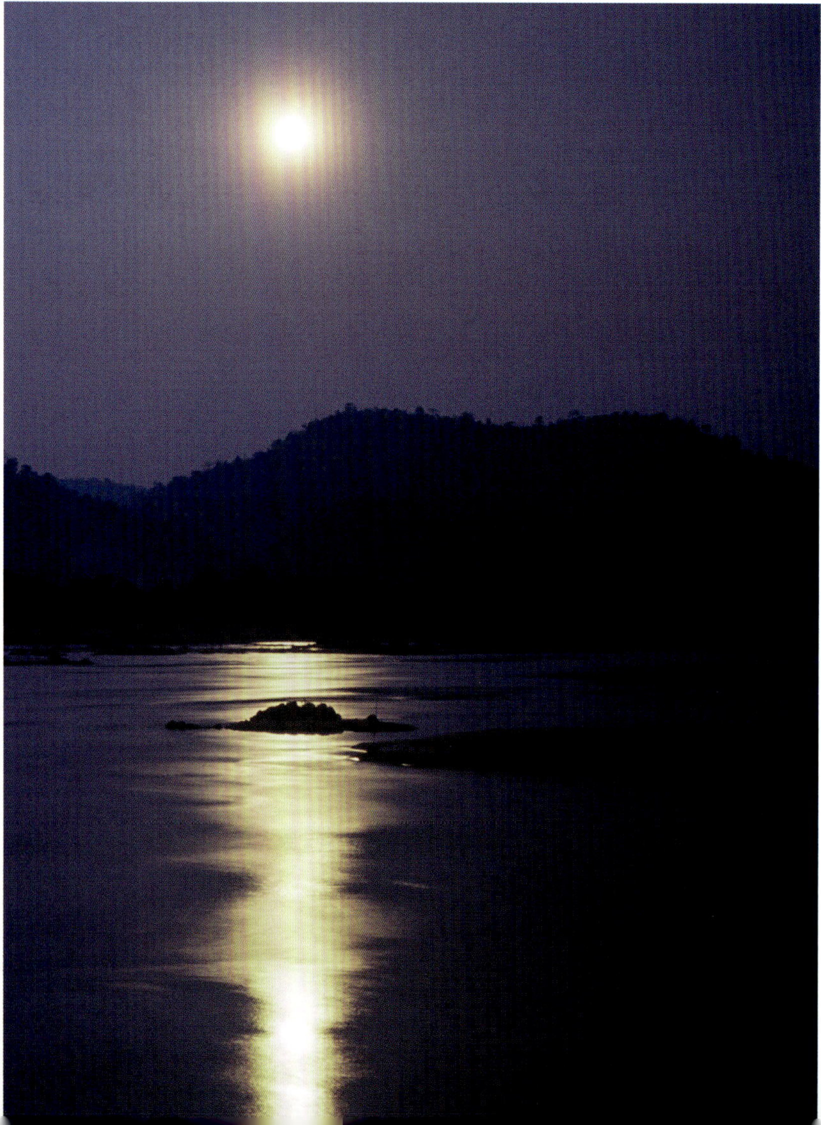

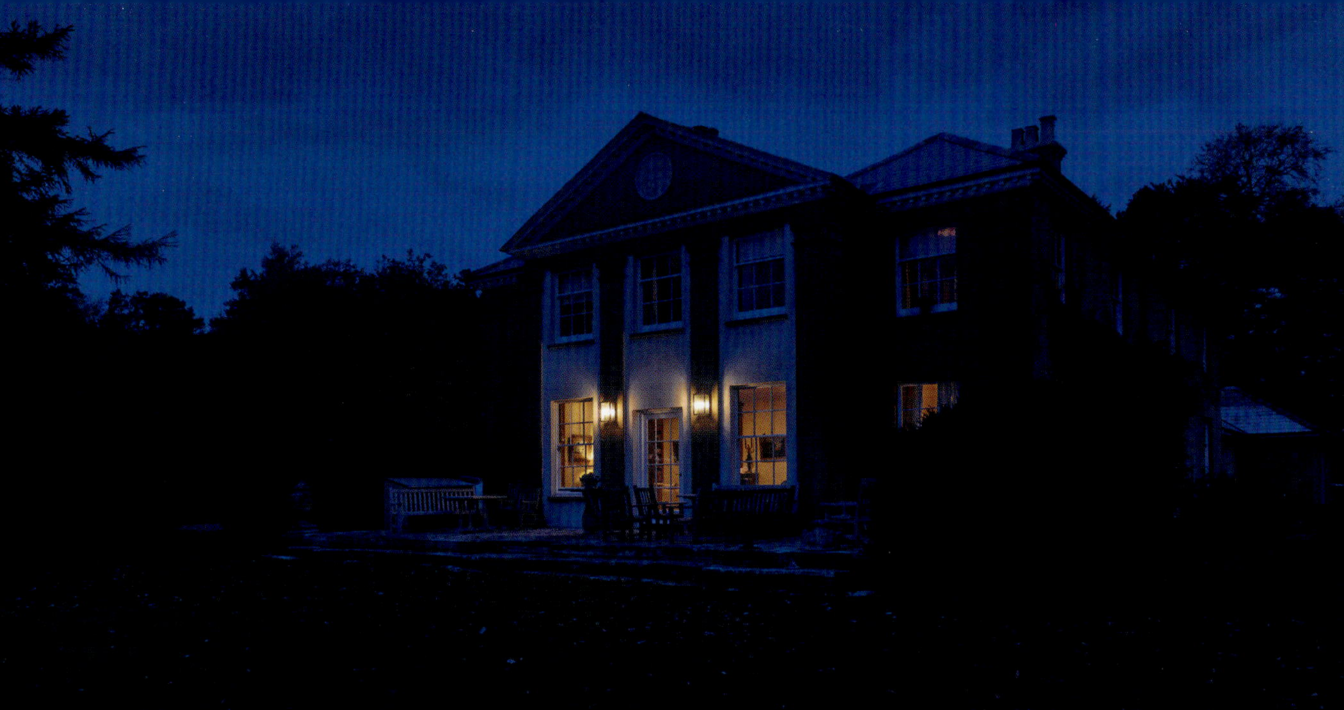

In fact, there are two very different kinds of night scene. The first, becoming less and less common, but familiar to anyone interested in astrophotography, is lit naturally, which is to say by moonlight and starlight. The second, increasingly common and more complicated, is the urban night-time scenario. Moonlit and starlit scenes are so dark – at best about 0.04 LUX – that the rods take over from the cones in our night vision, and they are not color sensitive. Our experience of night, after the 20 minutes or so for our eyes to become fully dark-adapted, is without color. Camera sensors, on the other hand, don't change their color response, and with a long enough exposure or a high enough ISO setting deliver pictures that simply look like daylight – which of course doesn't look right. However, neither does grey in varying shades, because we're so accustomed to seeing in color most of the time.

There are conventions for dealing with this in photography and film, mainly revolving around some kind of blue cast, but it's also interesting to see how painters have dealt with it. After all, painting starts with a blank canvas and the artist's imagination, so a night-time scene has to be created, not translated. Painters such as the Russian Arkhip Kuindzhi, J.M.W. Turner and Vincent van Gogh experimented with different color casts such as greens, blues, turquoise and yellows to create a slightly unworldly sensation, in combination with other techniques such as reflections of the moon and overall darkness.[†] These all work for photography, too, with the difference that you're reverse-engineering a fully colored digital image back to what gives a good impression of night. As I said, there are no standards, only interpretations of sensation. A deep blue cast has some justification, partly because this is our 'darkest' wavelength (see page 92), and partly because the last vestiges of light as a dusk sky turns to night is bluish. The last traces of blue evening light are in any case a common stand-in among photographers for night-time, not least because they help silhouette features in the landscape.

[†] The Night Sky: 10 Nocturnal Paintings You Will Love, *Daily Art Magazine*, https://www.dailyartmagazine.com/night-sky-paintings/

More usual, more complex and much more of a color question are urban night scenes, full of many light sources that are themselves colored differently. The box opposite lists the basic characteristics you can expect.

It's difficult to know where to start in deciding on the ideal – what such scenes should look like – as they're open to many interpretations. Indeed, the very colorfulness and contrast is for many people the main attraction of shooting cities at night, and realism doesn't necessarily have to come into it. Still, there are a few standards that most people would agree on, and the places to deal with them are at the time of shooting and during Raw processing. The first is that the setting is dark, even if the viewpoint and framing don't show much of it. In other words, what is not obviously lit by a lamp or some other clear light source, like the sky and shadows, should really be very dark, and even, in the deepest shadows, to the point of having no visible detail.

The second standard is what I call image integrity, which has mainly to do with being artefact-free. There's huge potential for this, including noise (we don't want any, but nor do we want artificial-looking smoothing), clipping edges around the larger light sources and color banding around light sources. Next is the dominant color – whether there should be one, and if so, what it should be. Here there's less general agreement, but one sensible principle is that if any surfaces look like they ought to be grey or white, they probably should be. Memory colors (see pages 70–1)

Light sources of different colors are typical of city night scenes, and the way they contrast is part of the appeal of shots like this of a movie production van parked in a Shanghai street during night-time filming.

Strong and harsh street lighting, combined with a black night sky, heightens contrast and intensifies the appearance of colors of a collective bus in Myanmar, with an additional wash of muted colors added in the foreground by blurred passers-by.

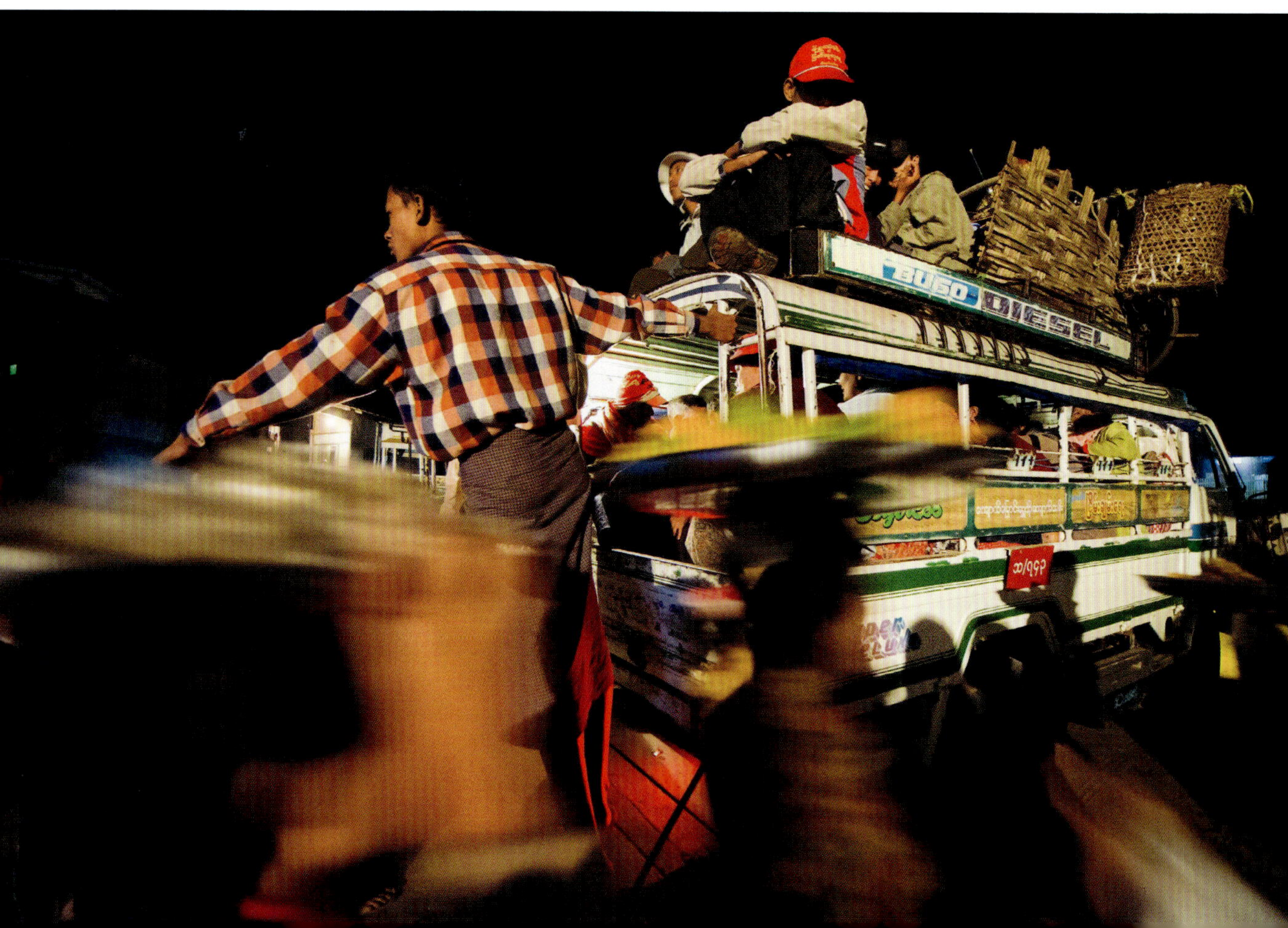

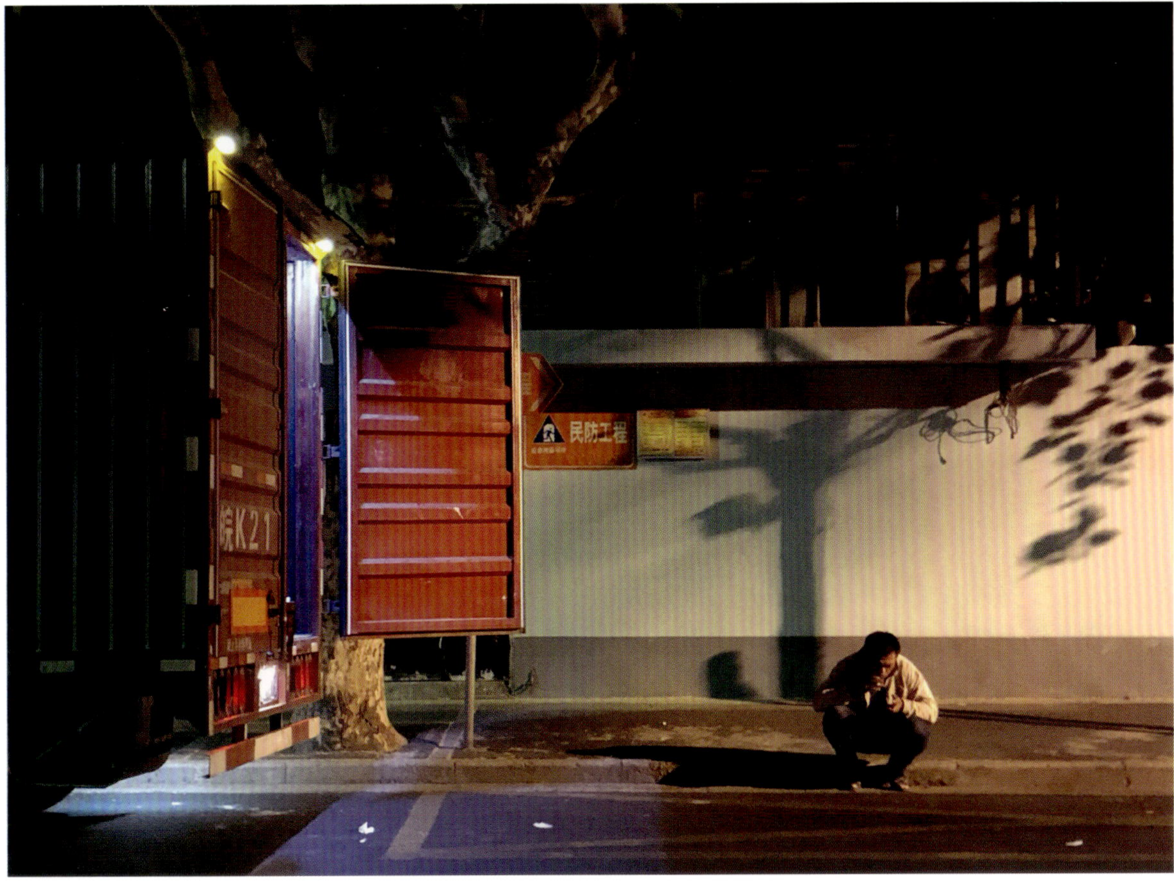

URBAN NIGHT SCENE CHARACTERISTICS

- Overall dark background/setting

- Several-to-many-point light sources and reflections

- Light sources of uncertain color and often multiple

- Often colorful

- Localized high contrast from light pooling, e.g., building floodlighting

can help. Roads, pavement, concrete in general, snow, clouds, steam and smoke all offer valuable clues. Even so, departing from these as grey anchors and letting them go in other color directions might simply be more interesting and attractive.

Colorfulness is largely the point of urban night shooting, but with all these bright-colored lights we soon hit some perceptual difficulties. I mentioned earlier the often-annoying issue with small over-saturated color patches (page 95). Night scenes are a breeding ground for these, because they tend to be full of smallish bright colors. Remember that brightness is what we perceive, and often not the same as what the camera records. The dark setting itself enhances the brightness of lights and lit patches, but more than that the Helmholtz-Kohlrausch effect mentioned earlier (saturation increases with brightness), together with what's called the Hunt effect (colorfulness increases with luminance) helps exaggerate small bright colors, and the result is often unrealistic. This is complicated by the color conversion and other algorithms that the camera manufacturer chooses to apply, but generally they need taming.

THE COLOR WHITE

Is white a color, or just the brightest of tones? This will seem a strange question if you've never thought about it before, and also if you have and have made your mind up.

The Ukrainian painter Kazimir Malevich was clear in his opinion: 'I have broken the blue boundary of color limits, come out into the white.' It's also one version of the bigger question in color photography: how colorful does any color need to be to be useful in shooting? Strong hues always attract attention and they don't create any uncertainties. They motivate many photographers to shoot for color in a scene, but also cause the opposite reaction in some – to reject and either reframe or ignore the scene. Or even decide to shoot in black and white.

Neutrals are their opposite, and so might seem equally clear-cut. White, greys and black have their uses as backgrounds, as on page 110. They can be the settings against which you can play with color patches, segments and accents, and in the next chapter on composition we'll see this in action. They are also supremely useful in judging, setting or eliminating the overall color cast of light over a scene, as on page 68. However, white is also at one end of a color scale: the B in HSB and the L* in L*a*b*. That alone qualifies it as a color, but if we stick to the idea that in photography it's the appearance of color that counts more than the numbers, it all depends on how you use white in composition. Composition is the theme of the next chapter, so here is the perfect place to consider whether to use white in that context – and black.

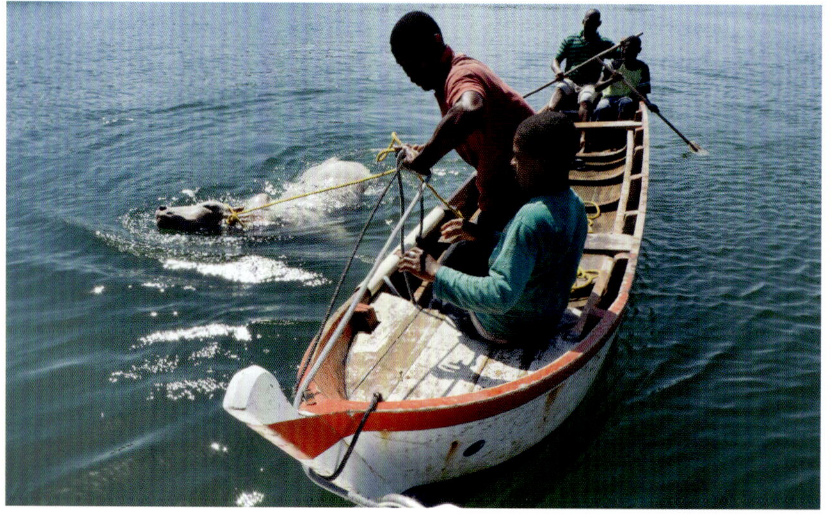

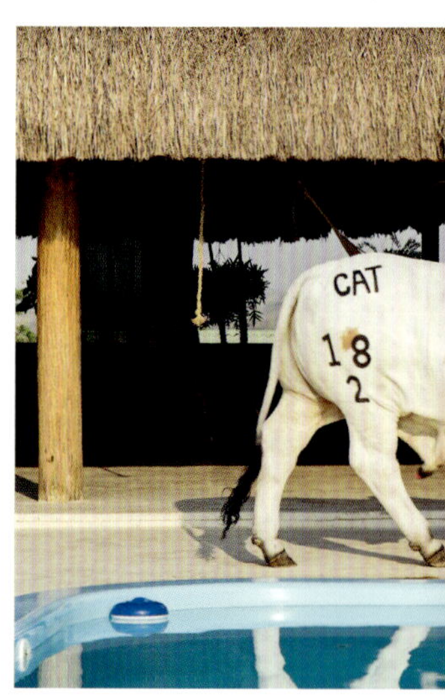

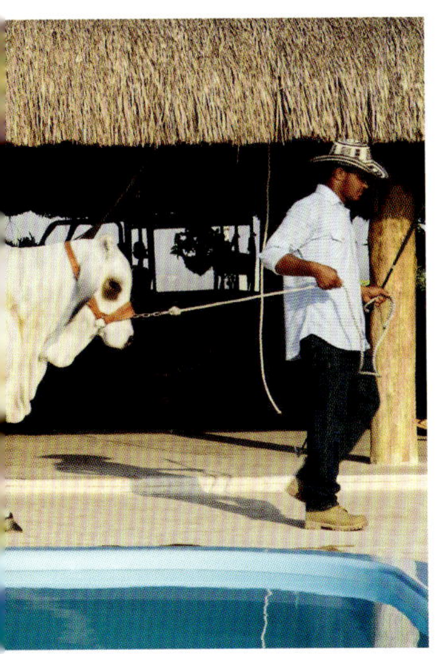

The photograph taken in Khartoum, Sudan, above, poses the question simply and clearly. It's obviously a picture about color, but which colors? Is it about blue and yellow with some less important neutrals hanging about, or is it about white, blue and yellow? Is it a pair or a triad, in the terminology of the next chapter? Even I'm not completely sure, because I was concentrating at the time on catching a man dressed in the traditional Sudanese *jelaba* in front of the blue and yellow street stall. In other words, he looked archetypical and therefore perfect for the book I was working on. The content was at the front of my mind. But *jelabas* are white, so ultimately it was, to me, a shot of white as a proper color.

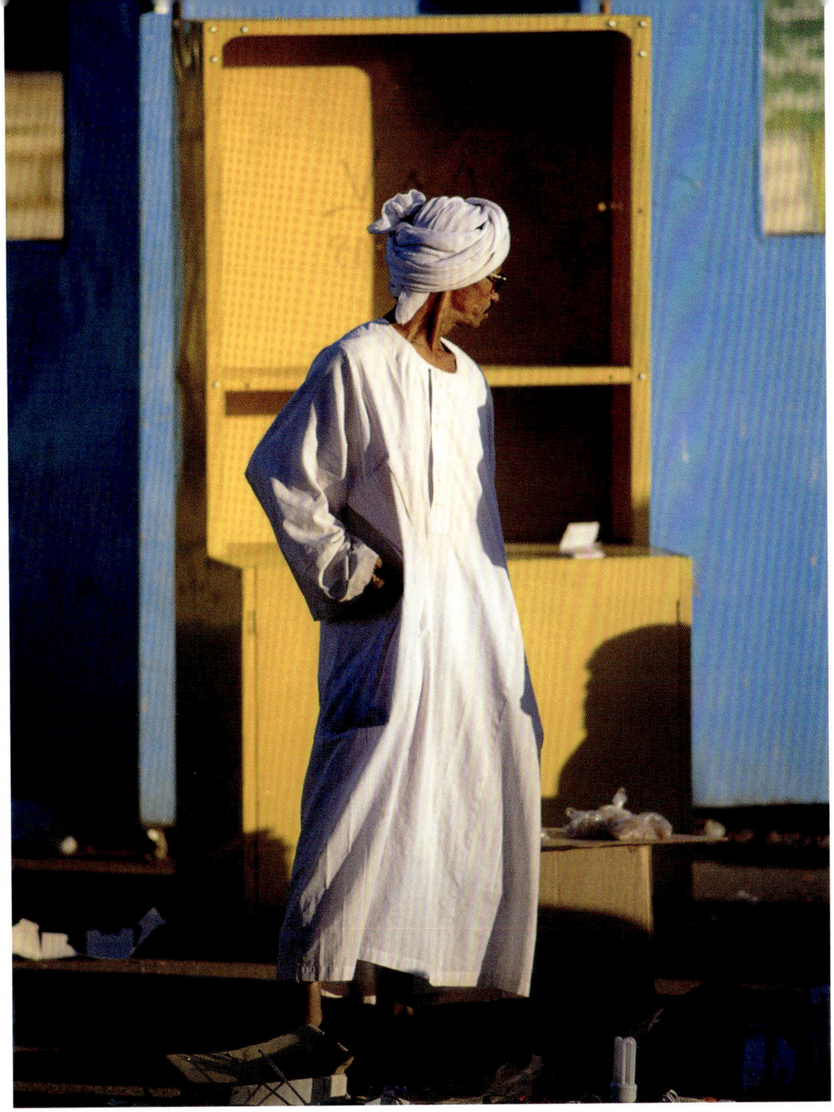

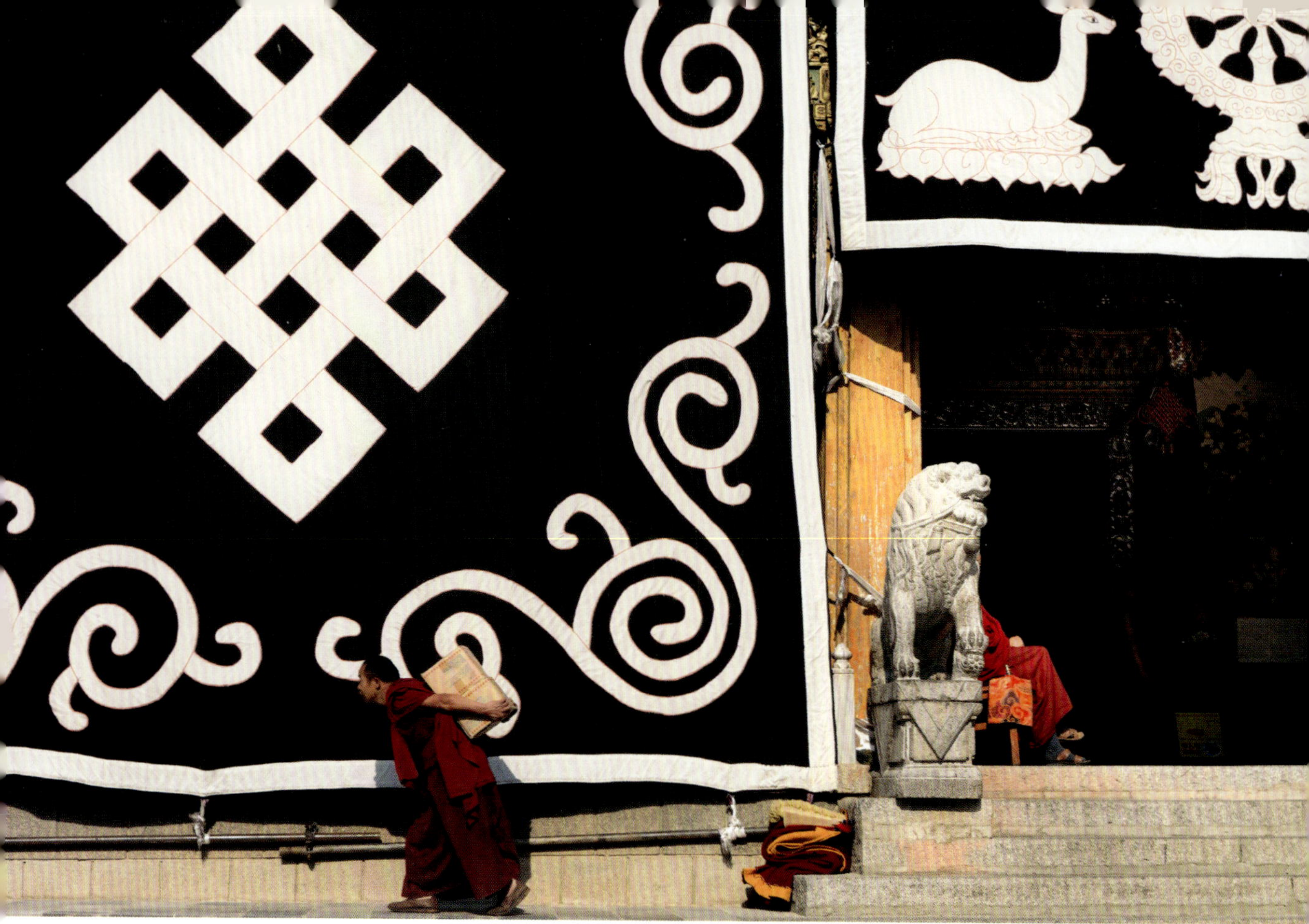

BLACK AS A COLOR

Just as white can be treated as a color that interacts with others, black has similar possibilities, and for this to work successfully, the same preconditions listed on the previous page apply. Perhaps more than white, black is very often in photographs as a background, as you can see, for example, on pages 84, 100 and 141.

You could just about argue that it's a color even in this way of using it, but background/backdrop is such a functional use that this overwhelms any other qualities. By definition, backgrounds are secondary, less significant.

Opinions vary, as you might expect. Édouard Manet was definite that 'Black is not a color' (and he was famous for black), but Pierre-Auguste Renoir wrote, 'I've been 40 years discovering that the queen of all colors is black'. In appearance, black has a wider range than white, both in tone and in color cast. This calls for some explanation. First, we are more sensitive to small differences of brightness

The sheer size and graphic power of traditional cloth hangings at a Tibetan Buddhist temple and monastery near Benzilan in western China make black arguably the subject of this geometric shot.

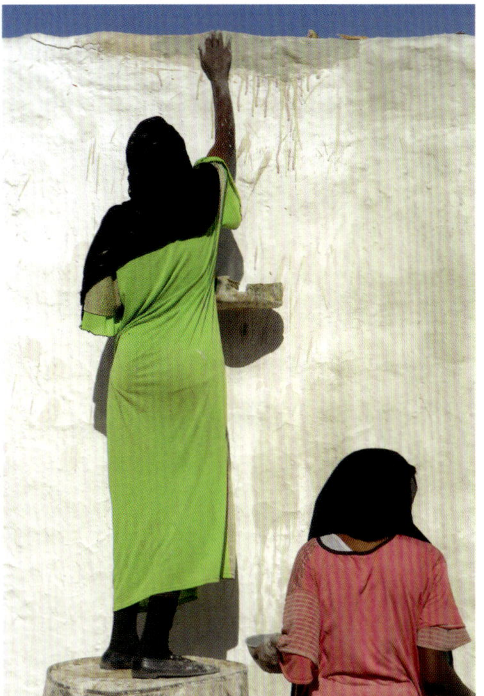

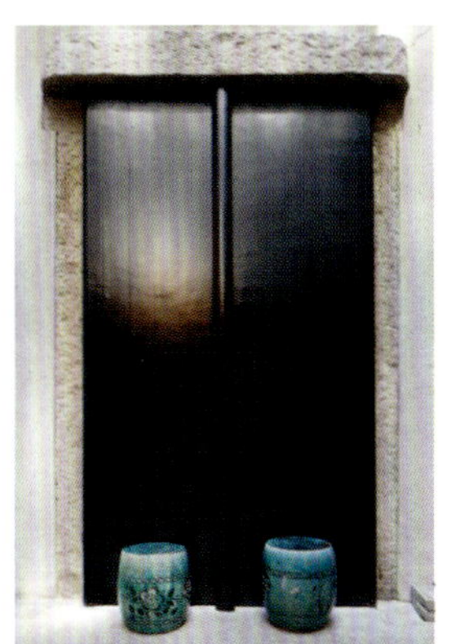

in shadows than we are in highlights. That's simply how our eyes and vision have evolved. Second, while there is a clear cut-off point at white when the photosites in a sensor fill up, at the lowest light levels there are always a few photons being captured, so that what sets the limit for black is noise – called the noise floor. The more efficient the camera sensor, the more fine shades of difference in the deepest shadows. There's more about our perception of shadows and the different types in the Shadowlands chapter of *Michael Freeman on... Composition*, but the important takeaway is that what we call black and what we think of as black are a little flexible. The black in the two main pictures here contains lighter shades that reveal the folds in the cloth, but most of us would still call the entire area black.

Above all, though, when black is tied to a significant subject and has edges, it's easiest to identify it as a color, and the nuances within it, whether tonal or subtle color tints, actually help its color sense. As a glance back at the color chart on page 94 shows, the darkest colors, even fully saturated, converge on black, and so black can contain other colors and not lose its blackness. It might even be more interesting because of it, as in the picture of the Chinese door (below, left). To return to Kazimir Malevich, his famous *Black Square* from 1915 has color tinges under the top layer.

Coincidentally, the example above is, as white was on the previous pages, a scene from Sudan, and they make an interesting pair. Both are traditional dress – white *jelaba* for men and, in this particular part of northern Sudan, black for the women's headscarves – and there are two other bright and colorful hues making up the composition. Note, incidentally, that the whitewashed wall really is a background, stretching on three sides out of frame, so doesn't register for most viewers as a color.

COMPOSING WITH COLOR

5

When colors occupy definite places in the frame, it's time to think about the possibilities of composition. The entire first book in this series focuses on composition – how it works, techniques, effects and styles – but here I want to look at the very specific way in which colors interact with each other spatially. Composition is, of course, all about space: where things are in the frame, how the eye moves between them and what they seem to mean to each other. What color brings to this is all that we've seen up to now, the triggers that different hues, different saturation and different brightness pull in our minds. Especially, the many different relationships between colors, what they do to each other, starts to come alive when you compose with them.

The end of the last chapter, looking at both white and black treated as colors, was a foretaste of the dynamics of color composition. I mentioned some preconditions, and want to elaborate on these in the following pages. There is first the need to be actively thinking about color as a prime ingredient in the picture. Ultimately, it's for each photographer to say whether the intention is color. Following this, the colors, even if there's only one, have to occupy a definite space in the frame. Clear edges help to do this, also compact and identifiable shapes.

To my mind this is the practical, creative heart of the book, and if that seems an odd turn of phrase, it may be because to many ears the two words sound at odds with each other. 'Creative' invokes inspiration and twists of imagination, and that's true enough, but making it real calls for some practical steps. Composing with color is a strangely under-written and under-discussed area of photography – strangely for me anyway – but once color starts to take over as the key ingredient in a picture, then by pitching one color against another, or some colors against others, all of the ideas in *The Photographer's Eye* and *Michael Freeman on... Composition* come into play. Practically speaking, when you have a frame and areas of color inside it, where they fall and how they react to each other can make (or even break) the picture.

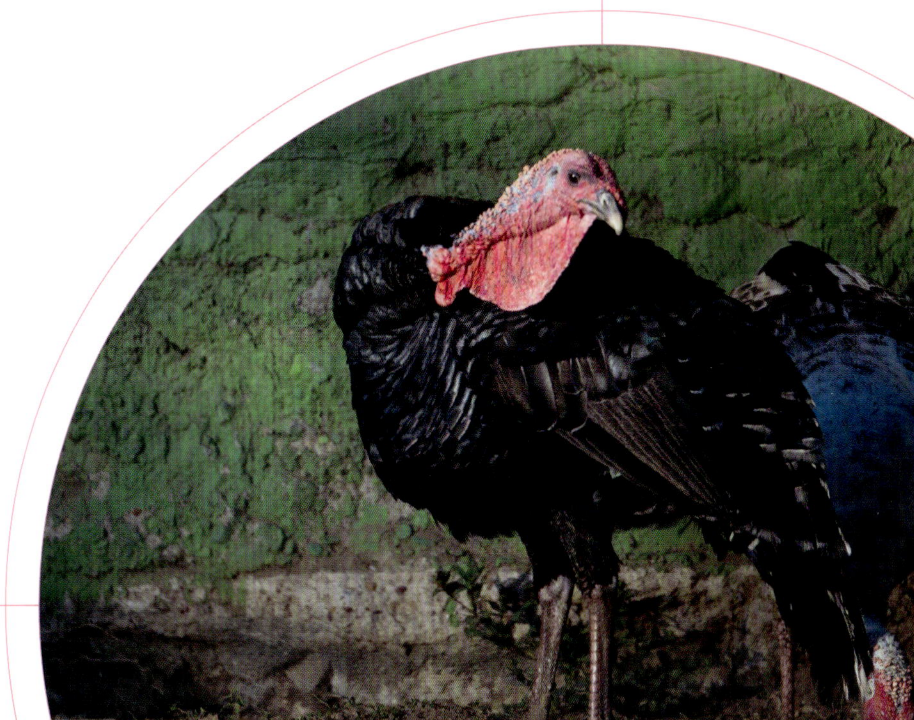

SHAPES & SEGMENTS

There are many ways of using color in photography, as you can see throughout this book, but one of the most deliberate, and interesting, is compositionally. Before anything else, it depends on having distinct units of color, and that means they need to have some kind of recognizable shape.

The actual shape isn't important – they don't have to be simple shapes like circles and triangles – but they do need to stand out from their surroundings. That generally means having clear, sharp edges, and the less complicated, the better. They also need to be more or less mid-sized, meaning large enough to be obvious but not taking over most of the frame. The idea is, like chess pieces on a board, we can 'move' them around the frame and relate them to each other. We can juxtapose one color unit against another, or against the background. The methods are all those laid out in *Michael Freeman on... Composition*, by changing viewpoint, changing the lens focal length, angling the camera, showing more of the scene or less, making them balance or deliberately unbalancing them. It's composition by placement.

All of this goes back to the idea of salience that I talk about in the first book. In pictures, salience is usually about content, and as the eye-tracking experiments we did in that book confirm, certain recognizable things such as faces, figures, animals, vehicles and so on, almost always catch our attention early on. This isn't quite the case with color shapes. Of course, a figure walking through the scene with a brightly colored coat is going to be very salient, catching immediate attention partly because it's a person but partly also because of the color. That would be a double reinforcement, but in the color-forward photography we're looking at here, it's usually more interesting and creative to rely mainly on the colors to make the point.

As well as clear shapes, there are segments and divisions possible. The example opposite is a very obvious one – rectilinear with rectangular frames and a dividing color bar at the top – but even simple bands of color can work. The simplest of all, the horizon line between sky and land or sea, verges on the obvious, but still allows you to choose the division by placing it higher or lower. The Italian colorist photographer Franco Fontana made a distinctive body of work doing this, using longer focal lengths and views that excluded obvious objects and structures to create highly abstracted landscapes.

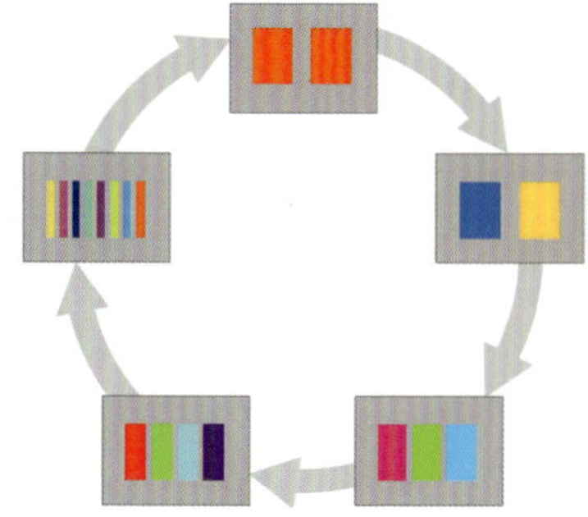

The relationships between color segments change according to how many there are, starting with just one color on a neutral ground (top), then (clockwise) a pair of colors, three, four, after which there are too many to have individual relationships and the image simply works as polychrome.

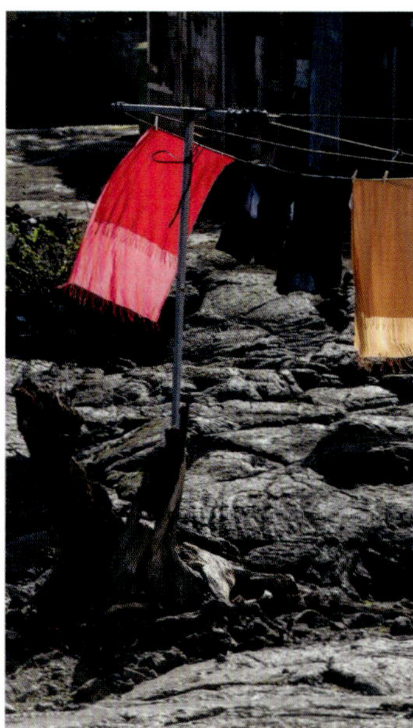

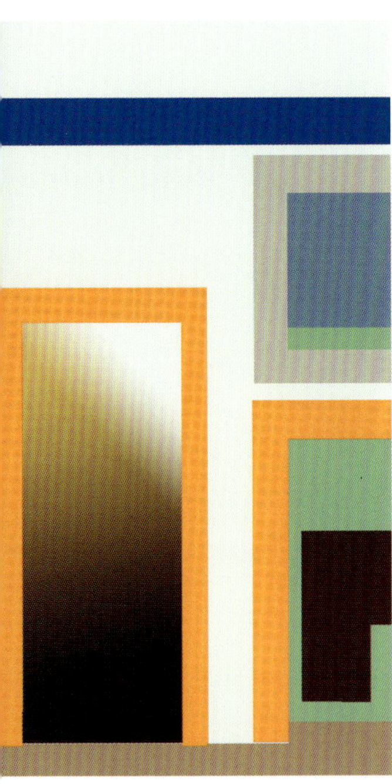

In Bogota's La Candelaria district, doorways and windows arrange themselves into a set of colored rectangles which, from a face-on viewpoint, interact with the picture frame.

Backlit washing hanging on a line becomes an arrangement of two colored rectangles against the neutral dark grey of a recent lava flow on the island of La Réunion.

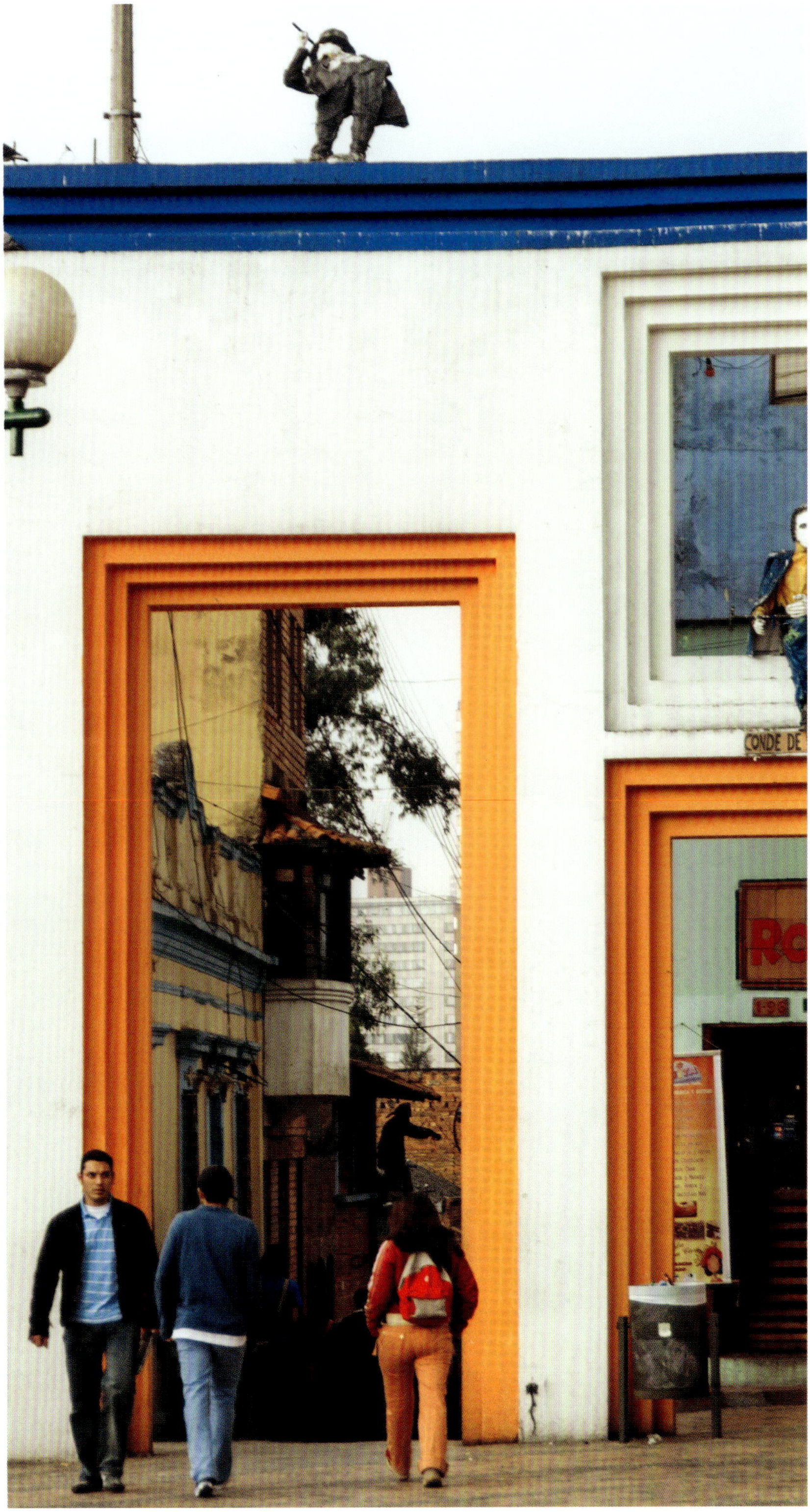

SOLITARY COLOR

T he simplest situation of all is a single color against a
more-or-less neutral background. To work effectively,
the unit of color needs to have a reasonably clear shape, as
in the examples here, because that's the only way for it to
stand out as an element that catches attention.

It also, as just described on the previous pages, needs to be a certain size, and in
particular not so large that it takes over the frame. We're not talking here about a
dominant color that suffuses the entire picture, as on pages 22–3, but an element
that sits clearly against a background. This background is the second actor in the
photograph. It has a supporting role, but is still very influential. First, there's the
matter of neutrality. It has to appear colorless, otherwise the relationship with
the single color would morph into one of the other kinds of relationship that we
explore next. There's arguably some latitude here, because a tinted grey as the
setting for a vibrant color may still appear to most people as colorless, simply
because the single color overwhelms it. In the shot of a foot resting on the wooden
block of a tricycle cart, the background has a blue tint, but the yellow is strong
enough to make it seem neutral. In processing, you could neutralize it completely,
but the difference would not be great.

Colors take on a different appearance according to whether the neutral background is dark, as in the close-up (left) of a tricycle cart rider's foot in Cartagena, Colombia, or bright, as below in a Colonial-style Singaporean house. The strip below with three identical yellow squares shows how not only does the color pop out the most strongly from black, but seems brighter than when against white.

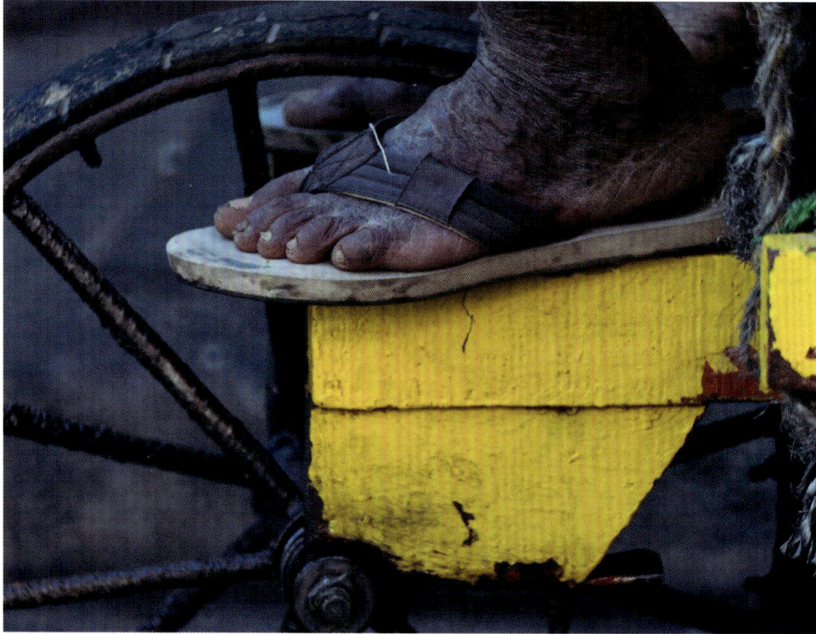

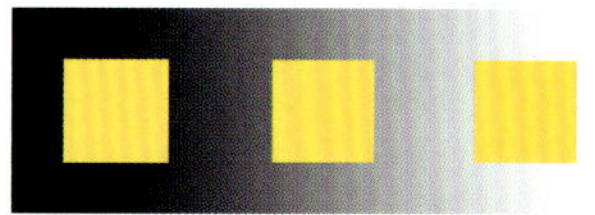

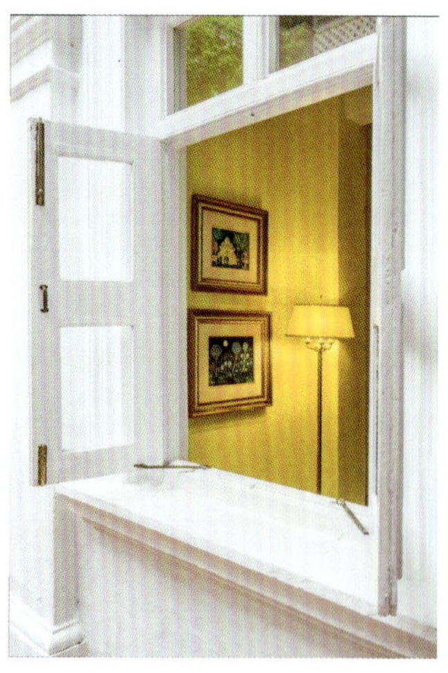

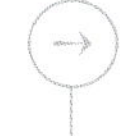

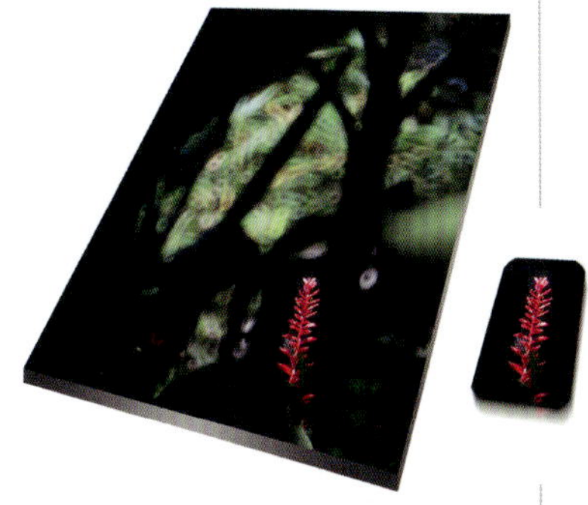

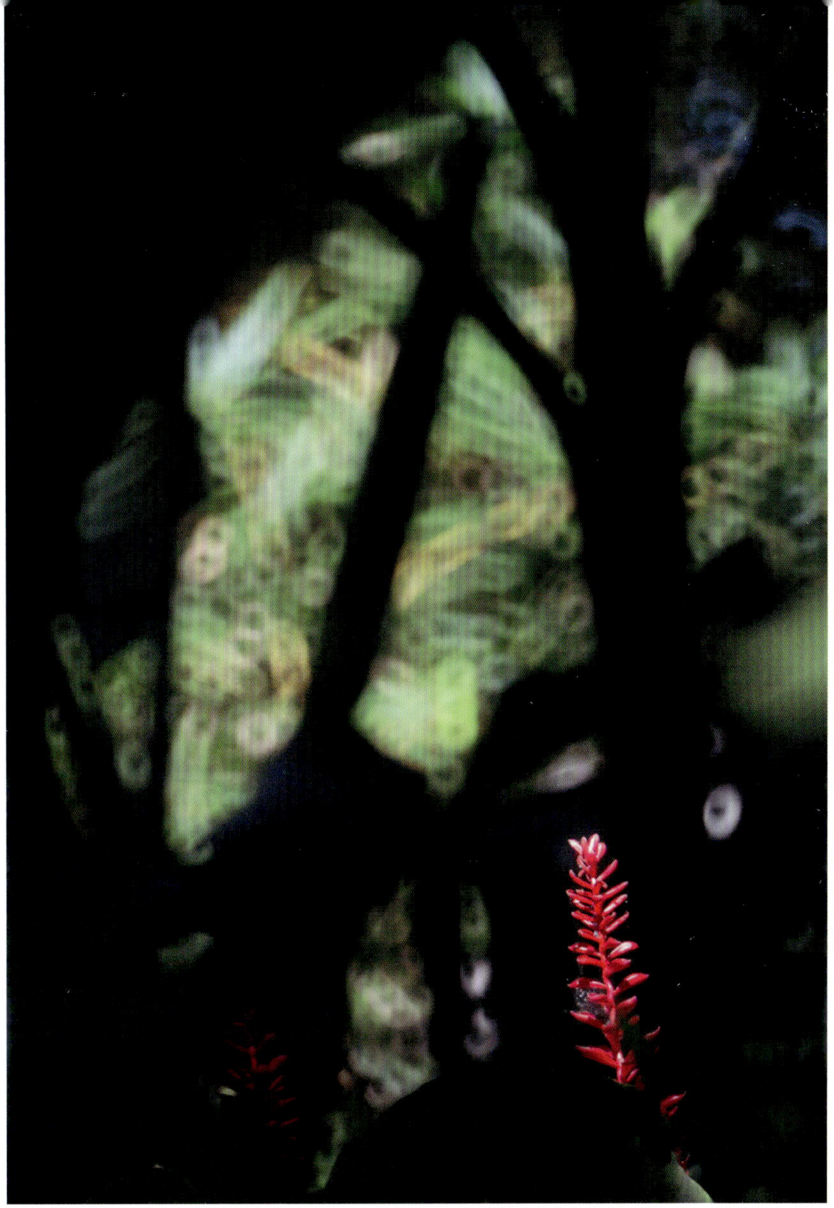

This raises the larger question of what counts as color in a picture. If that sounds at first a bit silly, consider that often we simply discount a weaker color in favour of a stronger one. In the picture on page 117, how many colors would you say the picture is dealing with? There are often borderline cases like this, and not everyone will treat them in the same way, but it boils down to a judgement on whether it's one color on its own, or two colors in a relationship.

Second, the brightness of the background has a strong effect on how the color looks to us. We already saw something of this in the picture of the tulip on page 60, a reminder that color is always relative. The same color against a dark background or a light background doesn't appear the same. Against dark it seems brighter and more intense, while against white it falls back and seems more delicate. This is the illusion called simultaneous brightness contrast, described at the start of *Michael Freeman on... Composition*. It's not a question of better or worse, just different.

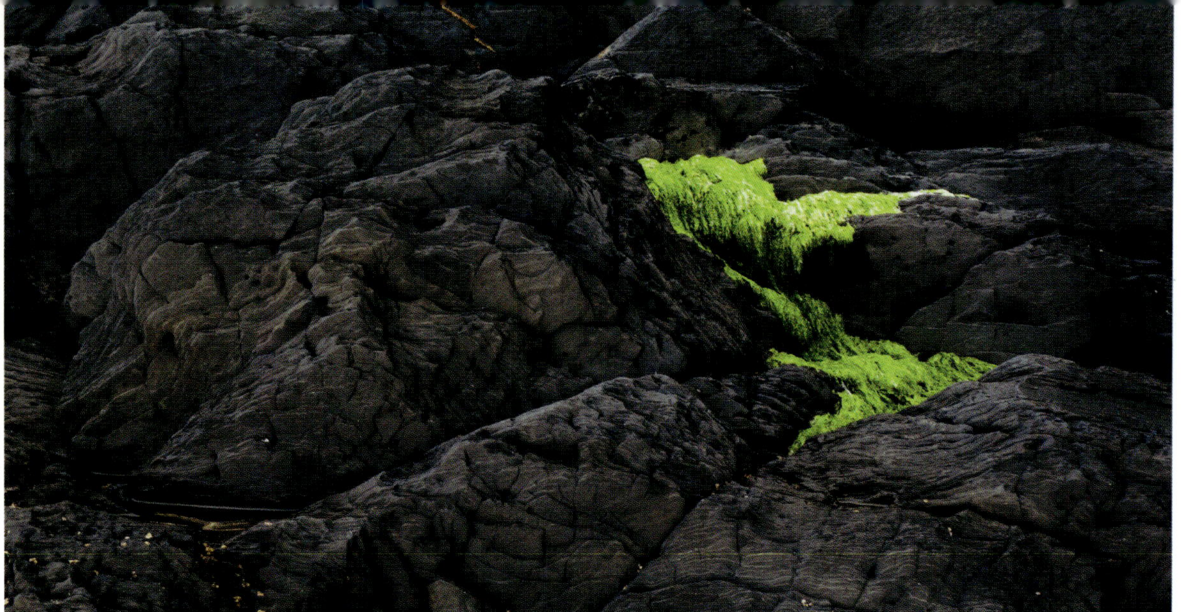

The nature of this kind of picture begins to change when the size of the color unit shrinks. It becomes more isolated but, strangely enough, not necessarily less noticeable. Paradoxical though it may sound, making a color smaller in the frame is actually one way to intensify it and make it more important. There are quite a few ifs, but the strategy is to isolate a single color object against large areas of contrasting color and tone.

These surroundings are the key to making this work, because it's the contrast between small colorful and large less-colorful that creates the energy that this kind of color picture has. It's often also called spot color or color accent, which hint at this. To quote the painter Henri Matisse, 'A thimbleful of red is redder than a bucketful'. That sounds a little provocative, but from all we've seen so far, one of the lessons is that color comes alive when it's noticeably different to what it's next to. One color against another, or against a colorless setting, and if there's also a big size difference in this contrast, favours the color even more.

This is a pop-out effect, and if you've already read *Michael Freeman on... Light & Shadow*, it's obviously similar to the localized pop-out style described there. Technically, pop-out happens in a visual search when the viewer quickly and without thinking notices one small element that is different from the surroundings. A small object brighter or darker than its setting is one way explored in the other book, but doing it with color brings in likes, dislikes and even emotion.

Bright seaweed in a Welsh sea cove takes on a shape organized into horizontals and diagonals that echoes the pattern of fissures in the rock.

In contrast to the single units of color in the other pictures here, this shot of a church on the island of Grand Manan in Canada's Bay of Fundy attempts a composition of red segments *around* the frame, offset against white.

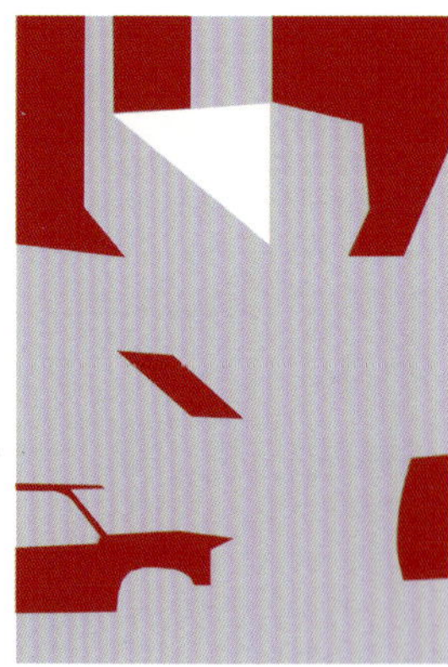

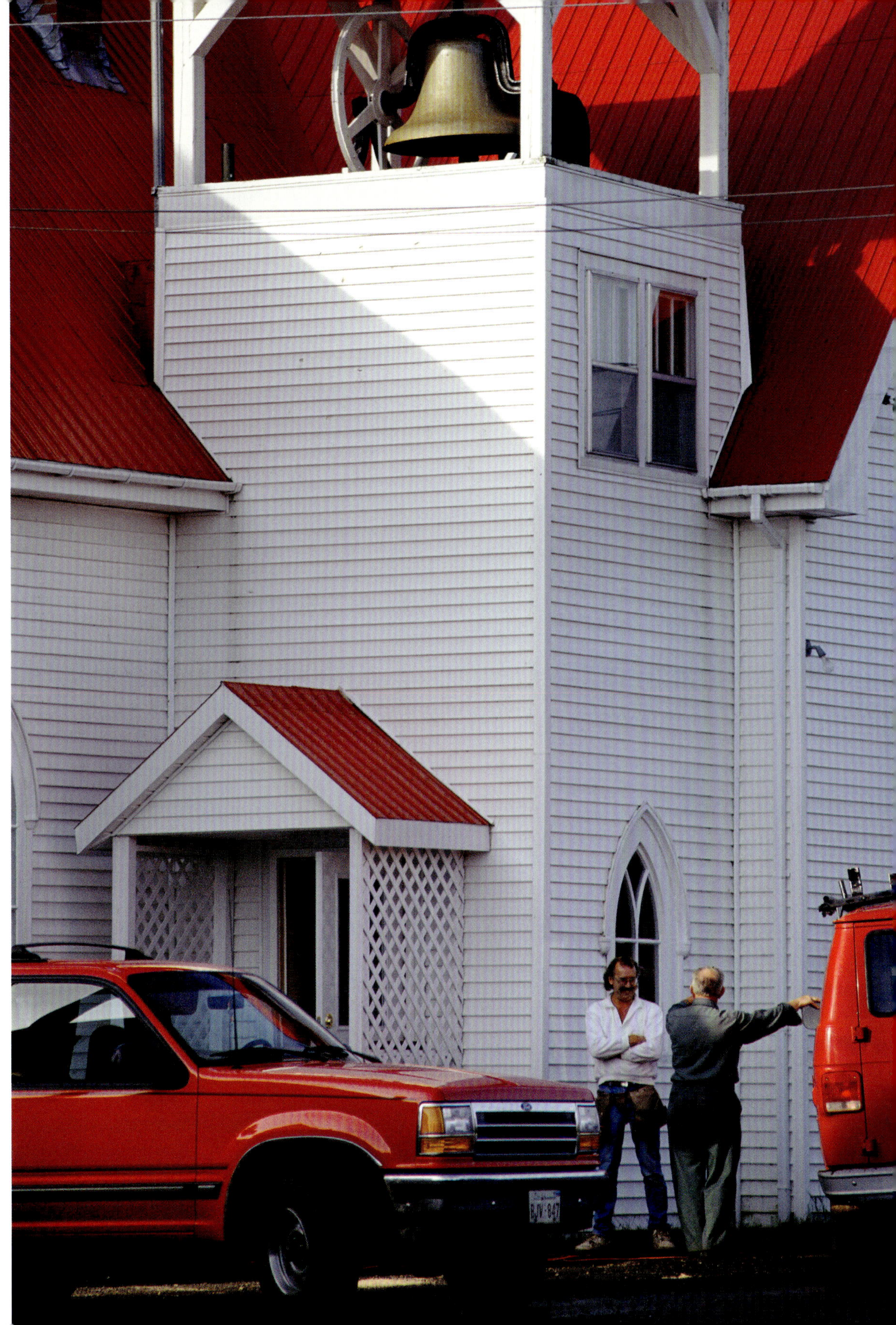

THREE RELATIONSHIPS

The simplest color relationship in a picture is between two hues. Even then, there's a considerable range of combinations, because they can differ from each other in brightness, saturation and size, and also we can stretch the definition of hue to cover several degrees around the color circle.

In other words, red can become reds, one green can be several greens, and as we're photographers rather than color scientists, exactness doesn't matter. In addition to this, the smaller that color patches are against a background, the more possibilities for their position in the frame, which takes us right back to the opening chapters of *Michael Freeman on... Composition*. More often than not there is some kind of less colorful background or setting, and it's worth considering the tipping point between a setting for two colors that is just a background and one that actively contributes its own color. Backgrounds, whether neutral or mildly tinted, work in the same way for two or several colors.

With all this in mind, the way in which two colors interact depends most on how far apart they are around the color circle. The boundaries are necessarily fuzzy, but there are three basic relationships, or pairings, and in color language they are Adjacent, Opponent and Tangential. Adjacent colors are those that most people would consider being in the same segment, and their relationship is essentially one of similarity – variations on a theme is another way of looking at it. This varies according to the color in a way similar to the tolerance we looked at on page 62, so that around orange-yellow, for example, colors considered similar would be within about 30 degrees, but around green could take up a full quarter of the circle.

We've already seen Opponent colors at work in how the brain processes (page 34) and in the L*a*b* color model and space that attempts to mimic this (page 44). Any two colors directly across the circle from each other are opponent – or opposite – and they are also complementary, which we'll look at in more detail shortly. This kind of relationship is the most contrasting, and according to one widespread opinion is in a sense harmonious.

In between Adjacent and Opponent are color pairs that are distinctly different from each other but without a fixed, locked relationship. They lack complementarity, but there's no reason to think of that as some kind of ideal. Instead, such Tangential color pairings offer less expected combinations, and when you find them you can work with them as a more personal expression. More on this soon.

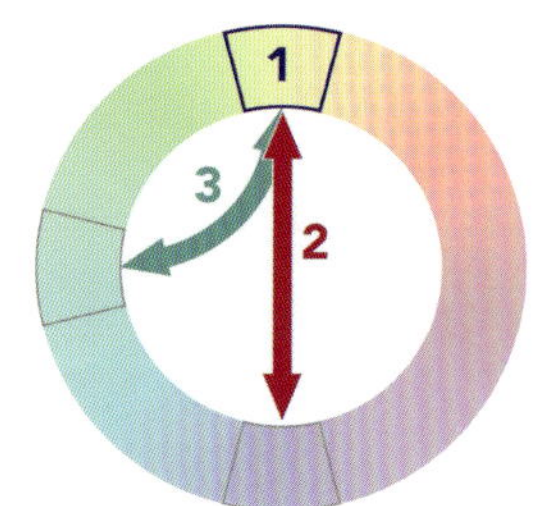

Color relationships are easiest to appreciate when mapped against the color circle, and fall into three groups: adjacent to each other (1), as in the picture of monks' robes drying under an old Thai monastery (far right); opposite each other (2), as in the interior of a café in Colombia (lower right); and at a tangent to each other (3), as in the painted statue in a nat shrine in Myanmar (near right).

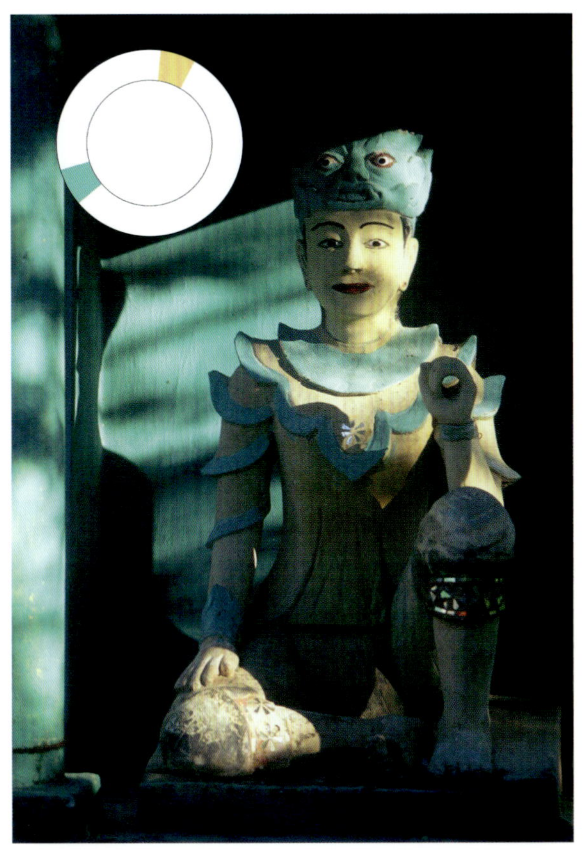

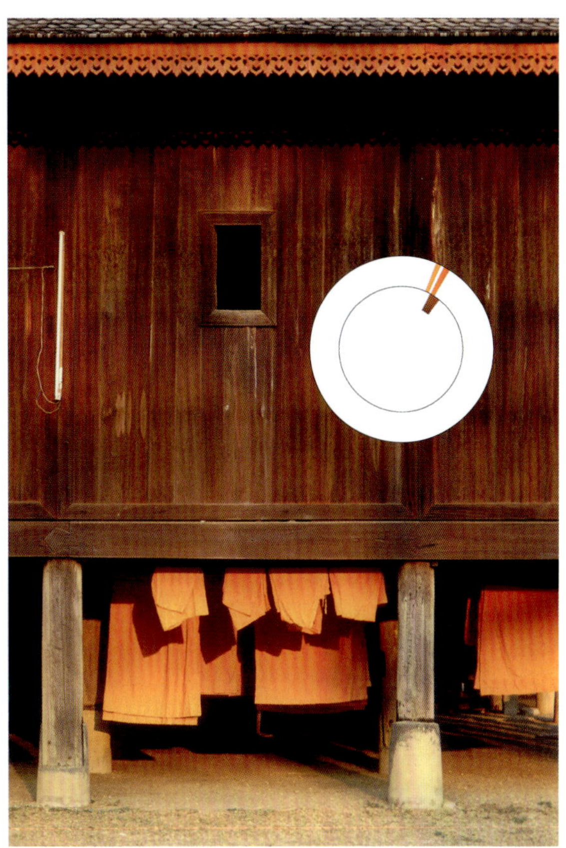

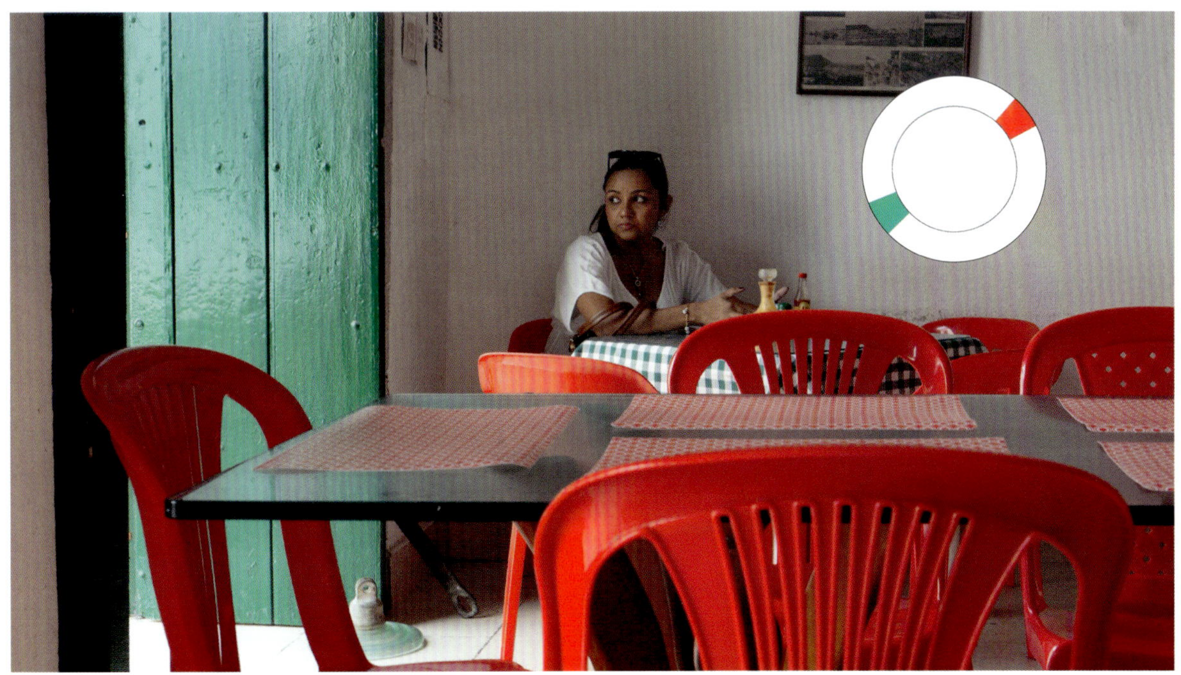

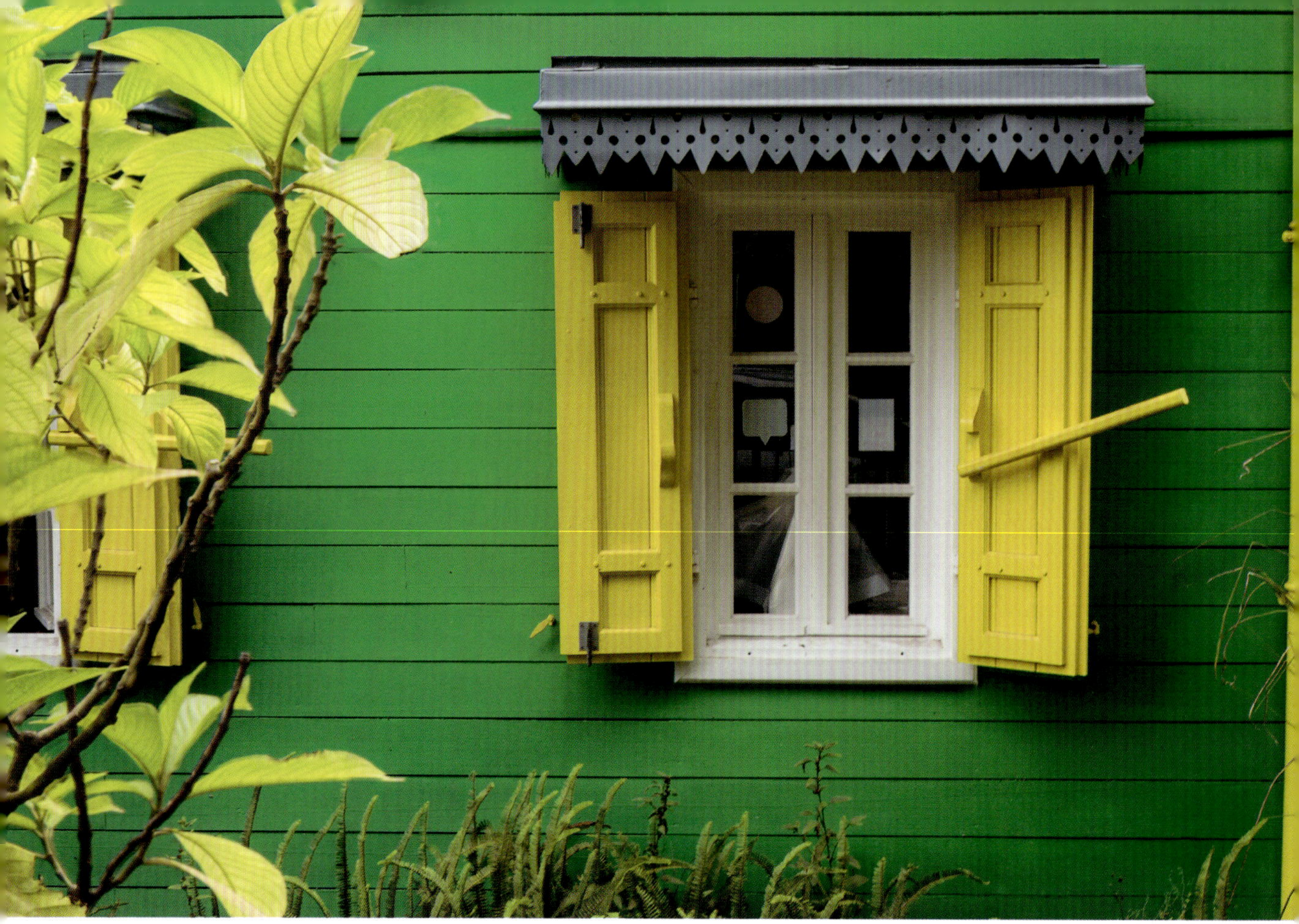

ADJACENT COLORS

Possibly the least complicated relationship between colors is when they are simply next to each other, or close to each other, on the color circle. Also called analogous colors, their obvious similarity makes them 'go well' together. It's an easy harmony.

There are no fixed limits, just what's generally agreed by most people as being similar. The limit is simply when most people would say that two colors seem 'apart'. However, this is affected by which part of the color circle we're talking about. While a range from reddish to purplish (I'm deliberately not being precise) and also from greenish to bluish could comfortably take in more than a quarter of the circle, yellow is more problematic. Yellow towards reddish works perfectly well, as does yellow towards greenish, but spreading in both directions quickly reaches a limit because greenish and reddish appear very different to each other. Lime-green and orange, for example, are only about 60 degrees apart, and yet they don't seem similar at all.

Entre-Deux in La Réunion is known for its colorful houses. Leaves from yellow to green take up a quarter of the color circle, but note how this feels fresher than the combination of adjacent colors in the other photograph, which runs from yellow to red.

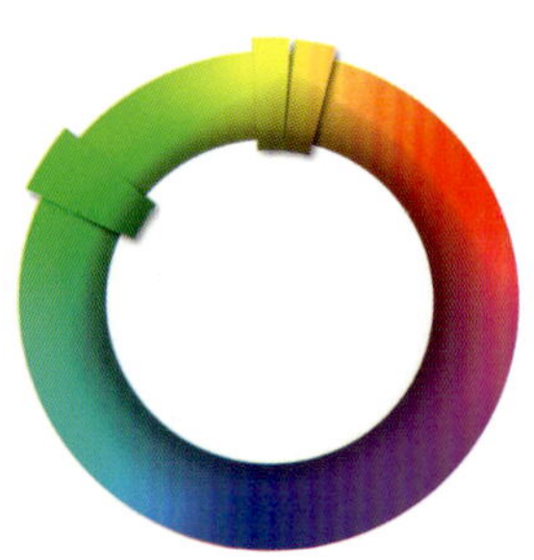

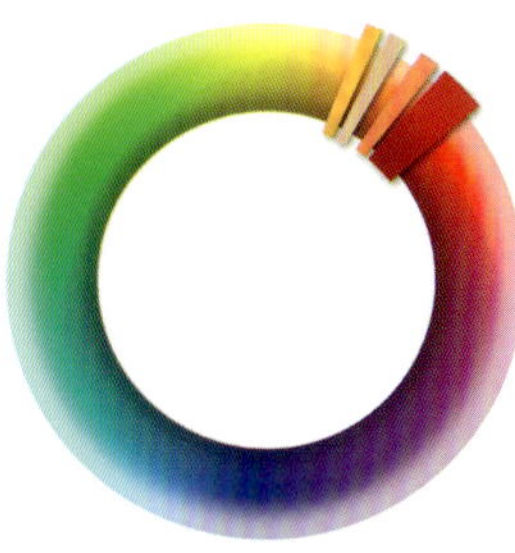

The pink blouse of a flower seller in Mandalay's Maharani Temple, Myanmar, and her skin tone fit into the interior's color scheme, which ranges around a deep orange, from yellow to red and taking up just a sixth of the color circle.

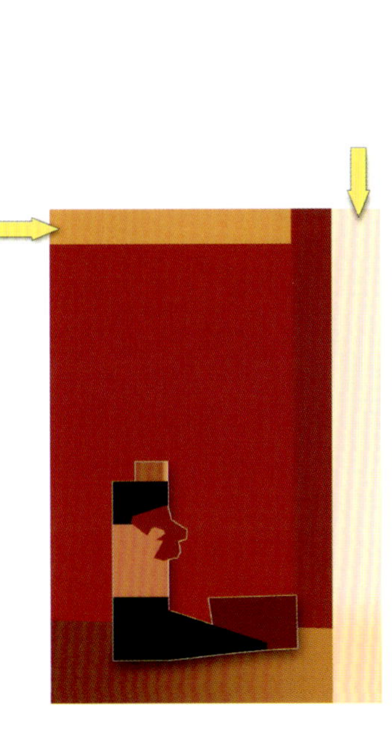

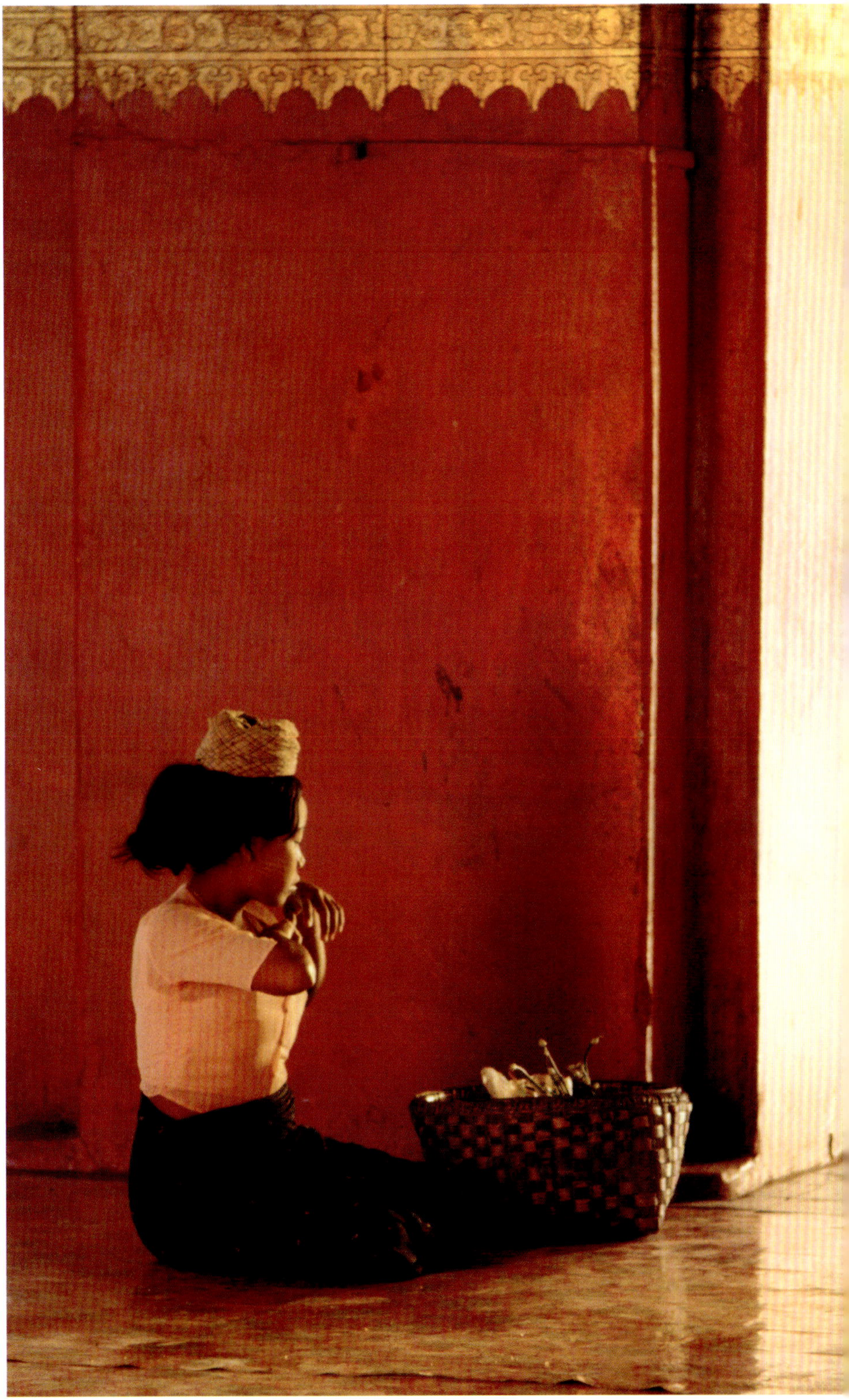

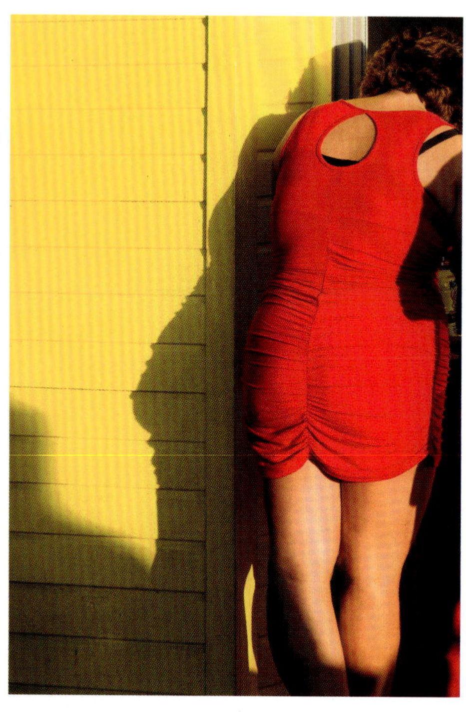

All of the above has been about hue, but there are other ways of being adjacent, and one of the most important is brightness. The picture of the Thai monastery wall on page 115 is a good example of how this usual definition of adjacent colors – hues next to each other – breaks down. Brown and orange are certainly colors and certainly similar, but what separates them is not actual hue, but brightness, as their places on the color circle show. A more useful color circle for adjacent colors is the one here, varying in brightness as well as hue.

As we'll see throughout this chapter, the most 'compositional' use of color pairs and groupings is when the colors are in clear, separate units. This makes it possible to play with their arrangement in the way you frame them, as in the monastery wall picture with its cluster of orange rectangles low in the frame and squared up to the camera, and also as in the picture on the previous page of the Burmese girl selling flowers in a temple, where she's positioned neatly against the red wall, and the gold frieze and the bright side of the wall frames the scene top and right. The other main picture, of a ruined stone hall at Angkor, Cambodia, is less distinct, and the range of adjacent colors, from blue-green through green towards almost yellow, is 'smeared'. That doesn't make it better or worse, just a different way of arranging the colors.

A simple, two-block color combination on Santa Monica Pier, California, of yellow and red. Separated by a sixth of the color circle, they appear to be more similar than different.

The colors of collapsed masonry in the 12th-century temple of Preah Khan in Angkor, Cambodia, have an overall sense of yellow-greenish cohesion from moss, lichen and reflected light from the forest outside. The reddish blocks of laterite in the foreground, however, have a less certain relationship – they could be seen as part of the whole, or possibly contrasting. The mingled colors are mapped on the circle below.

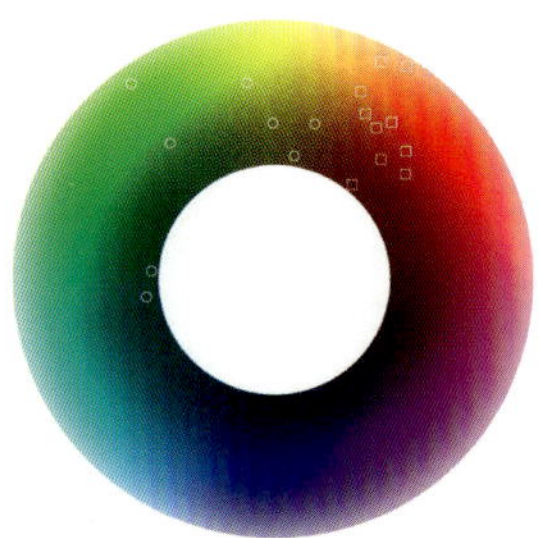

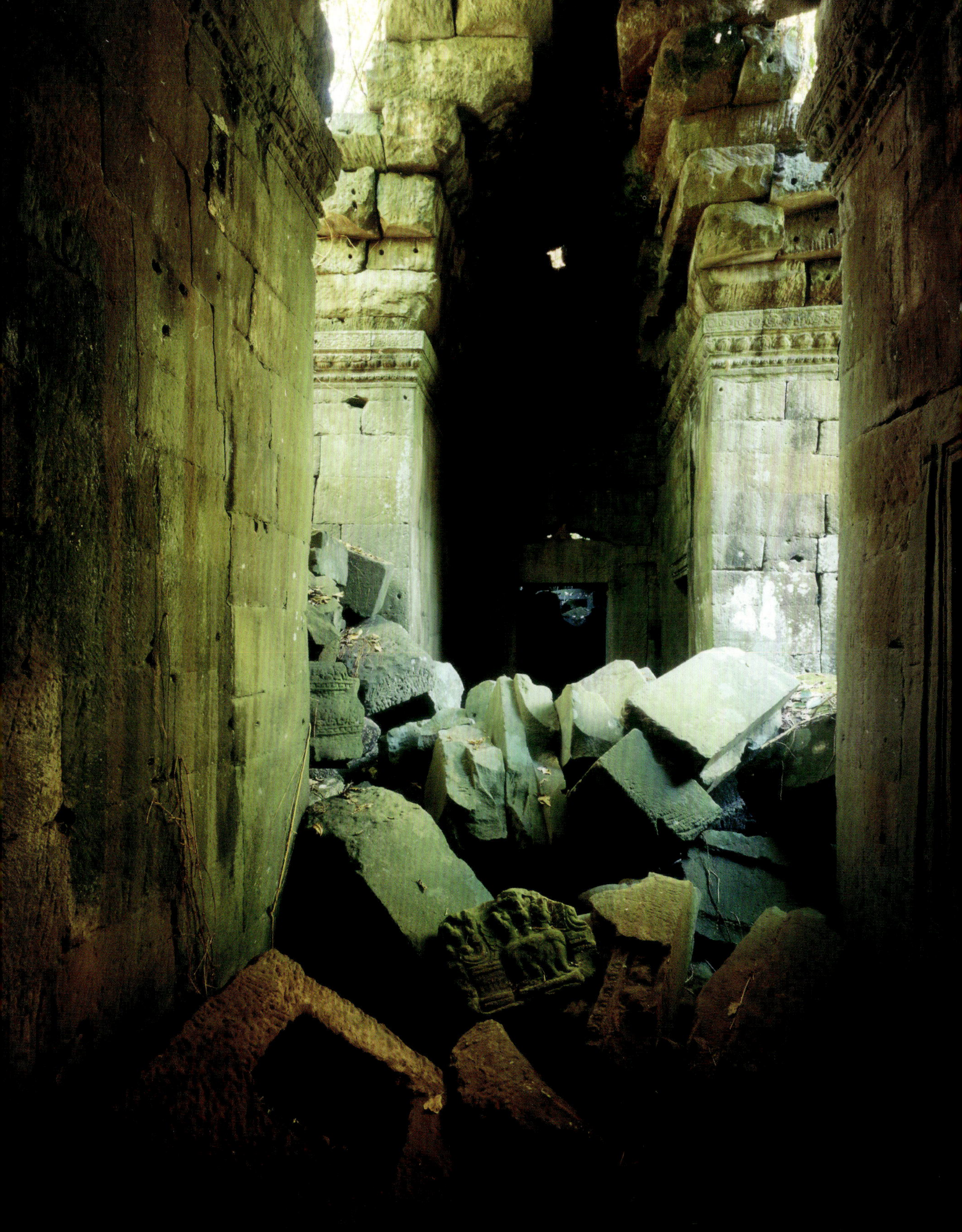

OPPONENT PAIRS

C olors directly opposite each other on the color circle are called complementary because they mix to make a neutral. This is academic for photography, but what is important is that to the eye they have a special relationship as a pair.

As opposites they reinforce each other. When they're together they each look stronger than if they were next to another color. This is easy to show: the green in the three squares (right) is the same, but looks stronger against its opposite, a purple, than against grey or a nearby color.

All the photographs on the next few pages work on this color opposition, and it's a way of being more definite about color, about pushing it forward to the viewer even when the colors themselves are subtle, as in the picture of the Indian girl at a bathing ceremony. As we saw on pages 34–5, this is the way the mind processes color, and again that's easy to show. The little experiment with successive color contrast on page 44 creates a pale after-image of opposite colors.

It's not often that a pair of colors completely fills the frame, unless you're cropping in very tightly, so what about the rest of the picture? For two opponent colors to dominate a shot, the background needs to be fairly neutral – that is, desaturated. The Sudanese woman pouring water into earthen jars is a case in point. The surroundings are brownish and whitish, and the shadows also colorless, and so they fade in visual importance in comparison with the bright blues and red. In fact, there are two blues – the blue-green of the woman's dress and the pale blue of the table, but they are close enough in hue to read as a set that's opposed to the red.

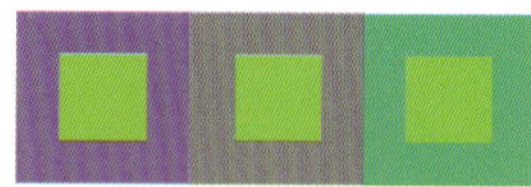

A yellowish-green square appears differently depending on its surround. Complementary light purple boosts its strength the most, more than a neutral grey and much more than a close color, blue-green.

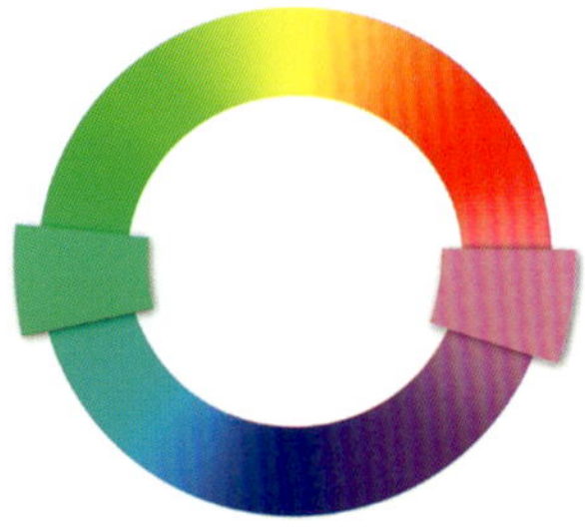

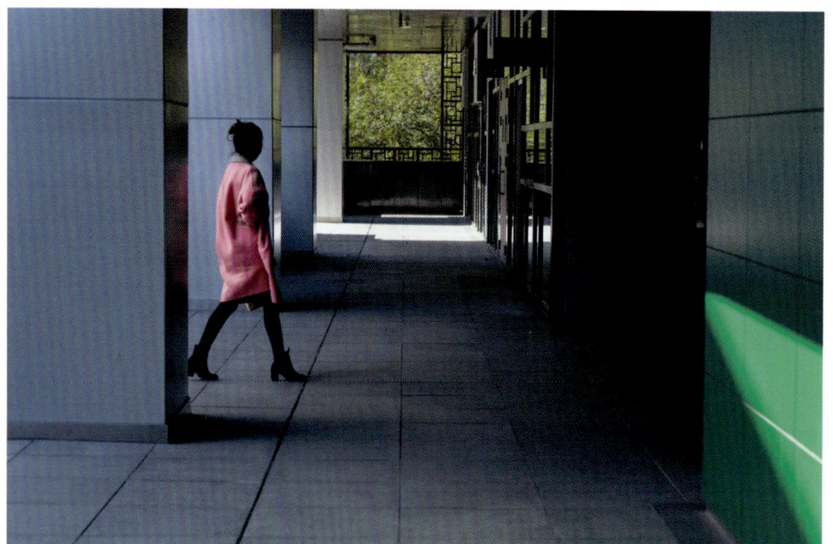

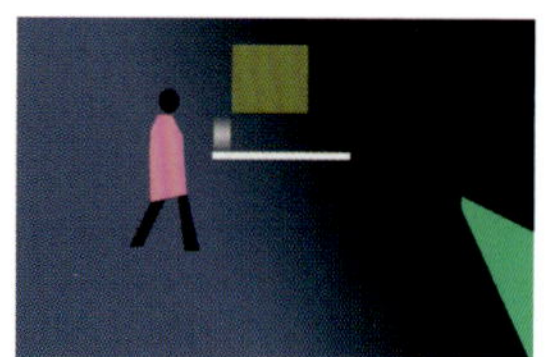

Corridor in a shopping mall. Two strong and opposing patches of color set against a dark and neutral background draw attention to themselves all the more for being small and apart.

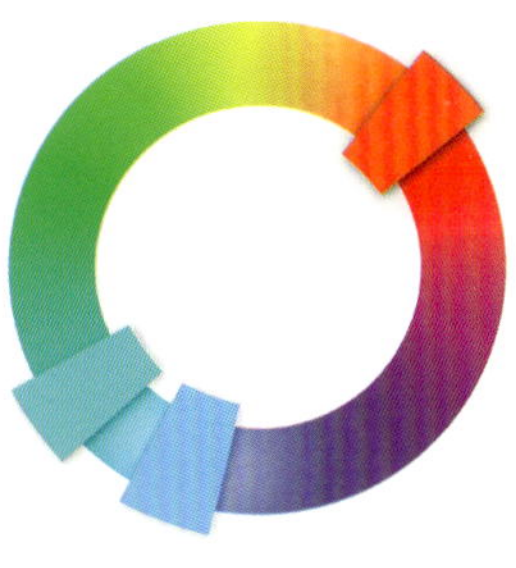

A woman fills water jars for passers-by in a village in the Nubian Desert, Sudan.

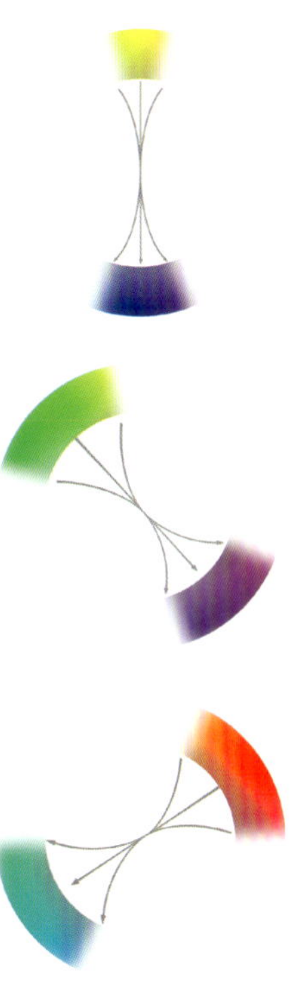

The complementaries to green, red and yellow cover a band of the circle opposite. Note that yellow has a much narrower place on the circle than the spread that most viewers would assign to green and red.

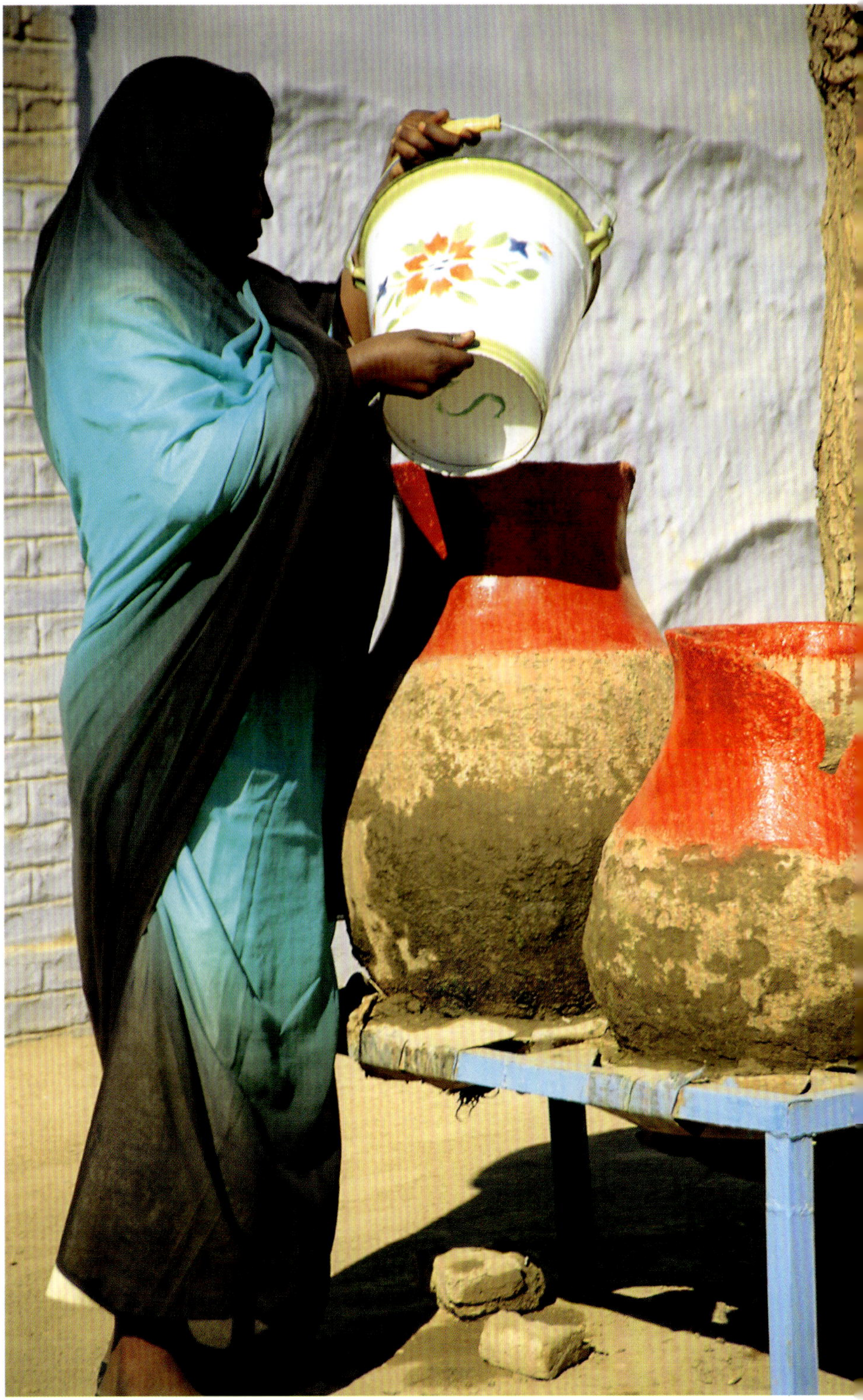

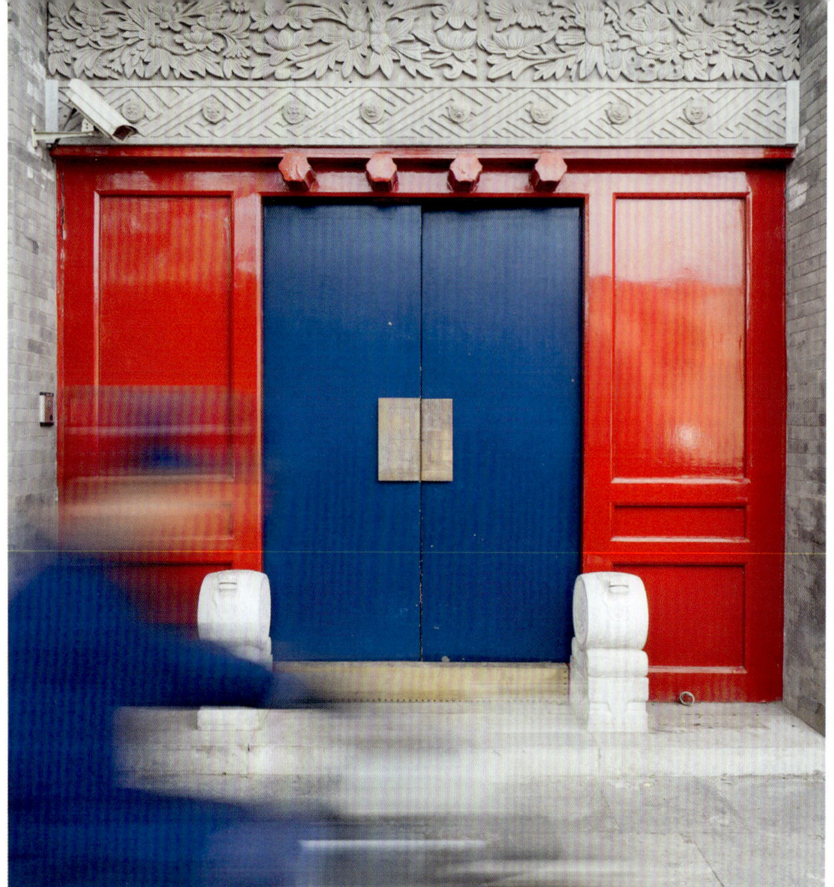

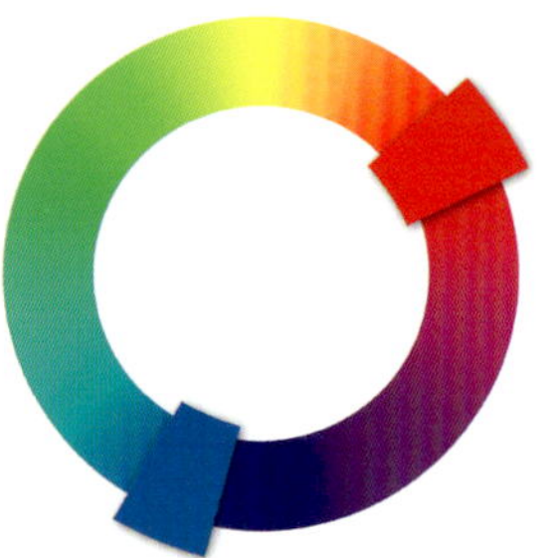

A motion-blurred cyclist passes a blue and red doorway in a Beijing *hutong* (a traditional lane neighbourhood). Despite not being complementaries, the blue and red seem approximately opposite to most people.

Under Solitary Color on page 110 we already saw how the size of a patch of color in the frame doesn't diminish its impact, provided the background conditions are right. The same applies when there are two color accents, with the added element of a pairing and a relationship. In fact, you could argue that the very isolation of two opposed and separated colors makes them stand out all the stronger, and the viewer is made all the more aware of their positions. In a picture like that of the woman in a pink coat with a splash of light on a green wall, there's much more of a sense of deliberate composition than in the larger color areas of the woman with the water jars. Processing, as we'll see in Chapter 6, can do a lot to support the effect, not by interfering with the image but simply with overall controls to keep shadows down and to keep the tonal range of the setting more even.

How accurate does this opposition across the color circle have to be? Or, to put it another way, by how much can the hues be off and still work as complementaries? The more exact, the stronger the effect, obviously, but this is photography, not painting, so the practical answer is 'more or less'. The door and blurred passing cyclist in a Beijing *hutong* is a good example, because while the blue and the red aren't exactly complementary by any means, most people read them as opposites. If the two are way off being opposite, they become tangential, as we'll see in a few pages, but for that they really do need to be almost at right angles to each other.

Strong colors like these examples make these kinds of relationships definite, and at the same time are very obviously colorful. Subtle colors with less saturation or through being darker or paler still work together in the same way. We'll see later in the book, under Style in the last chapter, that there are deep-seated differences in taste when it comes to strength of color. Strong colors are too obvious for some people, and there's arguably more pleasure to be taken from restrained colors such as those making up the photograph of a young Indian girl at a religious bathing ceremony. The saturation and tones are way down, but there is still the same basic interaction between opposites, with the browns of her skin surrounded by an area of dark blue-green. This pairing brings a surprising richness to the image without being heavy-handed about it. This, incidentally, was shot on Kodachrome, which handled darker rich tones very well.

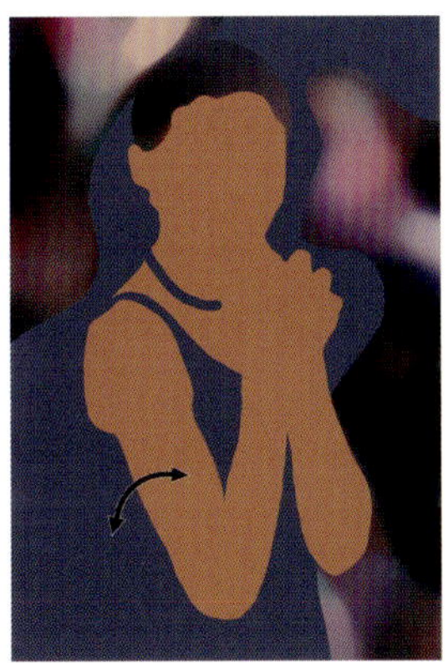

An Indian girl at a bathing ceremony to Krishna, Venupopale Swamy Temple, Karnataka. The two main groups of color – her skin and the immediate surroundings – are complementary, and even though muted, they reinforce each other for a rich effect.

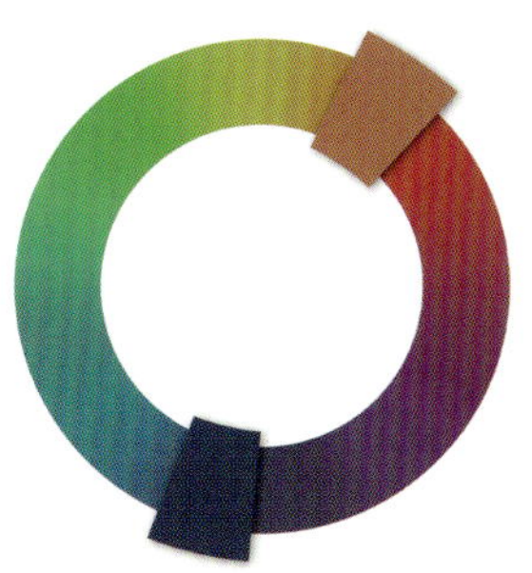

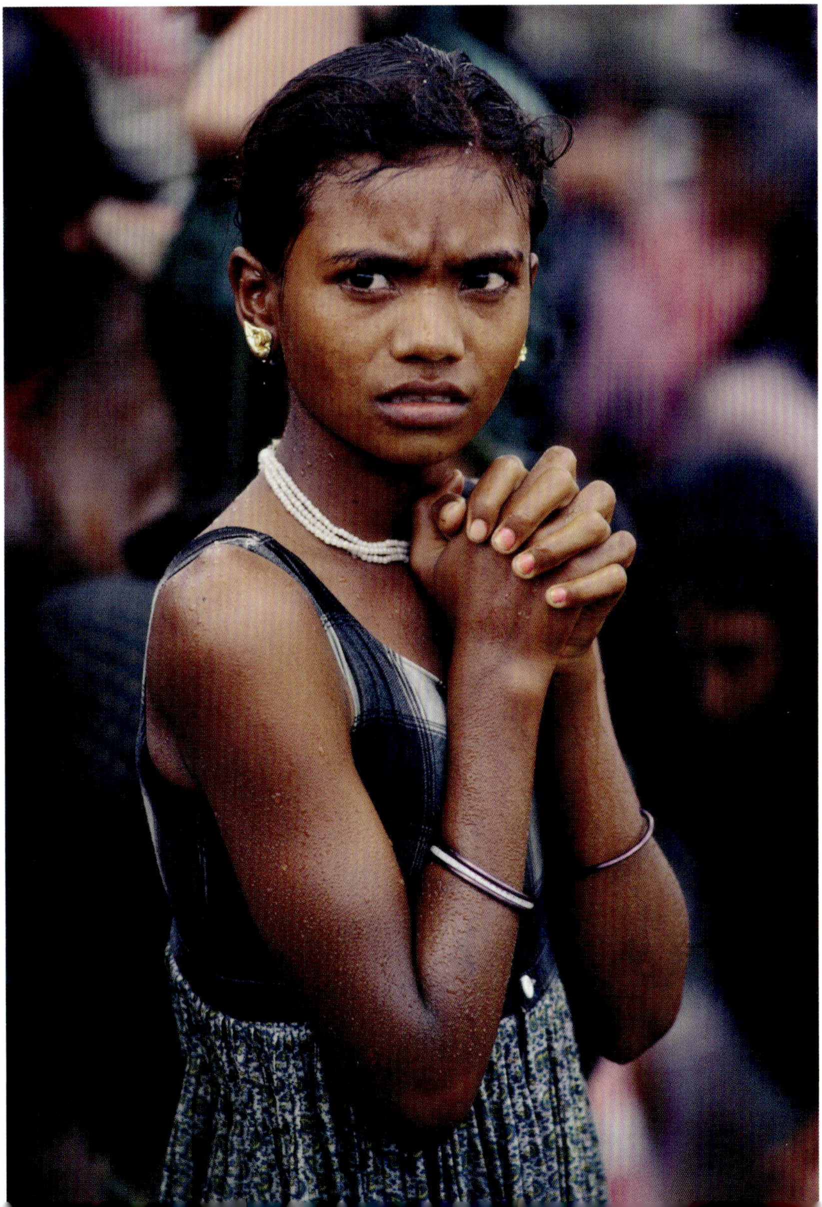

WARM-COOL OPPONENT

There's another color opposition that's both important to photography and fundamental – between warm and cool colors. The associations are obvious, with the sun and fire on the warm side, and it's reinforced by the daily cycle of light and color that humans have evolved under.

As the sun sets, its color changes towards yellow then orange, while on the opposite side of the sky blue takes over, and the same in reverse at sunrise. The end-of-day color palette is embedded in our experience, and it's also, as we saw early on, on pages 14–5, a color opposition that most people find attractive, even evocative. This color opposition was reinforced throughout human evolution in the contrast between human-made light and the darkness outside. Right until the middle of the 20th century, lamps were incandescent, meaning orange-ish, and it's interesting that today, with LED lamps available in different color temperatures, sales for domestic interiors still lean towards the warmer-looking.

These daily conditions, in clear weather at least, make up most photography that features this opposition, as in the picture below and on pages 36, 65, 80 and 148. To make the most of it, consider viewpoint and framing that balances the areas of shadow with the sunlit areas. It needs a significant area of shadow in the frame, like the shadowed side of a building or mountain, plus the shadow it casts. Shadows take the

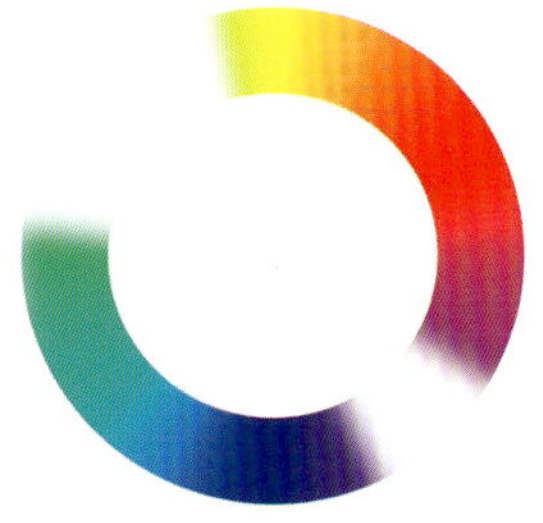

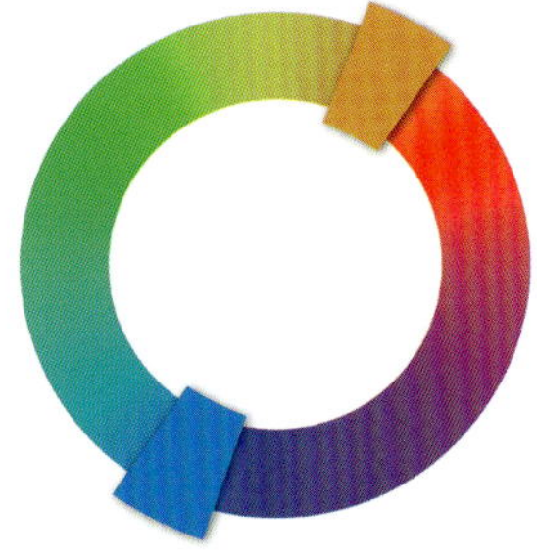

In terms of warm vs cool, the color circle divides into these two almost-halves (excluding green and purple, which are ambiguous).

A performer at a music festival on the island of La Réunion. A setting sun in a clear sky creates perfect conditions for an opposition of color temperature, between the warmth of the direct sunlight on his neck and the reflections of the blue sky in the colorless metal of the microphone.

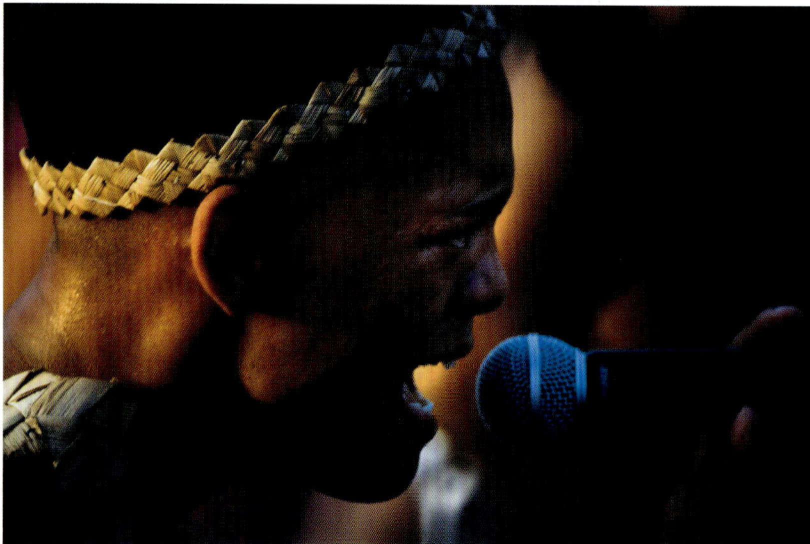

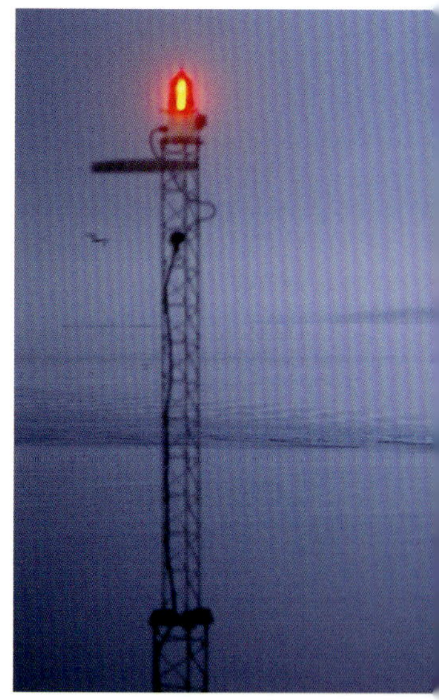

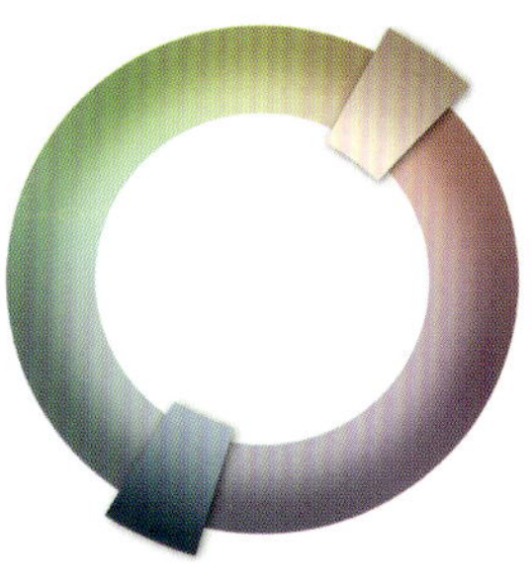

A slight haze mutes the early morning color contrast of cool shade against warm sunlight in a traditional farmyard in Mae Hong Son, northwest Thailand.

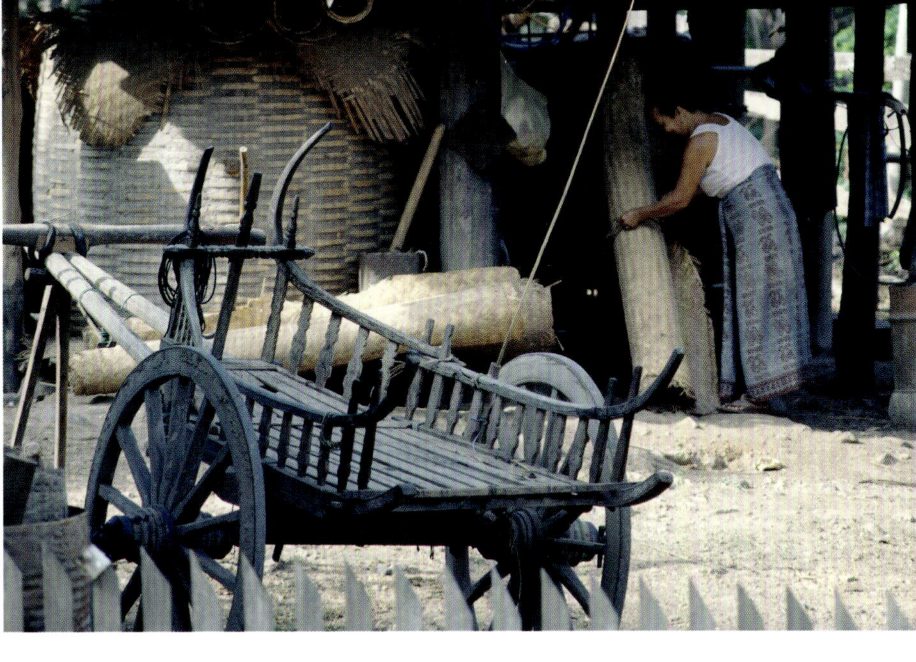

A harbour light creates an extreme version of a color accent (see also page 112), and its two colors, yellow and red, work together as a single opponent to the blue typical of pre-dawn light.

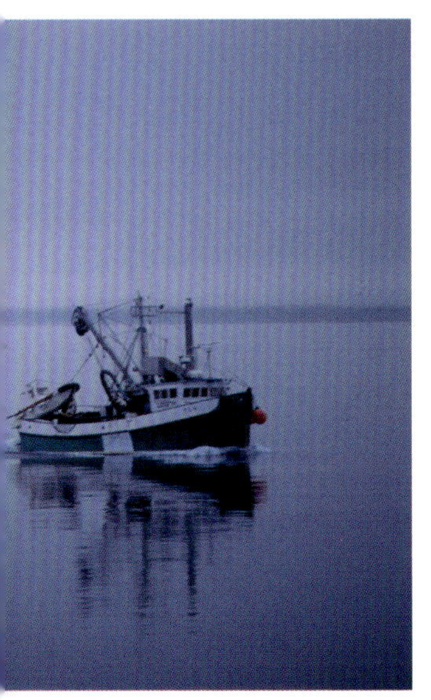

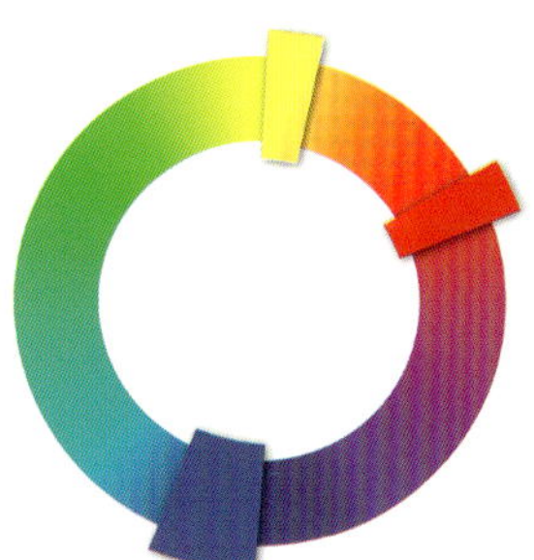

color of the sky opposite the sun – that is, blue in these conditions. Caution here: if you use Auto White Balance, when shooting, it's likely that this will render shadows neutral, whereas they should be bluish. Processing becomes important.

The exact time of day also makes a difference, because as the sunlight fades in intensity, the two light sources on opposite sides of the horizon become more equal, and so the color opposition more marked. Here's where the air quality matters. The lower the sun is, the more atmosphere its light travels through, and even a light haze weakens its color. The most intense warm-cool opposition happens in very clear air (such as desert or high altitude), and when shooting with the two color sources, sunward and blue sky, on either side of the frame – or angled a little towards the sunset/sunrise.

That's the approximate formula for maximizing this color contrast, but as with other color relationships, they can be just as interesting, maybe even more so, when less saturated. Then, as in the shot of a Shan woman with an ox cart, the color opposition has its satisfying effect without being obvious. Compare this with the picture on the previous pages of an Indian girl at a bathing ceremony.

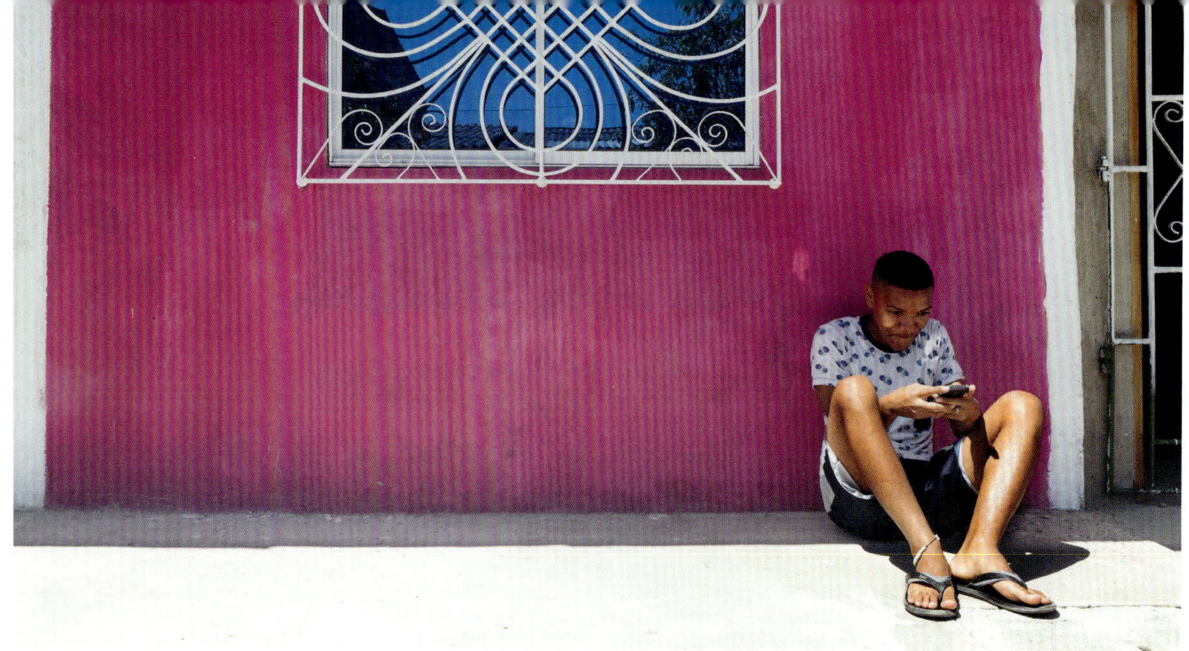

TANGENTIAL PAIRS

There's a strangely neglected pairing of colors that you'll be hard put to find mention of anywhere. The widespread obsession with color harmony focuses so much on complementary and adjacent colors that the in-between relationships are either ignored or condemned as being dissonant.

In other words, starting with any single color, take away the adjacent colors and also the complementary color opposite, and you're left with... what exactly? A choice of two colors, one on either side, that are clearly very different yet not complementary. As there's no standard name for this relationship, I'm calling them tangential pairs, and of course they exist everywhere, so they are very much material for colorist photography. First, it's necessary to get rid of the illusion that only complementary and adjacent pairings 'work' properly. The surge in the number of websites and software aimed at helping designers and others to choose colors is at least partly responsible for this, because they offer the same formulaic advice. At least one site calls the in-between area of the color circle that we're showing here the 'danger zone'. All of this is about as useful as such old sayings as 'blue and green should never be seen' and, in composition, the rule of thirds. Thoughtless formulae, in other words, even for designers who can choose colors, while we photographers in any case take what we can find from the scenes in front of us.

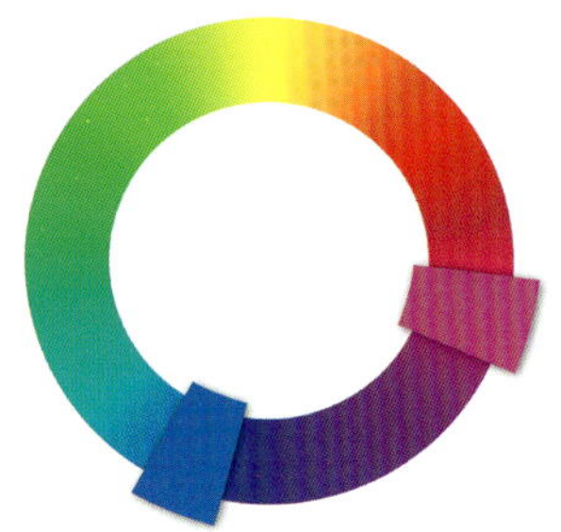

A brightly painted house front in a South American city barrio contrasts with the blue sky reflected in the window. As the color circle shows, they are about 90 degrees apart from each other, typical of tangential color pairs.

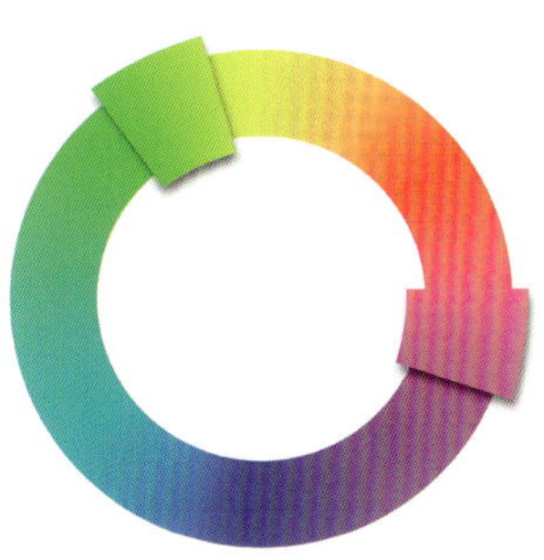

A Kerala Kathakali dancer donning costume before a performance. Green and pink are the two dominant colors (the only other strong colors – yellow and red – are too small to have much impact), and being a similar size and separated in the frame have an immediate relationship. It helps that they have the same saturation, around 50 percent.

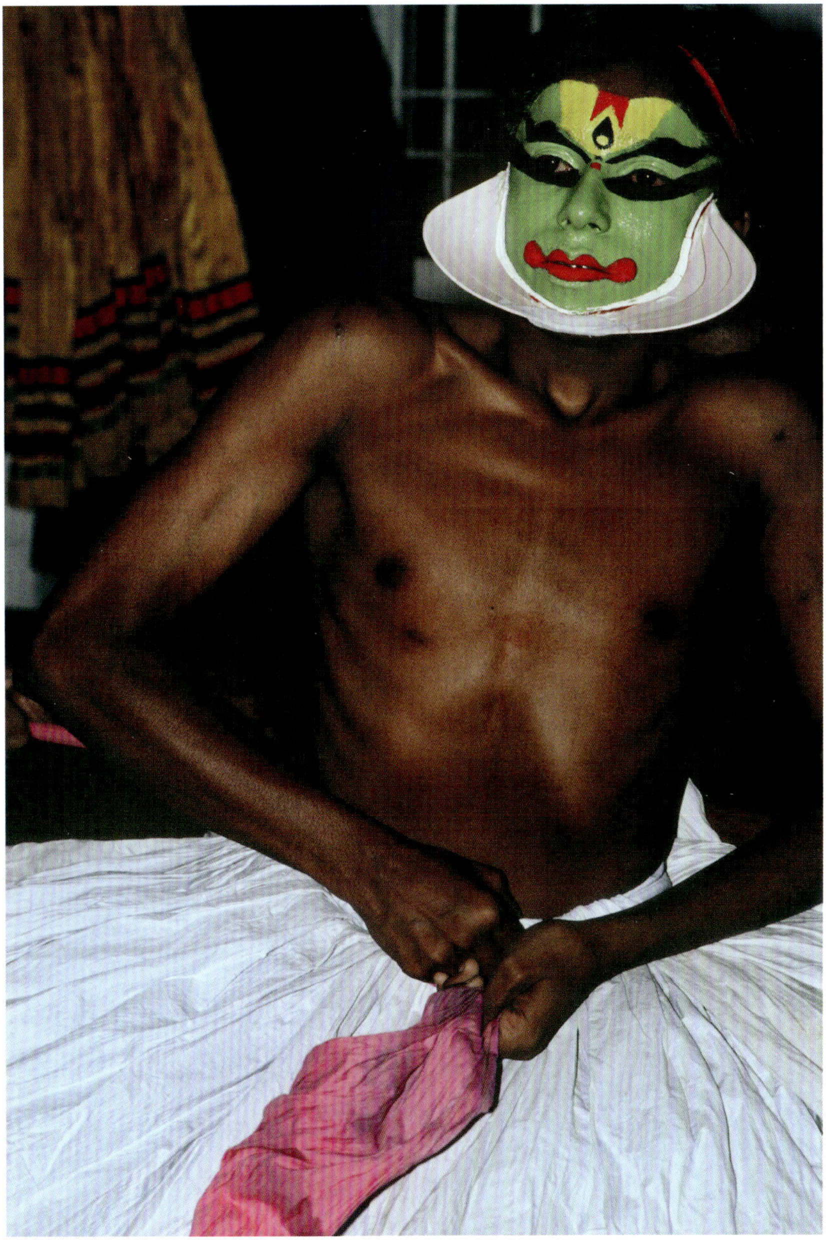

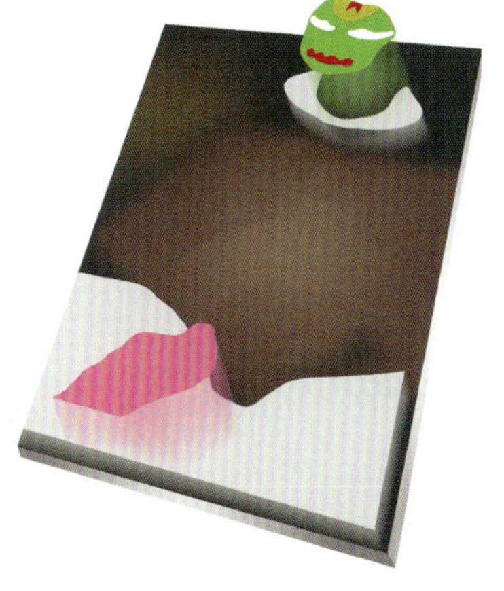

The case for searching out and experimenting with this kind of pairing (or just enjoying the combination without thinking about it) is that it's perhaps less predictable and might be more interesting. These off-axis pairings have the contrast of complementaries but without the exactness. In neither of these examples was I thinking at all about where the colors were on the color circle – who would? – but I certainly was attracted to the slightly unusual tension between the colors.

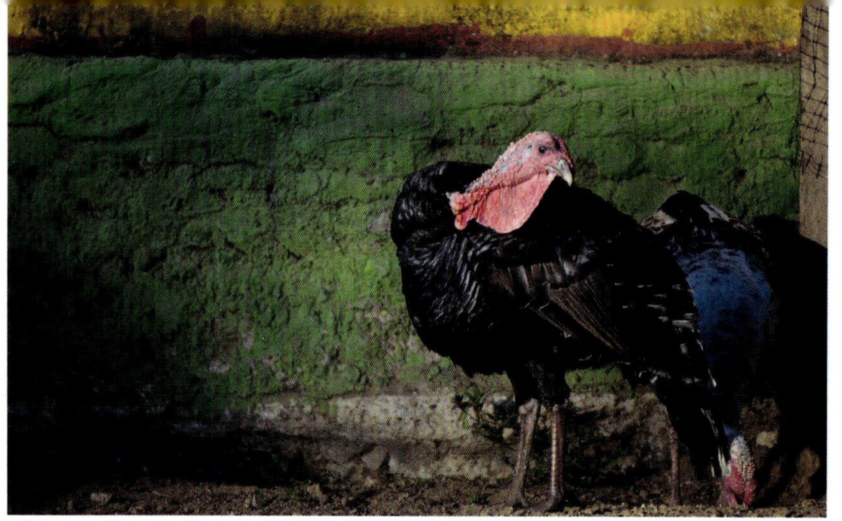

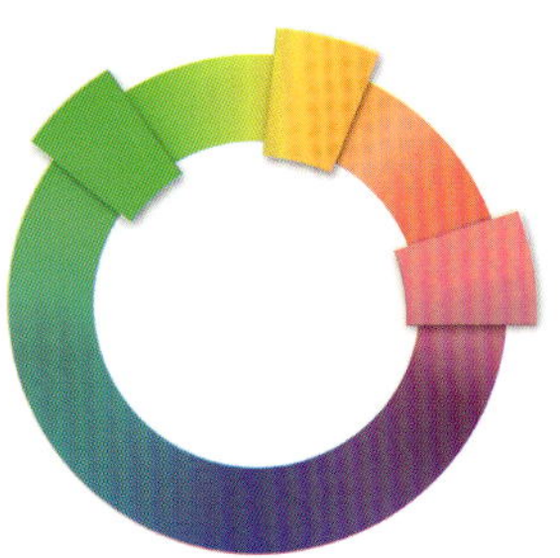

TRIAD

Introducing a third color changes the dynamic from a face-off between two colors to a kind of triangular idea, and as you can see in *Michael Freeman on... Composition*, triangles are a basic and generally satisfying structure.

This doesn't mean that there's any pressure to find an actual triangular arrangement of three shapes, although if you do manage to make this work compositionally, as in the picture below, it certainly reinforces the idea. Plotted on the color circle, however, for three colors to function independently and not seem similar to each other, they naturally tend to be well spaced from each other. This means that

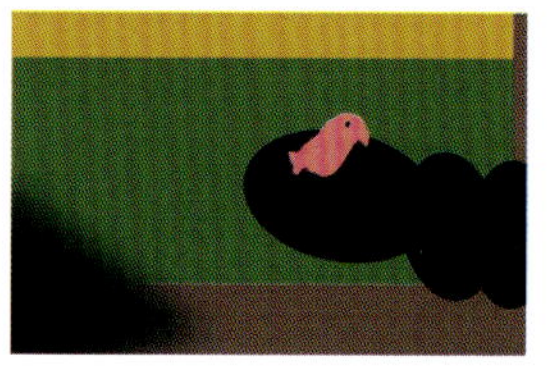

The pink wattle of a turkey catches the eye first because of its brightness and saturation, but the color interest comes from its relationship with the yellow and green of the wall, with the black serving as a neutral anchor (which also helps the pink to pop out).

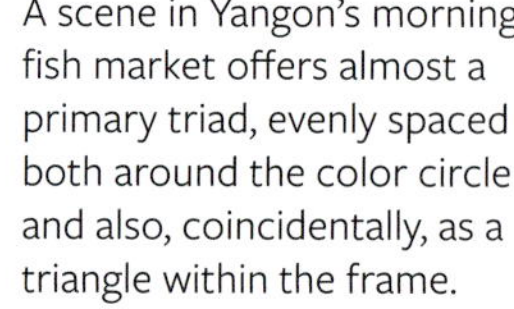

A scene in Yangon's morning fish market offers almost a primary triad, evenly spaced both around the color circle and also, coincidentally, as a triangle within the frame.

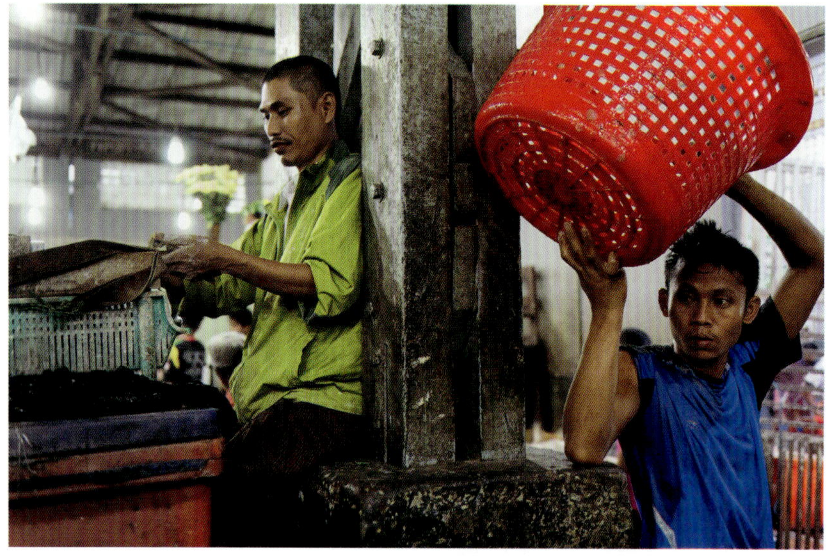

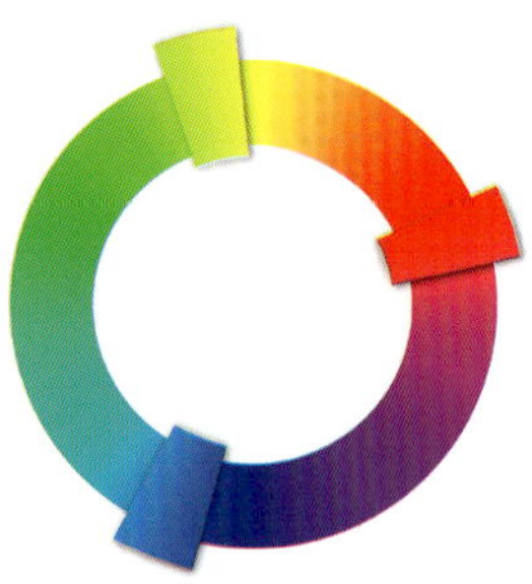

there's less opportunity for strong opposition, because if evenly spaced they would each be a third of the way around the circle, but what's gained is a more colorful composition in terms of number. If two of the colors are close to each other, they begin to act together in opposition to the third color, as is happening to an extent in the photograph of the Peruvian woman crossing Cuzco Plaza, although differences in brightness keep the purple and pale blue distinct.

As with all the pairings and multicolor combinations in this chapter, how you place them in the space of the frame adds an extra dimension to the color relationships. In the picture on the left, the brightest color (the pink of the turkey's head and wattle) is used like a color accent, on top of the rectangular arrangement of the green and yellow. The still life of a cocktail was an arranged shot, and there was time to adjust the glass and the camera so that the three colors are separated, with the very pale gold enclosed by the lines of pink and blue. The scene in a Burmese market mirrors the way the yellow, red and blue are on the color circle – in a spatial triangle.

The triad of a Peruvian woman's dress in Cuzco is a major component of this street shot (below).

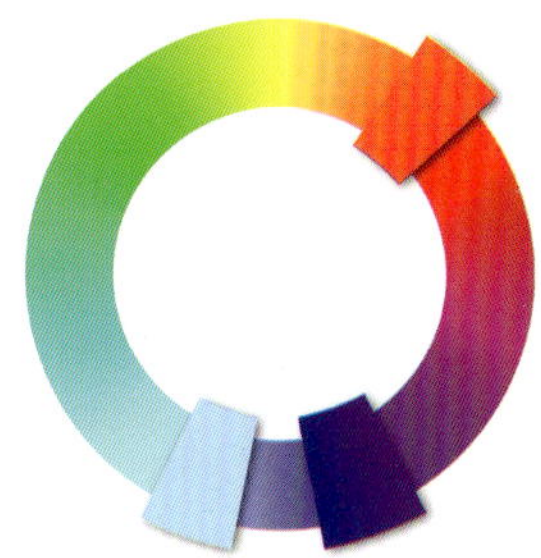

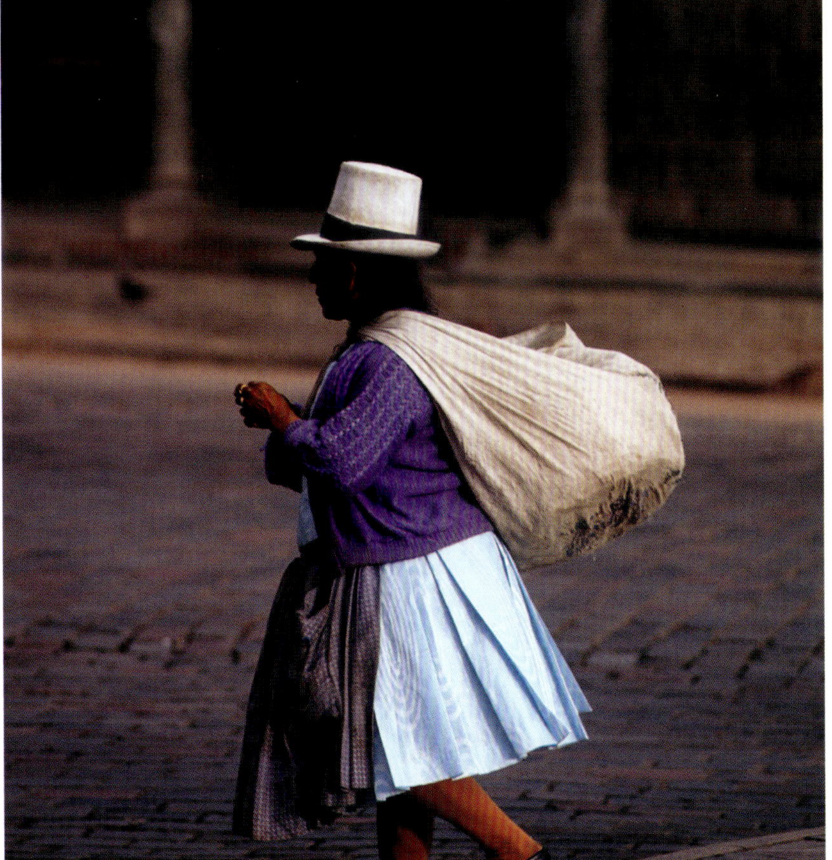

A cocktail shot makes deliberate use of reflections to set up a triad that makes the gold distinctive. Separating the colors focuses attention on the drink.

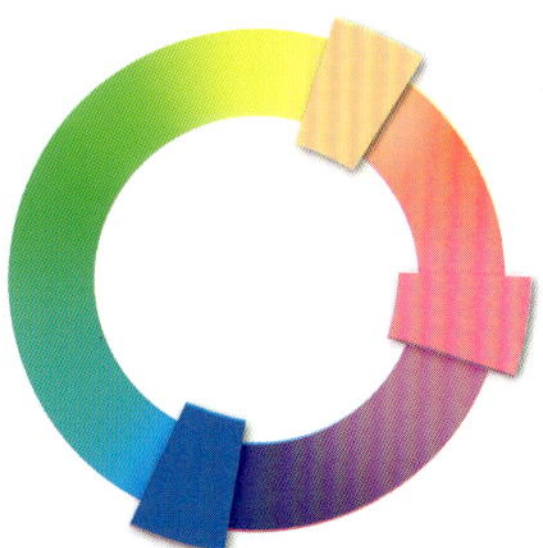

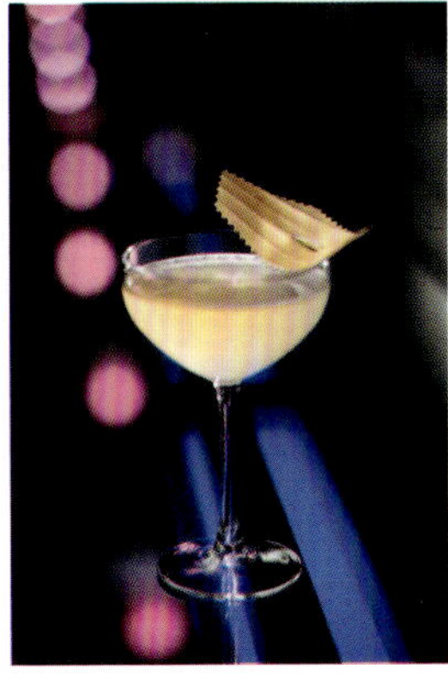

TETRAD

M oving up from three to four, a tetrad of colors is probably the highest number that still reads as distinct hues, and even then often comes across as simply 'several'. As with triads and the following poly color, more individual colors are naturally closer to each other on the color circle, and so less easy to discriminate.

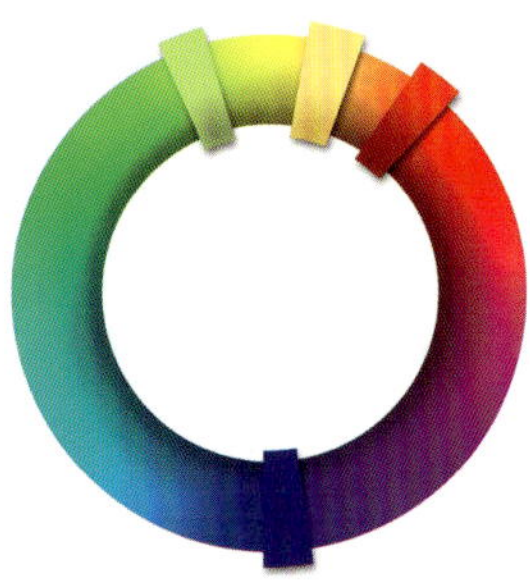

One of the basic questions with color used compositionally is how many colors actually count as individual, and with a tetrad it's usually less obvious. The reason is that there are more decisions to make in deciding what counts as the more-or-less neutral background. In choosing the colors that count, we automatically have to discount the rest. What always helps, and for a tetrad is probably necessary, is more saturation or brightness, or both. Separation between the colors is even tighter than for a triad – if they were evenly spaced it would be just a quarter of the circle between each – and there are more possibilities for a kind of grouping. This happens in the interior shot of a strikingly colored living room over the page, and while I'm showing the two pairs of colors on the color circle, it's perfectly obvious at a glance that the blue and the purple are related and act in opposition to the red and golden yellow.

As always, you have to decide which count as active colors and which to discount as either non-active neutrals or too small to register. It's straightforward in the case of the women in a Comoros market – shadows and the white shawl are neutrals – while in the vivid interior I'm discounting details that are either dark or pale. The Indian yoghurt dish is less obvious. Would you say there are three or four colors here? The questionable one is the green of the leaves. It's quite a bit duller than the yellow, blue and red, and in my judgement doesn't really count, making this a triad. You might disagree, and in any case it would be easy enough if you wanted to brighten up the green during processing. All of these color relationships are open to adjustment.

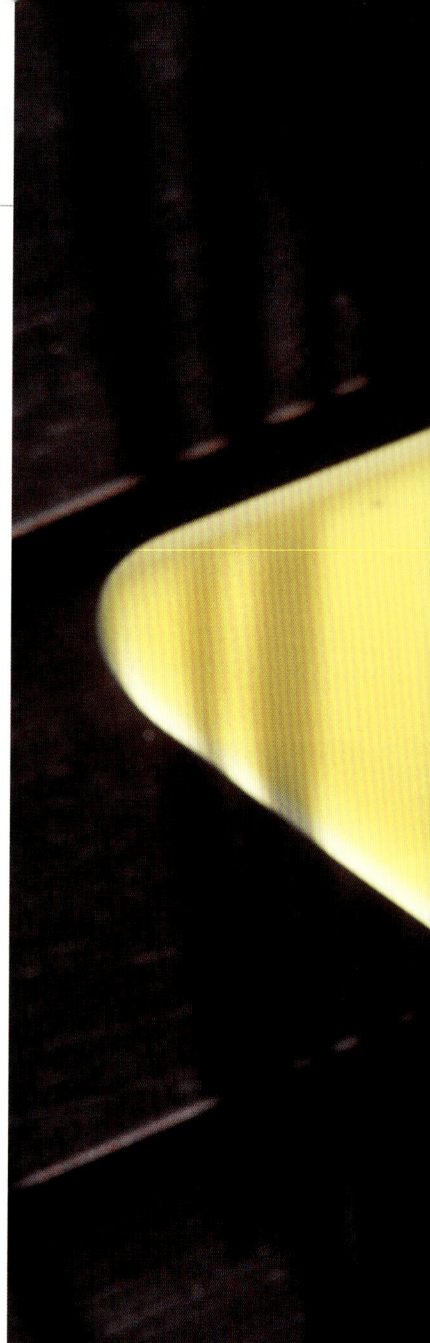

While yellow dominates because of the area it covers and its brightness, followed by the red chilli because of its saturation and central position, the blue and green turn this into a distinct four-color combination.

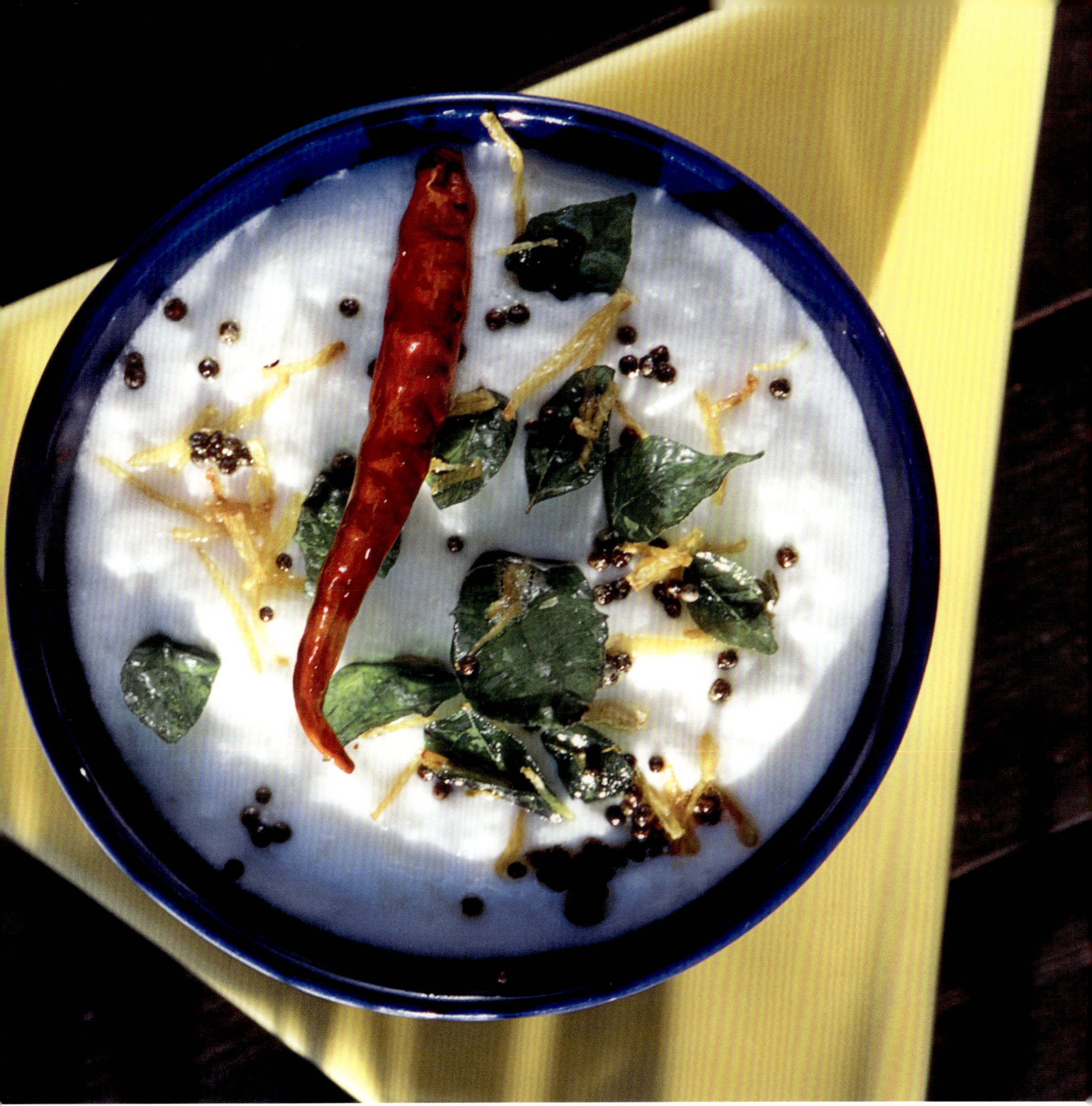

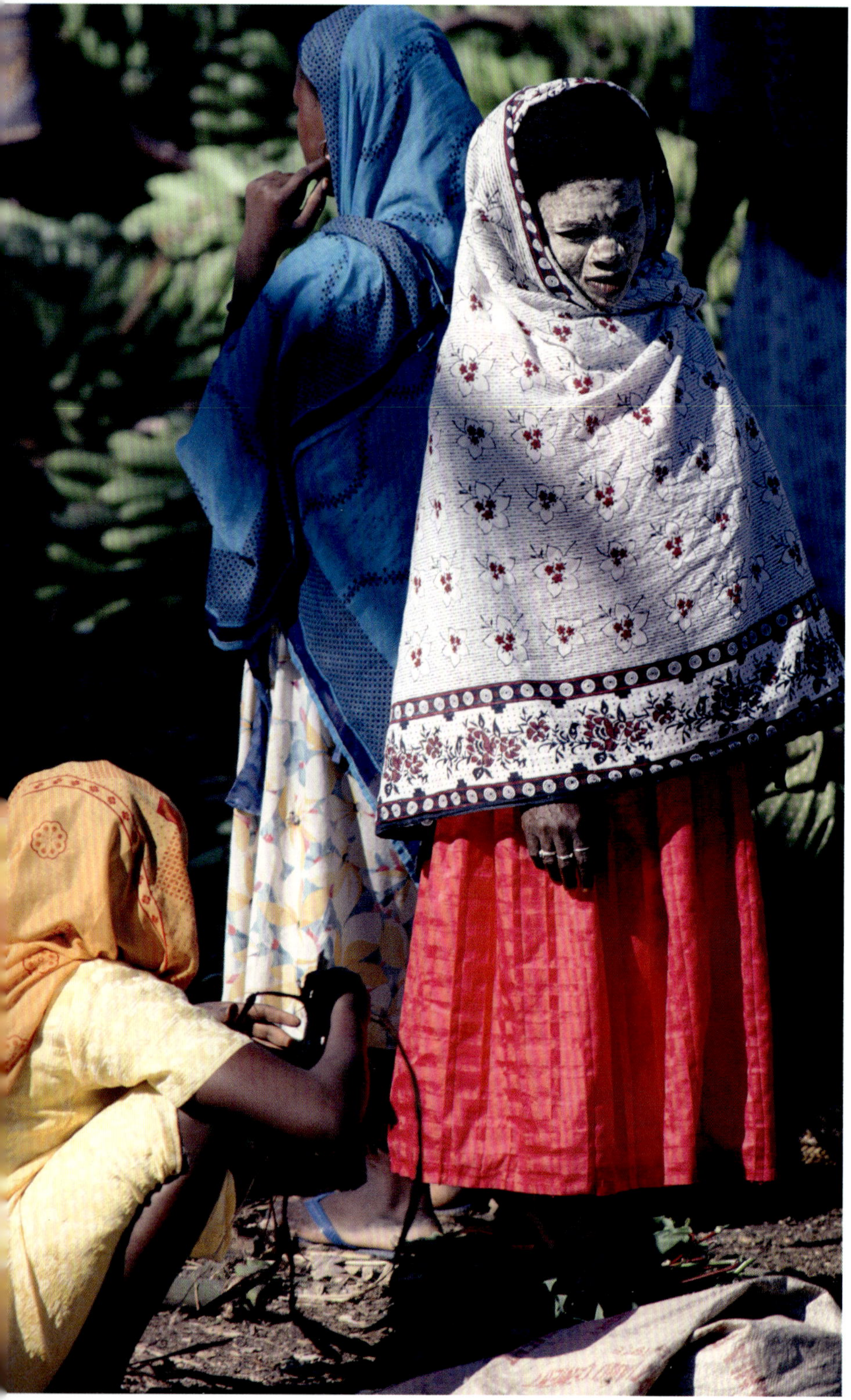

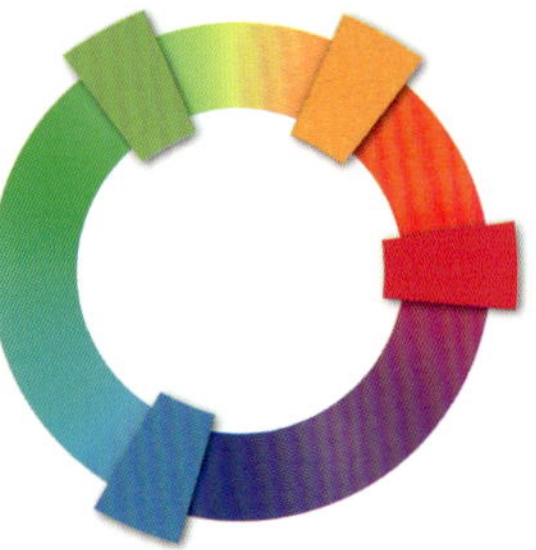

In a market on the Indian Ocean island of Grande Comore, large background piles of plantains turn the blue, red and yellow of the women's dresses (the white is neutral) into a primary-color triad. Clear separation of four colors around the circle is what makes tetrads work – and also makes them unusual.

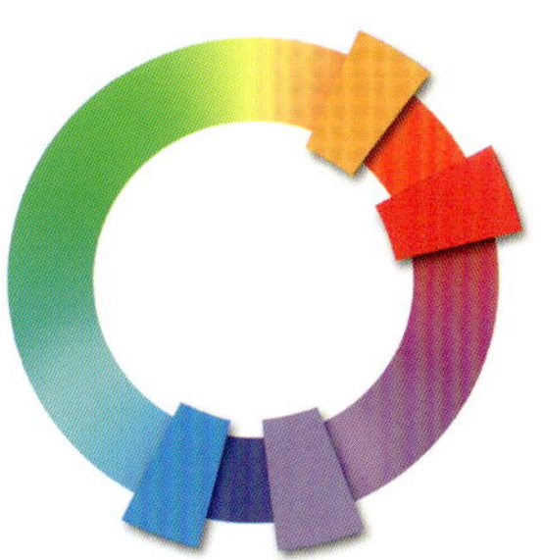

A different style of tetrad from the exuberant style of the interior designer of this Hong Kong interior, with the four colors arranged as two pairs. What we consider to be distinct colors depends partly on which sectors of the circle they are in.

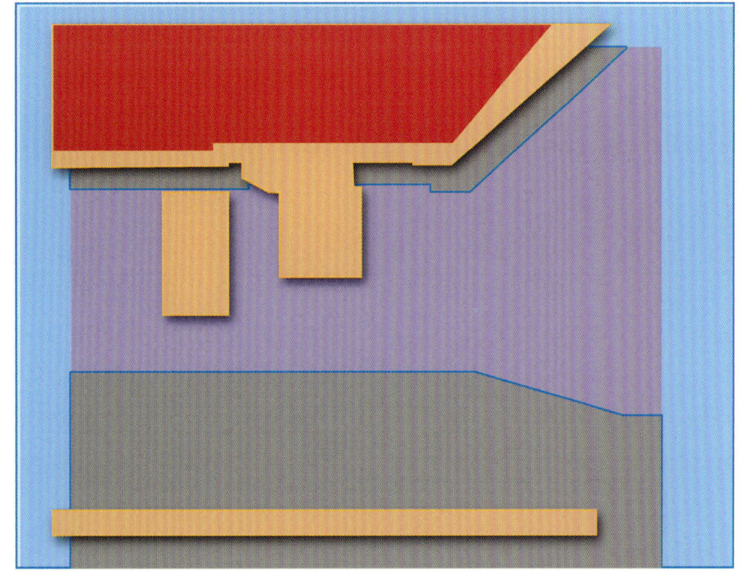

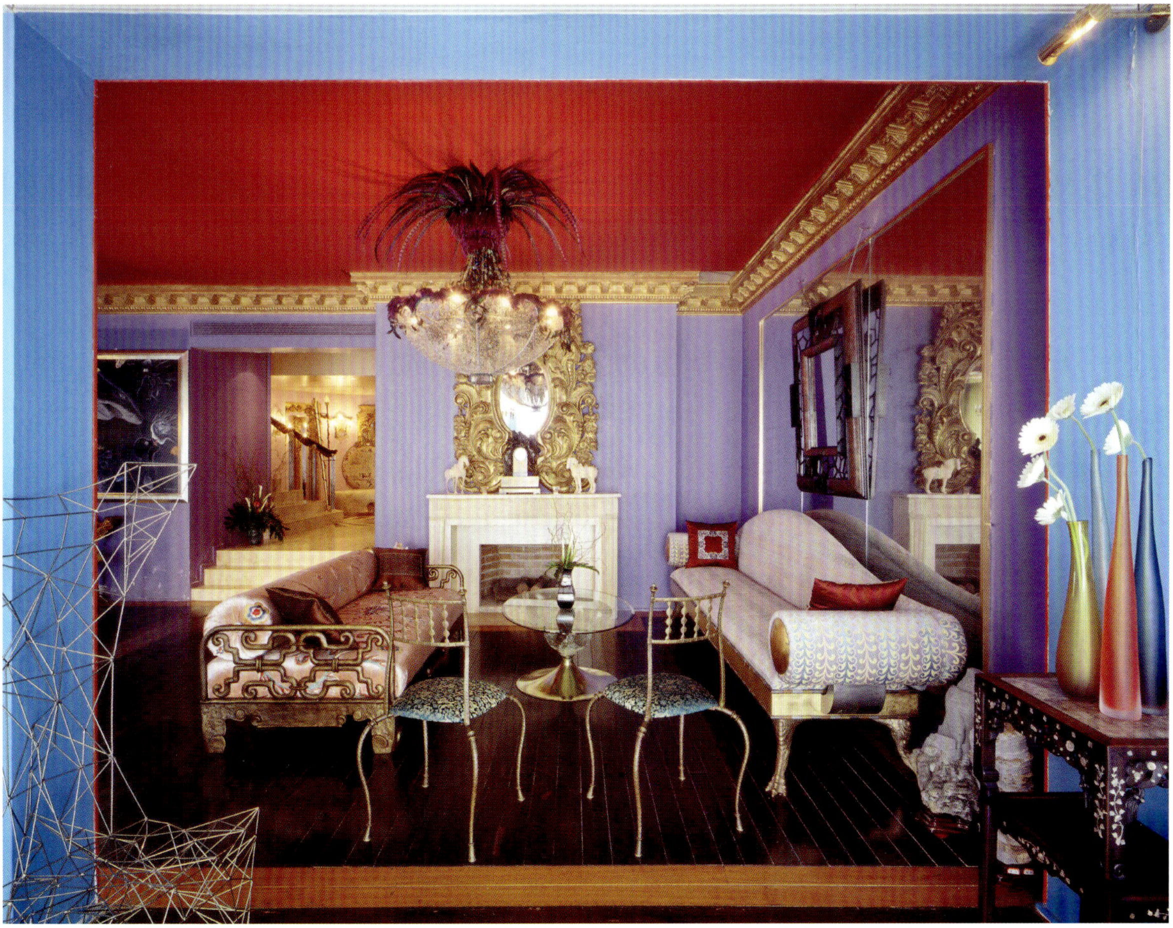

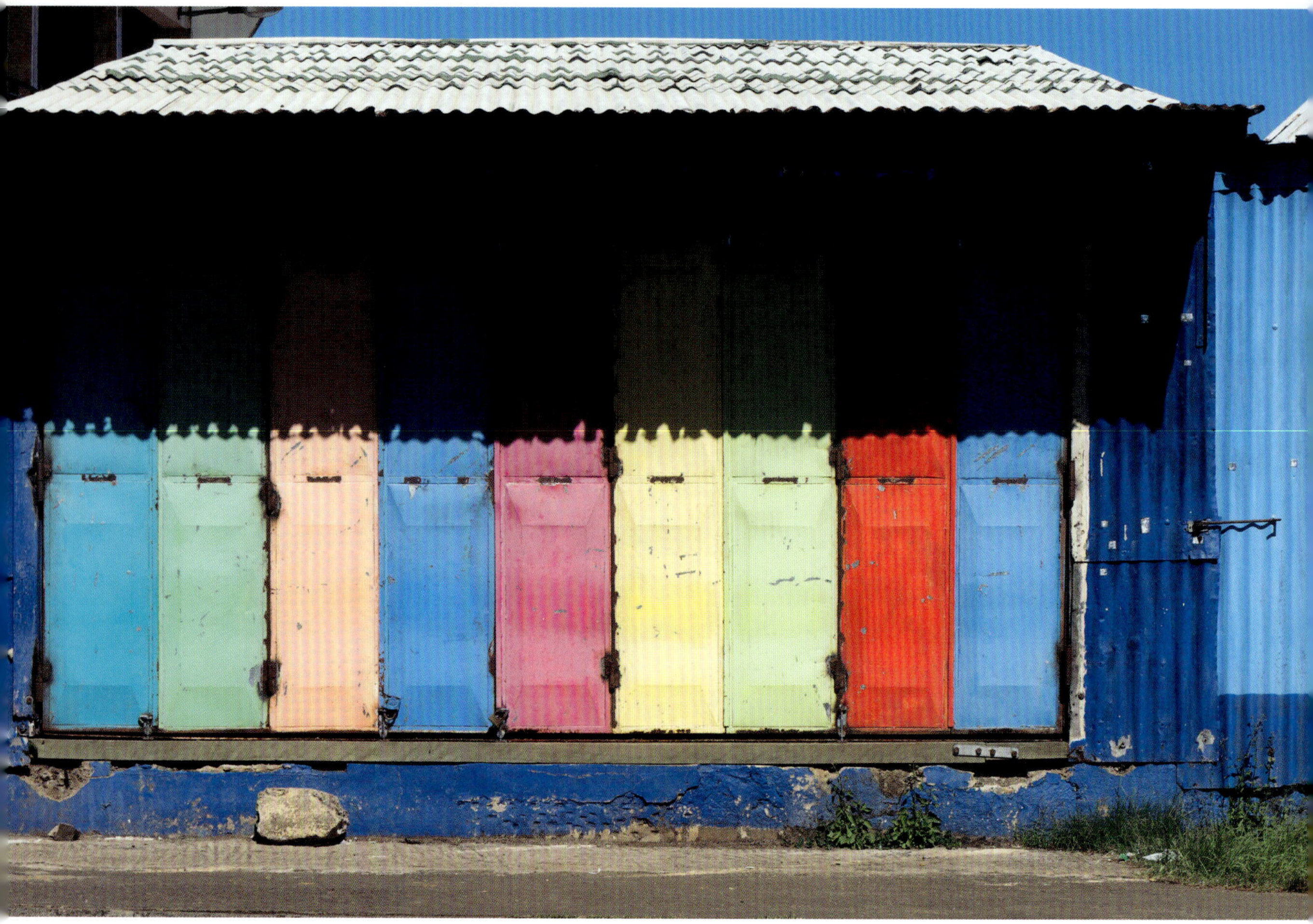

POLY COLOR

The more colors that you add to a scene (often simply a matter of framing to include more), the less clear the relationships they have. This isn't a drawback, but they do become something else, in the same way that a crowd of people seems fundamentally different from a few, and from a couple.

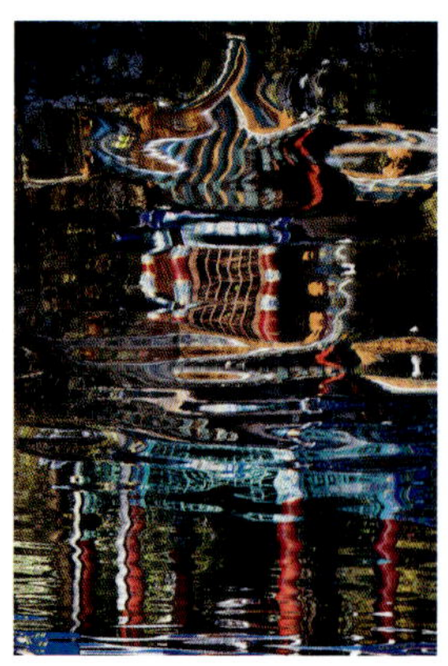

A polychrome photograph has several-to-many small patches of color, all different, and that means scattered all around the color circle. It's undeniably going to be colorful, but in a very particular way. The hues are varied, but by definition none of

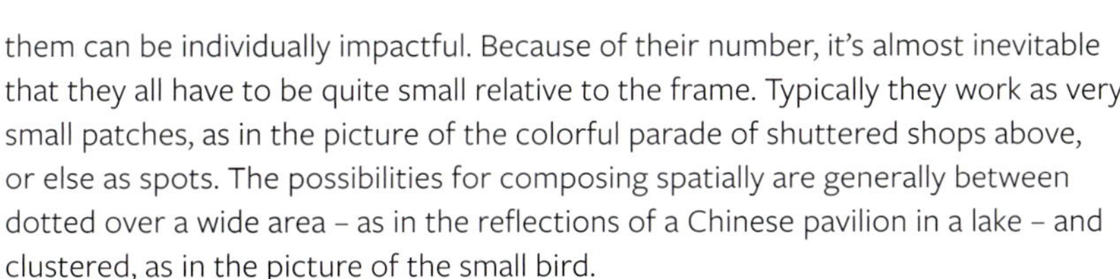

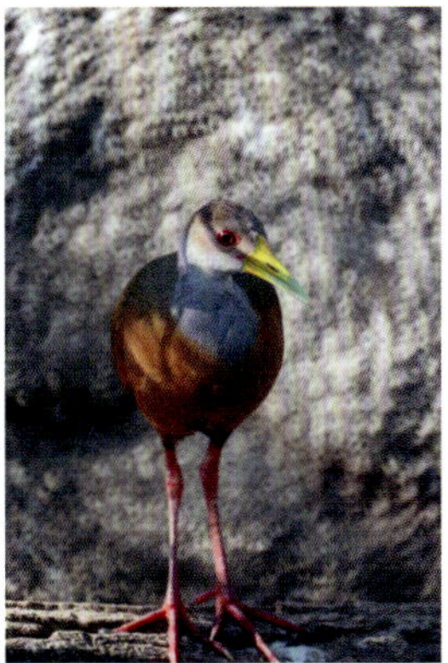

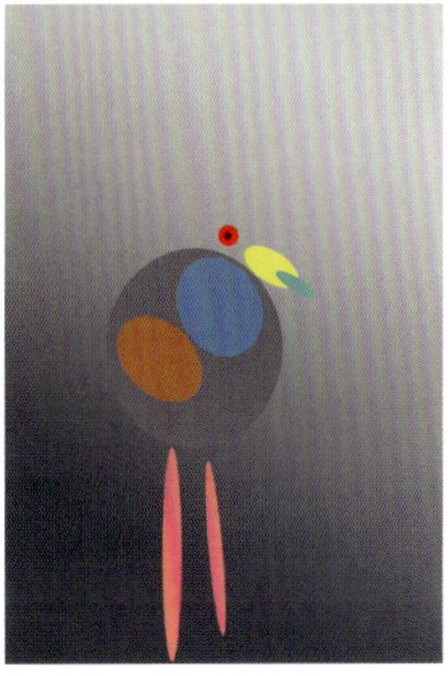

them can be individually impactful. Because of their number, it's almost inevitable that they all have to be quite small relative to the frame. Typically they work as very small patches, as in the picture of the colorful parade of shuttered shops above, or else as spots. The possibilities for composing spatially are generally between dotted over a wide area – as in the reflections of a Chinese pavilion in a lake – and clustered, as in the picture of the small bird.

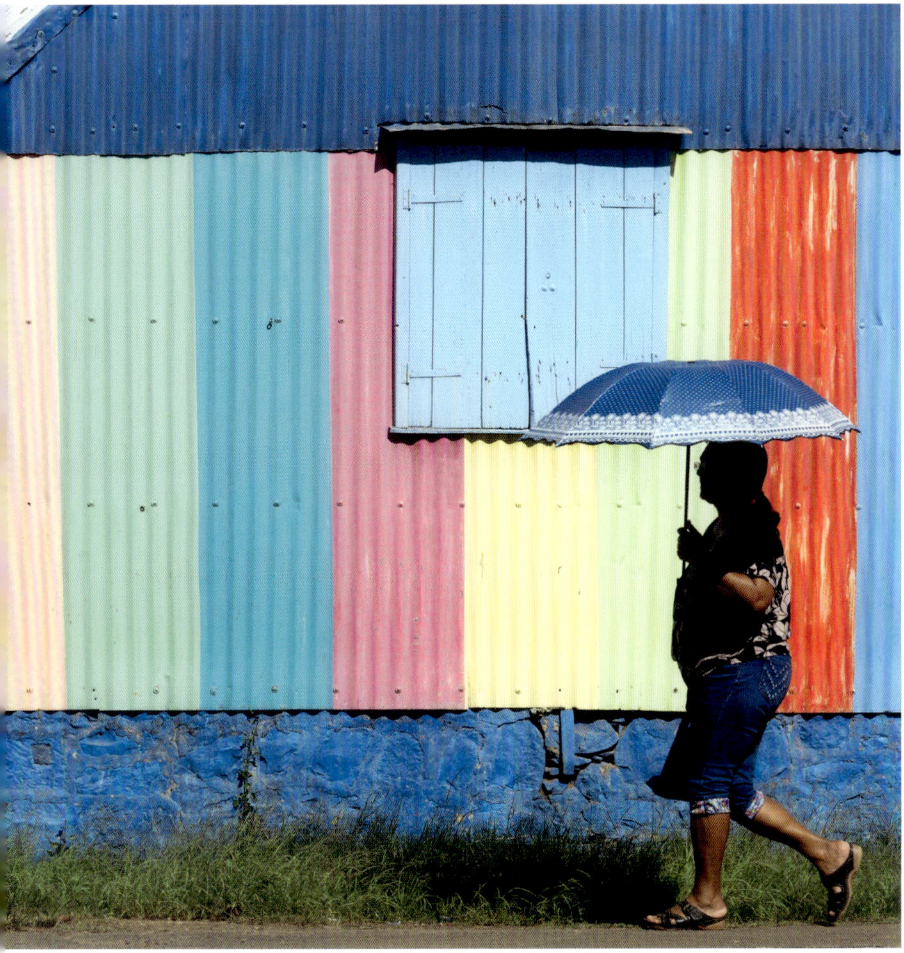

Again because of the necessary small size of the color elements, polychrome demands brighter and more saturated hues than even tetrads and triads in order to be effective. Concentrations of these are not especially common, the two main sources for shooting being some city streets, especially with signage, and some wildlife, and both are included in the examples here. Coincidentally, the small street where I live is a kind of polychrome (see page 67), with every house painted a different color, which makes it a popular setting for Instagram tourists.

Set against a background of grey stone, the colors of a wood rail are a well-separated arrangement of two muted and four saturated colors.

Street stalls on the island of Rodrigues in the Indian Ocean, shuttered for Sunday, provide an extreme example of a polychrome photograph.

Ripples in Green Lake in the heart of the Chinese city of Kunming rearrange the colors of an already brightly painted pavilion into a shimmering pattern.

DEFOCUS BLENDING

One useful way of moving a scene – or parts of it – to the realm of pure color is to defocus it. Blur is an essential component of selective focus, at its most effective with a very wide aperture and a longer focal length, and most people are familiar with the way that a defocused background helps concentrate attention on a small, sharply focused subject. Perhaps a little less familiar is the technique of blending colors in this way.

This is an optical effect, and works only with particular lenses and ways of using them. It doesn't work at all with traditional straightforward shooting in the sense of a wide-to-normal focal length, mid-range aperture and general scenes. Selective-focus shooting needs the maximum possible contrast between what's in focus and what's out. Four things contribute: a longer focal length lens, a very wide aperture such as *f*/1.4, a larger sensor or film, and a considerable distance between the focused subject and the background. (It could also be between the focused subject and foreground, but this is less easy to pull off successfully). Fast longer lenses are expensive, as are large-sensor cameras, so there's a cost factor involved.

A still life of a dessert combining purples and violets, placed against a defocused background of complementary green in a patisserie. A lens of 85mm at *f*/1.4 gave the blurring.

Foreground color wash from a 500mm mirror lens contrasts with the pink skin of the man's head.

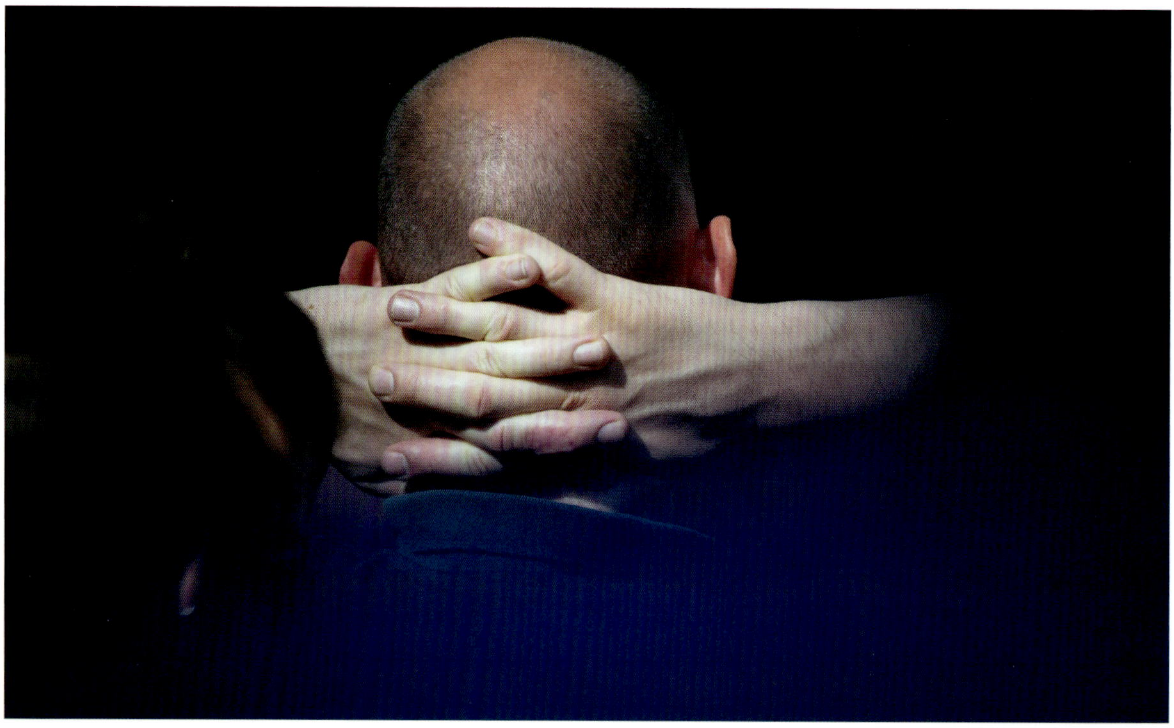

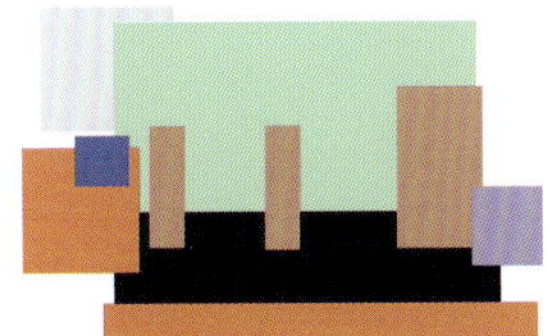

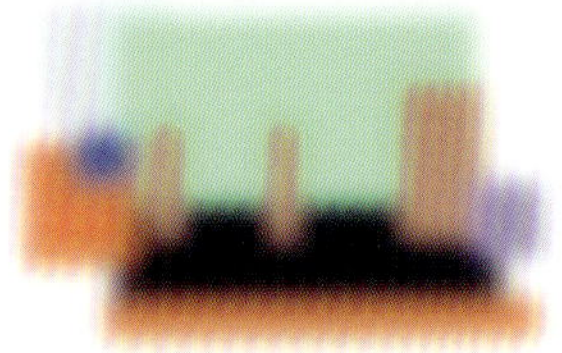

A telephoto lens at full aperture (400mm at *f*/2.8) typically smears background colors when they are at a sufficient distance, here in a park in Kunming into an attractive wash of yellows and greens.

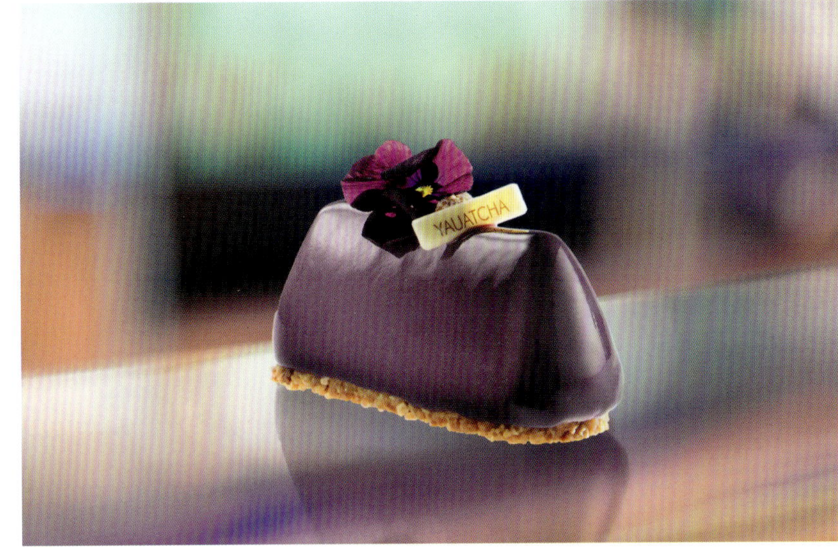

The quality of blur matters, and this often gets overlooked in the common obsession over sharpness. To read most opinions – and promotion – about lenses, you'd be forgiven for thinking that the sole purpose of a lens was to get things exquisitely sharp. In reality, there's a limit to how much sharpness we can perceive, and like the amount of detail in an image, it depends heavily on the size of the image as we view it. For the vast majority of photographs as they're displayed, that limit has long been passed. Also, most close-up photographs have more of their image area blurred than sharp because depth of field is limited at these distances.

Lens manufacturers generally make less of this, but at the top end a lot of effort goes into balancing sharp focus with smooth blur. There's a conflict between the two because of spherical aberration. In lens design, the more this is corrected, the better the sharpness – but the worse the blur looks. Spherical under-correction gives a more pleasing blur and a smoother blending of colors. You can't have both, and so lens designs vary.

In practice, blending background colors means defocusing to the point where not only are the colored objects totally unrecognizable, but they merge pleasantly. That's entirely a matter of judgement, but less blur tends to separate them while extreme blur loses the area of change from one to the other.

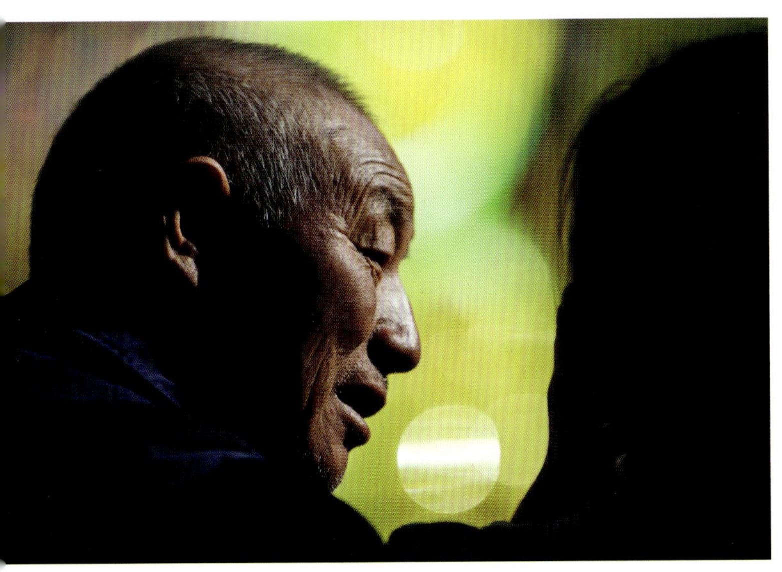

PROCESS & GRADING

6

Shooting Raw files has the overwhelming advantage that you preserve the maximum image data, which is why all serious photographers do it. This inevitably makes processing an essential part of photography, and software such as Lightroom, Photoshop, Capture One and DxO PhotoLab (there are many more) allows colors and tones to be adjusted without limit. This is at once liberating and problematic, because while you can control color absolutely, you can also ruin it. This is a special issue for color, because as we've seen, it depends on perception so much more than light, shadow and tonal distribution do.

At the very least, it needs to be monitored very carefully during a normal processing operation. Tonal adjustments also affect color, though not necessarily in the way you want. Increasing contrast, for instance, can increase perceived saturation if the color doesn't change in brightness, but if it does become brighter from a contrast adjustment, it can seem to weaken. Processing purely by the numbers (HSB, RGB or L*a*b* values, for example) is no guarantee of a successful result. The colors have to look right to an experienced eye, and that may mean overriding the numbers. One of the best examples of this is the light at the so-called Golden Hour and Magic Hour – when the sun is respectively low in the sky and just below the horizon. As we saw earlier, on pages 80–1, there's no standard agreed white balance for these conditions, which leaves color processing very much to the eye and judgement of whoever's doing it. Of all subjects, landscape scenes at these times of day vary the most in the way they are processed, as tests have shown[†]. This is an extreme example, but it demonstrates that color processing involves interpretation. It always does, to a greater or lesser degree, simply because (at the risk of flogging the phrase to death) color is in the mind. That means in the mind of each photographer doing the processing.

[†] MIT-Adobe FiveK Dataset, 2011, https://data.csail.mit.edu/graphics/fivek/

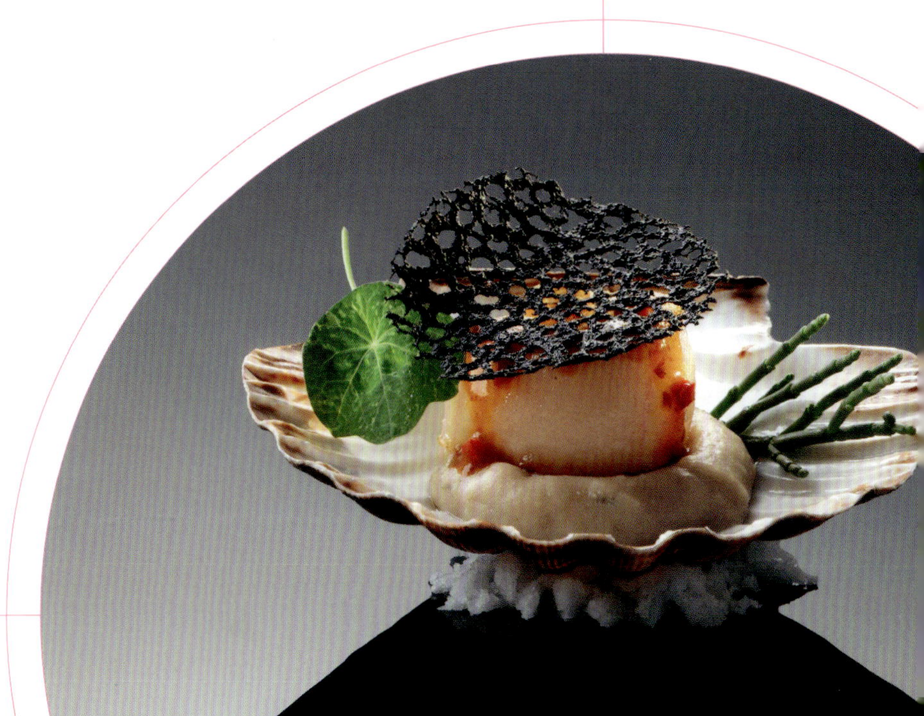

HOLD, ENHANCE, SHIFT

A professional approach to processing means integrating it into the entire shoot-to-result pipeline. Knowing what you want from a color at the start gives processing a purpose. For color, it gives it three possible purposes. One is to hold the color as you shot it. Another is to enhance some properties of the color (such as saturation or brightness). A third is to shift the color in one direction or another, and because of the way we typically think about color, that means a hue shift, such as moving a green more towards blue or more towards yellow.

HOLD

Maintaining a color isn't an automatic procedure. Whatever changes you make for other reasons may alter the color, and to avoid that may mean some compromise or tweaking with different sliders. An example is the picture of the gold lapel watch on the following pages. It was shot under controlled lighting with a large-sensor camera that has good color management, and the hue of the gold (nuanced and always important) was perfect. Although very little needed to be adjusted in processing the Raw file, raising the exposure even slightly to reveal a little more of the black-on-black embroidery in the jacket material weakened the perceived color of the gold. The solution in this case was to use the Highlights control just a little to recover.

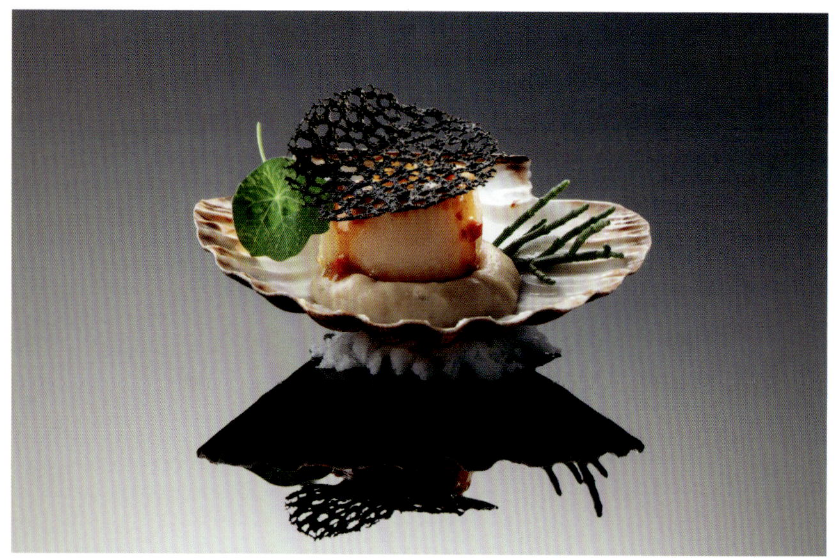

Another large subject group that demands accurate color is food, because we're very sensitive to how it should look and so to even slight departures from normal. It's good practice to shoot a color target, or at least a white balance reference (see pages 66–9), at the start of a session.

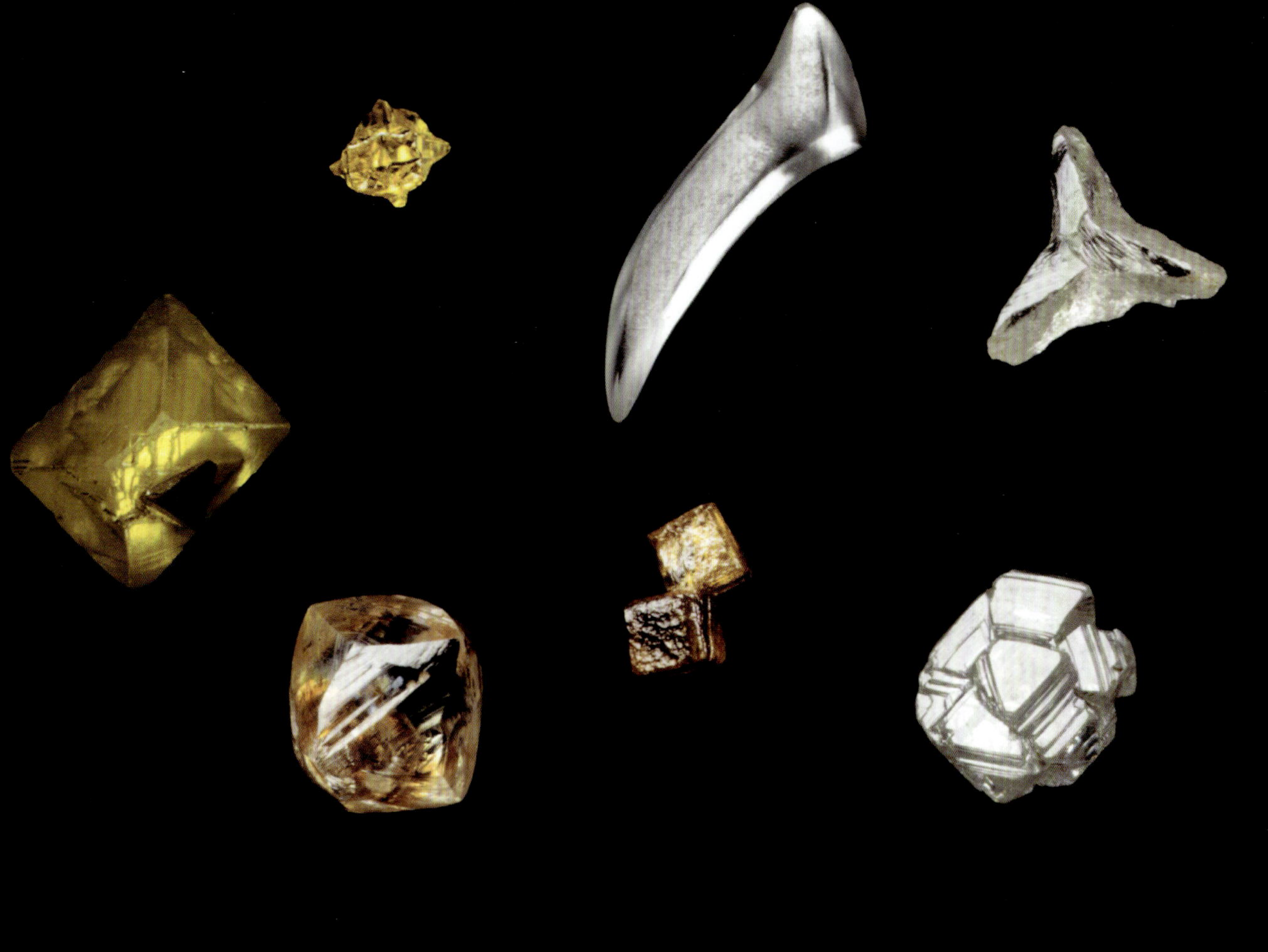

An assortment of baroque (that is, misshapen) diamonds in the De Beers collection. As most diamonds are clear and neutral in color, any hues are important, and this is a class of object that needs absolute color accuracy when photographing.

In fact, as we saw in Chapter 3, making sure that colors stay as they should isn't completely straightforward. Using a color target (page 66) is a good start when real accuracy is important, and involves a pre-processing step in which you open the image file in the manufacturer's software. This creates a color profile to save and apply in Lightroom, Adobe Camera Raw or whatever other processing software you normally use. Even then, colors need to match the way you perceived them when you shot, because color is perception. As we saw on page 120, what surrounds a color or is next to it affects the way we see it. That may be a reason for adjusting so that it looks right as in the picture on page 124. This doesn't always mean targeting and adjusting the color itself – working on the surrounds may be just as effective.

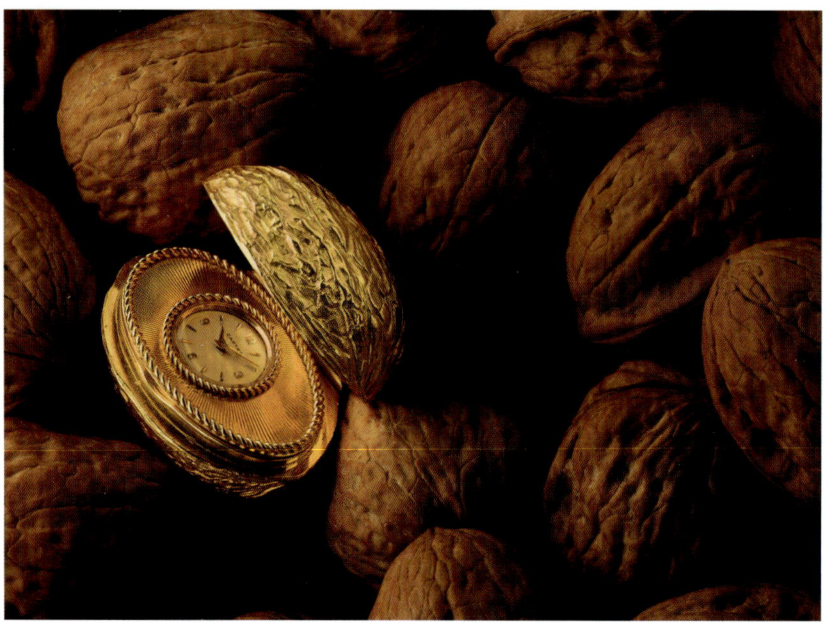

ENHANCE

A step beyond holding is enhancing, which means increasing some quality of a color from the way it looks when shot, and that normally means altering saturation or brightness or both. Even if you're not striving for accuracy, as a colorist photographer you're entitled to present colors as you wish, such as more saturated or darker (or both). Or to reduce those qualities. This isn't a processing manual, but every processing software offers more than one way of adjusting the saturation and brightness of a particular color or a range. A global adjustment may do it, or some method of targeting. This is all a matter of taste, so the more you enhance, the more likely it is that not everyone will agree with you. Enhancement runs aesthetic risks.

There are different ways of enhancing. The most straightforward is the Saturation slider, but Adobe, for example, offers the slightly more subtle Vibrance. This applies more saturation to muted colors than to stronger ones, so acts as a kind of moderating filter. Then, as we saw on page 88, the brightness of a color affects its intensity, and making it darker or lighter is also a way of enhancing its appearance. And as colors in a photograph are rarely solid, increasing the contrast within an area of color does more enhancing. In Photoshop, using layers in different blend modes has a special effect, and was used in the picture of a walnut-shaped clock above. I wanted a richer color to the walnuts, so made a duplicate layer and blended it into the original as Overlay at 40 percent, and this blend mode has a multiplying effect.

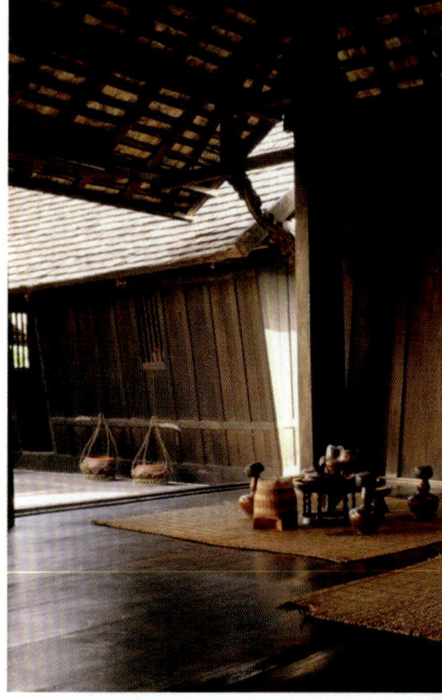

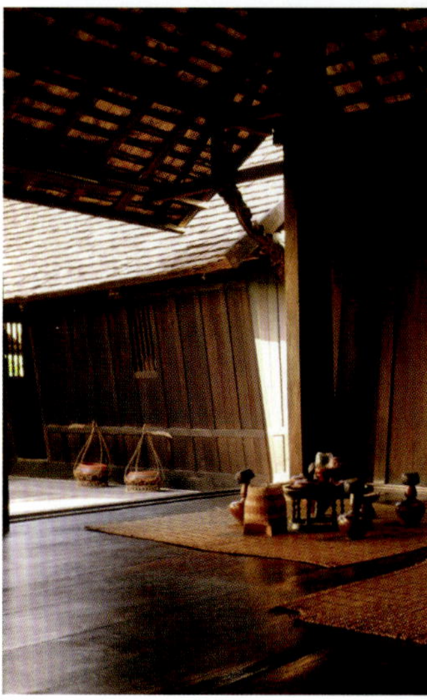

A watch encased in a gold walnut, which was modelled from a real nut chosen from a large number for its 'perfection'. As shot, the actual walnuts that form the background were more pale, and overwhelmed the watch visually. Adding a duplicate layer in post-production blended in Overlay mode made them richer and darker, more in keeping with the watch.

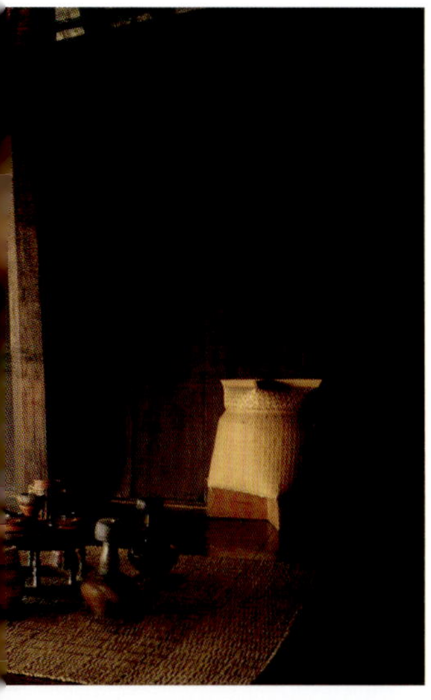

For an architectural shot in natural light, targeting the shadow areas and increasing their saturation enhanced the richness of the image without compromising the outdoor lighting beyond.

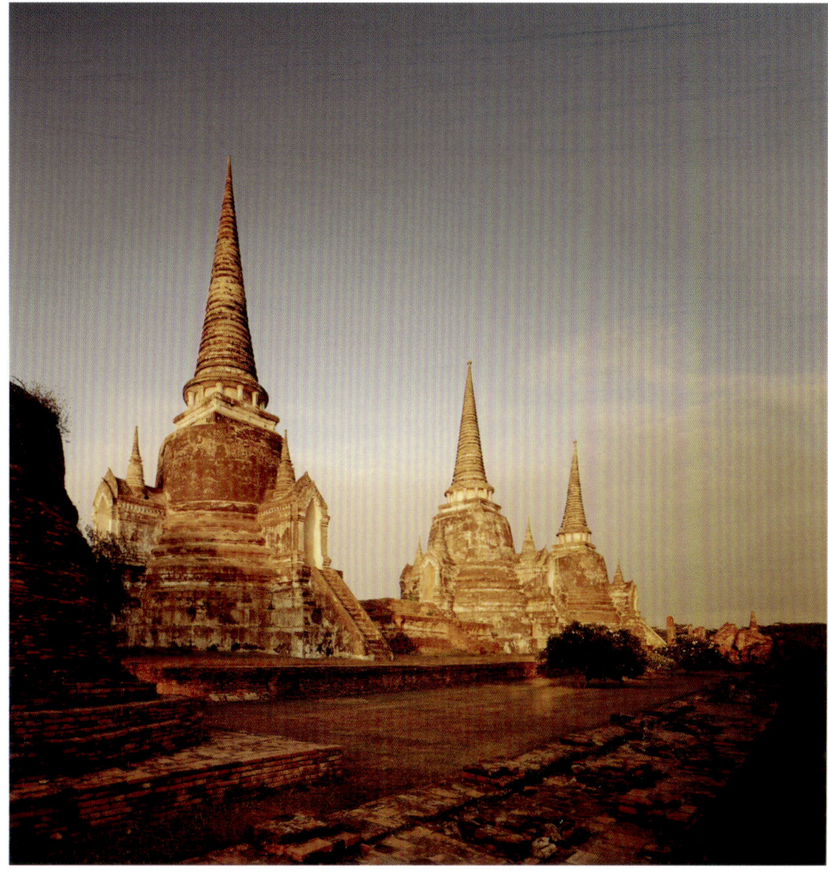

For this shot of three chedis in Ayuthhaya, Thailand, photographed on 4x5in transparency film, a Wratten 85 filter was used to neutralize the sky and enhance the sunlight.

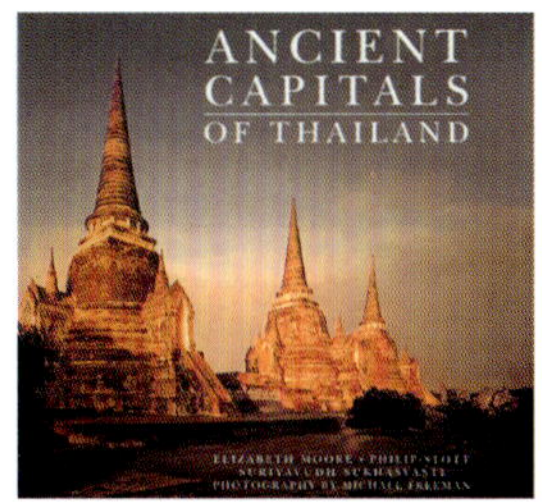

SHIFT

Thirdly, there's shifting the hue itself, which for most people is the biggest kind of change. As with enhancement, the reasons for doing this are usually for personal taste, and understandably it runs even greater risks of looking strange or unrealistic. How you do this depends on the kind of color space you choose to work in – HSB, RGB or L*a*b* – and the particular controls that your processing software offers. The most obvious way is to raise or lower the hue angle, working in HSB color space. How far is, of course, critical. For a memory color like skin, one or two degrees is likely to be sufficient, but for colors that attract less judgement it could be as many as several degrees. For more on the limits of similar hues, see Adjacent Colors on page 116.

WHICH COLOR SPACE?

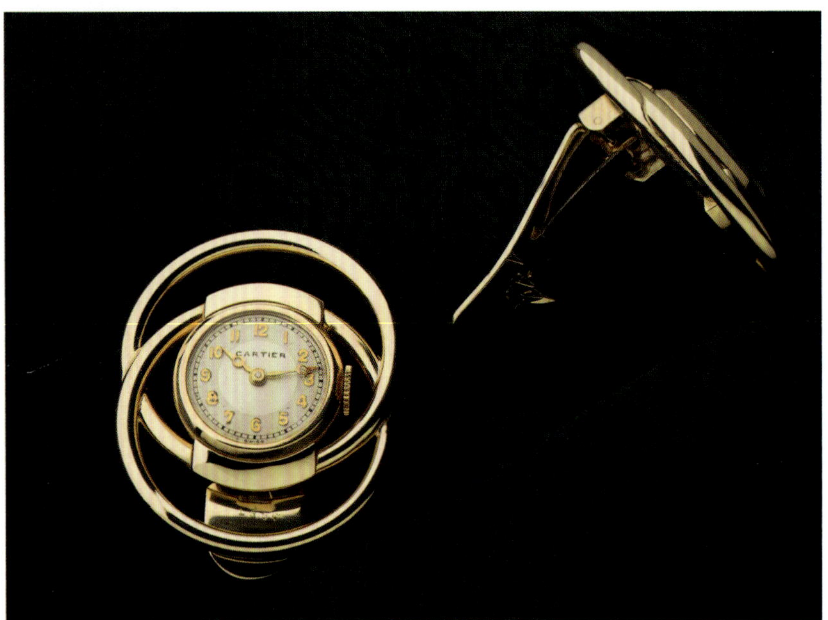

With a dynamic range of about 14 stops, this studio-lit close-up of a gold watch against a black embroidered silk jacket posed a problem not only for the tonal range but for the color of the gold, which needed to be held and not allowed to roll off into white. The ideal treatment was a high dynamic range medium-format sensor, a 10-bit monitor and ProPhoto RGB in Adobe Camera Raw, all in order to maintain the full range.

As we saw in Chapter 2, color spaces are specific versions of color models, and for processing Raw files there's a choice of three: sRGB, Adobe RGB (1998) and ProPhoto RGB. All three are overlaid opposite on the horseshoe-shaped CIE chromaticity diagram, which is a slice taken out of the 3D model.

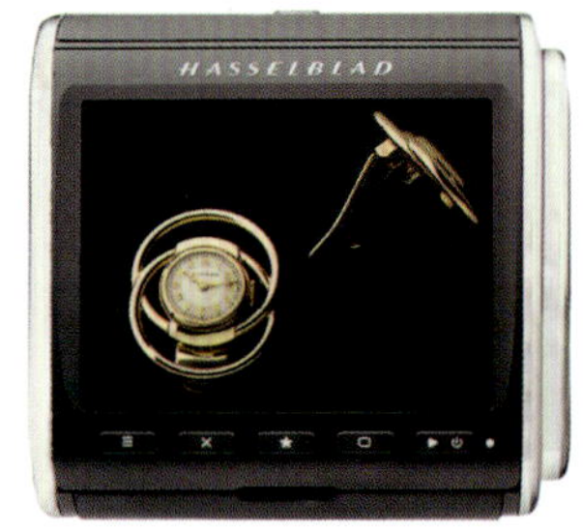

Remembering that this entire area is the total gamut of human vision, it's immediately obvious that there's a large area of greens and blue-greens that we can see that are not available, even to the largest of the three, ProPhoto RGB. The point of shooting Raw is to preserve the maximum color and light information, and that means processing in software such as Lightroom, Adobe Camera Raw or Capture One. At this point you need to choose which color space to work in, even though it may not be the one you finally convert to.

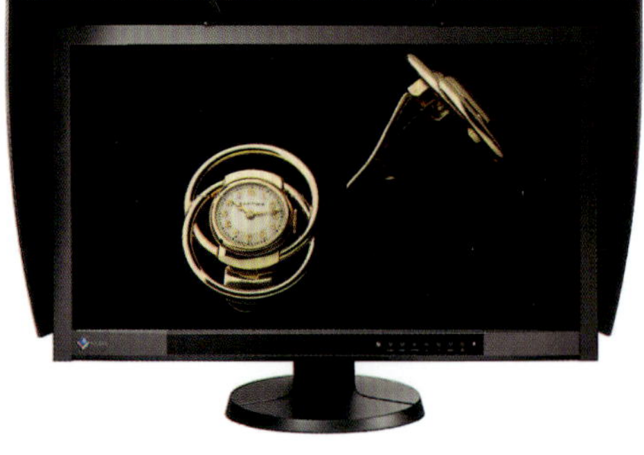

The space used by web browsers for rendering images is sRGB, so that alone makes it the most widely used. Adobe RGB (1998) is the industry standard for printing, and it's a considerably larger space. However, if you display an image that's been made and processed in Adobe RGB (1998) on the web without taking any precautions, it will look duller, less vibrant, for the obvious reason that a web browser cannot show all the colors in the original. Much larger than either of these two is

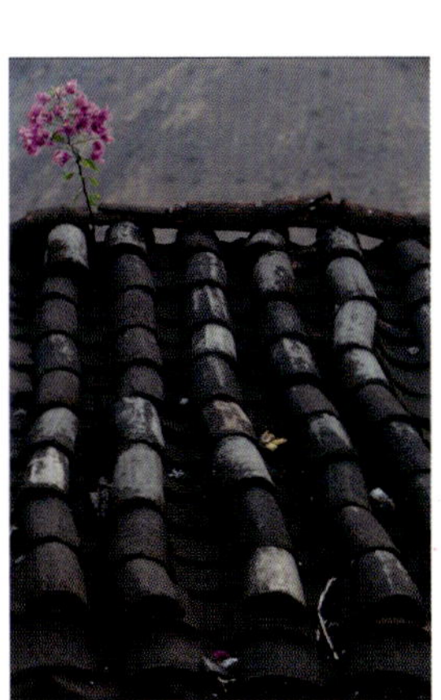

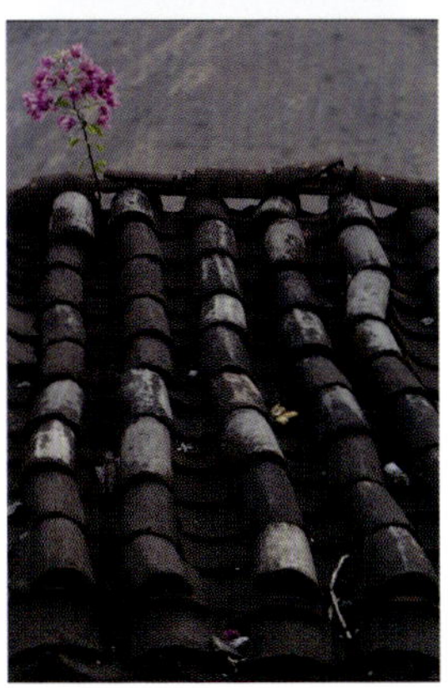

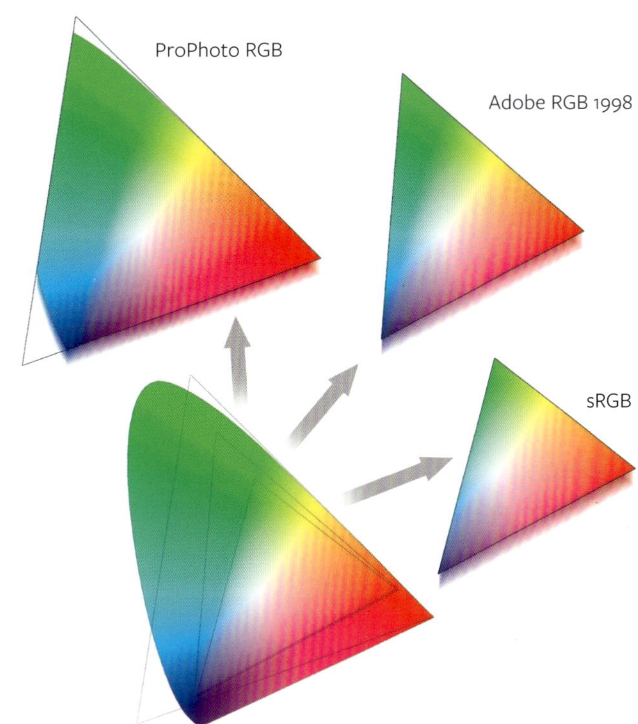

ProPhoto RGB, and it's big enough to hold all the colors captured by any camera, even high-end medium-format backs that deliver 16 bits and have a dynamic range of over 14 stops. That makes it the best choice for processing high-quality images, especially those with saturated colors and a high range, and the studio shot here of a gold watch against black embroidered silk cloth is a good example.

You can choose which color space to use in Preferences, and any of the options will, naturally, fit within this underlying space. This is a powerful argument for keeping maximum color information and using ProPhoto RGB. However, as the same colors from the camera are now being spread over a wider gamut than Adobe RGB (1998), you must work in 16 bits, otherwise you're likely to get banding. It's worth noting that in Adobe Camera Raw and Lightroom, the underlying color space is ProPhoto RGB in any case, which you might take as a seal of approval. And, of course, take the extra step of converting the image to either Adobe RGB (1998) or sRGB before sending it anywhere.

That said, in most cases and with most cameras, Adobe RGB (1998) is sufficient for working. Just remember that if the picture is going to be posted on the web, convert it first to sRGB. Also remember that you can convert from a larger color space to a smaller, but not the other way around.

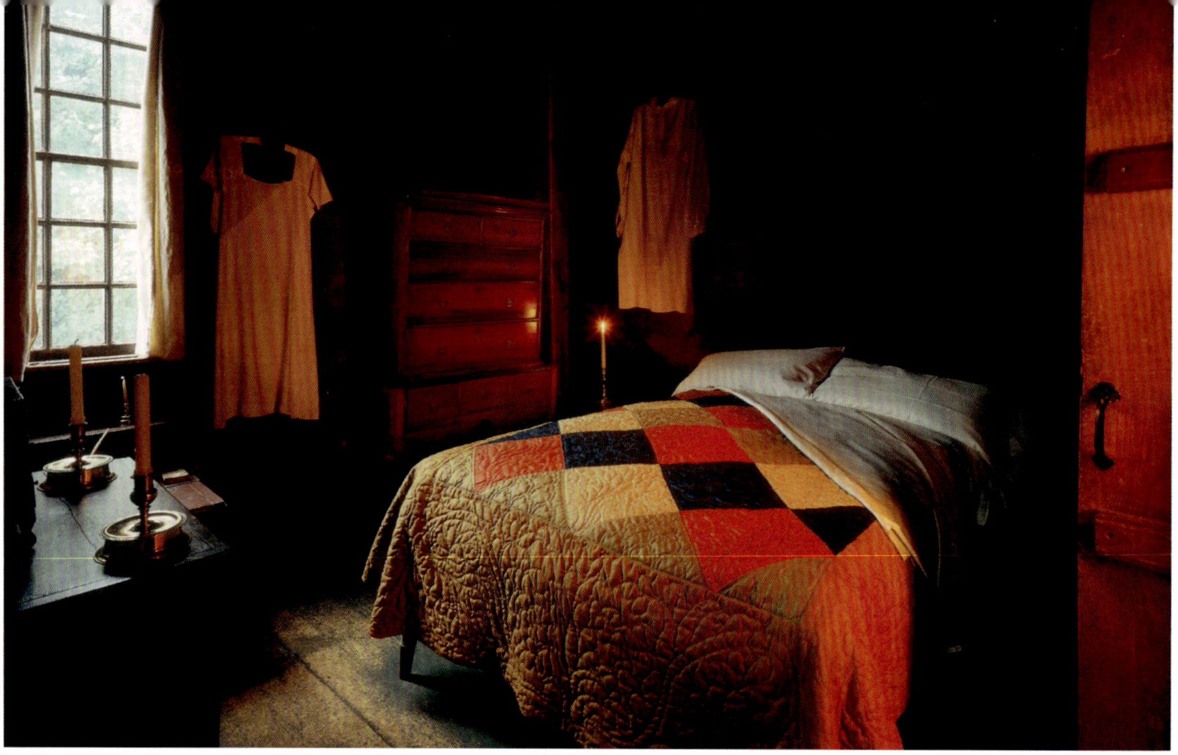

COLOR OPPONENT PROCESSING

D espite sounding unfamiliar and a bit unwieldy, this is in fact the default offered by processing software, and for good reason. Talking about color and perceiving it are actually at odds with each other.

While we easily say red, yellow, blue and so on as our main means of identifying a color, and saying it's strong or weak, light or dark, these aren't quite so intuitive for adjusting color. That was the HSB model, but it's not very practical for basic overall changes to an image. Color opponency as described in Chapter 2 on page 34 feels much more natural, and that's what Lightroom, Adobe Camera Raw and others offer.

Taking Adobe software as the example, the very top slider (the general idea is to work from top to bottom) is color temperature, called simply Temperature. This is traditionally, from the days of color film, the most common value that needs to be fixed, first because it's on the daylight scale that we're most familiar with, from blue sky to warm low sun, and second because until very recently, interior lighting was incandescent, and so orange-ish. All that's then needed is an opposite axis, from greenish to reddish, called Tint by Adobe. Now, these two are not the same as the a* and b* axes in L*a*b* color shown on page 44, and the reason is that the scale of color temperature is different from the b* axis – on the CIE color space on page 37 you can see that it follows a curved line that goes through neutral white. Practically

A bedroom in the Sheldon-Hawks House, Massachusetts, preserved in its original Colonial-era form. Interior shots that mix daylight and artificial light (here candles at a very low 1,500 degrees kelvin) call for a decision on which color temperature to prioritize. Usually, a very warm-looking artificial light is more acceptable visually than a bluish daylight, unless at evening.

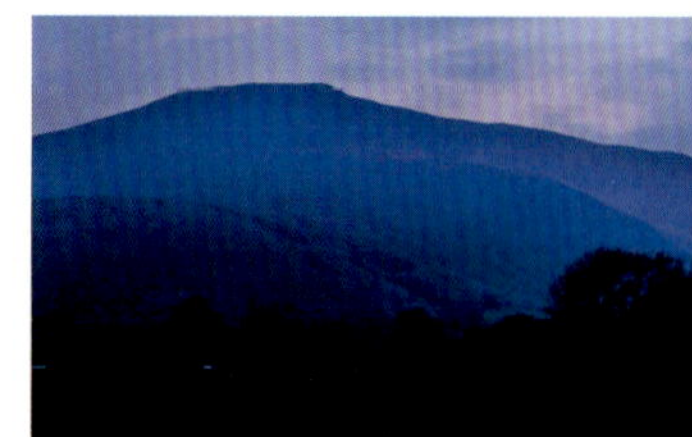

Golden Hour (see page 80) is the classic case that allows for different processing opinions. At one end (top) are the color temperature settings that deliver what looks like white light. At the other (bottom) are the warmer settings that go as far as you think realistic. The circles mark the white points used.

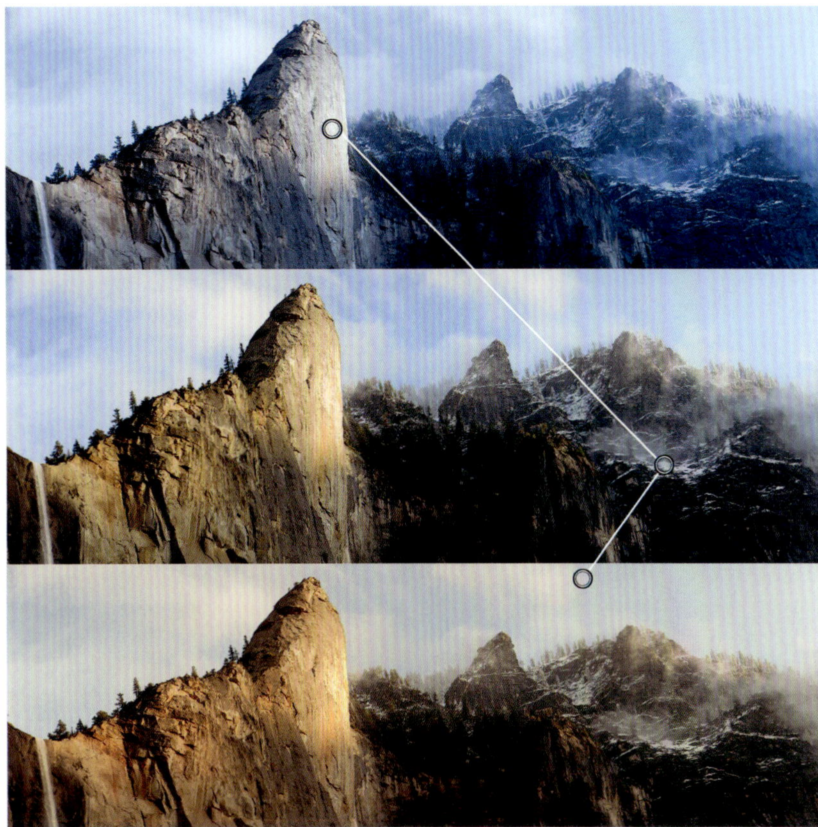

Shot at dusk, this panorama of hills in Cumbria, northern England, was color balanced for a slight hint of pink in the sunset, which rendered the landscape a distinct blue, which is acceptable because it accords with most people's idea of blue evening light.

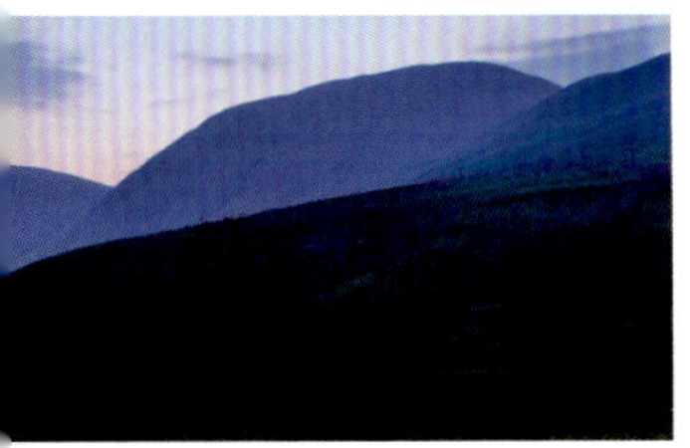

this doesn't matter at all, as Temperature and Tint together will sort out most common color shifts that you're likely to encounter.

A Raw file has the color balance as a separate setting, so regardless of which white balance you set the camera to (or set it to automatic), these controls give total freedom to adjust. In fact, Auto White Balance early or late in the day with a low sun is a typical scenario for needing adjustment, as the landscape above shows. The Auto White Balance averages the entire frame to neutral, and while there's nothing wrong with that, most people expect to see such a scene suffused with some warmth.

This is almost always the basic first step in processing for color – to get the overall color bias looking right. More often than not that means no bias at all, looking as if the entire scene is bathed in white, colorless light, as from a midday sun. Tools such as the Eyedropper help set the two sliders to this in a click, provided you can identify an area in the picture that should be neutral (see page 68). There are reasons other than color temperature why it might be off. The photograph on page 61, for example, was shot through an aircraft window that had a slight greenish tinge.

TARGETED COLOR

M oving a little deeper into processing, you can be as selective as you want when it comes to adjusting a color, and this naturally changes the actual relationships between the different colors in a photograph.

Traditional photographic processing and adjustment is global, meaning across the entire image. Color changes are across the board, and most of the time that's all that's needed. The alternative is more precise and specific – to target a particular range of color, usually narrow. All good processing software allows you to target a color and adjust it independently if you want, and there are many ways – too many to spend time on here debating which is more accurate or more convenient. There was a time when targeting a color range was an operation for Photoshop after the initial processing stage, but now, Raw processing engines such as Adobe Camera Raw handle it at the Raw stage.

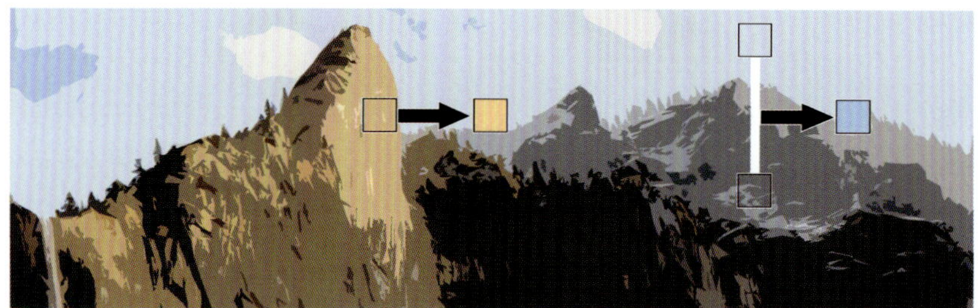

In the main hall of the National Museum of Natural History, Washington DC, the lighting is a mixture of artificial and daylight from the dome above. Without targeted correction, parts of the elephant including its tusks are an unwelcome orange. Brush masking in ACR allows a higher local color temperature.

The same Yosemite panorama as on the previous pages, but here processed to enhance the color contrast between lit and shaded parts of the landscape. Using sky detection in ACR and reversing the selection, these two areas can be targeted independently, and given lower and higher color temperatures respectively.

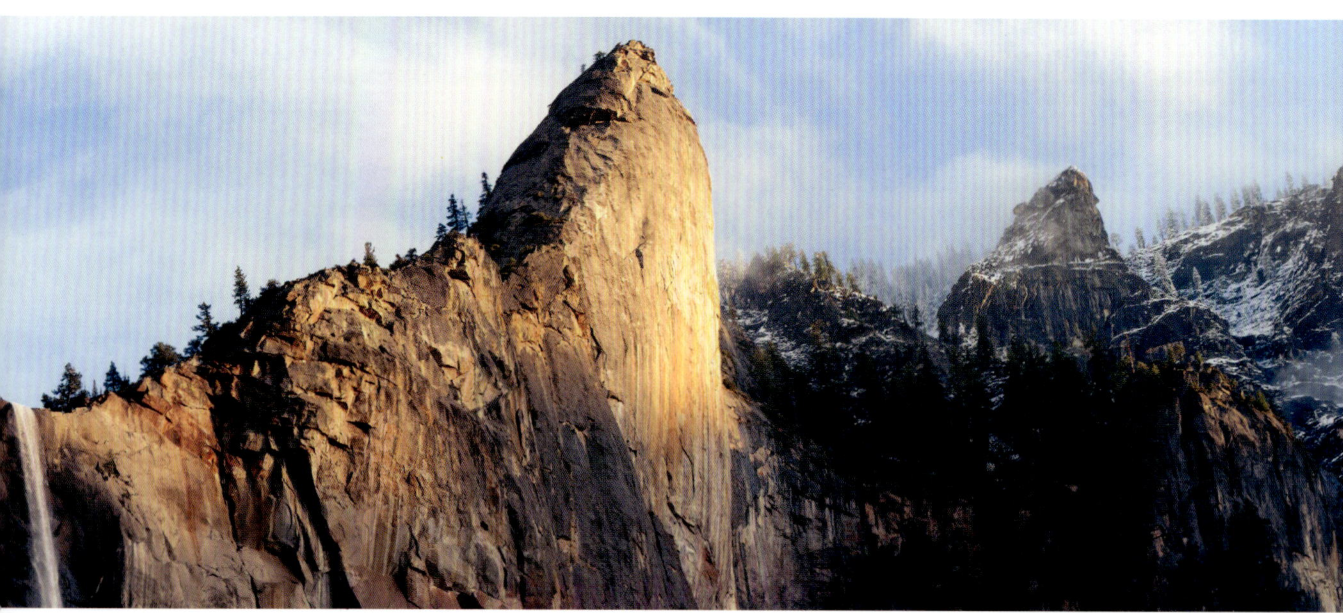

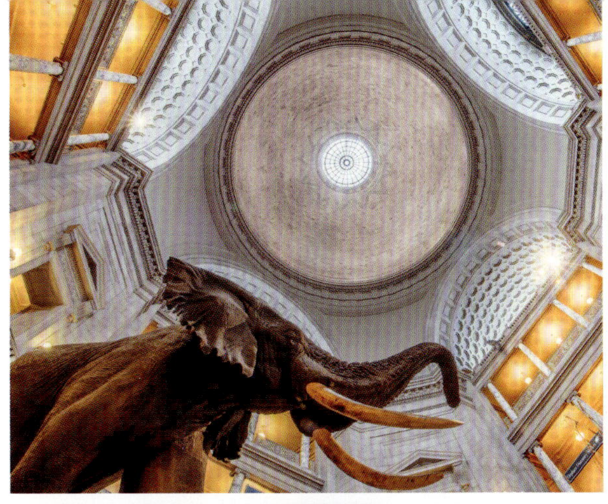
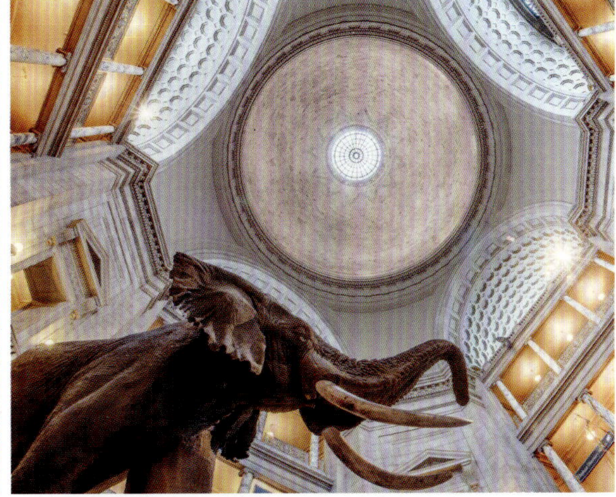
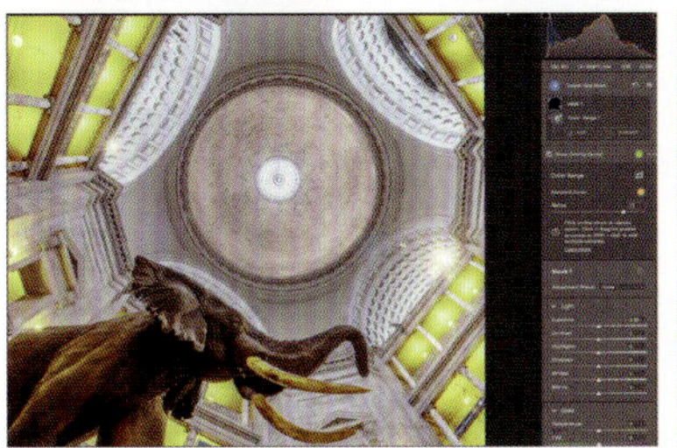
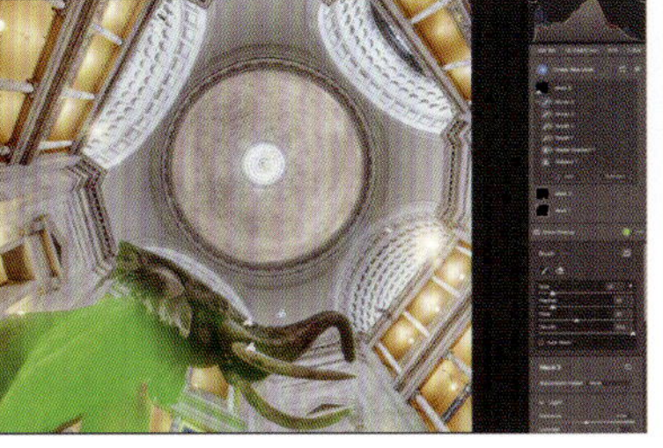
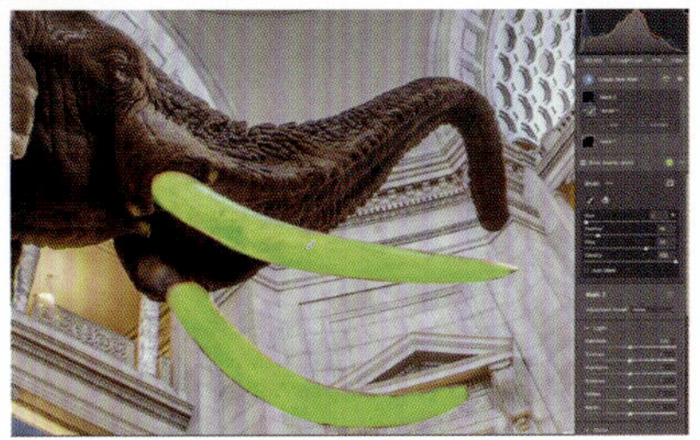
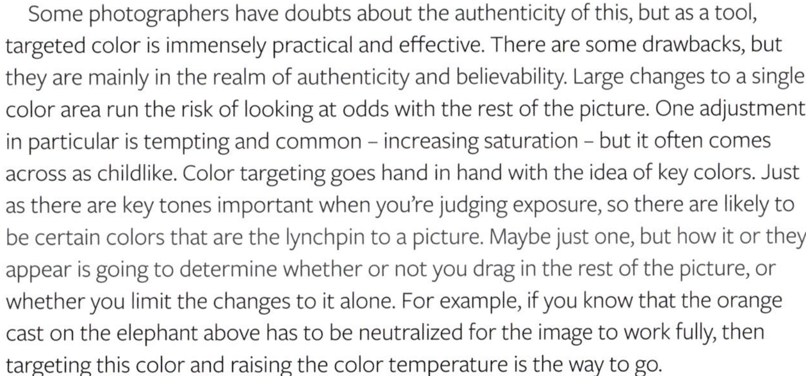
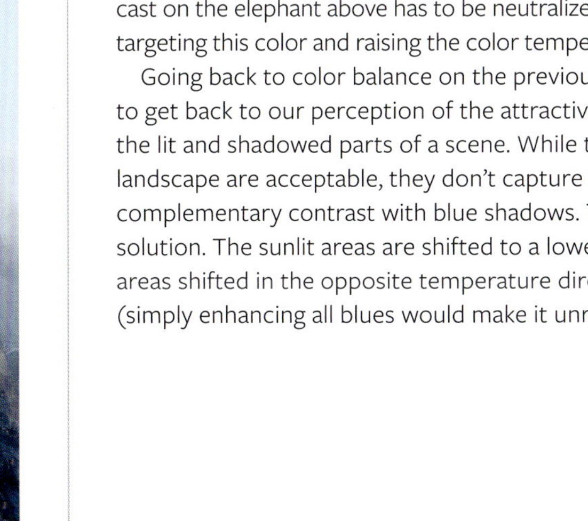
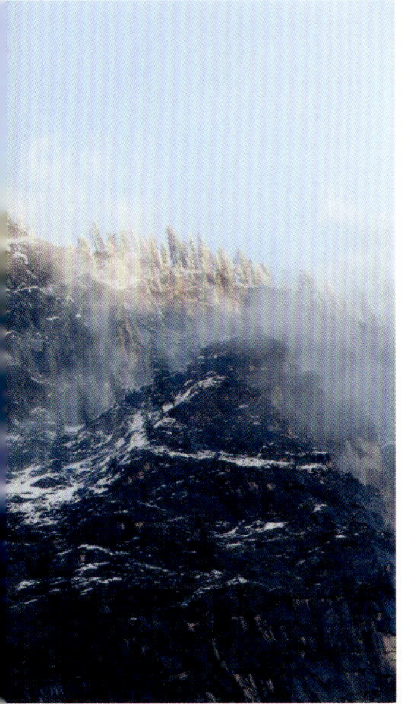

Some photographers have doubts about the authenticity of this, but as a tool, targeted color is immensely practical and effective. There are some drawbacks, but they are mainly in the realm of authenticity and believability. Large changes to a single color area run the risk of looking at odds with the rest of the picture. One adjustment in particular is tempting and common – increasing saturation – but it often comes across as childlike. Color targeting goes hand in hand with the idea of key colors. Just as there are key tones important when you're judging exposure, so there are likely to be certain colors that are the lynchpin to a picture. Maybe just one, but how it or they appear is going to determine whether or not you drag in the rest of the picture, or whether you limit the changes to it alone. For example, if you know that the orange cast on the elephant above has to be neutralized for the image to work fully, then targeting this color and raising the color temperature is the way to go.

Going back to color balance on the previous pages, targeting may be the only way to get back to our perception of the attractive color opposition at Golden Hour of the lit and shadowed parts of a scene. While the three versions of that Yosemite landscape are acceptable, they don't capture the impression of warm lit areas in complementary contrast with blue shadows. The re-processed version here is one solution. The sunlit areas are shifted to a lower color temperature and the shadow areas shifted in the opposite temperature direction, while the sky is left untouched (simply enhancing all blues would make it unrealistically vivid).

NIGHT SCENE PROCESSING

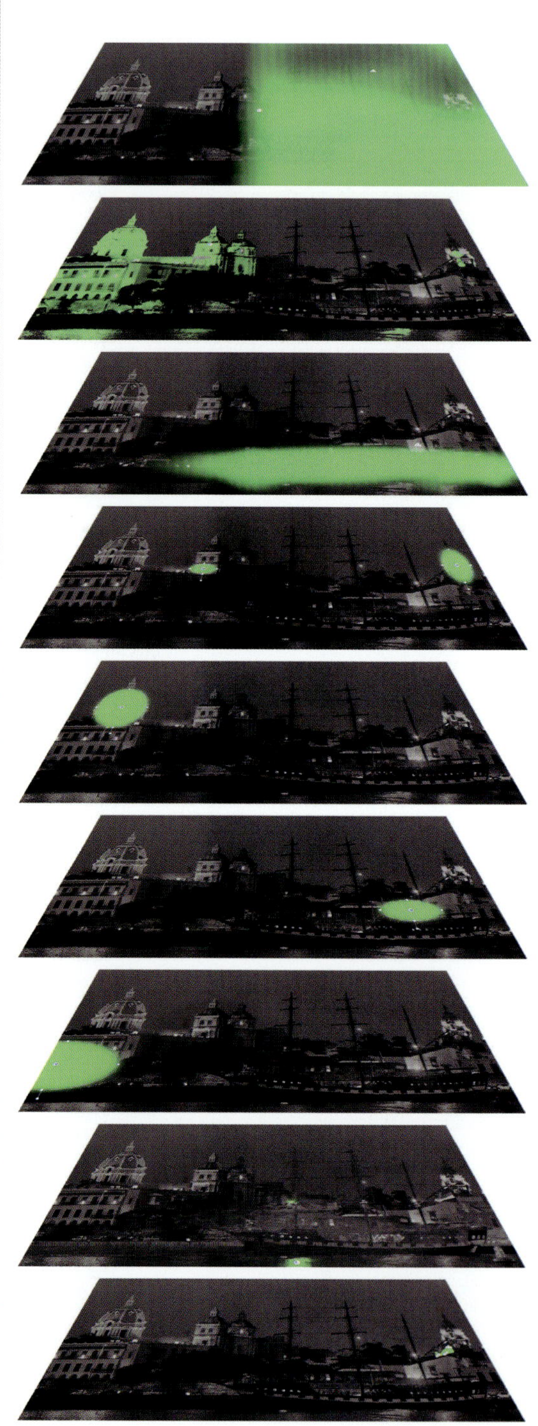

W e already looked at the uncertainties of color in urban night scenes on page 99, and they're worth a second, more detailed look at how to process them. Because you can never be sure of what the main light sources are – and there may be more than one in a single scene – the choices of color balance are wide open.

What I'm presenting here is a standard procedure, and it leans heavily towards working on different segments of the picture, but the balance you choose for each one is going to be personal. In principle, start with the dominant lighting, or at least the area you consider the most important, and first set the color balance of the entire image for that. With that as a base, you can then target other areas to adjust their color balance. At some point, you'll also need to make a basic overall tonal setting, typically a basic Exposure or Brightness adjustment followed by overall highlight recovery and shadow lifting, with the aim of bringing the different areas more into line with each other. To keep the look more photographically natural, use these two sliders (Highlights and Shadows in Adobe Camera Raw and Lightroom) in combination with an increase in Contrast. One limit to how much brighter you can make the darker areas, including the sky, is noise, and you may have to compromise one way or the other.

Next, expect to make a few or even several targeted color adjustments to deal with local areas, including point light sources which may need to have the clipping reduced – if they flare apply some de-hazing. Radial gradients retouched with a brush are generally the most useful and natural to work with, but color range, luminance range and even sky detection methods can work better in some instances.

A night scene in the Colombian port city of Cartagena, fully processed in ACR, with (right) the local adjustment plan superimposed over the default version. The stack of nine layers shows the masking used for individual local adjustment of various kinds (lightening, raising white points, desaturation and hue shifts).

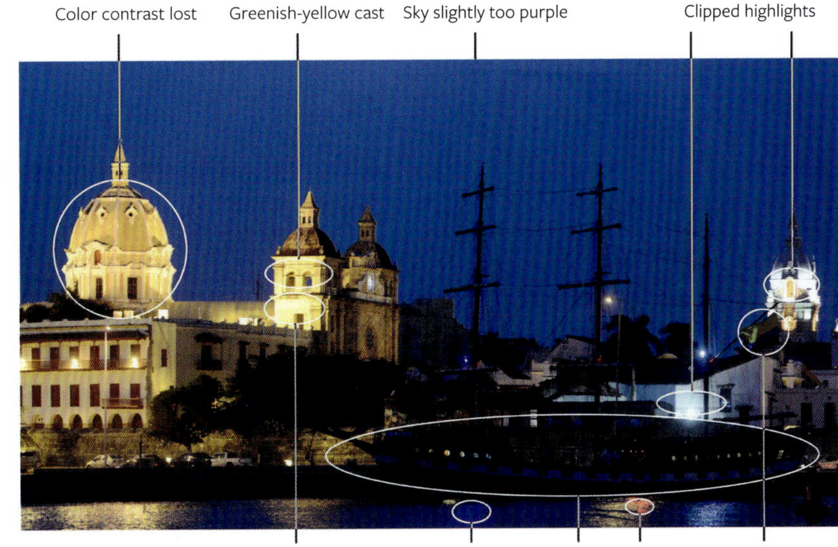

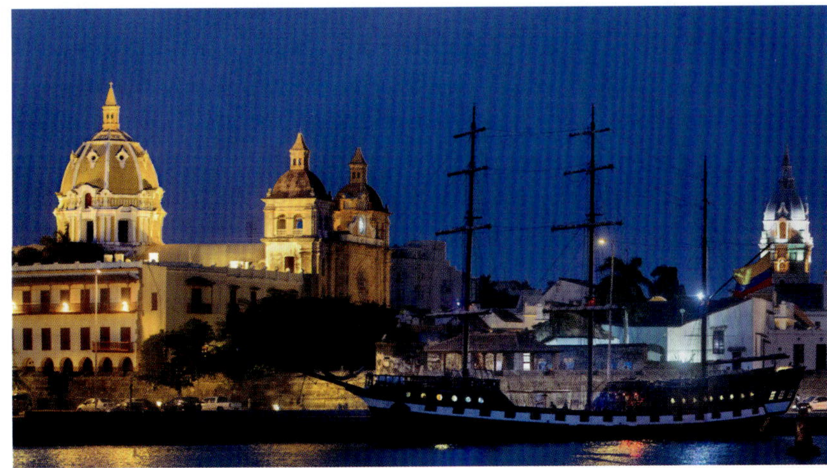

DECISIONS

1. In the lit areas (there's likely to be pooling of light), is there one overall lighting color? If so, eye-drop that to neutral and use the color balance sliders to alter that to taste.

2. If there are two or more differently colored light sources, either choose one of them to eye-drop to neutral, or strike a color compromise between them, whichever looks best.

3. Avoid any greenish cast in lit areas.

4. Set the basic overall Exposure or Brightness, then recover highlights and lift shadows to taste, together with raising contrast to keep these two effects natural-looking.

5. Work locally on point light sources like street lamps and other over-bright areas, bringing them down, but realistically.

6. Choose which over-dark areas you want to lighten, and adjust with caution (night scenes need healthy contrast).

7. There are likely to be small, highly saturated spots of color. Target these and reduce saturation to moderate.

8. If the sky has any tone (late evening), consider a deep blue.

9. If there are areas of flare, consider applying moderate de-hazing to these.

10. Finally, take an overall decision on how colorful the scene is. Typically, an urban night scene should be colorful, though without extremes of saturation. Adjust as necessary.

CINEMATIC GRADING

A t the far end of color processing, way beyond trying to get colors to look as they should or at their best, are the large-scale adjustments that alter the entire mood and sensation of the image.

Cinema has had the largest influence on these processing techniques that aim to stylize a photograph. Despite the similarity of the word, this has a different meaning from Style, used as the title of the chapter that follows. Style is an aesthetic preference developed over time by individual photographers. To stylize an image is to give it a distinctive appearance that is non-realistic, and in the professional world it means making the photograph conform to an established color recipe. In other words, it's not especially creative or imaginative, but it does serve a useful function, for cinema at least. Called color grading, it's used to give a consistent look to a movie regardless of the different lighting conditions under which all the footage was shot. It's also used to set up a mood, atmosphere or emotion that helps the film's direction. Simple examples are a teal-orange overlay for Hollywood action films, a washed-out look for apocalyptic films, dark and cool for horror films.

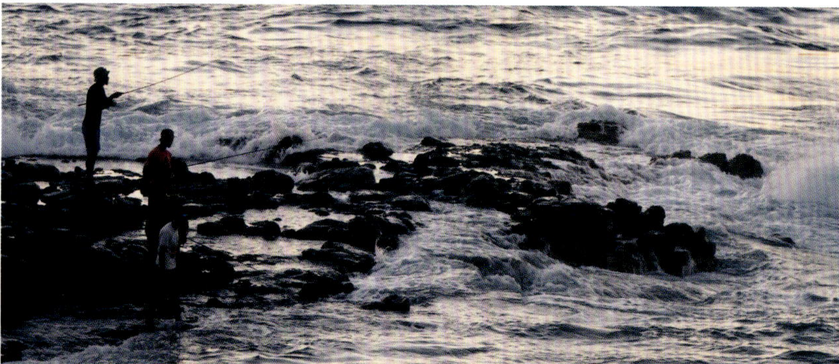

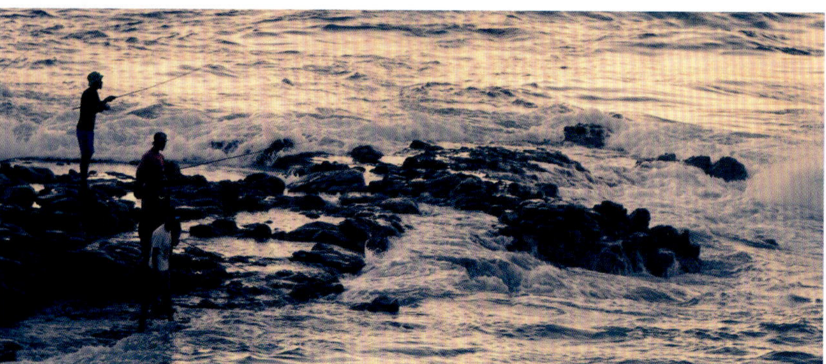

Color-grading tools allow highlights and shadows to be shifted separately, typically in opposite directions. This shot of fishermen on La Réunion has sufficient contrast to make this color divergence effective.

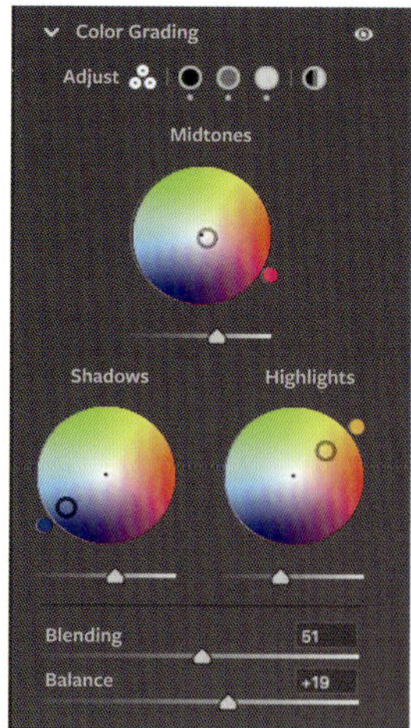

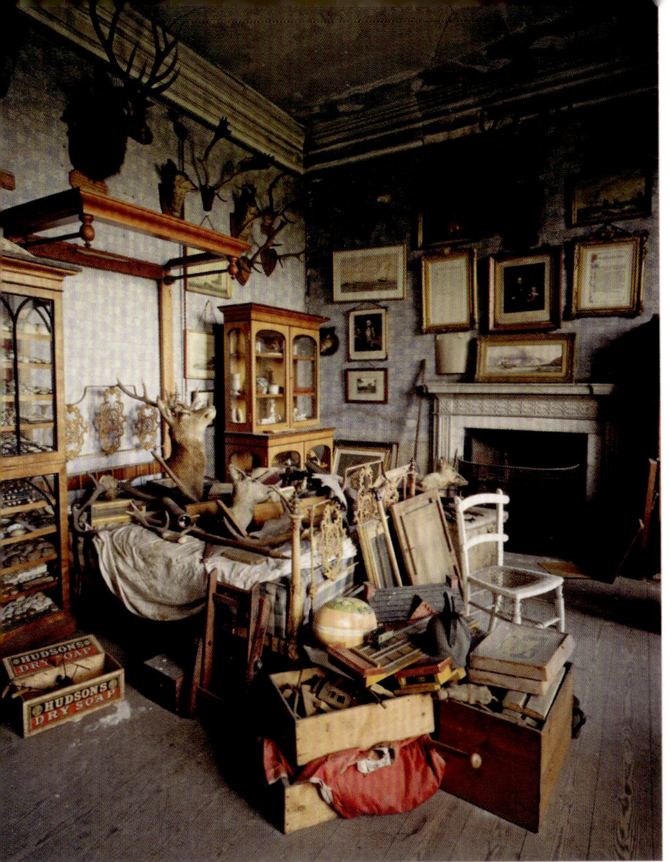 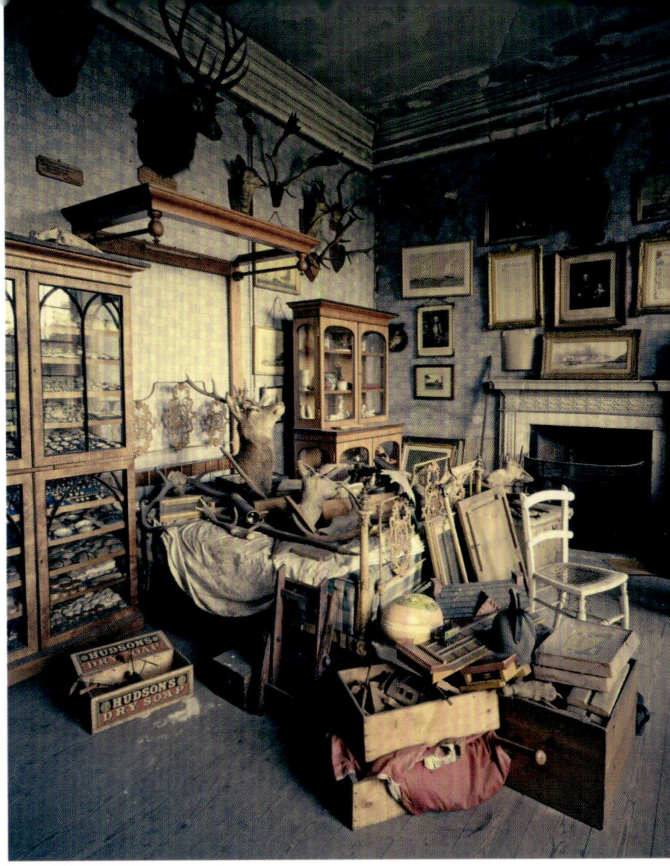

The bedroom of an English country house that remained untouched for over a century is given an old-fashioned, faded appearance by using the color wheels as shown below.

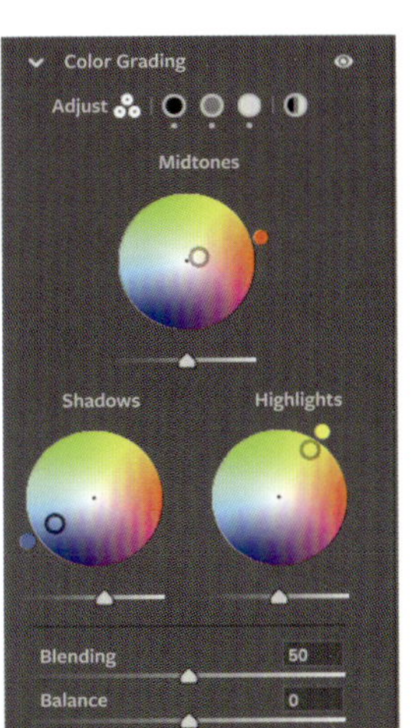

For still photography, the most common tools are color wheels for shadows, mid-tones and highlights, operated separately. Photoshop's Adobe Camera Raw and Lightroom's color grading wheels are modelled exactly on this, so that for the hue part of color grading, the result is almost always a shift of highlights in one direction and shadows in another. The well-known teal-orange cinematic style has shadows shifted towards a darker blue-green, so that the orange-shifted highlights pop out strongly. Moving highlights and shadows in opposite directions usually makes them complementary (see page 120), which tends to be attractive to audiences.

Because color grading aims at a particular mood for particular genres of photography (landscapes and portraits especially), there is a commercial market in the form of presets. These are loaded into the processing app such as Lightroom and save time – for a price. A sampling of names from the market gives a good idea of the popular ones: Cool and Moody Landscape, Soft and Desaturated, Teal Orange, Brown, Aqua, Vintage, Retro. They follow prescriptions, which appeal to many people, though you could argue that they just make photographs more similar to others and less distinctive.

7

STYLES

What makes a color style is an elusive concept. It involves technique, of which we've seen a great deal in the book so far, but that alone isn't enough, otherwise it would be just down to craft and skill. It also involves a preference for a particular color palette – in other words, certain combinations of specific colors – and knowing how to find them or create them. Essentially, it's an aesthetic preference. This applies to any creative work, not just color in photography, but somehow the underlying difficulty of getting to grips with color in the first place makes it more difficult (for me at least) than with composition or light and shadow.

Nevertheless, there are photographers who for one reason or another, including having the good fortune to be recognized and talked about by the wider community of photography, have been influential for their recognizable way with color. If you're interested in how to define style, I'd recommend spending time looking at the work of the following photographers, some historical, some contemporary. In date order, they are: Paul Outerbridge, Eliot Porter, Ernst Haas, Saul Leiter, Franco Fontana, Pete Turner, William Eggleston, Harry Gruyaert, Denis Waugh, Jan Groover, Eric Meola, Rolph Gobits, Stephen Shore, Nadav Kander. It's a highly selective list, but these, to me, have developed distinctive ways of handling color, sufficient for their work to be recognizable. I should say that very few of them actually said they had a particular style; they just got on with shooting – organically, you could say, naturally and as suited them. Most photographers don't explain, which is probably as it should be.

Style is a vastly over-used word in any case, simply because it sounds good and mature, and as most people can't be bothered to explain what they mean by it, it's a handy term to throw about. I'm not sure how good a job I'll do to define it, but I'll try, and can at least offer some examples that are themselves explainable. My approach to color style (any style, actually) is ridiculously empirical. If I can identify the photographer from just looking at a few pictures, then that's a style and I can set to and work out what's gone into making it.

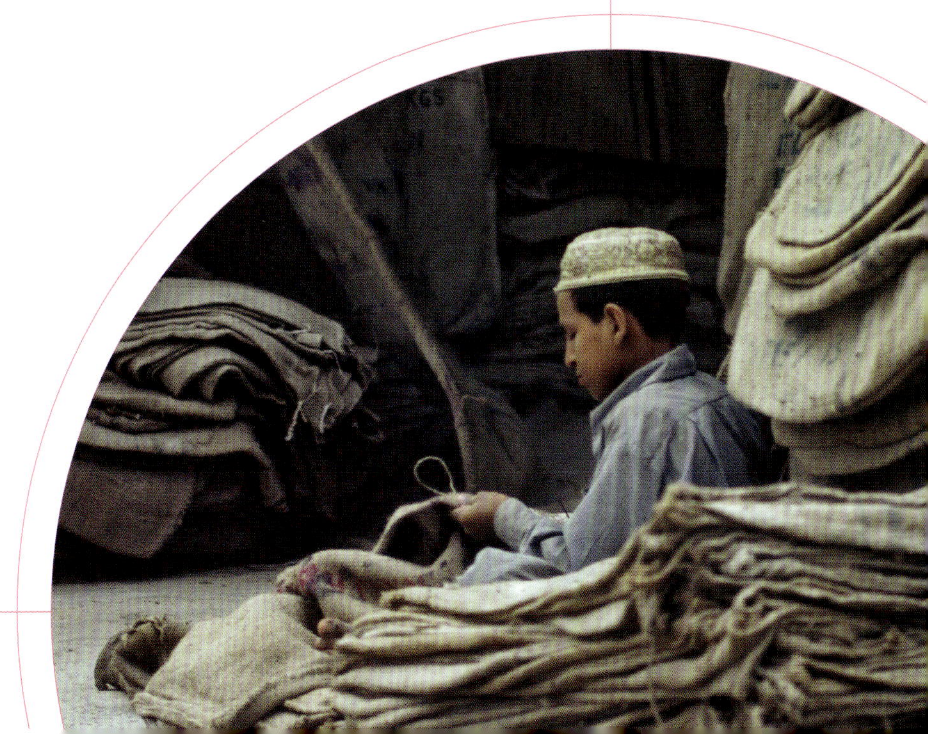

DIFFERENT PALETTES

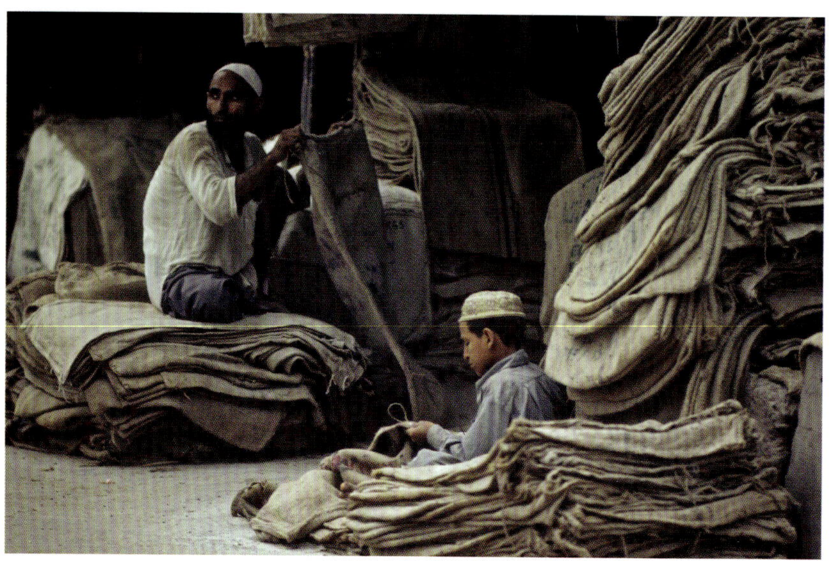

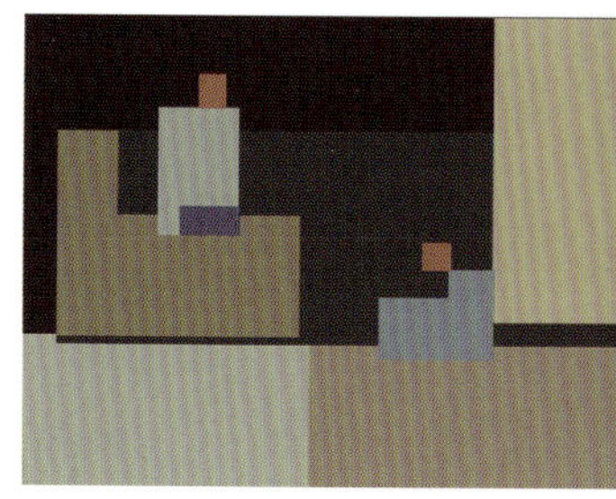

In the market area of Peshawar, in Pakistan's Northwest Frontier Province, where bags are being stitched for carrying produce, the extremely muted warm and cool greys establish a sombre palette.

A color palette is easy to understand in the context of painting, where pigments are first chosen and then used. Photography doesn't work in quite the same way (outside the studio, at least), but it's still possible to work within a certain range or pattern of colors.

There are three parts to the equation: seeking out the scenes and lighting that will deliver, framing and exposing to make them work, and processing to support all of this. I've little doubt in my mind that the first two are the more important because they're at the heart of the creative process, but processing can't be dismissed, even though it provides a craft element rather than creative input.

Finding your preferred palette out there in whatever part of the world you have access to isn't necessarily easy, but that's a key part of what photography is. Also, there's feedback involved, meaning that what's available may influence what you like. If you're a landscape photographer, the available palette is going to be quite different if you live in the American Southwest than if you're in the British countryside. If you're in a city there won't be much of the subtle greens and browns on page 167, but more vivid colors in details of signage, clothing, vehicles and so on. If you prefer to construct images, as in a studio, the choices are far greater, because you can choose your subjects and also introduce color through lighting. This is much closer to the painter's way of thinking and coloring, even though the genre, such as food or portraits or fashion, means that the ingredients bring their own colors.

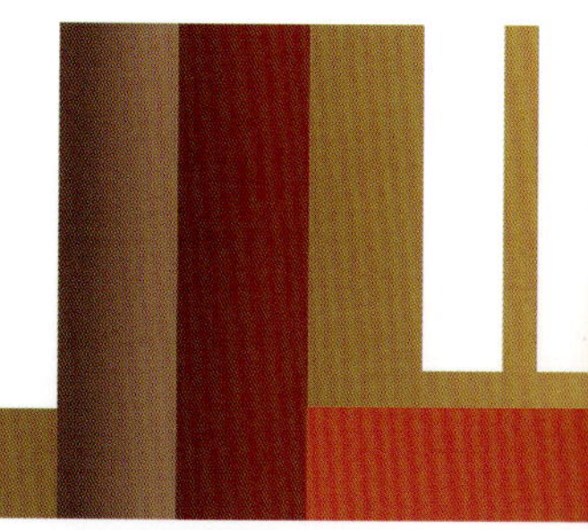

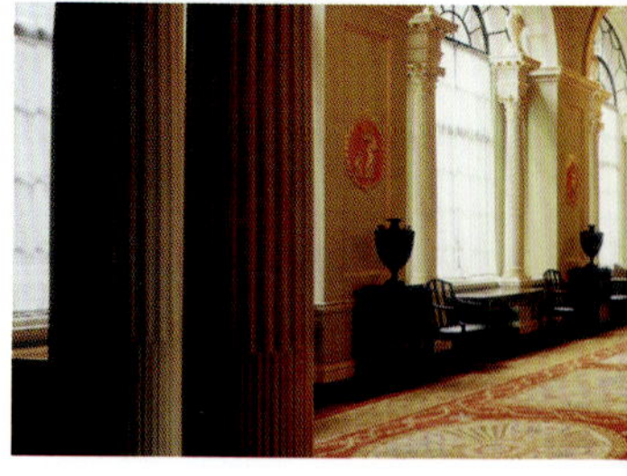

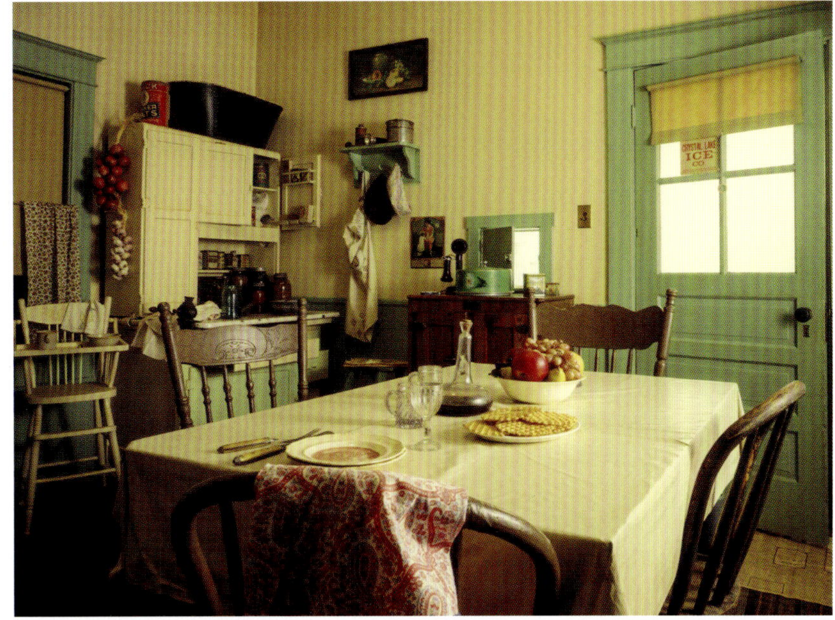
An Italian-American kitchen from the 1920s, preserved and re-installed in the National Museum of American History in Washington DC, has a color palette that reflects tastes of the day, featuring a pale green and cream.

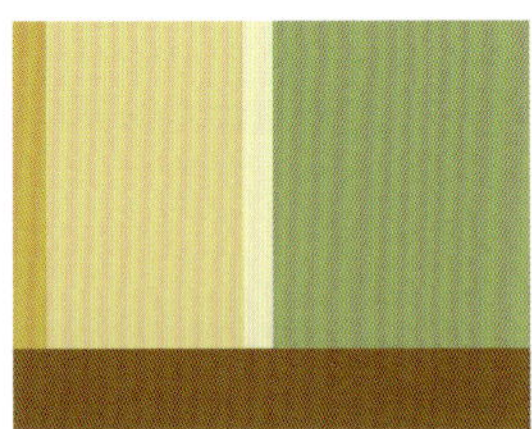

The boardroom of the Bank of England, shot on transparency 120 rollfilm balanced for daylight and with no further adjustment to the color. The size of the room and the single wall of windows made chandeliers necessary throughout the day, and the resulting palette is both sombre and slightly warm.

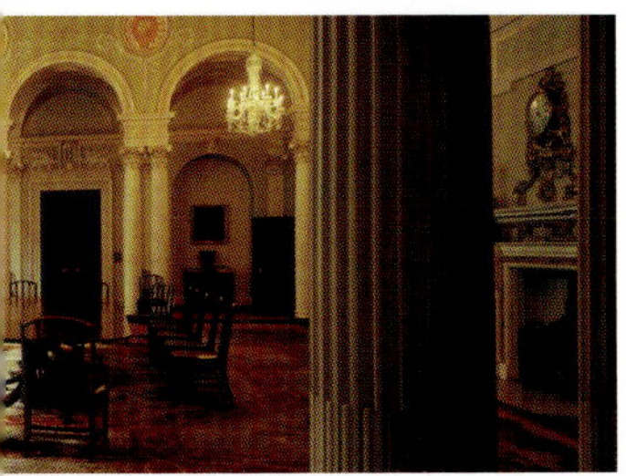

In fact, across the board there's much to learn from painting when it comes to palettes. At a glance, the palettes of Raphael, Vincent van Gogh and Claude Monet are wildly different, yet in themselves easy to define. We'll see shortly how some color styles in photography echo those of painters and schools of painting, even though unwittingly. This is also where the actual process comes in. The palettes of master painters were developed within the context of what pigments were available at the time (and the more costly ones like ultramarine, based on lapis lazuli, on what the client could afford). The varied palettes of painters were, of course, a matter of taste and feeling, but at the same time they were influenced by what other painters of the time were doing, as well as materials.

This sounds at first quite different from color in photography, where computational and advanced processing software allow us to do anything we wish to color, but there are genuine parallels with the chemistry of film, and we'll look at those shortly under Emulsion Color. Less genuine, but quite pervasive these days, are the various looks offered by presets, some of them included with the camera, others for sale to use in post-production. I'm not a great fan of these because I'm not interested in plugging in someone else's color algorithm, but they're available.

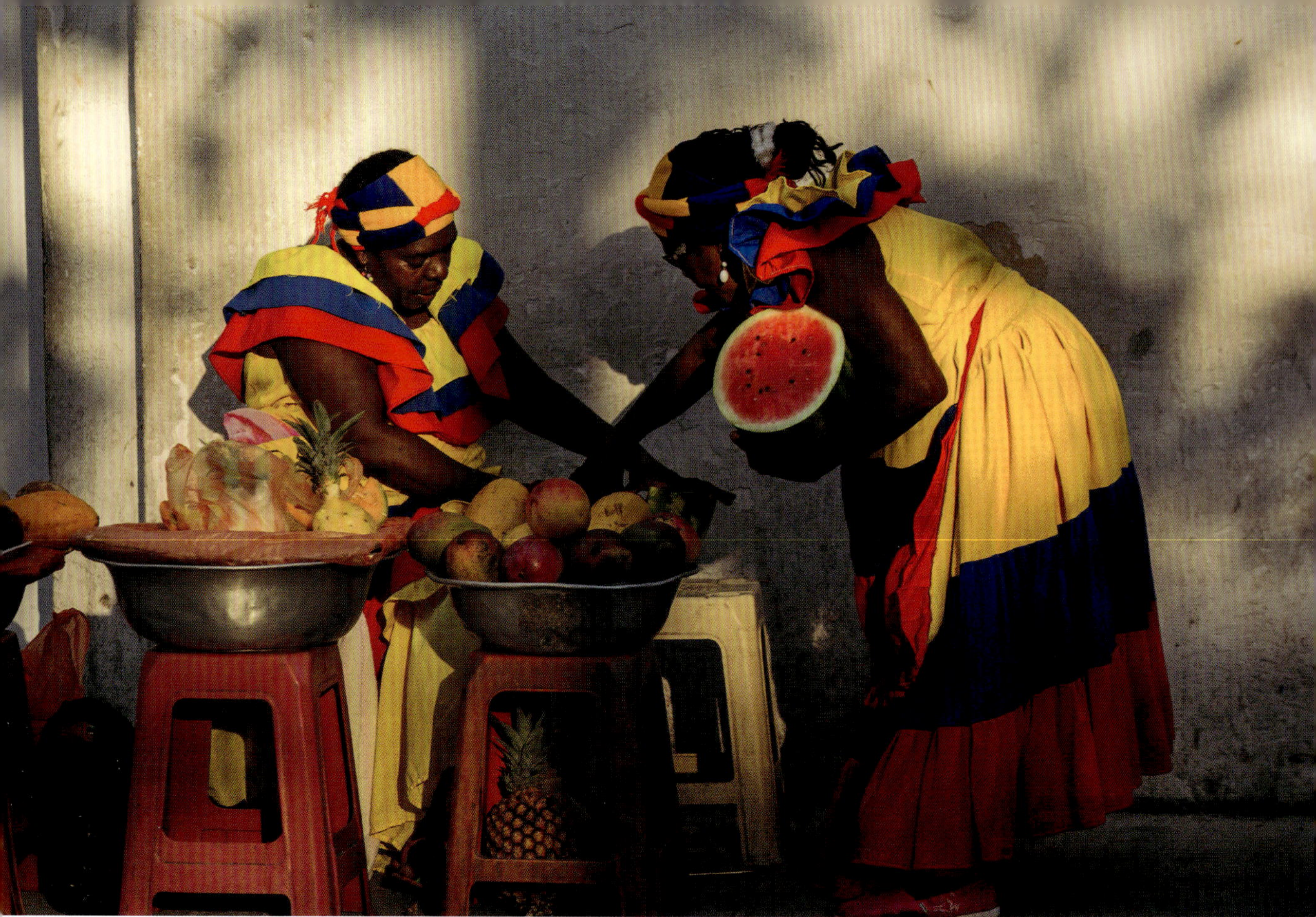

RICH

'm unashamedly using a loaded word to describe a style
that many admire for its intensity and strong use of color,
yet which is easy to get wrong and let slip into garishness.

That last is a second color-emotive word, and as we saw in the first chapter on
pages 28–9, how you describe a color effect often influences the way other people
will see it. At the centre of this issue is saturation, and how much of it makes an
attractive photograph. This is why it has everything to do with style, because style *is*
personal preference. If only a few people like your style, then it's a limited one, but
no less valid for that.

This style of rich color happens to be attractive to many, and therefore popular, but
needs some explanation. In particular, what sets it apart from such restrained styles
as Nuanced Nature on page 166, and perhaps less obviously from Vivid on page 162.
While it clearly has more saturated colors than the natural tints of rocks and leaves,
how it differs from Vivid is not so straightforward. The main difference is that rich, as
I'm using the word, is about strong saturation in mid-to-dark tones while being fairly

Fruit sellers in the Colombian
port city of Cartagena, called
palanqueras, wear dresses
in the colors of the national
flag. Almost horizontal clear
sunlight in the late afternoon
heightens the intensity of
the red and yellow, and it's
the red, being darker, that
contributes most to the
sense of rich color.

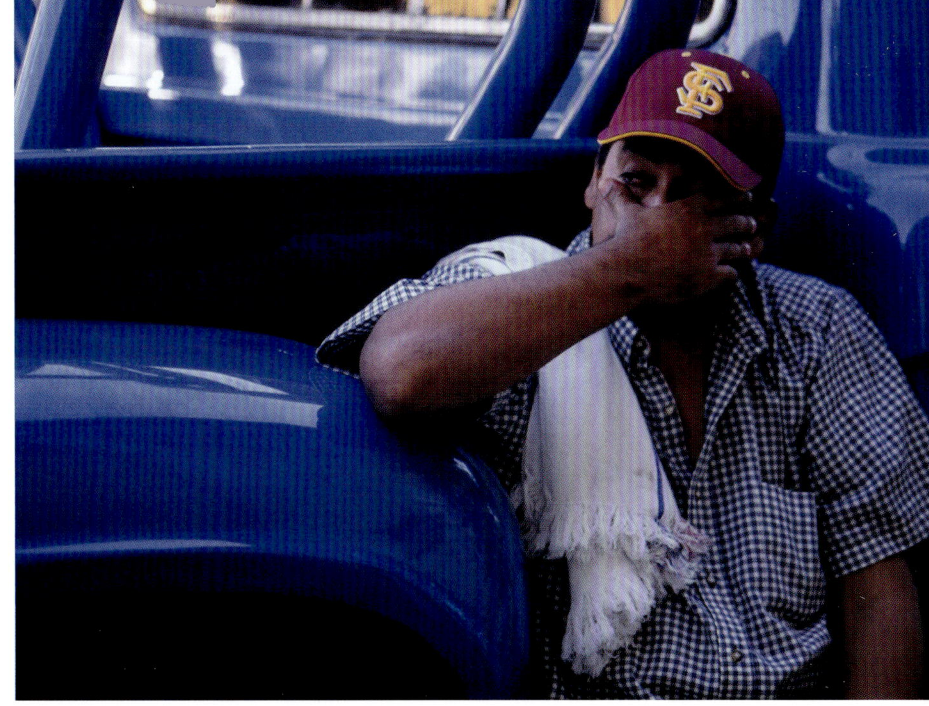

Blue, which as we saw under Naturally Darker (pages 92–3), is traditionally seen as a darker color and also delivers the sense of richness, especially when slightly underexposed. Shot on Fujichrome Velvia film, which was formulated to give saturated blues and greens in particular.

In an entirely different situation, in southern Sudan, a red headscarf brings the same intensity and richness, shot on Fujichrome Velvia.

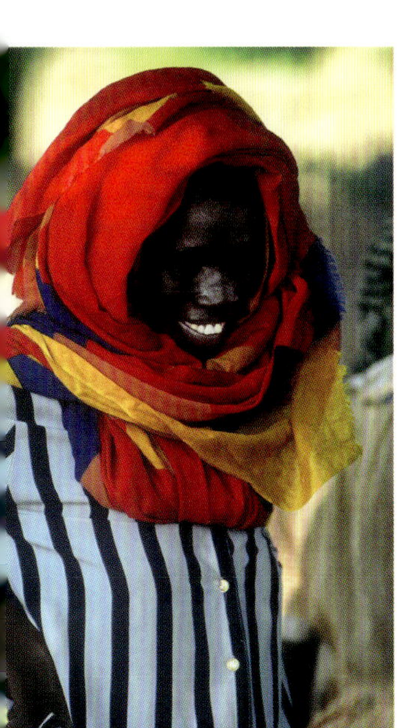

moderate in bright tones. In other words, it draws on an understanding of how colors interact with tones – the theme of Chapter 4: Color & Tone.

It might sound as if this has to involve processing to modify saturation, but in practice by far the most important controls are what you choose to shoot, how you frame, and keeping the exposure a little down. All of these, of course, applied to shooting film, and as I'm stressing elsewhere in the book, including in Emulsion Color in this chapter, Kodachrome delivered rich results extremely well, particularly in warmer colors, and its reputation rested largely on this.

Richly colored style got caught up in the big New Color debate of the 1970s, because it appeared on both sides. The difference was how it was described by the promoters of New Color, such as John Szarkowski, Sally Eauclaire and Max Kozloff, with William Eggleston leading the new and Ernst Haas representing the old. However, just look for yourself at the bodies of work of these two influential photographers on opposite sides of the controversy at the time, and see the same love of color richness. In fact, both used Kodachrome, which Eggleston then paired with Kodak's dye-transfer printing process, famous for not just printing control but intense color dyes (he later moved to color negative, but made his name with Kodachrome).

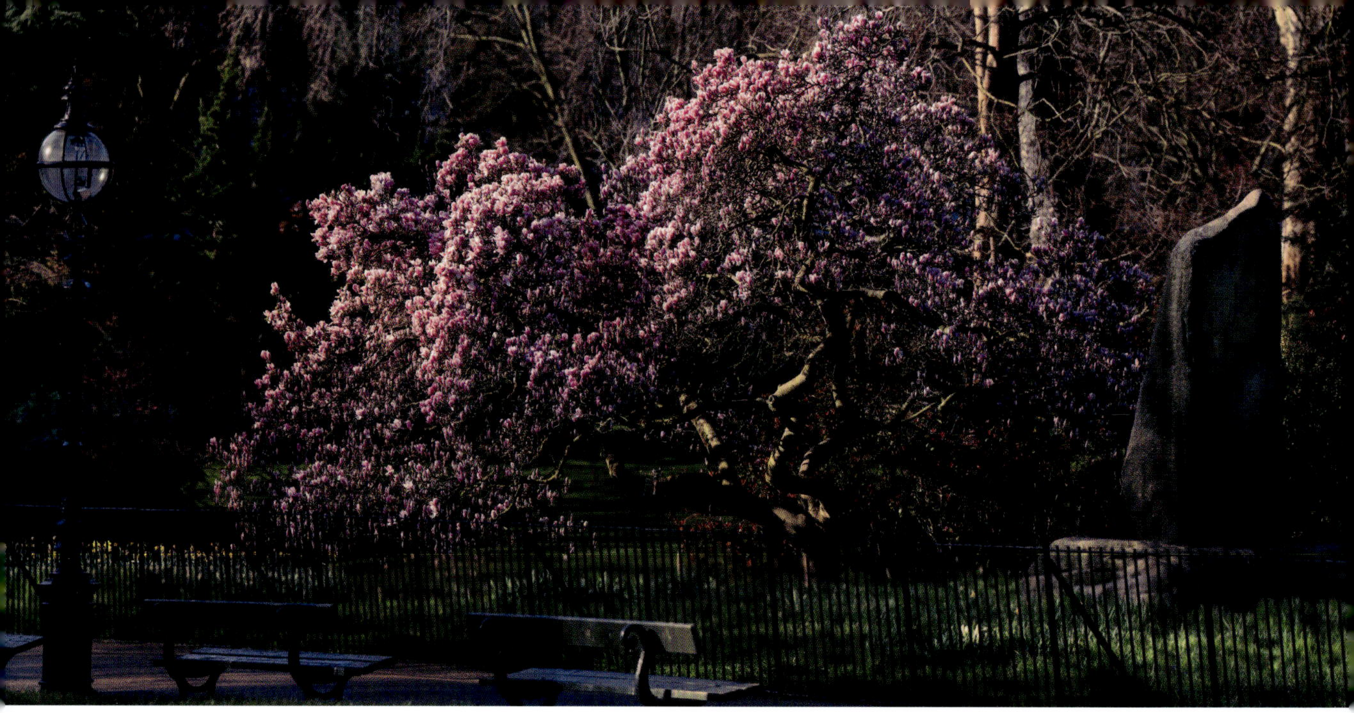

TONAL DRAMA, COLOR RESTRAINT

There's no snappy name for this style, because it calls
for a deliberate and controlled balance between
tonality and colorfulness, and most photographers don't
think in this way. Color and tone, in other words, are
working in opposite directions.

I suspect that most photographers who use this style don't mentally divide tone
from color in the way that I'm analyzing it here (I certainly don't), but a histogram
and a greyscale image side by side certainly help to show how it works. More
important, I think, is that the *opposition* between the two goes a long way towards
explaining why it gets a reliably favourable reception among audiences. There's
an inherent drama in a strong tonal range (in the way I'm describing that), while
limiting the color in area or range is the opposite. Putting them together in the
same image is more intriguing than the more obvious alternatives of having both
dramatic or both muted. It certainly sets it apart stylistically.

I'm being deliberately loose with the adjectives, because there are different ways
of interpreting 'strong' and 'restricted', yet most of them fit within this identifiable
style. Strong tonality means a high range, but with significant darks, even an overall
bias towards dark. With film, this always meant shooting to hold the highlights well
under control and not worrying about how dark the shadows might go, sometimes
with judicious use of grad filters. Digitally there are more exposure-plus-processing
choices, but staying well away from clipped highlights is a must, while processing

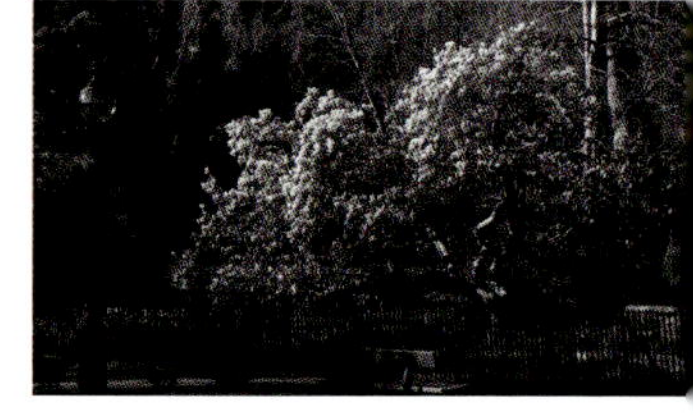

A magnolia in full bloom in
London's Hyde Park, shot
in early morning sunlight
for strong contrast, as the
monochrome version shows,
and processed to lower
shadows (see histogram).
The color is untouched,
and even the most colorful
magnolias are no more than
50 percent saturated, yet
the overall impression is of
richness and intensity.

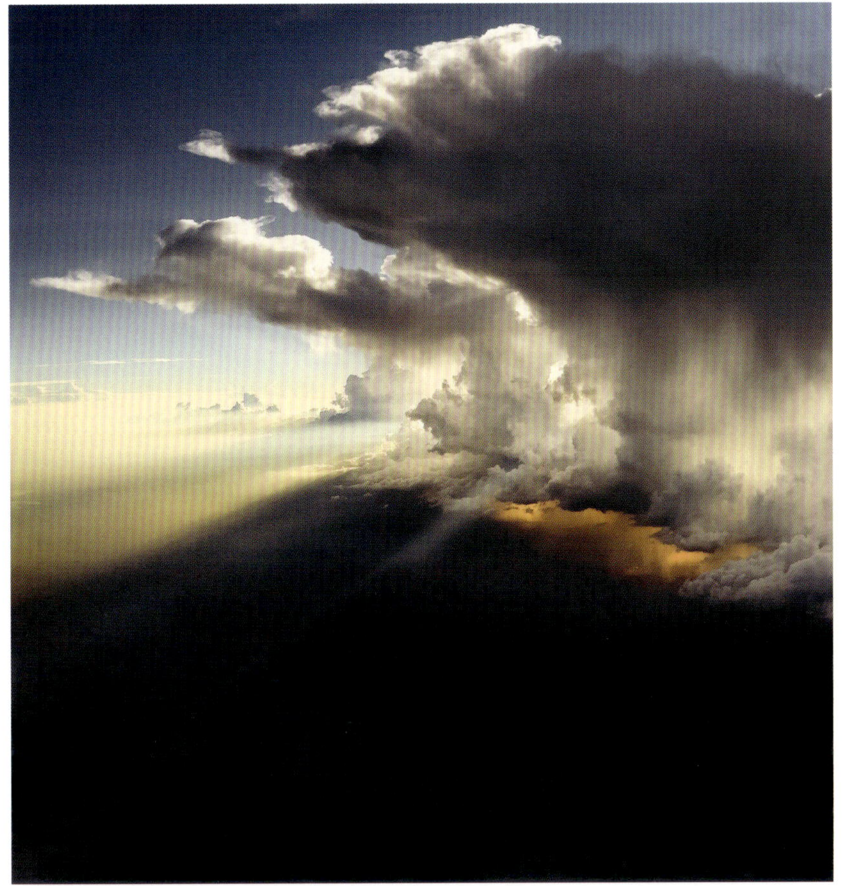

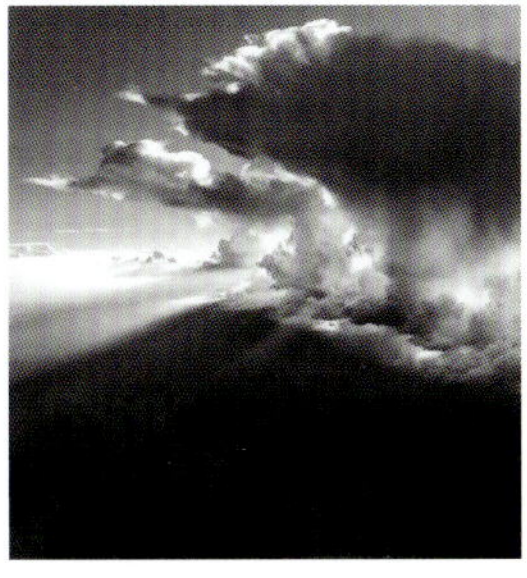

Anvil-shaped cumulonimbus clouds building over the Magdalena River, Colombia, in the late afternoon. The tonal contrast is even higher than the magnolia shot opposite, but the colors are similarly restrained, with the blue sky actually lowered slightly in saturation during processing.

mid-shadows downward and keeping the darkest shadows in the 'mystery' area of Zone I is a typical procedure. It's worth looking at the Shadowlands chapter of *Michael Freeman on... Light & Shadow* for more examples, particularly the Basic Rich, Receding Shadow and Chiaroscuro types.

Restricted color doesn't necessarily mean restrained color, although that can work, but it does mean limiting some of the qualities. For instance, narrowing the range of hues is one method, as is keeping the color very localized against neutrals or darks, and perhaps keeping the color itself darker rather than mid-tone or light.

VIVID

F ew preferences in the world of color excite quite so much opinion and argument as a liking for bright, saturated and exotic colors.

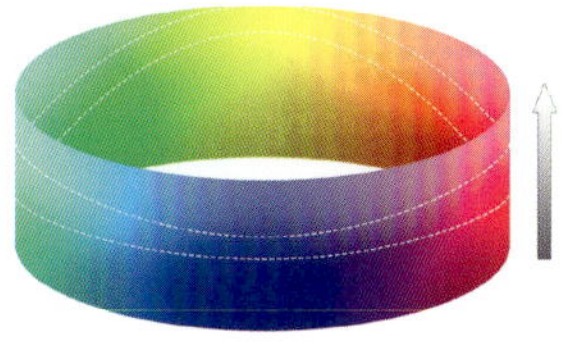

Vivid is the positive word, but there are plenty of critical descriptions, from gaudy to vulgar, and what's perhaps most interesting about this style is how it exposes conflict of taste among photographers, artists and designers. Vivid hues are the Marmite of color photography – you like them or you really don't.

Going back to our color circle, you can see above that vivid belongs in the outer rim of strongly saturated hues, but more than that, it depends also on brightness and the actual hue. The dotted band shows how different hues around the circle have different sweet spots of vividness. Yellow needs to be bright to be vivid, but

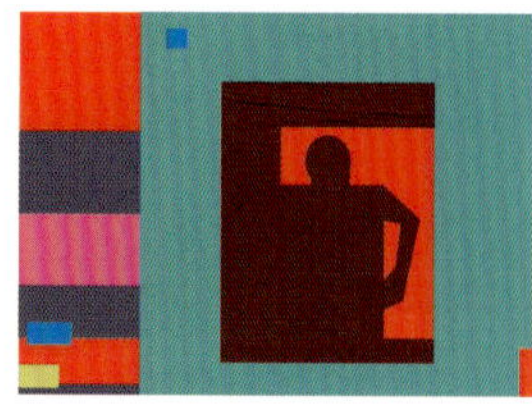

A gaudy and far from harmonious set of colors in a bus station scene on La Réunion. The particular hues – pink, orange-red and teal – are, like the colors of the other pictures here, particularly prone to being cast as vivid in our minds.

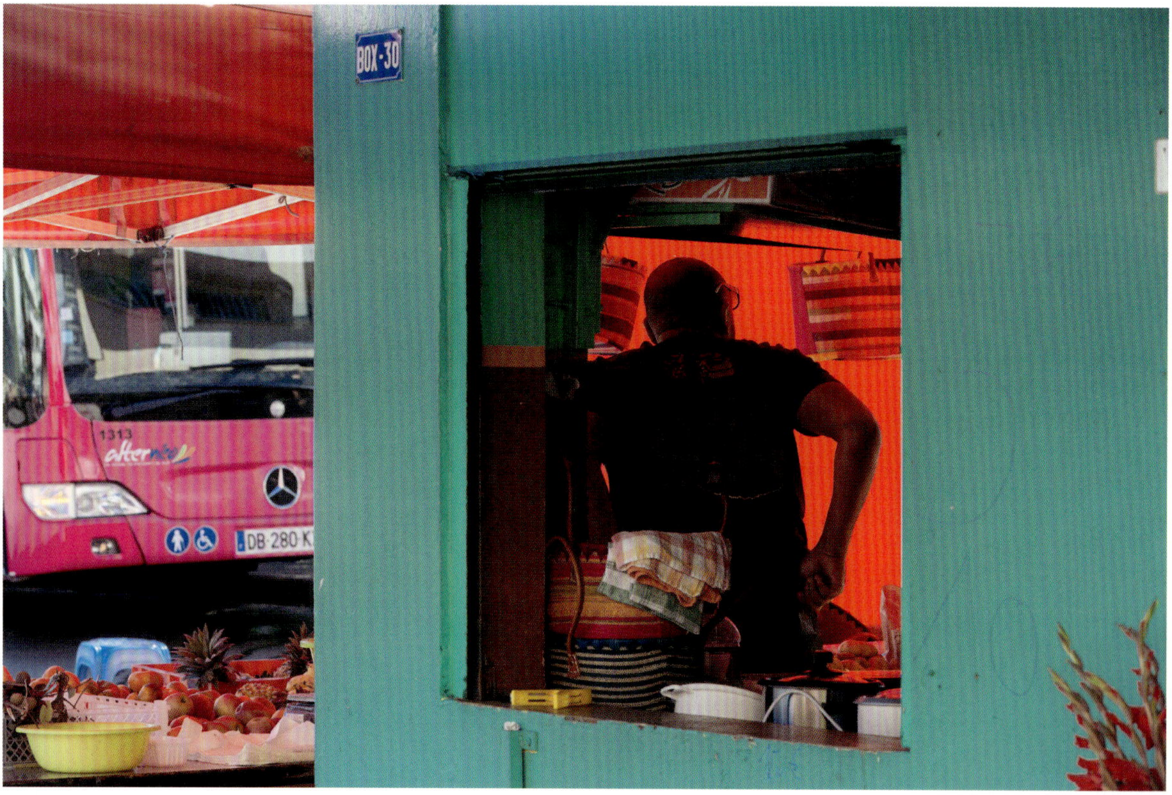

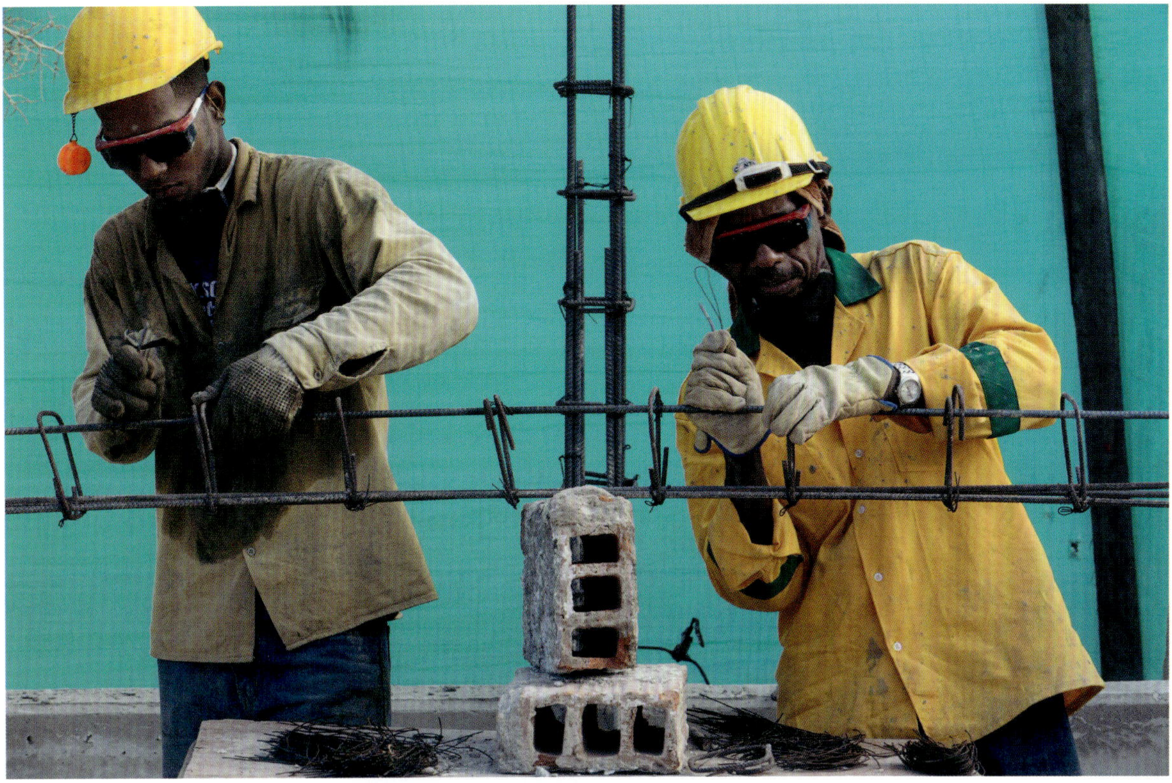

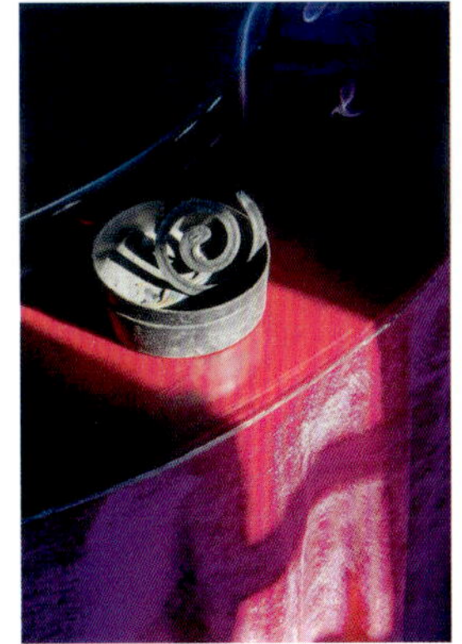

Cyan is a reliably gaudy color in almost any situation, the more so when it's paired with a near-opponent color such as yellow.

A mosquito coil sitting on a table draped in a synthetic velvet cloth of a color that's difficult to define and to process digitally. In a part of the spectrum that's challenging for the camera sensor – between magenta and the 'line of purples' – it appears purple in shade even though magenta-to-pink in direct sunlight.

blue needs to be closer to the middle. That's because a darker yellow just becomes muddy and turns towards olive, while a light blue becomes pale – there's more about this on page 88 in Colors to Us.

In fact, some particular hues are linked in our minds with vividness (or garishness, if you don't like them), and the prime candidates are bright blue-greens on one side of the circle and bright magentas and pinks on the other. You can see examples here, and the reason for this strong association is probably because they're not so easy to find. There's a hint of the exotic in vivid, not to mention obvious drama.

In nature, vivid colors are restricted to details, notably in flowers and some insects and bird feathers. For more general shooting, you can find them most easily in the urban environment – signage, clothing, vehicles and so on. This puts vivid color style into a specific framework – almost, and I'm not being complimentary, a lifestyle choice.

TRANSLUCENT PRIMARIES

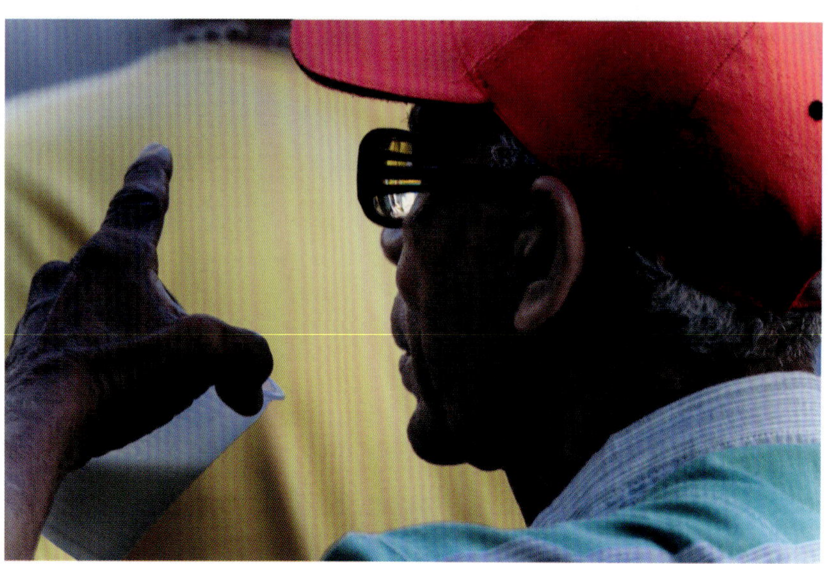

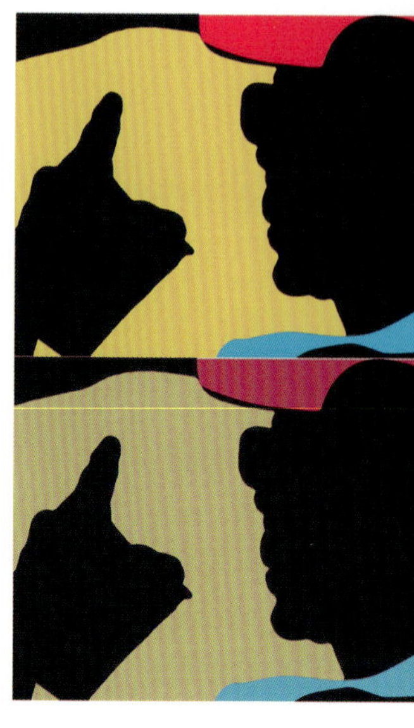

I haven't used the term 'primary color' much, because of the usual confusion between additive and subtractive color, which frankly isn't useful in photography, but here it's relevant when we're dealing with three or four strong colors together. This goes back to triads and tetrads on pages 128–33, which depend on being well separated in hue. Inevitably these are going to be some variation of red, green, blue and yellow. As we saw just now with vivid colors, the problem with these is they're aggressive and punchy, and far from unified when together in a frame.

In order to work in a kind of harmony, primaries need to be moderated in some way. One method is to keep them darker, but that locks us in to an overall dark and rich appearance. Going lighter is a more delicate operation if the goal is brightly colored without being vivid. Finding or choosing such colors in the first place is a first step, although not easy to manage outside the studio, and then composing them, but more than anything, this style relies on delicate processing. Translucent isn't a very practical description, belonging more to painting than photography, but it evokes the right feeling. And classical painting offers clues about how to do this.

Possibly the master of this method was the Renaissance painter Raphael, contemporary and rival of Michelangelo. His distinctive handling of pigments (these were the early days of oil painting) produced a style in which colors were luminous

It would be temptingly easy to push the vibrancy of tropical colors (top illustration) in this street shot in Cartagena, Colombia, and there would be nothing wrong with that. However, I preferred a more subtle and moderate effect (lower illustration) by tempering the saturation of the three principal colors. A side-benefit is that the tiny colors refracted in the man's glasses, which were left as saturated, gain extra impact.

The colors of Raphael's painting of the martyred Saint Catherine of Alexandria (about 1507) are striking for their pearly restraint, even though they are a combination of the four primaries. The purity of the pigments combined with the moderate-to-low saturation and pale highlights in the folds has a compelling translucency.

A traditional Burmese *zat pwe* dance, shot on Kodachrome. The two color bars, with the colors arranged in proportion to the space they occupy, are (top) as shot and reproduced, and (bottom) as they could be enhanced by increasing saturation, as happens often in social media postings.

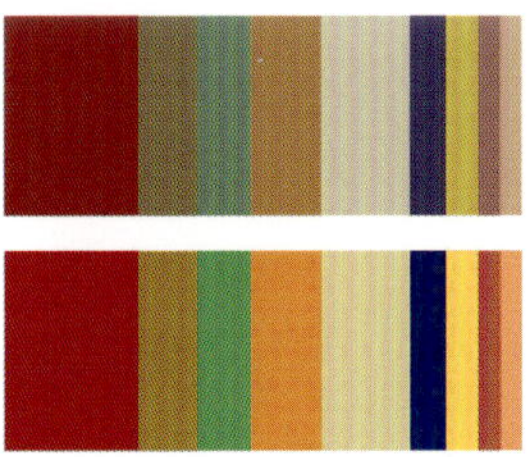

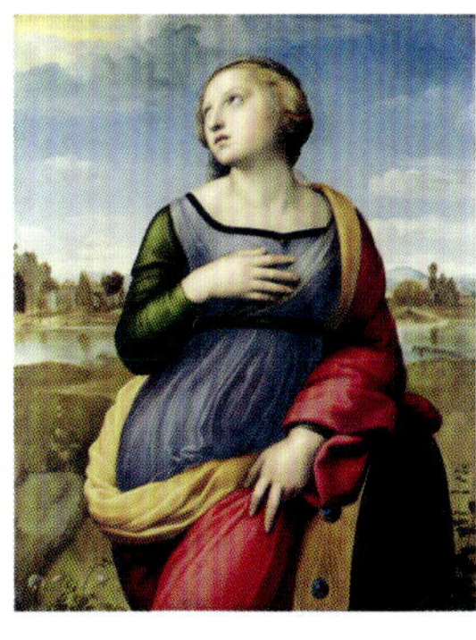

and subtle, despite often being primary hues like red, yellow, blue and green, as in the 1507 painting *Saint Catherine of Alexandria*. The delicacy of distinct separated colors is down to Raphael's technique of many translucent layers and thin glazes of white and powdered glass, which give the luminous effect.

This isn't of any use in photography, but it shows the beauty of delicate rather than strong primaries and suggests ways of controlling and enhancing it. Obviously it begins with the scenes and subjects you choose to shoot, and one help here is arrangements of colors that are distinctly separated and in clear shapes, with no merging (in complete contrast, for example, to the de-focus blending on page 136). Then, in the processing, you can target each color and work with three sliders: increase the Brightness (Exposure in Adobe Camera Raw), lower the Saturation only very slightly, and lower the Contrast significantly (which 'spreads' the color over a larger area).

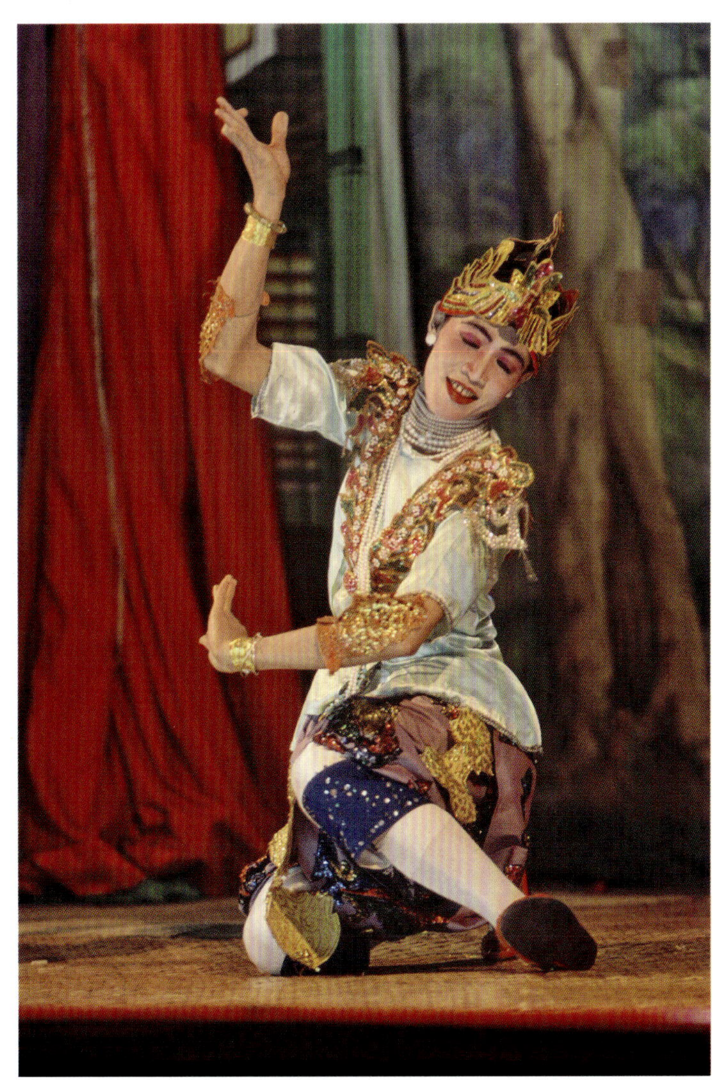

NUANCED NATURE

The colors of nature cover the full gamut possible, but there's a strong association with subtlety, and especially in relationships between colors that you might not have expected. This kind of natural color inspires a definable style.

It's a style based on discovery and on looking hard, often at our feet and on scales more modest than the full step of a grand landscape. As Joel Meyerowitz says in his book *Cape Light*, 'In a photograph you don't look *for*, you look *at*!'[†] If you put aside bright flowers (which, of course, are worth their own, different, exploration of color), then rock strata, mosses, grasses, sedges and leaves offer one of the most interesting broad palettes possible. This is a very contemplative kind of shooting that suits people who like observing slowly and taking their time, and who find pleasure in finding tints and shades. Small variations on greens, browns and greys are often enough to trigger a satisfying image.

Red sandstone, sculpted by flash floods and windborne particles, gives Antelope Canyon in Arizona its well-known form. The subtle range of color on the same stone comes from reflected light from both sunlit and skylit surfaces above.

Limpets and anemones bring natural splashes of color to a rockpool in Wales.

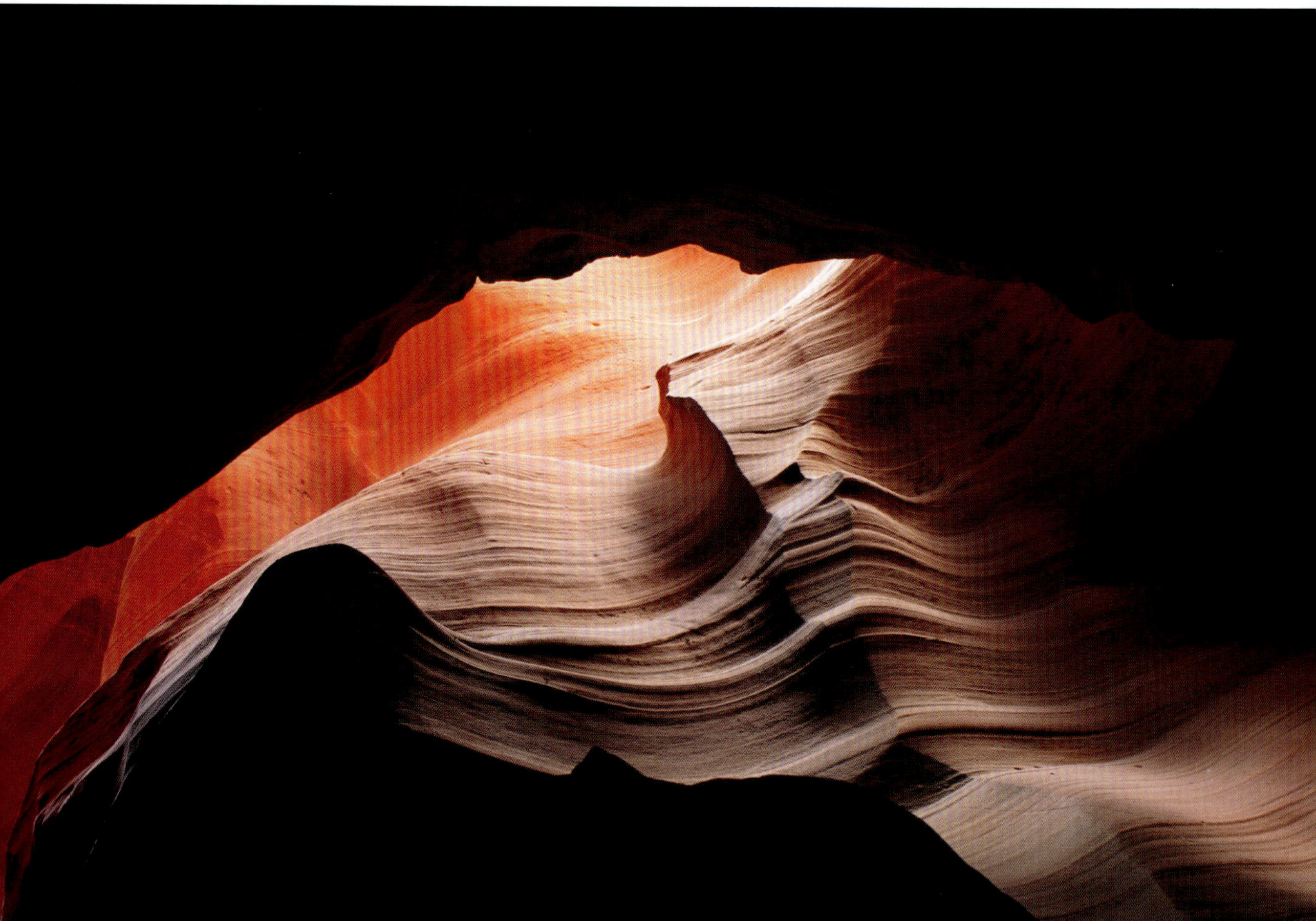

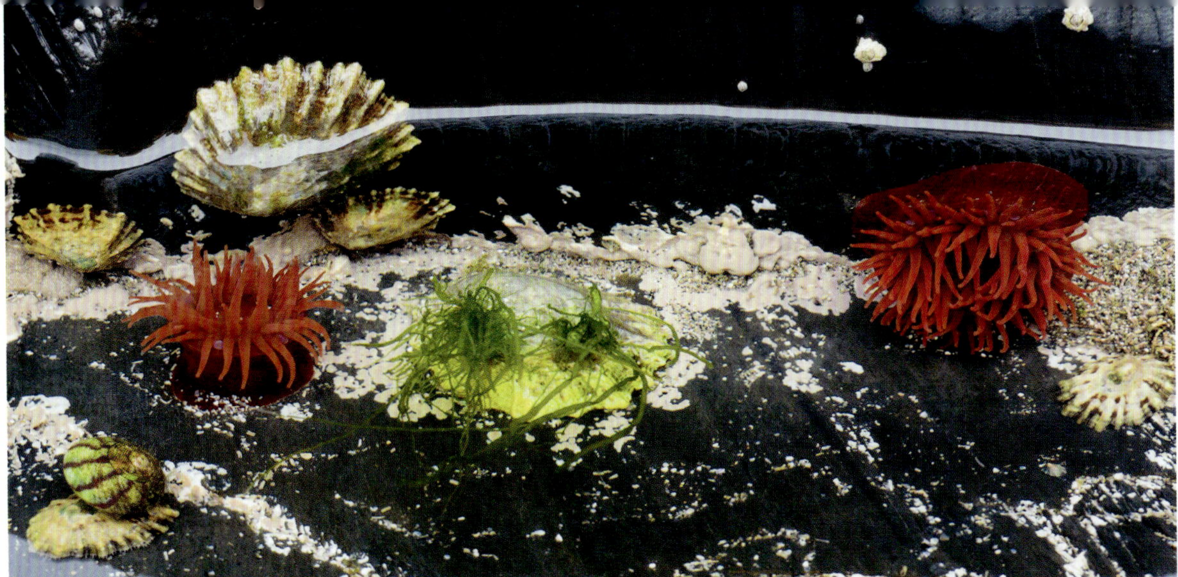

Also in overcast weather, which is almost essential for revealing the soft palettes of woodland, a hillside in Scotland shot on Kodachrome film displays a remarkably broad range of muted color covering a full third of the color circle, at low saturations between 15 percent and 40 percent.

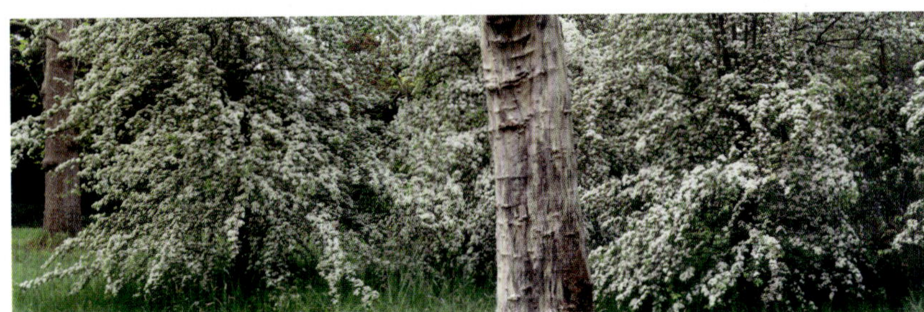

Probably the original master of this style was the American large-format photographer Eliot Porter. He was an early pioneer of color photography, using Kodak's dye-transfer process to make subtle prints that could sometimes be rich but, because of his preference for commonplace details of nature, were more usually restrained. The phrase he used, 'intimate landscapes', describes a way of exploring the natural world in close-up, reacting to details that 'exhibit the most extraordinary combination of shapes and colors, scarcely suspected on casual observation'.[‡]

He was strongly influenced by Henry David Thoreau, who wrote elegantly about the experience of nature and with an emphasis on color. The lesson from Porter's work is that nature at a local scale, including rocks, plants and water, offers color arrangements that can be surprising and beautiful if only you avoid letting strong objects take over the image. Porter acknowledged an element of abstraction in his work, and as we'll see in a few pages, fully abstracted color is just about as far as you can go in pushing color to the front of the stage in photography.

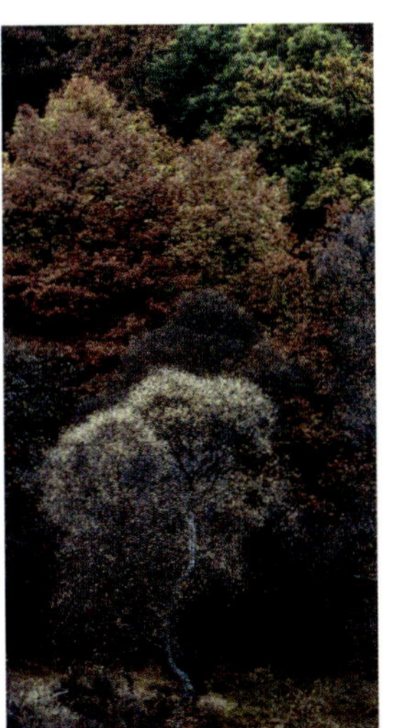

[†]Joel Meyerowitz, *Cape Light* (Museum of Fine Arts, Boston, 1978)

[‡]Eliot Porter, *Intimate Landscapes* (The Metropolitan Museum of Art, New York, 1979)

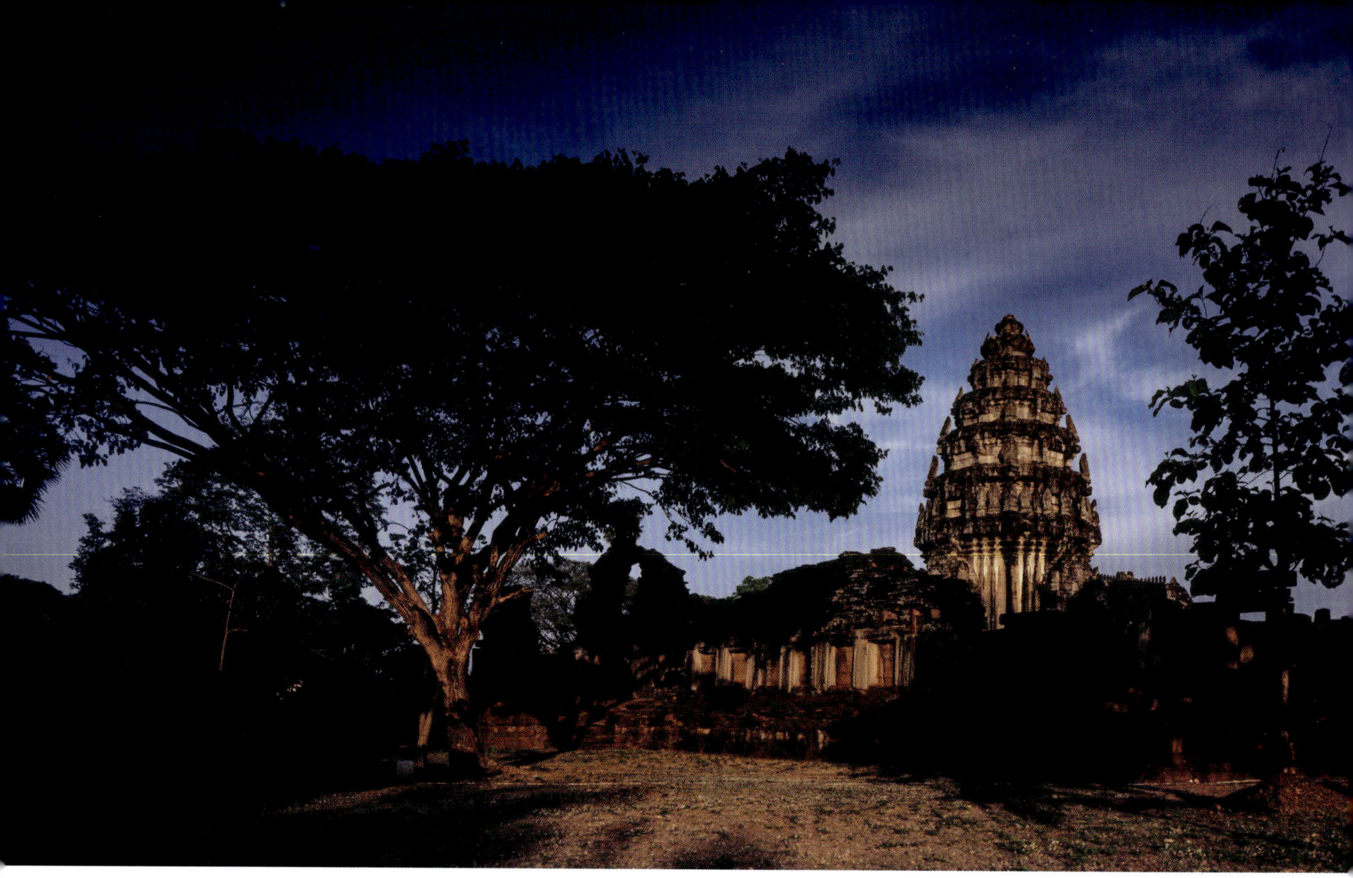

EMULSION COLOR

Different color film and print processes put their distinctive stamp on photographs, and while this now seems like a retro quality, some of it can be reproduced digitally during processing as one way towards a style.

Film chemistry was never perfect, which is why brands were always improving and competing, but then many photographers outside of commercial studios weren't demanding perfection anyway – just an attractive result. I've already mentioned the special color qualities that made Kodachrome popular, but they weren't a result of Eastman Kodak deliberately targeting specific consumer tastes, but a by-product of the company aiming for a good, accurate film. There were less-good by-products, such as the dull greens of vegetation and in later Kodachrome an unhappy shift towards cyan in overexposed skies. Not so Fujichrome, with Velvia (a portmanteau of 'Velvet Media') launched in 1990 as a direct competitor, with deliberately enhanced blues for the sky and greens for vegetation. The results were in fact a little unrealistic, but landscape and nature photographers loved them. They solved a longstanding problem that Kodachrome had, and then added extra juice. And for the Japanese market for a couple of years, there was an even more saturated, less realistic film, Fortia.

Kodachrome 120 film used in a panoramic holder on a large-format camera for a cover shot of an ancient Khmer temple in northeastern Thailand. The scan keeps the appearance of the transparency, which I valued for the low saturation of the blue sky shading smoothly towards grey.

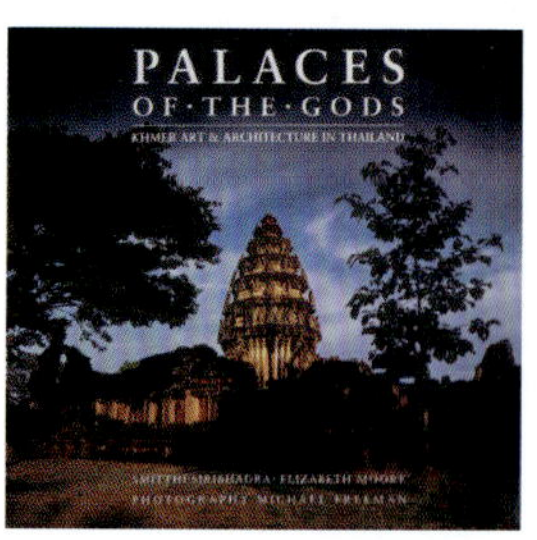

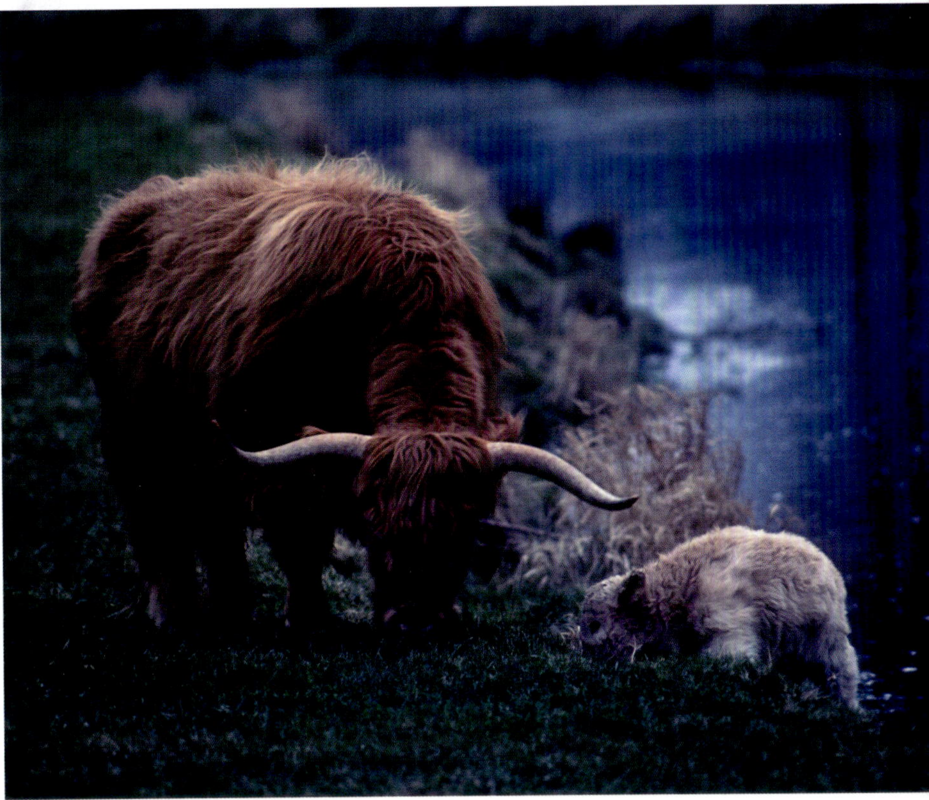

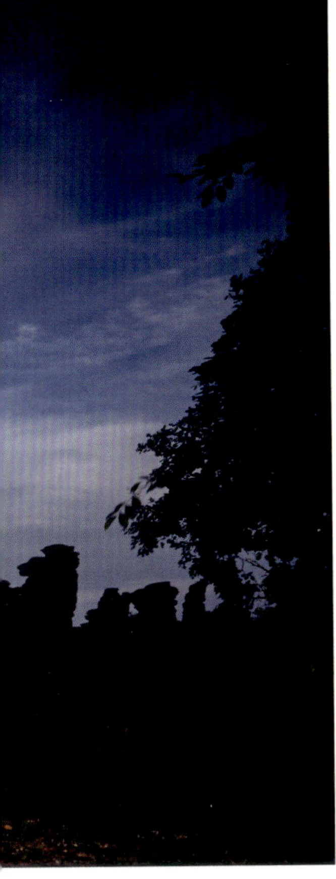

EP 120 High Speed Ektachrome, rated at ASA 160, used in fading daylight to photograph Highland cattle in Kent.

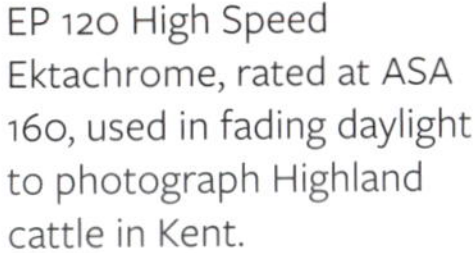

Polaroid SX-70 film on an overcast day in Glencoe, Scotland. The warm, creamy cast occurred occasionally and was difficult to predict.

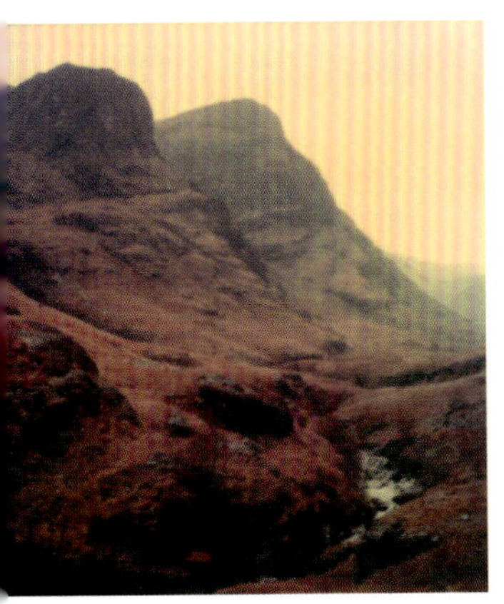

Indeed, that idea of customizing a look through chemistry is alive and well, albeit in greatly reduced numbers. Fine-tuning of the emulsions at a less dramatic level still continues in the (much fewer) color films available today, with manufacturers such as Kodak offering films that have their color optimized for skin (the Portra range). Digital nearly killed off color film for all the obvious reasons, which include cost (zero costs per image once you've bought the camera), efficiency in guaranteeing and adjusting color, and ease of distributing and displaying pictures in the medium that most people use (screens). But not quite, because first a few diehards stuck with what they knew, which allowed Kodak and Fujifilm to continue selling a few lines, and second because young photographers have discovered analogue from scratch, and in the last few years color film has seen a perhaps surprising uptake. There's hope yet for analogue, and that big names in cinematography insist on shooting with film stock (Steven Spielberg, Quentin Tarantino, Christopher Nolan and Wes Anderson among others) probably hasn't gone unnoticed.

The word 'organic' crops up regularly in praise of color film, and it hardly matters if color distinctions between films and between film and digital are subtle and difficult to pin down precisely. If shooting color film increases the photographer's personal engagement and pleasure, that alone improves the handling of color in imagery. There were in any case films that had very distinctive looks, and one of them remains, sort of. This is Polaroid, invented by Edwin Land in the 1940s, relying on a pod of chemical reagents to process an image within a minute. By the 1960s it was available in color. The most distinctive Polaroid look of all, however, was from the completely re-invented system of camera-plus-film launched as the SX-70 in 1972. The

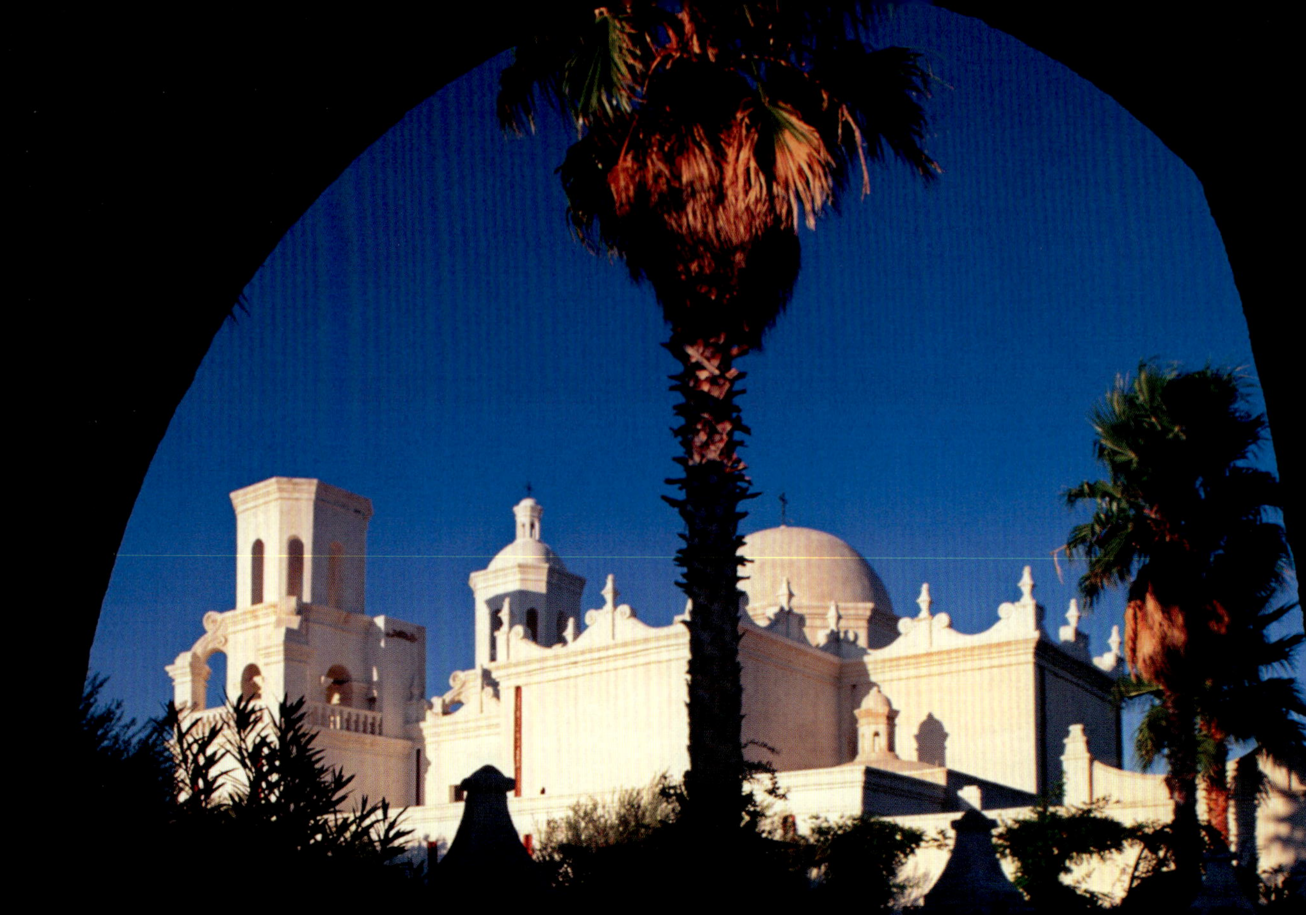

ejected film unit – a finished print, in fact – was made up of 17 layers, including thin polymers, protected by a mylar window, which contributed a slightly hazy, opalescent appearance to colors that were not especially accurate, but the combination was attractive and distinctive, and a great success. Since Polaroid's demise, there has been a manufacturing revival, though with less-perfect chemistry.

Definitely lost to history is Kodak's color infrared film, called at the time false-color film as it had one emulsion layer sensitive to infrared. The original purpose was camouflage-detection aerial photography, because green vegetation, which reflects strongly in infrared, appeared magenta in this slide film. In fact, the final colors depended on which colored filter was used over the lens when shooting, and at least some filter was necessary – yellow was recommended – because all three layers in the film were sensitive to blue. I use the past tense, as all production stopped years ago, but old stock is sometimes available. There is a digital equivalent, in the form of a sensor modification that removes the normal filter designed to cut infrared, to which camera sensors are sensitive.

The Mission San Xavier del Bac, near Tucson, Arizona, owes its intense color in morning sunlight to the dyes in Fujichrome Velvia, a transparency film launched in 1990 to compete with Kodachrome. It was formulated for high saturation, especially in blues and greens – the colors where Kodachrome was weakest.

An aerial shot of the Mazaruni River, Guyana, taken on the long-discontinued Ektachrome Infrared EIR 35mm film, designed to display healthy green vegetation as red.

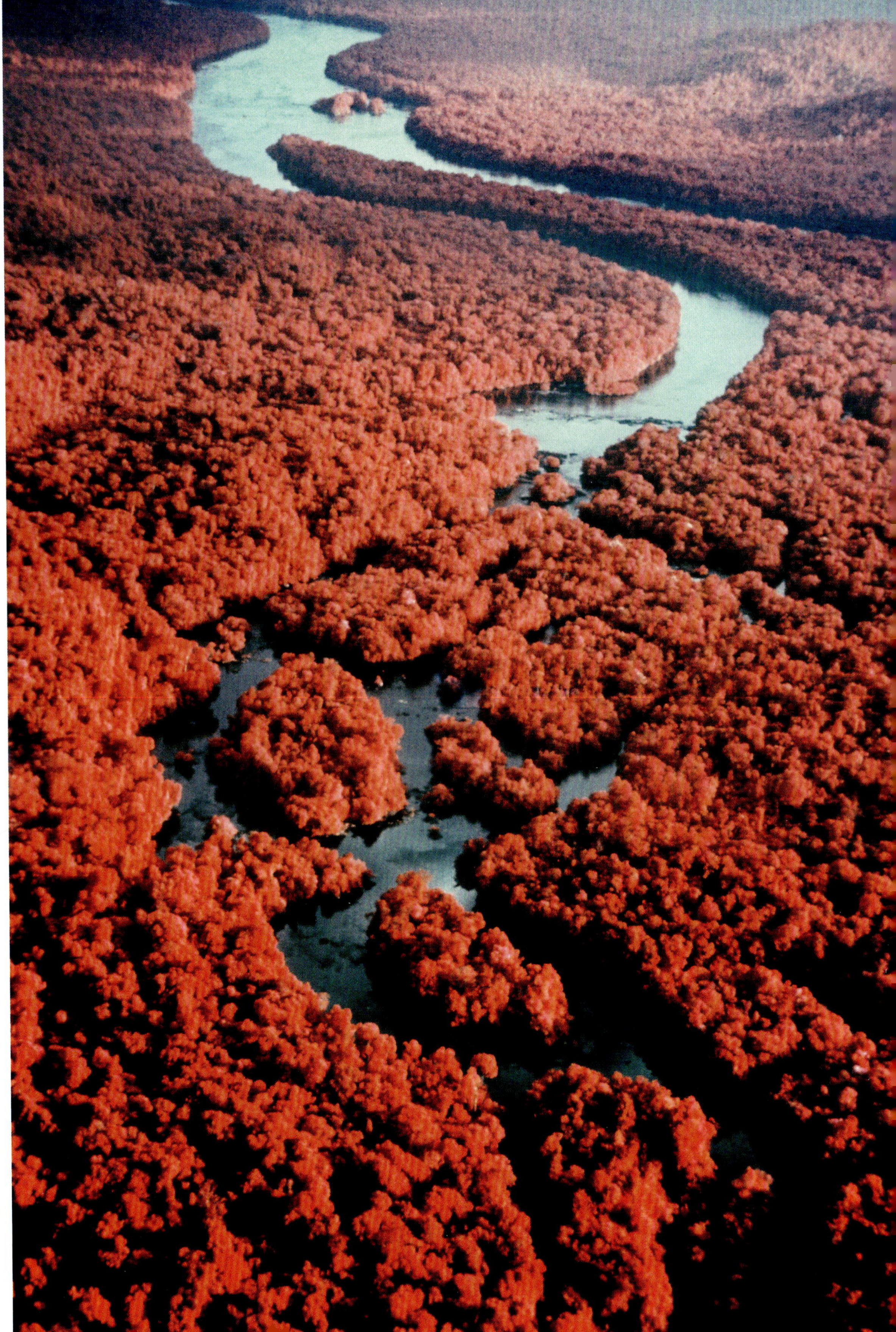

ABSTRACTED COLOR

Abstraction has a special appeal in photography because it's not completely natural. It takes some imagination to turn the regular recording of scenes in front of the camera into images that are not obvious. More than that, if you're looking to push color forward in shooting, this is a particularly good direction. Color responds very well to in-camera abstraction, provided that you have a way to make it unrecognizable – unlinked to reality.

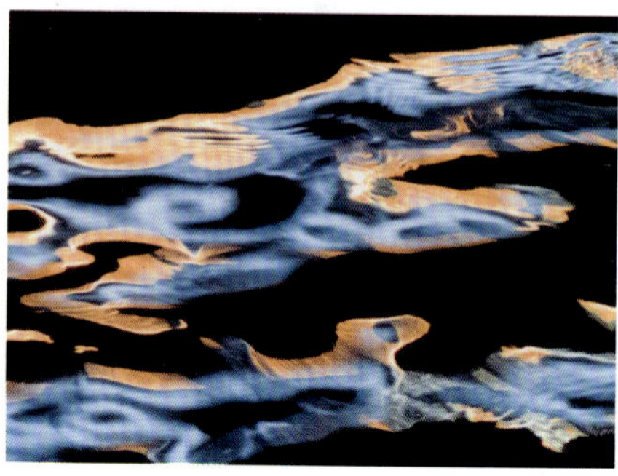

There are several ways, and they've been used from the beginning by the earliest color photographers to experiment, in the 1960s. This is when 35mm color film became widely available, and it became easy, for anyone inclined, to explore by playing with lens and shutter settings and with strange compositions. Abstracted color always fell under the heading of 'personal work', as it was of no use to art directors in publishing and the commercial world. Ernst Haas crops up again as an early influencer in color photography, as he often stepped aside for a few frames from his successful advertising and magazine career just to play. Only one or two made it onto the pages of *Life* magazine, and then in his book *The Creation*, but it took another half-century for his abstracts to get full recognition in the book *Color Correction*. By then, of course, serendipitous color experiments had become completely normal. Other photographers noted for deliberate abstraction are Franco Fontana, Wolfgang Tillmans, Lester Bookbinder in studio work, Gueorgui Pinkhassov and Ola Kolehmainen.

There are several tried and tested ways of removing reality and context from a photograph, and they fall into the two groups of distressing the image and unusual framing. For the first, de-focusing, which we already saw on page 136 as a way of blending different colors in backgrounds, is one easy option. Another, much less predictable, is a slow shutter speed combined with movement, either motion blur or deliberate camera shake. Reflections, which we saw on page 24, offer possibilities when they're distorted by the shape or the movement of the surface, such as rippling water, and also if you combine them in a layered picture such as a glass window. This last image is also a compositional style that you can see in the first book, *Michael Freeman on... Composition*. Experimental composition accounts for the other ways of abstracting color, basically cropping in and angling to isolate color fragments from scenes. Typically this works best with close-ups and with a long telephoto.

ABSTRACTED COLOR TECHNIQUES:

1. Defocused blur

2. Tight cropping, both close-up and telephoto

3. Distorted and layered reflections

4. High-contrast chiaroscuro, exposed down

5. Motion blur

Above and right, reflections in water give an infinite and unpredictable range of distortions.

Below, iridescent colors form on the polished surface of an abalone shell.

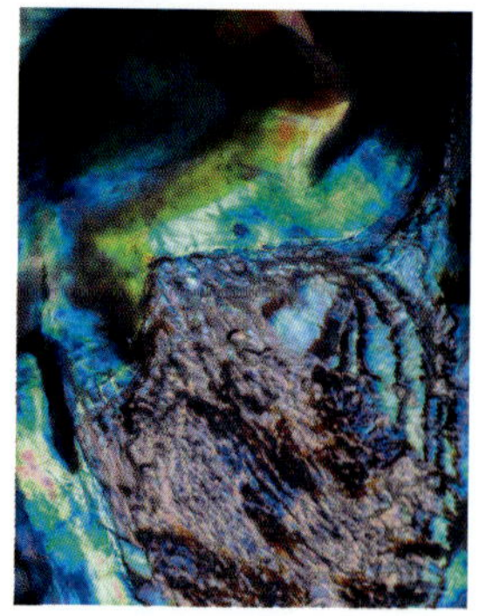

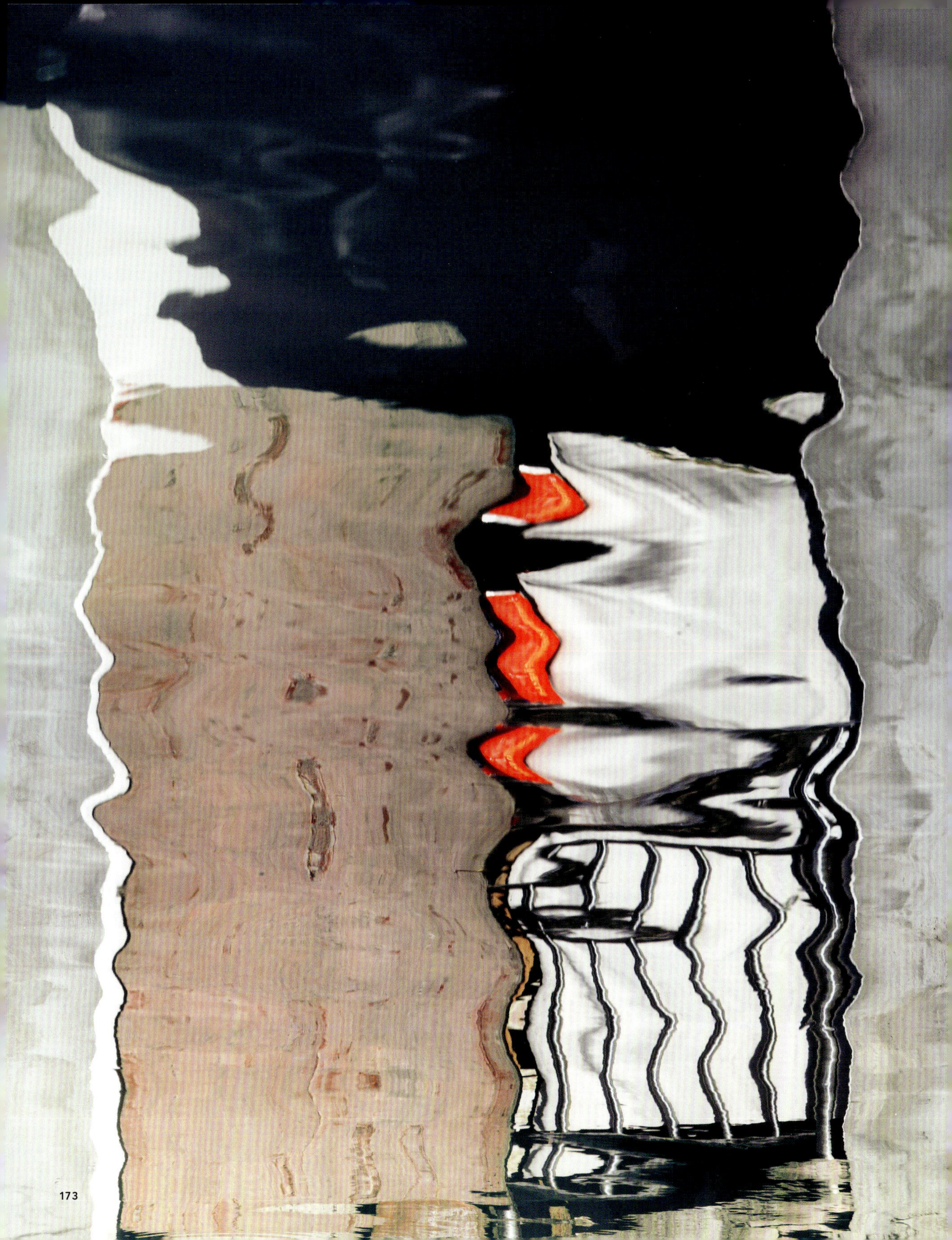